LLOYD GEORGE

A Diary by Frances Stevenson

Frances Stevenson—the photograph taken specially for Lloyd George

LLOYD GEORGE

A Diary
by Frances Stevenson

Edited by
A. J. P. TAYLOR

HARPER & ROW, PUBLISHERS
New York, Evanston, San Francisco, London

FIRST U.S. EDITION

STANDARD BOOK NUMBER: 06-014116-6

LIBRARY OF CONGRESS CATALOG CARD NUMBER: 77-160652

Contents

Illustrations

Preface

David Lloyd George remains the most fascinating, because the most elusive, of twentieth-century British statesmen. His career was a bundle of contradictions: the Radical opponent of one war who became the advocate of the knock-out blow in the next; the champion of the poor who became the associate of the rich; the oppressor of Ireland in the Troubles who then gave Ireland freedom. He helped to destroy the Liberal party, said that he had never got on with Liberals, and yet always asserted his own attachment to Liberalism. Bonar Law said at the end of the first world war: 'He can be prime minister for life if he wants to.' Less than four years later he fell from power for ever and at the end was left isolated and disregarded. He inaugurated the Welfare State, but in the inter-war years his fertile ideas fell on stony ground.

He was called the Welsh Wizard by his admirers, the Goat by those who distrusted him, the Big Beast in his years of power. Most of all he was the man from Outside—a humble Welsh solicitor, the only prime minister except Disraeli, as he mistakenly boasted, who had not gone through the staff college of one of the ancient universities. Tom Jones said at the time of his death: 'He could charm a bird off a branch but was himself always unmoved.' Professor Trevor Wilson writes in his introduction to C. P. Scott's Diaries (1970):

'Admittedly a vast amount has been written about Lloyd George. Yet the detailed scrutiny needed to understand him—the study in depth of his conduct during a series of key episodes—has largely been lacking. Those memoirs and diaries which have been published ... have offered much external information but little unravelling of his character.'

Even C. P. Scott, who knew and understood Lloyd George better than most people did, knew him only as a politician.

In the Diary of Frances Stevenson we have a record of Lloyd George as a man as well as a statesman. This Diary is a unique document—a claim often made but rarely with as much justification as in this case. Where else have we the detailed picture of a British prime minister by one who was at once his devoted mistress and his confidential secretary? The relations between Lloyd

George and Frances Stevenson were a secret, respected even by his bitterest opponents, during his life and for some years afterwards. Now there is no reason for concealment. Countess Lloyd-George, as Frances Stevenson now is, has told the full story frankly and movingly in her autobiography.[1] Her Diary commands attention if only as the monument to a deep and lasting love.

It has a larger value for the political historian. Frances Stevenson loved Lloyd George as a man. But she also shared his political interests to the full and was soon at home in the great world of public affairs. She was not his secretary in name only. She was a very efficient working secretary. The Lloyd George Papers, now in the Beaverbrook Library, bear witness to this. Until 1912, when Frances Stevenson took over, they are a slight chaotic collection. From the moment of her appointment they become incomparably rich. Frances Stevenson preserved everything, including the casual notes which ministers exchanged in cabinet and the doodles which Lloyd George made at international conferences.[2] She helped to compose Lloyd George's speeches and appraised them when they were delivered. She accompanied him on important foreign missions—to Rapallo in 1917 and to the peace conference at Paris in 1919. She met all the great statesmen of the day and negotiated on Lloyd George's behalf with the press lords, Northcliffe and Beaverbrook. She wrote down everything she heard and understood what she was writing.

Much of the Diary consists of Lloyd George talking. The critical historian, of course, bears this in mind. What Frances Stevenson records is often second-hand. She does not tell what happened in cabinet. She tells what Lloyd George said happened in cabinet, and it is therefore not surprising that he usually came out best. This Diary is very much Lloyd George's version of events. The same is true of his private life. Naturally he worked off on Frances Stevenson the irritation which he sometimes felt with his family. It does not follow that they were as tiresome as he made out or as she was led to believe. Indeed it is a fair surmise that there was a Welsh side to Lloyd George which cherished life at Criccieth with his wife and children. The estrangement between Frances Stevenson and the family seems to have increased later when it became clear that Lloyd George's attachment to her was no passing fancy. At first there were many contacts, and Megan even shared Frances Stevenson's room in Paris during the peace conference.

Frances Stevenson was an official secretary, on the government payroll, from 1913 until 1922. She began with Lloyd George at the treasury and moved successively, as he did, to the ministry of munitions and the war office. When Lloyd George became prime minister she and J. T. Davies were established in 10 Downing Street as joint principal private secretaries—the first time a woman had held the post. After Lloyd George left office, Frances

---

1. The Years that are Past, by Frances Lloyd George, Hutchinson, 1967.
2. Some of these are reproduced following page 146.

Stevenson was still involved in his political activities and, later still, organised the writing of his War Memoirs. Her political interest grew with experience. She was an educated woman with a good classical degree and incidentally with much better French than Lloyd George. She had enlightened views, to the extent of being mildly suffragist, and often gives the impression of having stepped out of a novel by H. G. Wells. But it was life with Lloyd George which gave her an understanding of life at the top.

This development is reflected in the Diary. In the first year or two which it covers it is mainly a personal document in which Lloyd George bulks larger than events. Throughout the period when he was prime minister the Diary is predominantly a political record, providing an invaluable though not always accurate supplement to other accounts. The later entries, which are more fragmentary, describe a politician out of office and take on political importance only in 1934 and 1935 when Lloyd George imagined that he was about to launch the British New Deal.

The Diary is tantalisingly incomplete. Like many diarists Frances Stevenson started each year with good resolutions and then broke them. At some of the most critical moments she was too busy or too tired to keep up her Diary, and it lapsed for weeks or months together. Occasionally she breaks off in the middle of a sentence. A dramatic story is often left hanging in the air. Thus the Diary does not carry the negotiations with the Irish in 1921 to a conclusion, though we know from other evidence that Frances Stevenson was waiting in an anteroom when the treaty was actually signed. Again there were long periods when Frances Stevenson and Lloyd George did not see each other. He was in Wales or she was on holiday. During the war, as the Diary makes clear, she was often worn down by overwork or maybe by the difficulties of her situation, and had to take a long convalescence. The long gaps in the years after Lloyd George's fall from power are less easy to explain. Apparently Frances Stevenson took up the writing of her Diary only when she felt that something important was happening and that she was again at the centre of events.

The later history of the Diary may do something to explain its fragmentary character. Lloyd George and Frances Stevenson married in 1943. When Earl Lloyd-George died he bequeathed to his wife all his political papers. Some years later Lord Beaverbrook was anxious to commission a life of Lloyd George and wished to use these papers. The simplest solution of copyright and other difficulties was for Lord Beaverbrook to buy the papers outright, and this he did.[1] Lady Lloyd-George threw in her own Diary and letters so far as they related to Lloyd George. It is thus possible that other parts of her Diary were discarded or perhaps lost. Frank Owen duly wrote a biography of Lloyd George[2] at Lord Beaverbrook's commission. Lord

---

1. The Lloyd George Papers are now the property of the First Beaverbrook Foundation.
2. Tempestuous Journey, Hutchinson, 1954.

Beaverbrook then came to regret that he had left the exploitation of the Lloyd George papers to another and resumed his own historical writing. He used the papers extensively both in Men and Power and in The Decline and Fall of Lloyd George. In the last work, particularly, the experienced historian will admire the skill with which Lord Beaverbrook presented in his own inimitable way anecdotes which he had in fact culled from Frances Stevenson's Diary.

Lord Beaverbrook kept his treasures to himself—a Nibelung hoard as D. C. Watt described them. Enquirers were told that the papers were in constant use, as indeed they were, and therefore could not be made available to others. Lord Beaverbrook also gave the impression that he had undertaken not to open the Diary to researchers until 1971. After his death I became honorary director of the Beaverbrook Library, to which all Lord Beaverbrook's papers were transferred, and, with the approval of the trustees of the First Beaverbrook Foundation, the Lloyd George Papers were opened to researchers, virtually without restriction. For some time I accepted the tradition that the Diary must remain sealed until 1971. One day, being curious to read it, I looked into the relevant legal file and found that the restriction applied only to the personal letters between Frances Stevenson and Lloyd George. The Diary was thus available for publication. As a matter of courtesy, I consulted Lady Lloyd-George who raised no objection to publication and indeed welcomed it. She read through the Diary, commenting: 'I had no idea I wrote so much', and gave me information about the more obscure persons. The editorial responsibility is solely mine, acting on behalf of the First Beaverbrook Foundation, the proprietors.

I have made a few omissions. These were principally remarks about individuals who are still living or whose families might be hurt. None of these remarks originates from Lloyd George or concerns him in any way. Even where Lloyd George is monstrously unfair to an individual, as often to Winston Churchill and even more to C. F. G. Masterman, I have let the passage stand. Lloyd George's own reconciliation later with both these men is the best evidence of his unfairness. Towards the end of the Diary I have made more extensive cuts for a different reason. Lloyd George in his retirement at Churt talked a great deal about his youth—his schooling, his contacts with nature, the preachers he listened to. Frances Stevenson set down all these reminiscences, often more than once. I have kept only the more interesting passages.

Most of the Diary, as it now exists, was recorded by Frances Stevenson in contemporary diary volumes. According to her own account, she tried to keep brief notes and then wrote up the full entries when she had time. Only a few of these original notes have survived. Some of the Diary, particularly for the later years, is on loose sheets of ruled paper, and it is probable that a good deal has been lost. Some twenty pages were provided by Lady Lloyd-George in a typed copy headed 'Extracts from Lady Lloyd-George's Diary'.

Editors of Diaries usually write out in full the abbreviations and initials. I felt that it recaptured the spirit of this very personal document to leave them alone. C. for instance expresses Frances Stevenson's relationship towards Lloyd George in a way that chancellor of the exchequer would not, and the same is true of the later D. Similarly I have kept down the notes and not attempted to provide in them a detailed history of the times. In conclusion, I am grateful to Lady Lloyd-George for her cooperation. I thank my daughter-in-law, Mary Taylor, for producing a clear typed copy. Most of all, I thank Veronica Horne, the secretary of the Beaverbrook Library, for her indefatigable labours in reducing the manuscript to order. This book is more hers than mine.

Beaverbrook Library   A. J. P. TAYLOR
London

Poem in Lloyd George's handwriting (?1913)

Beloved let us love so well,
Our work shall still be better for our love,
And still our love be sweeter for our work,
And both, commended for the sake of each,
By all true workers and true lovers born.

Diary 1914

David Lloyd George was born in Manchester on 17 January 1863. He was brought up at Llanystumdwy, a small village in North Wales, mainly by his uncle Richard Lloyd, a shoemaker. In 1888 he married Margaret Owen. They had two sons—Richard (b. 1889) and Gwilym (b. 1894)—and three daughters—Mair (b. 1890), Olwen (b. 1892) and Megan (b. 1902). Mair died in 1907 to Lloyd George's great grief.

His correct surname was 'George'. He disliked this and gradually imposed Lloyd George on his friends and the public. He was president of the board of trade from 1905 to 1908; chancellor of the exchequer from 1908 to 1915; minister of munitions from May 1915 to July 1916; and secretary of state for war from July to December 1916. On 7 December 1916 he became prime minister of a Coalition government and remained in power until 19 October 1922. He never held office again.

As chancellor of the exchequer he lived at No. 11 Downing Street and remained there during his two subsequent appointments. He had a modest house at Walton Heath some fifteen miles outside London, which had been given him by Sir George Riddell, and another at Criccieth in North Wales, where Mrs. Lloyd George spent much of her time. Lloyd George moved into No. 10 Downing Street when he became prime minister and was the first to enjoy Chequers, a country house in Buckingham-shire which Sir Arthur Lee (later Lord Lee of Fareham) gave to the nation, together with an endowment, for the use of prime ministers. After the war Lloyd George sold the house at Walton Heath and acquired a similar suburban house at Cobham, not far away. He did not stay there for long. In 1921 he bought a country house and sixty acres of land at Churt in Surrey forty-five miles from London and thereafter lived there for most of the time. He left Churt for North Wales in September 1944, was created Earl Lloyd-George of Dwyfor in January 1945, and died at Llany-stumdwy on 26 March 1945.

Frances Stevenson was born in 1888. After taking a degree in classics at London University, she taught in a girls' boarding school at Wimbledon. In 1911 she was employed to coach Megan during the summer holidays. In 1912 Lloyd George invited her to become a secretary at the treasury 'on his own terms, which were in direct conflict with my essentially Victorian upbringing'. At Christmas 1912 she accepted these terms and began a relationship which ended only with Lloyd George's

*death. She lived with her parents at Wallington until 1915 when she set up a flat
of her own in London. In 1931 she moved to Worplesdon near Churt and a little
later built her own house, Avalon, adjacent to the Churt estate.*

*Great Britain declared war on Germany on 4 August 1914. The British Expedi-
tionary Force crossed to France and, after the retreat from Mons, took part in the
Allied victory of the Marne. When the Diary opens, the Germans had come to rest
on the Aisne, the B.E.F. was moving north to Ypres, and the Belgian army was
beleaguered in Antwerp.*

1914

I am to make a diary. I began one three years ago when at Criccieth in the
summer—life was interesting then, as now. That diary did not last, but this
one is in a sense the outcome of that visit.

September 21st 1914

Last Saturday was the Chancellor's great speech on the War, at the Queen's
Hall.[1] There is no doubt that it was a tremendous success, but C.[2] was very
depressed after it. He said the audience made him sick—they were far too
stodgy and 'comfortable'—'you had to talk your way through layers of fat'.
He thought the meeting had not been a success, but the newspapers on Sunday put his mind at rest—most enthusiastic. They were loud in their praises
this morning. Tory papers loudest of all. He laughed at the exuberance of
The Times. 'These people become almost sickly,' he remarked, 'when one
happens to fall in with their ideas.' Many people say it is the finest effort of
his career. Masterman[3] on Sunday [20 September] pronounced it 'the finest
speech in the history of England'.

C.'s colleagues in the Cabinet help to reassure him as to success of speech.
The Prime Minister said with tears in his eyes that it was 'a wonderful speech'.
Sir Edward Grey said he wept when he read the peroration. C. is satisfied,
but very tired.

At breakfast today C. told me the story of Belgium's decision to resist
Germany. The Belgian Government were on the point of giving way, and
allowing the Germans to pass through their territory, when M. Vandervelde,[4] the Socialist leader, came to the Ministry, and taking a letter out of

1. 19 September 1914. This was the first occasion when Lloyd George spoke publicly in
support of the war.
2. In the early part of the Diary covering the period when Lloyd George was chancellor
of the exchequer, Frances Stevenson refers to him as 'C.'. When Lloyd George ceased to
be chancellor he becomes 'D.' (David).
3. Charles Frederick Gurney Masterman (1874–1927): Liberal M.P., 1906–14, 1923–4;
appointed chancellor of the duchy of Lancaster in 1914, he vacated his seat according to
current practice and failed to secure re-election; resigned 1915; worked in ministry of
information, 1918; closely associated with Lloyd George's social policy before the war;
estranged from him in 1915, but reconciled after Lloyd George left office and worked
with him again.
4. Emile Vandervelde, Belgian Socialist leader.

his pocket, said: 'Jaurès has been murdered: this is a letter from the French socialists asking me to go to Paris and lead them. Unless you can tell me that Belgium will resist violation, I will shake the dust of Belgium from my feet, and take my stand among the French—and France shall know the reason why.' This came to the ears of the Belgian King, who sent for Vandervelde, and together they turned the tide of feeling in the Ministry, and Belgium declared war on Germany.

C. is most indignant at the burning of Rheims cathedral, the news of which is in today's papers. It has moved him more than anything else since the outbreak of the war.

I returned from Walton Heath this morning with C., after the happiest fortnight of my life. Have been correcting Saturday's speech for publication. The family have returned from Criccieth, and I go home.

C. said this morning he wished I had kept the love letters he wrote me two years ago. But I promised at the time to burn them, and they are all destroyed, though, as he says, 'every word of them meant business'. It does not seem possible that it is two years ago this autumn, and yet such a lot of things have happened since then.

September 22nd 1914

C. is overwhelmed with letters of congratulations for last Saturday's speech. He is very pleased with a letter from Lena Ashwell,[1] and carries it about with him. He is quite content now, and begins to think that perhaps it was a good speech after all!

September 28th 1914

Have just returned from W.H., but go back there tonight, as C. is preparing his speech for Cardiff tomorrow. Yesterday we discussed what it would mean to C. if he retired from politics. We both know that he cannot do it. It would be treason if he did. He says it is only during the last few years that he has understood the words 'Woe be unto me if I preach not the gospel!' He must go on, and I will help him.

Today he has had a great tussle with Kitchener[2] in the Cabinet, and it has left him excited and rather angry. The question of sending Nonconformist Chaplains to the front came up, and Kitchener treated the proposal with contempt. He said it was impossible, but C. said the Nonconformists only ask to be treated as he would treat the native Indian troops, the Sikhs and the Gurkhas, who are allowed to have priests of their own faith in their regiment. 'If you intend to send a Church of England Army to the front, say so!' said C., 'but you cannot fight with half a nation'. Kitchener has given in. 'Just

1. A well-known actress of the day.
2. Earl Kitchener of Khartoum became secretary of state for war on 6 August 1914. He had been out of England for forty years and knew nothing of politics. He now attempted to run the war singlehanded, as he had run his victorious campaigns in the Sudan and South Africa. Strategy, supply, and recruitment were at first under his sole control.

write down a list of these denominations', he said in a half-contemptuous way. C. likes him really, all the more I think because he has an occasional scrap with him. K. was inclined to regard C. as a kind of curiosity at first, but he finds he has an equal to reckon with.

October 2nd 1914

I think L.G. made a good speech in Cardiff. He was much amused with the Welsh Bishops, who were thoroughly sulky, and would not look at or speak to him. They are very sick that the Welsh Disestablishment Bill[1] has been passed. I have come to the conclusion that L.G. never has been or will allow himself to be, a victim of circumstances. He will always overcome them somehow, and get what he wants in the end, in things great and small. That is the secret of his success and his happy nature, and in no other man that I have ever known of or read about has this characteristic been so marked.

October 9th 1914

Returned to the Office on October 7th, my birthday. On Tuesday C. turned in to see me, and we had a long chat together. He looked tired & worried at first, and I found that passing through Clapham had depressed him, calling up sad memories of Mair. He avoids Clapham as much as possible. He told me that Antwerp[2] was in a bad way. The Govt. had that day decided to send some 20,000 men over to Ostend, in order to march on Antwerp and relieve it. They discovered however that the Admiralty had mined the sea right up to Ostend, making a landing impossible. The difficulty was to be overcome by sending a pilot ship with the troopships, & landing south of Ostend. The pilot ship to be supplied by the Admiralty. Some time after troops had started, it was discovered that the pilot ship had been forgotten, & that our troops were therefore in imminent danger of being blown up by our own mines. A torpedo-boat was therefore dispatched at full speed to recall troopships. This was done, & ships eventually re-started safely with pilot, but only after some hours delay. I fear they will not be able to save Antwerp. I cannot sleep for thinking of the horrible tortures that Belgium is undergoing.

On Wednesday C. went to Committee of Imperial Defence. It seems that Kitchener fears an attempted invasion as soon as the two armies are 'stalemate' in France. Both the P.M. and C. are convinced that this could not be successfully attempted.

---

1. The Bill disestablishing the Welsh Church was passed under the provisions of the Parliament Act after being rejected three times by the House of Lords. Its operation was postponed until after the war.
2. The Belgian army had fallen back into Antwerp and was now attacked there by the Germans. Failing any more substantial Allied aid, Churchill went to Antwerp with a naval brigade and even proposed to take command. Antwerp fell on 10 October. The Belgian army retreated down the coast where it held a fragment of national territory throughout the war. Most of the British force were taken prisoner or interned in Holland, and Churchill was much criticised for his rash intervention.

C. & I had a very primitive dinner together at No. 11 (which is under repair) before C. departed for W.H.

Yesterday (Thursday) we dined again in the same primitive way. He was to have dined with Donald[1] & friends, but decided to go straight to theatre instead. We had great fun. C. gave me a beautiful set of Barrie's works for a birthday present. It is sweet of him, he was so keen about it, & it gives him such pleasure to give anyone a present. I was very touched. We hated leaving each other. C. said he might have been going to the war, judging from the parting we had.

Have not seen much of him today as he has been very busy in Board Room, with occasional flying visits in here. He has left for weekend at W.H. His last words. 'Same address. "Virtuous"—Walton Heath.'

Winston has returned from Antwerp, admitting failure, and blaming Kitchener & War Office for lack of foresight.

October 14th 1914
L.G. is still determined to go to France, and may leave on Friday. But the Lord Chief Justice[2] is also going, so I know he will be well looked after.

L.G. has for some time past been urging the Government to take precautionary measures for future home defence. He considers that a far larger store of arms and ammunition ought to be provided. Other arrangements he also considers inadequate. As a result of his pleadings, the Cabinet decided to institute a War Council to consider these matters. It met for the first time on Monday [12 October], and again Tuesday.[3] L.G. has promised to dictate to me an account of the proceedings to put with my other papers.

But in spite of his cautiousness, L.G. does not believe it is at all possible for the Huns to invade England. He says that if we, with 6 times the number of men the Germans have (assuming they bring over 200,000) with our fleet, with French[4] and his army to attack from behind, and with all our resources at our disposal—if we are not able to keep out the Germans under these conditions—then the Germans are the best men, and it is essential for the welfare of the world that men who have reached such a pitch of perfection should govern the world for the next century. But he does not think they have reached that pitch of perfection, and he believes with every other Briton that we shall win.

---

1. Robert Donald (1860–1933): editor of the Radical Daily Chronicle, 1902–18; supported Lloyd George until 1918 and then turned against him; dismissed as editor when Daily Chronicle bought by Lloyd George group, 1918.
2. Rufus Daniel Isaacs (1860–1935), cr. Baron Reading, 1914, Viscount, 1916, Earl, 1917, Marquess, 1926; lord chief justice, 1913–21; high commissioner in United States, 1917, ambassador, 1918–19; viceroy of India, 1921–6; foreign secretary, 1931.
3. This body was an adaptation of the peacetime Committee of Imperial Defence. It had originally eight members and gradually increased to thirteen.
4. John Denton Pinkstone French (1852–1925): commander-in-chief, British Expeditionary Force, 1914–15; of home forces, 1916–18; lord-lieutenant of Ireland, 1918–21; cr. Viscount, 1916, Earl of Ypres, 1922.

Churchill has been widely condemned for his action at Antwerp. It seems that but for his promise of British help, Antwerp would have surrendered a week earlier, and much loss and destruction would have been avoided. However, he blames Kitchener for lack of foresight.

October 23rd 1914 (Walton Heath)
C. spent last weekend in France. He left on Friday night [16 October], & returned on Monday night. I was very anxious all the time he was away, as there was considerable risk attached to the journey. We received a wire to say that they had landed safely at Dieppe, and another on Monday from General Headquarters in France. I was glad when I heard late Monday night that he had returned safely. I came down here with him on Tuesday, & since then he has told me all about the journey.

C. has been very busy since his return, & is fearfully tired, I fear that his health will give way unless he slacks a little more. But the work must be done, & though Lord Reading is invaluable in helping him & relieving him of a great portion of the work, yet C. must give the final decisions, which means that he must acquaint himself with the details. Last night in the car coming down, I was afraid he was going to be ill, he was so terribly done up. But he is better again this morning, & has gone up for meetings with the Bankers this afternoon.

C. is rather disgusted with Winston still about Antwerp, and thinks that the P.M. is too. Having taken untrained men over there, he left them in the lurch. He behaved in rather a swaggering way when over there, standing for photographers & cinematographers with shells bursting near him, & actually promoting his pals on the field of action.

They have been discussing the question of separation allowances in the Cabinet. The machinery is very badly worked, & many women are suffering in consequence. Then the question of giving relief to unmarried women who have lived with soldiers meets with a good deal of opposition. The Archbishop of Canterbury[1] signified to the Cabinet his disapproval that these women should receive allowances on the same basis as married women. Mr. Masterman was sent to see him on the subject. It appears that the Archbishop does not wish them or their children to starve, but he does not wish them to be openly treated as deserving of relief,—which is a piece of blatant hypocrisy. C. fought hard for these unmarried women, & the Cabinet have decided to make no distinction, if a woman can prove that she has lived with a man as his wife. The Archbishop wrote a strong letter of disapproval on hearing this, saying that the Government were dealing a death-blow to the marriage tie, and were encouraging immorality. C. in an interview with the Rev. Shakespeare & the Rev. R. J. Campbell[2] spoke strongly on the subject, & found them very reasonable. He represented that in Scotland these women

---

1. Archbishop Davidson.
2. Two Nonconformist ministers.

would, many of them, be legally married, whereas in England they are not, so that the 'holy institution of marriage' is purely a question of local convention. Many of them, he said, are not less purely & holily united because they have not been before the parson. Moreover, it is not right to take the lives of the men for their country, and after you have accepted the sacrifice to say that you do not approve of their morals and are afraid you cannot make decent provision for the women they have treated as their wives. If you are going to take this line, you ought to inquire into the morals of the man *before* you accept his life. Once you have accepted it, he has a right to *demand* an allowance for the woman he has lived with & their children,—provided it is a bona-fide union.

C. is very pleased with himself about the guns. England was very inadequately prepared, but now we shall have 3,000 cannon of an up-to-date type by next July, instead of the 600 which the War Office considered sufficient.

October 30th 1914
Have been at W.H. most of the week, & am returning there for the weekend. C. is very tired and worrying in case Gwilym is sent to the front, which he fears will happen soon. Yesterday he fought Kitchener again in the Cabinet, on the subject of the Welsh Army Corps. There has been a foolish order issued last week to the effect that soldiers may not speak Welsh on parade or in their billets. C. says that unless the order is withdrawn immediately & the Colonel who gave the order censured, he will go. He was very much upset by the occurrence during last week-end, also by the fact that Separation Allowances are being disgracefully administered all over the country. He therefore criticised the War O. freely in the Cabinet, and Kitchener got angry, & suggested that perhaps C. would like to take over the management of the W.O. Whereupon C. remarked that he (K.) was only one among 19, and must stand criticism in the same way as any other member of the Cabinet. He (K.) was not a dictator, and if things were not mended at the W.O., the Chancellor would criticise him in the House of Commons & in the Cabinet. They parted bad friends, as K. very much resented the Chancellor's remarks. The rest of the Cabinet, including the Prime Minister, were with C.

Dr. Christopher Addison[1] suggests putting the manager of Selfridge's at the head of the W.O.

On Tuesday [27 October] Mr. Murray[2] drove me down to see Paul.[3] We

---

1. Christopher Addison (1869–1951), doctor of medicine and social reformer; advised Lloyd George on social reform; recruited Liberal support for Lloyd George in December 1916; minister of munitions, 1916–17; minister of reconstruction, 1917–19; minister of health, 1919–21; minister without portfolio, 1921; directed 'Homes for Heroes' and was later saddled with responsibility for failure; went over to Labour and became ultimately leader of the house of lords; cr. Baron, 1937, Viscount, 1945.
2. Later Sir James Murray. He had been a Liberal member of parliament and was devoted to Lloyd George.
3. Paul Stevenson, Frances's brother, died of wounds 1915.

had a long talk with him, & left him rather happier. He is very anxious to get to the front, and thinks they will be moving soon, but is very much afraid in case he gets left behind, being only a junior officer.

On Wednesday C. dined with Robertson Nicoll[1] & others. They discussed the question of the unmarried mother & her status. One of the party said that at a recent gathering on the subject Mary Macarthur[2] & Violet Markham[3] had both spoken in support of her, & they had expressed the opinion that a woman had a perfect right to have a child from any man she pleases.

Last night I talked to C. about Women's Suffrage. He says there is no big woman at the head of the movement. Christabel Pankhurst[4] is clever & sharp, but not big. Mrs. P. is a big woman, but narrow. C. says the women have not yet learnt to fight flanking movements, i.e. make a fight for an object which does not lead directly to their goal, but which helps considerably to attain their object. He says that when the Civil Service Commission was appointed, women should have combined their efforts to get themselves represented on it, and could have made a big fight for women's rights which might have borne good fruit.

C. has just promised R. J. Campbell to speak at the City Temple on Nov. 10th.

We have lost a Dreadnought (Audacious) by a mine off the Irish Coast. The Govt. are going to keep this news back from the public, which I think a great mistake. C. thinks so too. He is depressed about the war. He says he feels sometimes that it will overwhelm him & that he must go away somewhere and get out of it all. War is not his work, and he feels that he has not the heart to deal with it. It is all so horrible.

November 2nd 1914
We returned from W.H. this morning. C.'s quarrel with K. of K. has been patched up. C. went over to the War Office on Friday afternoon [30 October], taking with him Colonel Owen Thomas, whom he asked to wait for him while he had a talk with K. They talked about the Welsh Army Corps, & the appointment of a General for N. Wales. C. suggested that the man whose name he thought would be submitted would not be at all suitable for the post. K. agreed, & asked C. if he had anyone in mind. C. suggested Col. O.T., & K. rather fell in with the idea. He asked where the Colonel was, & when he heard he was in the building, sent for him, & appointed him Brigadier-General on the spot. C. said it was a most dramatic touch, & very

1. Sir William Robertson Nicoll, editor of The British Weekly, gave powerful support to Lloyd George.
2. Mary Reid Anderson, trade union organiser; member of reconstruction and other committees, 1914–18; married W. C. Anderson, 1911.
3. Violet Markham, social worker; married James Carruthers, 1915.
4. Christabel Pankhurst, militant suffragette. 'Mrs. P.' is Emmeline Pankhurst, her mother, the suffragette leader. Mrs. Pankhurst and Christabel were now strenuously for the war. Sylvia, Mrs. Pankhurst's younger daughter, was as strenuous against it.

magnanimous on K.'s part, as he must have known that it was the Colonel who had been supplying C. with complaints, about W.O. & Welsh Army Corps. C. was very pleased with the appointment. The new Brigadier seemed rather dazed at the sudden elevation.

C. is at present engaged in preparing a speech for Nonconformists at the City Temple. He told me some of it at breakfast this morning, and it seems good. Everyone is very anxious for him to speak on recruiting, but, as he says, he will be fighting with them all again in a year's time. He told me how in 1910, after the Conference which was summoned to decide the House of Lords controversy, he had suggested to the leaders of both parties that there should be a friendly settlement on the subjects of Disestablishment, Home Rule, Insurance, the Land question, etc., and he also suggested a system of Ballot Conscription in this country. The Tory leaders were Lansdowne,[1] Balfour,[2] F. E. Smith,[3] Chamberlain.[4] The Liberal Leaders were partial to this suggested Coalition, & the Tory leaders seemed anxious for a settlement —all except Balfour, who refused to come to terms. He would not accept any of these propositions, and though the other questions have been since dealt with by the Liberal Government, the plan of the Ballot Conscription fell to the ground. C. says that Balfour came to No. 11 to talk the project over with him, & they sat there for 3 hours deliberating, Balfour saying from time to time: 'I wish I could do it—I wish with all my heart that it were possible—but it cannot be'. And then: 'I *cannot* be the Sir Robert Peel of my party', adding half-whimsically—'Though I cannot see where the Disraeli of the Party would come in—unless it were in my cousin Hugh!'[5] Subsequently Balfour proposed that he and C. should stand out altogether, and support the Government from outside. C. was quite willing, but even then B. would not come to any decision, & the whole scheme fell through. Such a plan, though it might have solved many difficulties & hastened many reforms, would not have been without danger to the Liberal party, for it would without doubt have been objectionable to a great many Liberals. But though the Liberal leaders were willing to take this risk, & C. was willing to give up his place

1. Henry Petty-Fitzmaurice, fifth Marquess of Lansdowne (1845–1927); formerly governor general of Canada, viceroy of India, and foreign secretary; minister without portfolio, 1915–16; Unionist leader in house of lords, 1903–16; advocated compromise peace in The Daily Telegraph, November 1917.
2. Arthur James Balfour (1848–1930), formerly Unionist prime minister and leader; first lord of the admiralty, 1915–16; foreign secretary, 1916–19; lord president of the council, 1912–22, 1925–9; cr. Earl, 1922.
3. Frederick Edwin Smith (1874–1930): solicitor general, 1915; attorney general, 1915–19; lord chancellor, 1919–22; secretary for India, 1924–8; cr. Baron Birkenhead, 1919, Viscount, 1921, Earl, 1922.
4. Austen Chamberlain (1863–1937): secretary for India, 1915–17; member of war cabinet, 1918; chancellor of exchequer, 1919–21; lord privy seal, 1921–2; foreign secretary, 1924–9; first lord of admiralty, 1931; Unionist leader in house of commons, 1921–2.
5. Lord Hugh Cecil (1869–1956), fifth son of 3rd marquis of Salisbury and brother of Lord Robert Cecil; cr. Viscount Quickswood, 1941.

in the Government, yet Balfour would not take the corresponding risk on his side. So the matter fell through: but had the Chancellor's proposition of the Ballot Conscription been accepted, we should have had a million men ready in this country on the outbreak of the war; and when the Tories say that it is the fault of the Liberals that we had not more men ready, they lie.

November 5th 1914

C. remains down at W.H. today, to think over speech for next Tuesday [10 November]. He is still pessimistic about war. Kitchener, he says, was also rather depressed when he returned last Monday [2 November] from the front. But K. said that the French generals are very sanguine. He saw Foch and Joffre.[1] He thinks that the former is a brilliant general, & this was the impression of C. when he met him also; but he (K.) has no very great opinion of Joffre—he is too slow—'always two days late and two divisions short'— Foch, however, said this battle on the Yser would be the decisive battle of the war. He is confident we shall win, & thinks that the Germans will then have to retire from France & Belgium. General French, however, says if he is to go on he must have more men. K. is worried because he has no Regulars to send, except rather a ragged Division gathered from all ends of the earth. But he is giving French the choice of this or Territorials. We have suffered very heavy losses in this battle. The Duc de Morny, whom C. met on Tuesday [3 November], says that our men are too reckless with their lives. They are too proud to crawl along to take cover when necessary, and until they become more cautious we shall continue to have heavy losses.

C. has heard that Gwilym may go to India in a few weeks. He (C.) is very relieved that he is not going to France.

C. & Kitchener are very good pals again now. In the Cabinet on Monday [2 November] Grey announced that the Italian Ministry had resigned. Someone asked the reason of this, and Grey replied that it was owing to a difference between the Minister for War and the Chancellor of the Exchequer. C. of E. looked at Kitchener, & they both roared with laughter, in which the others joined. 'Well', said C. 'I hope they will make it up as satisfactorily as we have done!'

The naval losses are heavy lately. C. says Churchill is too busy trying to get a flashy success to attend to the real business of the Admiralty. Churchill blames Admiral Cradock for the defeat in South America[2]—the Admiral presumably having gone down with his ship & so unable to clear himself. This is characteristic of Churchill. When he returned from Antwerp after his failure he said to the Cabinet, 'Now that the administration of such serious & important affairs lies entirely in the hands of a few of us—since Parliament is not sitting—it behoves us to be quite frank with each other.' Everyone

---

1. French commander-in-chief 1914–16.
2. Battle of Coronel, 3 November 1914, when two British cruisers were sunk.

agreed, thinking that he was about to confess to his mistake. Instead, he went on to shift the whole of the responsibility for the disaster on to Kitchener, who happened to be absent from the Cabinet that day.

November 16th 1914

C. is remaining at Walton Heath today, as he is not feeling well enough[1] to come up to town. Miss Hunter is down there this weekend, helping with the Budget, as that is her job. The weekend before I spent down there, & we were busy over the City Temple speech,[2] which was a great success. C. was so much happier there than at the Queen's Hall, & spoke brilliantly, though of course the speech has not received so much notice as the first one, simply because it is the second of its kind. There have already been 2½ million copies of the Queen's Hall Speech disposed of.

The weekend at W.H. was a most interesting one, though of course the jolliest kind is when we have it all to ourselves. However, this time there were visitors, among them General Owen Thomas who told many interesting stories of the S. African War. He & C. were joking together about the way in which Kitchener created him a Brigadier-General. The General said he had no idea of anything of that sort happening when K. sent for him. 'Of course', he said, 'I had to accept it. I couldn't say No.' 'My dear Thomas', retorted C., 'you weren't in a condition to say anything!' 'No', laughed Thomas, 'I remember I dropped my hat in my amazement.'

The other day Mrs. Rowntree brought M. Emil Vandervelde to see the Chancellor, & he spent a short time in our room. He is supposed to be the Lloyd George of Belgium, but I thought that he rather lacked charm, which is of course essential to a Lloyd George. However, I suppose that M. Vandervelde is very worried over the agony of his poor little country, & the distress of his people. I talked to a Belgian refugee yesterday, who had left Brussels after the Germans entered it. She said that one German officer, who was disposed to be friendly, told them that the German armies, whatever they had done, had not been a quarter as brutal as the Kaiser had commanded them to be. His order had been that they were to kill whomsoever they met —that not a single Belgian man woman or child was to be spared—there was to be no more Belgium, & no more Belgians.

An amusing incident happened here the other day. A man came to the Treasury & inquired for Lloyd George—he only wanted a word with him. Mr. Davies[3] told him that he could not possibly see C. but said he would take a message for him. The fellow said he was anxious to be made a Roman Catholic—he must become one within a month's time—it was vital—& so

---

1. Asquith called it 'one of those psychological chills which always precede his budgets when he does not feel altogether sure of his ground'. Jenkins, Asquith, p. 337.
2. 10 November 1914. 'The Righteousness of our Cause.'
3. John Thomas Davies (1881–1938), Lloyd George's principal private secretary, 1912–22; knighted, 1922; director of Suez canal company, 1922–38.

he wanted to see Lloyd George. Mr. Davies said 'Why do you come to
Lloyd George to be made a Catholic? You have come to the wrong place.'
'Oh, but I have come to *Lloyd George*', the man answered. 'A word from him
would do it.' 'But why don't you go to the Pope', said Mr. Davies. 'He is
your man, if you want to become an R.C.' 'Why, man!' said he, 'Lloyd
George is above the Pope!'

I am sorry 'Bobs'[1] is dead. For once the newspapers have consented to
make room for something beyond war news. Though I suppose this is a part
of the war news. The papers are full of biographies today. C. tells me that
these biographies are already prepared & pigeon-holed for months or years
before a public man's death; & that T. P. O'Connor[2] has already received
£100 for writing his (C.'s).

November 20th 1914

C. has just gone to W. Heath to spend a 'virtuous weekend'. However we
managed to have an evening there together this week on Wednesday—quite
unexpected, but enjoyed to the very fullest. C. was rather conscience-stricken
on the way down, as he was dying to get away from the House, & could not
give his mind to Budget discussions. He says he accepted any proposal which
was quickly dealt with, & persuaded them to leave Beer till today, which he
assured them would serve just as well. He is very tired this evening after a
very hard day.

The Budget speech was a great success, though I could not go to hear it
owing to a Red Cross Exam. Bonar Law on Monday night sent a note to the
P.M. begging him not to allow the Budget to be brought in, as it would
provoke bitter and dangerous opposition. However, C. flatters himself that
by a very artful & ingenious speech he has brought round the House—or
most of it—to his way of thinking, & thinks he will be able to see the thing
through.

Mamma went to the Budget Speech instead of me, & thoroughly appreciated it. C. also got her a ticket for Lord Roberts' Funeral. She needs to have
her mind occupied just now, as she is worrying about Paul. I think she is
getting more reconciled to the relations between C. & me, as she recognises
it is an honest love which will last, & not just a passing passion. She and C.
get on very well together.

I dined with Dorothy Brown[3] on Tuesday [17 November]. She wished to
know whether my feelings towards her brother were any different, as he is
still very unhappy. I told her that I had not changed my mind. I cannot

---

1. Frederick Sleigh Roberts, first Earl Roberts (1832–1914) field-marshal, victor in
Afghan and Boer wars; died while visiting British troops in France.
2. Thomas Power O'Connor (1848–1929), Irish Nationalist M.P. and journalist.
3. The sister of Stuart Kelson Brown, who had proposed to Frances Stevenson shortly
before she met Lloyd George. He subsequently married a friend of Frances's and occupied
a high post at the India Office.

explain how things really are, but feel that I am doing right in refusing to see him, since he may forget & marry someone else. I am sorry he is unhappy.

C. again referred to the love-letters he sent me two years ago, when he was wooing me: he says he wishes we could read them over together now. But they are destroyed. They were indeed very beautiful, but the things he says to me now are more beautiful still. Sometimes I am so happy that I tremble for fear it will not last. Our love will always last, but there is the dread that he might be taken from me. He is never tired of talking of that summer when he used to come to Allenswood, & we both felt there was something between us, though it was not yet expressed—and of the following autumn, when we used to meet once a week, and I hovered between doubt and longing, dread and desire: and of the time in the House of Commons, when I left him because I would not agree to his proposals, but returned soon after to say that I could not face life without him, & would do what he wished. I have never regretted the decision. It has brought me two years of happiness, & if Fate wills will bring me many more.

November 30th 1914

The work is a little more slack today, though C. has been busy this afternoon with the Separation Allowances and Pensions Committee. I am to keep his papers for this Committee, which I am glad to do as I shall know what is going on. A well-known lady of the Mrs. Humphrey Ward type, sent him suggestions for dealing with the case of the 'unmarried wives', to avoid treating them on the same plane as the legal wife. She said (or words to that effect) that it would be an incentive to immorality. C. pushed the papers away with an exclamation of disgust. 'Who is she', he exclaimed, 'to talk of immorality! Why, her husband lived on immorality. He was President of the Divorce Court.'

C. is in very good spirits after a week-end rest. Yesterday I went down to W.H. & spent the afternoon with him, & we had a jolly time. We have both been reading Wells' last book The Wife of Sir Isaac Harman and C. thinks it is his most brilliant work. Wells has modified his views considerably, though, since he wrote Anne Veronica!

C. made a clinking speech on Friday.[1] He had prepared the first part of it ages ago—somewhere in August—& we thought it would never really come off, as it was continually postponed. It was a most difficult subject to handle, much more to make interesting, but it has been highly praised. The L.C.J. was watching him intently from the Gallery. He is extraordinarily fond of C. —one would almost say he is jealous—not of C., but of C.'s other friends.

C. & I were counting up yesterday—as far as we could remember, he has

---

1. Friday 27 November 1914 on third reading of Government War Obligations Bill. On outbreak of war the government had proclaimed a moratorium and took over responsibility for bills on neutral and enemy countries. Lord Reading did much of the subsequent work on this for Lloyd George.

made 22 big speeches since I have been working for him here. We began with the Marconi speeches in 1913.[1] I remember him sending for me when I was in Scotland, when I had only been there a few days, urging me to come back, for a great trouble had come on him & was gripping him, so that he could not sleep at night, and he wanted me to be there with him. I had no idea what the trouble was, nor would he tell me until I came back, & even then I could not grasp the extent of it, did not realise the menace of the Marconi campaign. I do not think I fully understood all it meant until the thing was over. I only know that all that spring I did my best to drive the shadow away from him & make him as happy as I could. He says he will never forgive Massingham[2] for deserting him at that time. He (C.) is one who can never forgive an act of treachery or an act of deceit, however much he may want to.

C. has begun to worry again over Gwilym, who is not going to India after all. He is a terrible man for worrying where anyone he is fond of is concerned. He is much too sensitive for a man, much too tender-hearted,—though he can be fearfully hard too. He will not grant Mr. Rowntree's[3] request that we should give the Belgians half the money towards providing food for them, if they will find the other half. He says to do this would be to help the Germans. He says the Germans are responsible for the Belgian population in Belgium, & that they *must* feed them if no-one else does, but so long as they think that someone else will send food, of course they will not trouble. Mr. Rowntree, who is thinking only of the sufferings of the Belgians, says that it is a brutal view to take, & that the Germans will not feed them: but C. says they are bound to, though there may be suffering first, while they are 'trying on' their game of making other countries send food to Belgium. C. says he & Grey & Kitchener fought hard against allowing the food ship from America to go to Belgium.

I have just rescued from the Archives C.'s account of the propositions which he suggested to the Conference in 1910—the plans which a Coalition Government might carry through but which could not be carried by a Party Govt. Some of them, such as Insurance and Local Govt. have already been carried, others such as Land, are in the making, while some, such as pensions for widows, conscription, & certain schemes of Imperial policy, are in the dim future. I expect the Opposition were shy at it because there would be

---

1. Lloyd George and Lord Reading, then Rufus Isaacs, were accused of using information acquired as members of the cabinet in order to make a profit in Marconi shares. They pleaded that they had bought shares only in American Marconi, and not in the British company, which had prospects of receiving a government contract. Lloyd George also pleaded that he had lost money by the speculation. These pleas were accepted by the (Liberal) majority of a select committee.

2. Henry William Massingham (1860–1924), editor of the Radical Nation, 1907–23; though not a pacifist, opposed Lloyd George's energetic conduct of the war and advocated a compromise peace. In 1917 The Nation was, for a time, banned from foreign circulation.

3. Seebohm Rowntree, cocoa magnate and social reformer.

too much Lloyd George in it! He showed the schemes to Montagu[1] tonight. Montagu was amazed. 'Well!', he said 'I always thought you weren't really a Liberal!'.

We really thought that, after the hundreds of letters containing suggestions for new taxes that we have received during the last few weeks, the sources of new taxation had been exhausted. But this evening we receive still another— a man who thinks that the women of the country are not paying enough towards the War, suggests that there should be a tax on corsets!

December 3rd 1914

L.G. made a brilliant little speech on Tuesday night at a send-off dinner to the London Welsh Battalion. The speech was quite impromptu, and he thought there were no reporters there, so he just 'let himself go'. There is in it some expression of the passionate attachment which he feels for Wales, and which lies at the bottom of all his work.

L.G. is trying to get an honour for the Lord Chief Justice, who has been so splendid over the Financial business since the beginning of the War. He has been an enormous help to L.G., who could not possibly have stood the great strain without the L.C.J.'s invaluable help. Time after time I thought L.G. was on the verge of a breakdown, but because of this strong right hand he was able to take a day or half a day to rest, and all was well again. I tell L.G. that he deserves some recognition too, but of course, he will not take a title.

L.G. says I am quite wrong about the Welsh people quarrelling among themselves. He says they do not quarrel any more than all other people engaged in public work; and the more artistic of temperament a person is, the more inclined will he be to quarrel over trifles. He says there are no people more jealous and quarrelsome than those of the artistic professions. I expect he is right: anyhow, I would much rather believe that he is, for I love the Welsh, with all their faults. I seem to be able to understand them, and with understanding most difficulties are overcome.

December 14th 1914

Spent a very quiet Sunday [13 December]. On Saturday was down at W.H. working. On Friday, C. & I spent the day there alone. We have been very lucky considering all things. The previous Thursday & Friday we spent together & had a jolly time. C. arrived very tired on Thursday, having had a very unpleasant interview with the Belgian Finance Minister. He is asking for money from the British Government to feed the Belgians in Belgium, but C. contends that to do this would be to relieve the Germans of their responsibility for feeding the population in the districts they are occupying, & would prolong the war. He told the Belgian Minister that he would therefore not give one penny for this purpose. Thereupon the Minister grew angry, and

---

1. Hon. Edwin Montagu (1879–1924), Liberal M.P.; chancellor duchy of Lancaster, 1916; minister of munitions, 1916; secretary for India, 1917–22; opposed Lloyd George's anti-Turkish policy.

said that he could obtain the money from elsewhere. 'Very well', said C. 'You are at liberty to do that, but then the responsibility for prolonging the war will be yours, not mine.' C. contends that the money we have already raised for the war—500 millions—has been raised as a consequence of our determination to protect Belgium.

His anger was further aroused on Monday as a consequence of a letter which he received from the French embassy, informing him that the Belgian soldiers were practically all in France at the present moment, & were being fed & billetted & paid with the French soldiers, it being the intention of the French Govt. to keep an account of expenses thus entailed, and to present the bill to Belgium after the war. The Belgians, however, have been trying to arrange for an advance of several millions from the British Govt. in order to pay the expenses of their soldiers: whereas it would now appear that there are no expenses being incurred.

C. says that the French finances are in a hopeless muddle. He says that before the war they were at a loss where to turn to raise money, & owed already a large amount, so that when the war broke out they were faced with a large debt and the necessity for raising further large sums without delay. So that when the war is over they will have an overwhelming amount of unfunded debt. C. on the other hand has consistently refused to obtain money by borrowing, & has always paid his way by raising taxes. Even since the war he has not raised the whole of the money needed by a loan, but has obtained a considerable portion by means of taxes. So that our finances are more prosperous now than they have ever been, & our resources are capable of bearing huge drains upon them & still recuperate fairly easily. No one has had the courage in France to impose heavy taxation upon income, for fear of rousing the anger of the monied classes.

C. has given me a letter from Bonar Law[1] to the Prime Minister on the night before the War Budget, counselling the 'easiest way' for raising money. But C. says that that 'easiest way' is fraught with disastrous consequences, and he would rather face any amount of opposition and abuse than adopt it. He says his plan is better in the end for the people & for the country. At any rate, some of the French 'Deputés' who have been over here lately seem to wish that the same course had been adopted in France, for there is a bad outlook at present for French finance. They are already wanting to borrow 12 millions from us.

C. was feeling ill last Monday [7 December], & was rather concerned for the state of his health in general. I know he has cause to feel tired in consequence of his hard work, but I can't help feeling that this is partly a result of a foolish paragraph in The British Weekly to the effect that C. was looking

---

1. Andrew Bonar Law (1858–1923), Unionist Leader in house of commons, 1911–21; leader of Conservative party, 1922–3; colonial secretary, 1915–16; chancellor of exchequer and member of war cabinet, 1916–19; lord privy seal, 1919–21; Conservative prime minister, 1922–3.

ill & his friends were concerned for his health. It is always foolish to tell C. that he looks ill, for then he always imagines he is ill; but if you tell him he is looking well, he bucks up at once. It is fatal to sympathise with him too strongly—it is no kindness to him. After all, he *does* know how to take care of himself, & when he ought to throw up everything & rest, & he is suffi- ciently strong-minded to do so & act upon instinct. However, he decided that he was not well last week, & rested a lot accordingly, & I am really not sorry that he did so. He told me of how he wrote to Tom Ellis when he was taken ill in the South of France, counselling him to take care of his body, and his soul would take care of itself. But the letter arrived too late, for it was read to him on his death bed.

December 16th 1914
Continued from Monday [14 December]. Last week C. was still pessimistic about the war—said we were fighting better brains than our own—that there was not one really first-class man on our side. The Germans had shown that they had had better training than we, and he knew the value of training— he had seen examples of it in the House, when Labour members competed against men of better education than themselves—they were just as good fellows, but they hadn't the training. And C. says that it is training that is wanting on our side—among the generals. He says our soldiers are the best in Europe, but they are being wantonly sacrificed because those in authority do not know how to make the best use of them. However, our big forward movement, which has been so long coming off, seems to have definitely begun, & perhaps we shall have better news. The advance will be very very slow—300 yards yesterday!—and will involve enormous loss of life. It seems too horrible to think of.

    There has been great excitement everywhere today at the news that German warships are shelling towns on the east coast. At the present moment the engagement is still going on, but news comes from the Admiralty that they think our ships have cut off the Germans, & will make good work of it. It is a great chance for us to give them a good smashing. C. was very excited over it. He says that since the beginning of the war there have been three war councils,—the third having been held this morning—at the first one he expressed the opinion that the most likely move on the part of the enemy with regard to our coast would be to shell towns like Scarborough, Middles- boro & the Hartlepools on the East coast—at least, he said, 'that is what I should do if I were commanding the German fleet'. The other members of the Council said it was most unlikely that this would occur and Captain Hankey[1] laughed at the idea. At the second Council C. expressed the same conviction again, with no further result. Today Captain Hankey entered the

---

1. Maurice Hankey (1877–1963): an officer of marines; secretary to the committee of imperial defence, 1912–38; to the war cabinet, 1916–19; to cabinet, 1919–38; clerk to the privy council, 1923–38; knighted 1919; cr. Baron, 1938.

Council & said: 'Well! Lloyd George's raid has come off!' C. was also very elated because he had had an interview with the Roumanian representatives, & thinks, as he expresses it, that he has 'roped Roumania in'. He says too that if we have a victory today, Italy may come in on our side. M. Cambon, the French Ambassador, who has a very quiet, biting wit, is reported to have said, of the Italians, when someone called his attention to their attitude in the war: 'The Italians are a very brave people: you will find them all rushing to the aid of the victor.'

Mr. Davies spoke of a friend's servant who is going to get married, & he says she is such an awful specimen that he has written to his sister-in-law to tell her that there is still some hope for her! We are both of the opinion that these ill-conditioned women should not be able to get married & have children, whereas girls who would make splendid mothers don't get a chance of having children. Mr. D. says that his sister-in-law is head mistress of a defective school, & when the children are brought to this school the mothers have to give the life-history of their antecedents, & some of the details are perfectly shocking. One woman used to bring up an idiot child regularly once a year, until the head mistress got tired of it, & said to her: 'You are a wicked woman to have so many children!' 'Lor, Mum', returned the woman, 'don't be 'ard on us! It's the only pleasure we gets in life!'

The Prince of Wales' Fund still seems to be badly administered. Mr. Rowntree says it is a 'national disaster'. They say that for Balham & Tooting £13 were allotted, & 120 people were appointed to distribute it!

The Lord Chief Justice still makes his appearance daily at the Treasury, & stays until he cannot with decency stay any longer. They say he misses his political life, and finds his work at the Law Courts tedious. It is certain that he is always very glad to get to the Treasury & have a gossip with C. C. told him the other day that he was like a little puppy that he had, who could not hide his delight when he was allowed to come back into the room after having been kept out for some time!

C. was very annoyed yesterday morning with me for allowing Mrs. Swanwick[1] to come with Miss Marshall[2] of the National Union to talk to him about childless Widows & Pensions. C. rather likes Miss Marshall, but—all unknown to me—cannot bear Mrs. Swanwick. 'Yes, I *have* seen her', he said in answer to my inquiries, 'and that is why I don't want to see her again! Why, she has a beard!' I must say that she is rather queer-looking, but anyhow he was quite nice to them both. Miss Marshall teased him for having on the last occasion they corresponded, called her 'cantankerous'. 'Well, so you were', said C. They are going to send in a Memo. to the Pensions Committee.

Am to go down to W.H. tomorrow & C. is going to make a strenuous effort to come down in the evening.

---

1. Helena Maria Swanwick (1864–1939), social worker and international conciliator. British founder of Women's International League.
2. Catherine E. Marshall, former suffragette; opponent of war and of conscription.

December 22nd 1914

C. is going away tomorrow & we are fearfully busy preparing for his departure. But there is a Cabinet the following Wednesday [30 December], so that he will have to return on Tuesday, and then at any rate we shall have a few days together. I hate to part with him for a week, but shall have heaps to keep me busy, as Mr. Davies is going with him, & Hamilton is going down to the country, over the Xmas weekend. Paul is not coming home for Xmas, and Mamma is rather upset.

December 23rd 1914

C. has gone, and left me desolate. How long before next Tuesday? There will be plenty of work, though, to keep one busy. There seems every likelihood of my having to come up here on Xmas day, and certainly on Boxing Day.

Mamma has received a beautiful basket of fruit from C., and she is very pleased thereat. He sent me at the same time a dear little orange-tree. He has been giving me Christmas presents since the beginning of the month, and I hope he has stopped now. But he says that it gives him pleasure to do it, & therefore that it is purely selfish. It would be a good thing if selfishness always benefited others to that extent!

I was very sick to hear of the escape of the German raiders, though C. had already told me before I left the office that they had got away. He said we knew they were coming—we had an agent who let us know the minute they had started and we had been expecting them for days. The Prime Minister at lunch that day had boasted that they would never get back again. 'They think', he said, 'that this war is going to be decided on land. It is not: it will be decided on the seas: what is more, it will be decided today!' When he heard later on that they had got away, his only answer was a sniff of disgust.

Winston is very sick about the whole affair. He is now interfering with the French campaign, and planning, it would appear, a second Antwerp escapade. But he sent a note across to C. in the Cabinet this week: 'The French are behaving odiously.' 'Which means', said C. to me, 'that they refuse to alter the whole of their plans in order to add to Winston's personal glory.'

Diary 1915

January 17th 1915
I fear my diary has got very behindhand. The last three weeks have been so busy and happy that I have not had the opportunity for writing things down. C. returned from Wales on Dec. 29th and from then till now I have been with him at W.H., coming up every day to town, & going back in the evening. It has been like an idyll, but alas! came to an end yesterday, when the family returned from Criccieth, & I returned home. The longer we are together, the more our love and affection seems to increase, so that it is all the more difficult to part. But we have resolved not to be miserable at parting, for 'my true love hath my heart, & I have his' and happy memories will buoy us up till 'the next time'. C. told me of Harry—whose youthful crimes have pursued him during the whole of his life, until he is now at fifty years of age, a broken old man. 'You think', he said to Sir George Riddell,[1] 'You think it is the future that matters: you are mistaken: it is only the past that counts!'

There has been plenty of work the last fortnight. General French paid a flying visit to London the last week in response to an invitation by the Cabinet. He and Kitchener have come athwart each other, for French has the idea that K. will want to take the command of the New Armies when they are ready, and this F. much resents, seeing that he has borne the brunt of the war up till the present. He tried to convince the Cabinet that it is possible to break through the German lines in Belgium, whereas the Cabinet—that is to say, those members of it who have given any thought to this side of the question—have come to the conclusion that it is not. C. has prepared a memorandum in which he sets forth proposals for taking the New Armies to the East, and landing them in Bosnia, or that neighbourhood, at the same time attacking the Turks in Syria. This plan has met with warm approval by

1. George Allardice Riddell (1865–1934): chairman, The News of the World, 1903–34; press liaison officer at Paris peace conference, 1919; provided Lloyd George with house at Walton Heath; estranged from Lloyd George in 1921, either because he opposed Lloyd George's Near Eastern policy or because Lloyd George's dog attacked him; his diaries are an important source of information; knighted, 1909; cr. baronet, 1919, Baron, 1920; the first divorced person to be made a peer.

Kitchener and indeed everyone to whom it has been submitted, except perhaps Churchill, who favours an attack through the Cattegat, as involving more honour and glory to himself.[1] With C.'s plan we should remove our troops from Belgium, leaving the French to keep the lines there.

C. had a long interview with French. F. is very loth to abandon the Belgian campaign, but in the first place C. pointed out that he has under-estimated the number of the enemy on the western front, & the fact that they are bringing up fresh troops; in the second place, supposing the British succeeded in breaking through the German lines, how much better off would we be? French confessed that he did not know what we should find beyond those lines, or how he would then proceed. In the end, C. got him to his own way of thinking, explaining how much better it would be to extend the enemy's front by some hundreds of miles, which would be effected by an attack on the eastern side, and the subsequent probable overthrow of Austria.

At the Council on the following day it was agreed that French should be given facilities for an attempt to break through to Ostende & Zeebrugge, which he says he can manage at the beginning or middle of February with a loss of 5,000 men. (C. fears he is far too sanguine and that the losses will be nearer 50,000 if the attempt does not end in a disaster.) Meantime, preparations are to be made for an attack in accordance with C.'s proposal, which has Balfour's[2] and the P.M.'s support, in addition to K.'s, as already stated. C. said it was evident at this Council that K. and French were not on good terms. They were very short with each other. K. was 'insolent', C. says. All the same, C. is on very good terms with K. at present & manages to get most of what he wants out of him.

In all this I see more clearly than ever the *thoroughness* with which C. sets about accomplishing a plan when he has once conceived an idea. He is indefatigable in his efforts, probing every source from which he may gain information which may be of some use to him, scrutinising every difficulty which might present itself, and adopting flanking movements, so to speak, when a frontal attack is not likely to prove successful, 'roping in' persons whose influence is likely to prove helpful or whose opinion counts for something, seeking out those who are 'on the fence' and whose opposition would be dangerous, and then talking them round, using all the arts of which he is a pastmaster. He seems sometimes to the casual observer to be impulsive and impatient, rushing at things in h:s desire to get 'something done', but no one who has watched him tackling such a weighty project as this can fail to abandon that first impression. His patience in overcoming obstacles, and in returning again and again to their attack with undiminished cheerfulness and

---

1. Churchill is generally regarded as the great enthusiast for the attack on the Dardanelles. In fact, as this passage shows, he advocated a landing in Schleswig-Holstein and acquiesced in the attack on the Dardanelles only when the cabinet decided in its favour. I am grateful to Martin Gilbert for this correction of the accepted view.
2. Balfour, although a Unionist, attended the war council at Asquith's invitation.

confidence, his tirelessness in examining and arranging for details, above all his complete self-effacement in his desire that the idea which he has conceived for the general good shall not fall to the ground and escape fulfilment, all these characteristics indicate the real greatness of the man, the motive power through which he has accomplished where other men have failed. And I think the greatest of these is his self-effacement, his absolute disinterestedness which gives him such a clear vision. He knows when he has hit upon the right idea, when his plan is the one which ought to be followed. And then he will never give in: he never despairs of accomplishing what he has in view. He clings to his object with a tenacity which is almost incredible, & which is only equalled by his confidence and cheerfulness. He is afraid, he says, of becoming biassed in this war, afraid that the day will come when the enemy will rouse him to hatred & fury, & he will no longer be able to see the issues clearly. 'The nearest I have come to this', he said to me, 'was when they bombarded Scarborough & Whitby. But I dare not think what would happen if any harm should come to Gwilym.'

I think he has shown great unselfishness with regard to Masterman & the Swansea affair.[1] C. was not consulted by the Whips as to the desirability of letting Masterman stand. Had he been, he would not have given his consent, for he objects to foisting English ministers without a seat upon Welsh and Scotch constituencies. However, after M.'s name had been put forward, C. was told that M. would stand a much better chance of being nominated locally if C. sent a letter to recommend him. This C. did, knowing the humiliation M. would suffer if he were not nominated. But in doing this, C. laid himself open to criticism by his own people. However, he risked this for the sake of his friend. But lo and behold! after being nominated, friend Masterman thinks that after all he will not stand, not having the courage to tackle the divided opinions in that constituency and having no doubt one eye upon Shipley. This again lays C. open to the taunt of the futility of his intervention. All this time C. has not had a word of thanks from Masterman, or of regret that he has let him down badly, or of explanation why he has done so. At present the relations between them are rather strained.

Mr. Donald, the Editor of The Chronicle, has just come back from Paris, interviewing the French ministers. He says that the French are much more united on the subject of the war than the British. He says a Keir Hardie[2] would not be tolerated there—he would be shot immediately. He says they realise too, that the war will be only beginning when the French get on to German soil, but that they have no doubt as to the ultimate success of the war. C. is to go over there in February to meet M. Ribot & the Russian financiers. He says the feeling in Russia is not very pro-English at the present time. There is a feeling that we are not doing enough, & are 'on the make'. They say, 'Oh

1. Masterman was still trying to find a constituency.
2. James Keir Hardie (1856–1915), socialist leader; founded I.L.P., 1893; first leader of parliamentary Labour party, 1906–7; opposed the war, 1914–15.

yes! England will fight to the last Russian!' C. says we did attempt to drive too much of a bargain with them over the financial transactions. Pals and partners do not lend each other money at 5%! But he will try to remove that feeling, & bring them to a more friendly basis. He at any rate, understands the political values of this war. He has got the cabinet to consent to having correspondents at the front, which French was very keen on.

January 21st 1915

C. is not very well today. He has been working very hard, but personally I think he is suffering from too much 'family'. He was very upset on Monday [18 January] because not one of them had remembered that it was his birth- day on Sunday. They did not think of it until Sir George Riddell came in at 7.30 in the evening & wished him many happy returns, & then it suddenly occurred to them. He always remembers their birthdays, however busy he is, and goes to a lot of trouble to get them something which will please them— he takes a delight in doing it. 'They take me for granted', he said to me rather bitterly. 'They treated me as someone who must be just tolerated because I provide money for everything they want. But they don't seem to remember that it is through me that they have their education and position and that if it were not for me they would get very little notice taken of them.'

C.'s plan for an attack in the East of Europe is progressing favourably. K. is keen on it, and so is the Prime Minister, but Winston is opposed to it for reasons afore-mentioned. People are beginning to get rather dissatisfied with Winston, as they accuse him of not holding Inquiries on ships which are lost owing to some fault of the Admiralty, but only in such cases where the Admiral or commander can be blamed. Lord Fisher,[1] too, is complaining that he overrules everyone at the Admiralty, even those who have far more experience than he, and that even Admiral Jellicoe[2] is beginning to get uneasy at the orders that he receives from Winston. The latter now wishes to take some of the finest ships in the North Sea for operations in the Mediterranean & Jellicoe says if he does this the Grand Fleet will be inadequate for the North Sea. Fisher says they try to argue with him at the Admiralty, but he simply overrides them and talks them down. If he continues in his domineering course they fear there may be a catastrophe.

It is just two years since C. & I were 'married', and our love seems to increase rather than diminish. He says I have taken the place somewhat of Mair, 'my little girl whom I lost' as he always calls her. He says I remind him of her & make up a little for her loss. I have always wanted to make this loss seem a little lighter to him, and he seems now to be able to speak of her with less pain than he used to.

1. John Arbuthnot Fisher (1841–1920): first sea lord, 1904–10, 1914–15; cr. Baron, 1909; his resignation in May 1915 provoked the fall of the Government.
2. John Rushworth Jellicoe (1859–1935); commander-in-chief, Grand Fleet, 1914–16; first sea lord, 1916–17; governor of New Zealand, 1920–5; cr. Viscount, 1918, Earl, 1925.

C. is going to Paris to meet the Russian & French finance ministers at the beginning of February. He wants to take a little holiday off at the same time in the S. of France, but does not know yet if it can be managed. He has promised me not to go to the front this time.

January 25th 1915
On Saturday [23 January] C. motored down to Walmer Castle to see the P.M. I went with him & we had a jolly run. In London the weather was terrible—a black fog and snowing, but out in the country the scenery was glorious—everywhere white, and so still and beautiful. C. had just been having words with Sir John Bradbury[1] who objects to C. giving instructions to Treasury officials without first of all consulting him. C. remained down at Walmer till Sunday and I came home by train. The journey back was dreary—lots of stoppages, and noisy soldiers everywhere. But still it was worth that for the run down. I went to Downing St. yesterday evening to await his return, & we had a tête-à-tête dinner. He talked to me of lots of interesting things. He had been speaking to the P.M. about Masterman. C. has finished with Masterman, who he says has betrayed him, and conveyed as much to Masterman through Whitehouse, M.'s henchman, when he came to sound the Chancellor on behalf of Masterman. C. says Masterman now ranks for him in the same category as Massingham, who deserted him over 'Marconi's'. Once a man has betrayed C. he can never take him back again, try how he will. On the other hand, if anyone has proved himself a friend in need, C. can never forget that either, & will do anything he can for him ever afterwards. He was telling me that during the Boer War he had a struggle to make both ends meet—he was publicly boycotted, he could not play on any golf links, he was howled down & persecuted, & his political & financial prospects seemed to dwindle from day to day. One day he was in the tea room at the House of Commons, when Lord St. Davids[2] came up to him & said, 'Look here, old chap! Money's a strange thing. Sometimes we have plenty of it, other times none at all. I happen to be pretty flush just at present —things have been going rather well with me. If you should happen to want to borrow—say £500, just say a word to me & you shall have it.' C. was mightily touched, for he says the man had nothing to gain from this generous offer then, nor could he know that C. would ever be in a position to repay him. But although C. did not accept the offer, yet he has never forgotten St. Davids' generosity, and St. D. will never ask him for anything in vain.

C. told me many things of his experiences during the Boer War, how many times he went with his life in his hands for the things he said— denouncing the British Army, mocking at their defeats & saying it was just

---

1. John Swanwick Bradbury (1872–1950), joint permanent secretary to the treasury, 1913–19; his signature appeared on the first treasury notes; K.C.B., 1913; cr. Baron, 1925.
2. John Wynford Philipps (1860–1938), thirteenth baronet; financier and former Liberal M.P.; cr. Baron St. Davids, 1908, Viscount, 1918; gave much private financial advice to Lloyd George.

retribution. 'But you were glad that we *won*?' I asked. '*We didn't win*', was his reply. 'The Boers—the Dutch—are the rulers in S. Africa. We had to give them back their land to rule—for us! And more—for whereas they had ruled the Orange Free State and the Transvaal, they were given in addition Cape Colony and Natal to rule. Had we not done this', he continued, 'we should now have been driven from S. Africa. C.-B.[1] was wise enough to see that safety lay in giving them autonomy. Had we not done so, Botha and the others would have gone back to their farms, and waited for the moment—this moment—when all our energies were wanted elsewhere, to drive us from S. Africa. We didn't win the Boer War!'

But to return to Masterman. The P.M. says they won't have him at Norwich, and that he really can't keep him any longer. He says that he is lazy, conceited, overbearing, that he expects his friends to work for his success, while he himself sits still and looks on—and if they don't do what he thinks they ought to, he turns round on them. C. says Insurance is in an awful muddle, & told the P.M. exactly what *he* thought of Masterman. He considered he (C.) was entitled to speak out, as he had given Masterman a warning. 'To give you my honest opinion', he told the P.M. 'I think it will do Masterman good to throw him into the water. His rapid promotion has been the ruin of him, until he is satisfied that nothing can touch him, and has become impossible. It is not fair to the nation to keep such a man in the Government.' The P.M. agreed, & will probably put Montagu to look after Insurance. I know C. was justified in saying what he did. No one else realises what a friend he has been to Masterman—how, during the last year, he has borne with him patiently, encouraging him, counselling him. But M.'s blatant treachery over Swansea cut him to the quick and though C. never *seeks out* an opportunity to pay off a score, yet he owns that he is vindictive when the opportunity presents himself, he takes it. 'And', he concluded yesterday evening, 'I have knifed Masterman today.'

C. is busy preparing for his journey to Paris for the Conference between himself & the Russian & French Finance Ministers. There is jealousy in the Treasury as to who shall accompany the Chancellor. It is extraordinary how jealous and petty these permanent officials can be. They seem to have no sense of proportion, and magnify their little grievances while they forget the really great affairs of State.

The King has just sent for C. to go and see him on Wednesday [27 January] morning. C. says 'I wonder what my little German friend has got to say to me!' 'It may have something to do with the wonderful document that came about Pensions & Separation Allowances—about as futile a document as I have seen.' 'Yes', said C., 'but everything that comes from the Court is like that. But then, as Balfour said to me once, "Whatever would you do if you had a ruler with brains?"'

---

1. Sir Henry Campbell-Bannerman, Liberal Prime Minister, 1905–8.

January 28th 1915

I forgot to mention an incident in connection with the Boer War. When things were looking very black, a prominent politician came to C. and begged him not to go on with his line of action any longer. 'You will ruin yourself', he said. 'I know that Rosebery expects to form the next Ministry and he means to put you in it but it will be impossible for him to do so if you go on like this.'

Masterman was asked to send in his papers yesterday, but cannot bring himself to do so.

If he has to resign in the end, it will be with humiliation and discredit. Today he again begged for an interview with the P.M., 'in order to be allowed to put his own case once more'. I do not yet know what the result of that interview is. Can it be possible that a man should cling so to office when everyone is telling him to go? When the Marconi rumours began to be ominous, and it was clear that things would be very unpleasant for the Government, C. and Lord Reading—Sir Rufus Isaacs then—went to the P.M. and offered to hand in their resignations to him. They said that they themselves had no right to burden the Government, and the Prime Minister had no right to saddle himself with such a responsibility, at a time when the Government was going through very grave times, with Home Rule & Disestablishment, etc. They said that they knew the P.M. would prefer to stand by his friends, but they thought it was his duty to the Party to accept their resignations. However, the P.M. would not hear of it, but said he wished to fight the thing through, but at any rate they had the satisfaction of knowing that they had done the right thing.

There is great excitement about the Paris visit. C. is having a brand new suit—which he hasn't seen yet, as he had no time to look at patterns; so that Mr. Davies and I had to choose for him—we hope he will approve. Mr. Davies has invested in a pair of beautiful new boots, which are too tight for him, but which he wants to stretch before he goes. He is also wearing a suit that is positively indecent, as it is rather out-of-date & he has expanded considerably the last year or two. But the more up-to-date suits are being pressed, and apparently it doesn't matter what you look like in London so long as you are chic in Paris!

The War Council have been very strenuous today. C. has just gone to the third meeting since this morning. He was telling me some amusing stories about K. It appears he has a little habit of appropriating articles which take his fancy when on visits—he has no scruples whatever. Thus he went to a shooting party at Lord Derby's but failed to bring rifles with him, and Lord Derby lent him two. They went away with K. and were never returned!

It is said too, that he used to visit the house of an Indian Prince who possessed some very fine old specimens of swords and knives. There were two in particular that K. coveted, and he asked the Prince to let him have them. The Prince however replied that they had been handed down in his family from generation to generation, and he could not bring himself to part with them. Each time K. went there he made the same request, and was met with a refusal. At last he offered in exchange for the swords a pair of beautiful antique vases, and the offer was accepted. K. sent over the vases & received the swords in return. A friend congratulated him on his bargain—K. turned to him with a smile and said: 'I did him! those vases were faked!' This story however was repeated to the Prince, but he took it quite calmly. 'Oh, that's all right', was his reply. 'The swords were faked too!'

February 8th 1915 (Walton Heath)
C. came back from France on Saturday [6 February]. He went there last Monday, & since then I have been trying to cure a bad cold, & at the same time allay my anxieties with regard to enemy submarines in the Channel, & the destruction of peaceful shipping. But however they returned quite safely without any mishap, & C. is thoroughly pleased with all the aspects of his visit.

I do not understand all the details of the financial conference, but I gather that the French have been induced to set free the 160 millions of gold which they were hoarding, & to bear their share of the financial burden of the war, whereas Russia is to be helped to set free the immense stores of grain in her country, and is to be allowed to borrow money on the English market. C. wants to propose that we should help her with the interest on this loan, as she is unable to borrow at a low rate of interest, and at the same time C. does not think it quite fair that we should exact a high rate of interest from an ally. 'When you are fighting with another country as ally', he said, 'you've got to make them feel that they are your pals.' He was very pleased with M. Bark,[1] & says that they understood each other from the first, and got on extremely well. Mr. Davies tells me that C. insisted upon going *alone* to the first conference, leaving the Governor of the Bank[2] & Montagu to kick their heels. The old Governor was very sniffy, and said he 'didn't know why he had come at all'. However, C. evidently knew what he was about, & probably wanted to prepare the way in a manner which only he is capable of.

C. saw a good many of the French Ministers, & also Clemenceau,[3] whom he says is a quaint old boy, 'born', as Briand[4] remarked, 'with a stock of "bienveillance" sufficient to last for only one day, and which he soon exhausted on himself!' They say that he is very excitable and impatient, & they tell an amusing tale of him & Caillaux[5] (for whom he had no great respect)

1. Russian Finance Minister.
2. Lord Cunliffe, governor of the Bank of England, 1913–18.
3. Georges Clemenceau, French politician and journalist; premier, 1906–9, 1917–20; presided over Paris peace conference, 1919; at this time agitating for a more energetic conduct of the war.
4. Aristide Briand, French politician; premier, 1909–11, 1915–17, 1921–2.
5. Joseph Caillaux, French premier, 1911–12. In 1917, at the instigation of Clemenceau, his parliamentary immunity was suspended. In 1920 he was indicted for 'plotting against the security of the state' and lost his civic rights for ten years. They were restored by an amnesty in 1924.

when the former was Prime Minister & the latter Finance Minister. Caillaux, whose head is completely bald on top, and had a little ridge of scanty hair behind, was excusing himself from the Cabinet one day on the ground that he had to attend a Budget Committee downstairs. 'Oh, go!' retorted Clemenceau, 'and take your forty hairs with you!'

Caillaux, it appears was forced to leave France on the outbreak of the war, as he would probably have been murdered had he stayed. The impression is that it is he who is responsible for the unprepared state of the Army.

But by far the most important part of C.'s mission to France bore on the military question. When Millerand[1] was over here he was tackled by C., Grey, and Kitchener on the subject of sending over two divisions to Salonika to help bring in the Balkan States & at the same time come to the assistance of Serbia. The plan cannot be carried out without the sanction of the French Government, as Joffre has the ordering of our expeditionary force.[2] Millerand evidently did not approve of the plan, but promised to bring the matter before the other ministers. C. however, thought at the time that he was not sincere, and told Sir Edward Grey so. Since Millerand's departure they have heard nothing of the plan from France. When C. was over there this week he spoke to the President & several Cabinet Ministers on the subject, and he found that they had not heard a word of the plan or the conversation he had had with K., C., and Grey on the matter. They were very much annoyed. C. subsequently learnt that the whole of the French Cabinet *except Millerand* were in favour of it, and they were willing to co-operate provided Joffre gave his consent. They said it was incredible that if 80,000 men from the W. could bring in 800,000 on the E., any general would refuse his consent to such a proposal. Briand has undertaken to persuade Joffre, who, he says, is rather a difficult customer. He says that Joffre when the Germans were advancing South in September, said he could not undertake to defend Paris. The Govt. however, were firm, & insisted on its being defended, saying that if Paris were lost, France herself would be lost.

C. called on French on the way back to Boulogne, as Grey had requested him (C.) to undertake to persuade French to release two divisions for the East. French was very amenable, and consented to do so provided that Joffre consents. C. explained to him that nothing would be done without his (French's) consent and that if he did not give it, his judgment would not be overruled from London. French, not being on good terms with K., is under the impression that his interests are being undermined in Whitehall, and that he is merely a puppet, but C. assured him that this was not so, and that it was French's decision that would remain. French ended by being in favour of the

---

1. Alexandre Millerand, at this time French minister of war, when he protected Joffre from civilian interference.
2. This was not technically correct.

plan & asked to come to London to discuss ways & means at the War Council. C. was introduced to General Robertson, the Chief of the Staff,[1] whom C. considers by far the ablest general he has met—except Kitchener—since the beginning of the war. Robertson pronounced the plan to be 'good strategy', and convinced French of its soundness so that the meeting ended quite happily, & C. hopes that the Expeditionary Force to the East will start within a fortnight. Churchill is still against the plan, as it does not give him a look in. He still wants to get in through Holland, or some such fool way.

C. said he was travelling with Lord Grimthorpe not very long ago, & the conversation turned on Churchill. Grimthorpe was a great friend of Lord Randolph Churchill, and knew him well. He compared the father and son. 'It is just the difference', he said, 'between great capacity and genius. Winston has great ability, but he has not the genius of his father.'

C. has brought me back the sweetest little brooch—diamonds—& a big sapphire—from Paris. He said he spent all his spare time walking the streets to find something to bring me home. It gives him such intense pleasure to give presents and he was so pleased with this one. It was sweet to watch him. He was very annoyed yesterday, however, over a paragraph in the Sunday papers, to the effect that 'Mr. Lloyd George, after a hard day's work in Paris, drove to the Latin quarter in the evening to see what life there during war time was like.' C. was furious, as he never went near the Latin quarter the whole time he was there, & he says it is exactly as if a Russian paper made the announcement that 'M. Bark, (the Russian finance Minister) while in London, after a hard day's work, spent his evening in Leicester Square . . .' The Central News (who circulated the statement) were told that they are to be struck off the Treasury list of Press Agencies who receive notices from the Treasury to the Press, & they have been asked to contradict the statement in England & in France. C. says that the idea that a Minister who goes to Paris on important business, & takes that opportunity for having a 'lark' is the very thing to create ill-feeling in the country. Moreover, if it were true, it would be scandalous & the nation would have a right to object.

I am staying away from the Treasury for a few days in order to get my cold quite well. C. has gone up to London, but I am expecting him back every minute. It is such a relief to have him back safely again.

February 11th 1915
Returned yesterday from W.H., where I had been staying for a few days, not feeling very fit. C. was very worried on Monday night [8 February], as no definite measures had been taken by the Government with regard to the Balkans, and he feared from the telegrams in the sections that it would soon be too late to do anything. It is now 5 weeks since C. wrote his Memo for

---

1. William Robertson (1860–1933), chief of staff in France, 1915; chief of imperial general staff, 1915–18; knighted, 1913; cr. baronet, 1919. Lloyd George's favourable opinion of Robertson was not maintained.

the Cabinet on the advisability of bringing in the Balkan States by sending an expeditionary force. It was approved by the W.O. and Lord K., & yet nothing has been done & all the time the Germans are planning and plotting against us there.

On Tuesday [9 February] General French came over to a meeting of the War Council, and at this meeting C. told them everything that was in his mind. He said that it was weeks since the subject had been broached, that there was absolutely no reason to prevent some definite measure from being decided upon—everyone knew that it was absolutely necessary—but they all seemed to be afraid of doing anything. Someone remarked that the French Government were against it. 'There you are wrong', replied C. 'I know that the majority of them are in favour of it. 'There is that fussy little haberdasher, Delcassé,[1] who thinks he knows his own mind because he has no mind except that of Joffre. Are we to allow things to become impossible simply because one man chooses to dictate what our policy is to be? I don't know that it is not already too late for us to do anything. It is like a man who is sick, whom a slight operation this week will save, but if that is not done immediately, then a week later a serious operation will not save his life. It may be even now too late, but for God's sake let us do something. If we fail, and the Germans get the upper hand in the Balkan States, we shall go down to history as the nation that could not make up its mind, and that dilly-dallied until it had bartered away the safety and co-operation of the small states who were looking to it for help.' General French made some remark about the French Ministry being in the hands of Joffre. 'Yes, Sir John', said C. laughingly, 'Joffre has the good fortune to have a tame secretary of State!' Whereupon Kitchener smiled broadly.

In the end, however, a telegram was sent at once to Greece, offering a Division of our troops, while France promised another Division & Russia also a small force.

Churchill, who is now in favour of the plan, is furious at the delay there has been. He is most furious with the Prime Minister, who has simply waited on the chance that something might happen. 'He is very good at passing judgment on things after the event', said Churchill to C., 'but he is incapable of making up his mind to action.'

Everyone is immensely pleased with C.'s visit to Paris, and none more pleased than himself. Lord Murray[2] has written to him from Paris to say that Paris can talk of nothing else but the energy & capacity of our Chancellor of the Exchequer. Bark cannot find words to express his admiration. On his visit to Buckingham Palace he expressed this admiration to the King, saying that had it not been for C., his eloquence, persuasiveness and patience, the Conference would have broken down. 'But he never once lost heart', said

1. Théophile Delcassé, (1852–1923) French foreign minister, 1898–1905, 1914–15.
2. Lord Murray of Elibank (cr. 1912): as Master of Elibank, Liberal chief whip, 1910–12; involved in Marconi affair.

Bark. 'He proposed one thing, and if Ribot[1] would not have it, tore it up & threw it into the fire and proposed something else.' 'Yes', answered King George, 'when he went to the Exchequer he did not know very much about finance, but he has been doing remarkably well of late.'

February 14th 1915
I returned from W.H. yesterday morning. C. called for me on Friday morning [12 February] & we motored down there & spent the day together. We went for a glorious walk in the afternoon on the Heath, & wandered about for hours together without meeting a soul. It was the kind of afternoon that comes as a herald of Spring—the leaves not yet quite in bud, & the branches still bare & the bracken quite brown, and yet there was a feeling of coming life in the air, as though the earth were waiting to give birth to the spring.

C. talked of what he would like to do when the war is over. He sometimes feels that he would like to give up politics & try his hand at writing on his own. 'But the idea I have got now', he said, 'is to be made Governor of Mesopotamia when it comes under our rule, and direct operations there, turning its barrenness into fertility, & making the desert to blossom like the rose.' 'I would love the climate', he continued, 'and there is scope for any amount of energy in a scheme like that, in organising and promoting irrigation, etc.

'But I know in the end', he said, 'I should never be able to give up this job I have taken up of bettering the lives of the poor. "Woe be unto me if I preach not the Gospel!" I cannot help myself. I see my way so clearly that I should be full of reproach for myself if I turned to anything else, or devoted myself to making money, which would be easy for me now.

'I think it was Victor Hugo's book Les Miserables that decided me to do what I could to alleviate the distress and suffering of the poor. That story gives you such a vivid picture of the under side of life, all the wretched & sordid details of the troubles of the poor—troubles that could be lessened. I know a great many people think that it was because I was born and lived among poor people that I turned my mind to reforms & schemes for alleviating want & suffering. But they are mistaken. The people in the village where I lived were poor, but there was no real want or privation. Our little cottage was humble enough, but we had enough to live on. There was no *wretchedness* in our district. The homes that you might think poor I used to look on as comfortable—homes where they used to have cake, and treacle on their bread—luxuries which we children rarely enjoyed! But I never saw there any of the privation & suffering which is depicted in Les Miserables. It was not until I grew up and left Wales that I realised what poverty really meant and what a need the poor have of someone to fight for them. And I know that I must keep on with the job. After the war there will be more than ever of that to do, and it will not be for me to indulge in my Mesopotamia dream!'

---

1. Alexandre Felix Joseph Ribot, at this time French minister of finance; premier in 1917.

But what I want him to do is to go outside *party* politics—to direct great reforms from the outside, impartially, & not waste energy on party strife. He could do it now, for his reputation is established, and both sides admit his capacity. He could leave his party & the Cabinet without it being said that he had been obliged to leave it, as they would surely have said after the Marconi affair, or at any other time when his schemes were meeting with opposition. If he were to leave now, however, he could promote schemes which are favoured in some form or other by both parties, such as land reform. He could earn enough for his needs by writing, for he is a man of simple tastes and prefers a simple life and simple fare to luxury. He has often hinted at this himself, and if he ever does it, this will be the time.

C. is speaking in the House tomorrow, and I am going up to Downing St. this afternoon to take down notes for his statement. C. & I have spent a lot of time together this week but I am returning to the office tomorrow to my official duties as Private Secretary.

February 23rd 1915
Last week was a most eventful one. On Monday [15 February] C. made his statement in the House on the subject of the Paris Conference. It was a very neat little speech. I met him afterwards & we motored down to Walton Heath together. He was very pleased with a story he had heard about Ribot, who remarked to one of his colleagues that the mistake he had made over the Conference was to put M. Bark & Mr. Lloyd George in the same hotel. 'I thought Lloyd George was an Englishman', he said. 'I did not realise that he was a Celt, and not English at all. Consequently, I found that when we met at the Conference, M. Bark was already in Lloyd George's pocket!'

The situation is very grave at present, & C. is very worried. The Russians seem to be completely worsted, and it seems that they are knocked out for some time to come, as they have no reinforcements. I went to a very interesting lecture by Belloc,[1] on the situation in the East. He seemed to take a grave view of the situation, but said that time was everything to the Germans, & if the coup were not immediately brought off, it would end in disaster for them. C. has written a very strong paper on the position, and our action subsequent to the Dardanelles movement.[2] Some of the cabinet seem very dubious as to the success of that movement, but it will be disastrous for us if it fails, as the Balkans will certainly not then come in. Greece even now will not be tempted by the offer that we sent her, saying that 'the position is changed'.

C. came up Saturday night [20 February], and dictated the 'phenomenal

---

1. Hilaire Belloc (1870–1953), novelist and political writer; Liberal M.P., 1906–10; contributed weekly surveys of the war to Land and Water; his military opinions were always self-confident and usually wrong.
2. On 13 January 1915 the war council approved a naval expedition against the Gallipoli peninsula. On 19 February British battleships bombarded the outer forts. Meanwhile Lloyd George continued to press the alternative of a landing at Salonika.

document' (as Lord Fisher calls it) to me, and I came up to the Treasury on Sunday morning and typed it and sent it down to C.

March 11th 1915 (Walton Heath)
The last fortnight has been too dreary and unhappy to write of. I am down here now to recover from the effects of it. My people have been trying to separate us—trying to make me promise that I will give up his love, the most precious thing of my life. They do not understand—they will never understand—they do not see that our love is pure and lasting—they think I am his plaything, & that he will fling me aside when he has finished with me—or else they think that there will be a scandal and that we shall all be disgraced. I know they are fond of me, and think it is for my good that they are doing this, but I have always held different ideas from theirs, & it was bound to come to this, or something akin to this, sooner or later. I am willing to pay dearly for my happiness, but I will not give it up. I fear that in the end I shall have to leave home, for they will never cease to urge their views upon me, & it will be almost intolerable. Besides which, they will never speak of C. except in unfriendly & contemptuous tones & that I will not endure. I cannot give up the hold upon life, & the broader outlook, which I have gained since C. & I came together. I can't help *hating* myself for making Mamma so miserable. The thought haunts me all day long, and I would do anything to prevent it. But what *can* I do? Some years ago Harold Spender said to C. 'You are the most lonely man I know.' I think I have changed all that now, & I cannot think that I have done wrong. I am not vicious or evil, and my only fault, in this matter and his, is love. 'Love justifies many audacities.' I think the justification for these audacities is the length of love's duration & I know C. and I belong to each other for ever. I should be so happy were it not for the fact that I am causing unhappiness to two people whom I love and who have been so good & loving to me.

Lloyd George to Frances Stevenson (undated)
> Go *now* a little beyond House of Lords
> I am off to Walton.

In addition to distress of mind, I have been ill, which increased my misery. Finally C. insisted that I should come down here & have absolute rest for a few days, & be free from worrying surroundings. I agreed to this all the more willingly as I could see that C. was making himself ill through worrying about me—several times I thought he was on the point of breaking down; but he has been better since I have been down here & have shown signs of recovering.

I do not think I can ever repay him for his goodness to me the last fortnight or three weeks. He has been husband, lover & mother to me. I never knew a man could be so womanly & tender. He has watched and waited on me devotedly, until I cursed myself for being ill & causing him all this worry.

There was no little thing that he did not think of for my comfort, no tender-ness that he did not lavish on me. I have indeed known the full extent of his love. If those who idolise him as a public man could know the full greatness of his heart, how much more their idol would he be! And through it all he has been immersed in great decisions appertaining to this great crisis, until I have trembled for his health, & loathed myself for causing him trouble at this time.

In the midst of all this he found time to prepare and deliver a speech at Bangor,[1] which many think is the greatest speech of his life. He says that the anxiety and trouble helped him to make a great speech, for when his mind is disturbed his whole nature is upheaved, and it stimulates him to greater power of expression. He is very pleased that The Nation should have praised it, saying that as an orator he is unequalled. He tells me that from his youth it has always been his ambition to become a great orator, rather than a states-man or politician. And it does now seem as though his ambition has been fulfilled. He deserves that it should be, if ever any man did. I do not think that there is any man in England who is working more unselfishly for our victory in this war, than he is. He does not cease from one week to the next to devise some means for advancing our interests: and when a plan is thought of, he does not hesitate until it is carried into practice, & with the right men to work it, & a word of advice, a hint, suggestion, or word of encourage-ment, he leaves it in full swing. And the fruits of his tireless brain have been so diverse that it seems impossible that one man should have been responsible for them, & carried them into effect, and still be 'going strong'.

His Bill[2] yesterday for commandeering factories, etc., for making muni-tions of war, was, as he expresses it, the 'first fruits of the Bangor speech'. He is very pleased with his new phrase 'Victory as usual', instead of 'business as usual', & all the papers this morning seem very pleased with it too. The next step is for the Government to take over all the public-houses, but I fear this will be a more difficult job.

There was a good deal of opposition at first when he proposed to speak on a Sunday at Bangor, but the meeting went off without any unpleasantness, in fact, he had a wonderful reception. Speaking afterwards to Lord Boston he commented on the fact that he had been allowed to speak in Wales on a Sunday. 'Ten years ago that would not have been possible', said C. 'No, & it would not have been possible now for anyone but yourself', was the reply. 'You seem privileged to roam about the field, while we poor devils are not even allowed to look over the hedge!'

Paul is under orders to go to France. They were to have left Southampton on Tuesday [9 March], but there appears to be some difficulty in getting the

1. 28 February 1915. 'Through Terror to Triumph.'
2. Defence of the Realm (Amendment No. 2) Bill gave power to control factories and engineering works not at present on war work but which could be used for war production.

troops off, & they have not yet gone, but may leave at any moment. Mamma and Dada are naturally upset about it, & it seems very hard for them that their troubles should come all at once. I do not want to add unduly to their trouble, so must make up my mind to a little self-sacrifice for some time to come so as not to upset them too much. Nevertheless I will never, never, give C. up. 'Leave all for love!'

C. tells me that Italy is coming in in April.[1] That is good news. Things will begin to move then.

March 25th 1915

Paul went to France last Sunday week. I went home for the weekend, and was glad I did so, as Mamma was very upset about it. She is quite sure he will never come back. She is very bitter as to the disappointment that one's children bring. She says, 'Everything is turning out so differently from what we had expected. Dada & I have had 27 years of happiness, and now we have got to pay for it.' Poor Mother! She cannot realise, & I fear she never will, that parents cannot control their children's lives for ever—that children exist for their own and the next generation, and not for that of their parents, which is past. However, it is hopeless to argue with her; but I fear she will never be happy unless she takes a wider view. What is more, if she is not careful, she will lose the sympathy and respect of her children.

We have had several letters from Paul, and he seems in excellent spirits. The casualties lately have been very heavy & I hope this will not continue. I cannot help thinking of the awful terror that must come over some of these boys when they are under fire for the first time. I pray that Paul may be spared that.

We are fearfully busy again at the Treasury. C.'s Bill for the State control of factories went through successfully. He tells me that the Prime Minister said he would never get it through, and was for giving up the attempt. He (the P.M.) would not take it on himself, because he feared what the consequences might be with such a drastic measure. The Bill met with very little opposition. C. says the House loathed it, but dared not say anything against it, and had to stifle other criticism by the criticism that it 'ought to have been passed six months ago!' The P.M. said that if the Bill was to go through, C. was the only person to do it. Mr. Balfour supported C. whole-heartedly. The two of them are very friendly just now. I am not sure whether there is anything behind Balfour's friendliness—it is quite possible that it is a case of the 'velvet glove'. But for the present at any rate Balfour says that C. is the only man in the Cabinet who can *do* anything—the others just talk.

After the Bill was passed, C. had to conciliate the trades union people. They were here for 3 days last week, overrunning the Treasury, but in the end they consented to the suspension of the Trades Unions Rules for the period of the war. They are a very unsatisfactory lot of people, however, and

---

1. Italy entered the war on 23 May 1915.

one cannot help feeling that it is a danger for the working classes to be in the hands of such incompetent and narrow-minded—for they *are* essentially narrow-minded & selfish—men. However I suppose the working classes will work out their own fate; but one cannot help feeling that their unpatriotic attitude in the present crisis will deprive them of sympathy when the war is over, and when the working classes will be in need of consideration owing to the effects of the war.

March 26th 1915

The number of letters that we had from men who claimed to be the 'super-man'[1] required by the Chancellor was simply amazing. Unfortunately, the choice will not rest with C.; in fact, I fear he is going to wash his hands of the whole business. After he had successfully tackled the Trades Unions people, and subsequently the Engineers, the Prime Minister suggested that a new Department should be formed, with C. at the head as Minister of Contracts. C. was doubtful about the proposal at first, as he thought it might involve his leaving the Treasury, and if he kept on the Treasury work, he did not know how he would be able to take on extra work, being over-worked as it is. But everyone seemed so keen for him to take it over (excepting McKenna[2])— everyone—including Mr. Balfour said he was the only one to make his Bill a success, and put the factories of the country to their full use—that C. at last consented to think about the scheme. In the meantime, however, Kitchener had considered the proposal, and—as I believe—urged by Von Donop,[3] put forward conditions by which the W.O. were to have control over the new Department it was proposed to set up. K. said of course the W.O. would be very glad to have the co-operation of the new Committee, but . . . and then followed conditions and restrictions which would have rendered the Committee quite ineffectual. So C. has declined to have anything more to do with it and has turned his attention to the Drink question.

I fear however, that the powers granted by the Amendment to the Defence of the Realm Act will not be used to their utmost. As C. pointed out to K., there will be endless labour troubles in dealing with the question, & the W.O. will have to deal with them.

Kitchener was only too pleased, however, for C. to make his Bangor Speech in aid of increasing the output of munitions, and to have the Chancellor's help in dealing with the question so far as he (K.) was concerned. Before making his speech in the House of Lords on the subject, he came to C. with the MS. He stalked into the Board Room, walked over to the desk, fixed on his huge glasses, & saying severely, 'What do you think of this?'

1. Lloyd George had said publicly that he was looking for a superman to take charge of Munitions—'a man of push and go'.
2. Reginald McKenna (1863–1941): Liberal M.P., 1895–1918; home secretary, 1911–15; chancellor of the exchequer, 1915–16; subsequently chairman of Midland Bank.
3. Major General Sir Stanley von Donop (1860–1941): Master-General of Ordnance, 1913–16; much criticised by Lloyd George for his tardiness in producing munitions.

proceeded to read the speech at the top of his voice. After he had finished, he proceeded to the P.M. and read it to him. 'He shouted it at me', said the P.M. to C. afterwards, 'as though I had been on Parade'. 'Yes', said C. 'He rehearses it to you and me as he ought to deliver it in the House of Lords, but when he gets up to speak in the House of Lords, he delivers it as he should have delivered it to us.' They say he is so nervous when he gets up to speak that it is difficult to catch what he says.

'I suppose', said Tennant, who happened to be with the P.M. 'that K.'s speech was well tessellated?'

'Oh, yes!' said the P.M.

'What does that mean?' asked C. puzzled. 'Well it means this', explained Tennant. 'It has a foundation of Creedy (K.'s private sec.) then a layer of some General or other, then a layer of Von Donop, and so on, until the construction is completed by a touch or two of K.'

March 29th 1915
I have before me a telegram message intercepted by the W.O. Censor on August 4th at 9.5 p.m. It reads:

To . . . German Ambassador . . .

From . . . Berlin.

'English Ambassador has just demanded his passport shortly after seven o'clock declaring war.'

(signed) Jagow.

On the back of this sheet of paper there is a little conglomeration of triangles and circles which I recognise as the product of the hand of C. when his mind was occupied with far weightier matters. Around this same sheet of paper sat four anxious ministers late in the evening of August 4th—the Prime Minister, Sir Edward Grey, McKenna and the Chancellor of the Exchequer. An ultimatum had been sent to Germany, and if no reply were received before midnight, then England would be in a state of war. It was a terribly anxious period for those upon whom the decision between peace and war had rested, but the uncertainty was minimised by this message which had been intercepted, announcing that our Ambassador was leaving Berlin. This, however, was the only intimation that had yet been received; no message had come direct from our Ambassador; and the ministers were accordingly forced to sit in the Cabinet Room and wait until the expiry of the period in which it was possible for Berlin to reply to their ultimatum. The Prime Minister sat with darkened face and dropped jowl; Grey's countenance was care-worn and haggard with the strain of the last few days, he sat with his head between his hands: all were silent, for the gravity of the situation was oppressive. They had calculated that midnight in Germany would be eleven o'clock by London time, so they waited on till that hour should strike. At last Big Ben chimed, and the first note of eleven rang out with a deep boom that re-echoed through the night air. Not a word was uttered till the eleven strokes had clanged forth their fateful message, and when the echoes died away the Ministers knew that Britain had embarked upon a war, the consequences of which it would be impossible even to guess at. Those eleven strokes must have reverberated through the minds of those who waited, as marking the most solemn crisis they had faced. No one of them liked to be the first to break that long silence, and they sat there mute, regarding each other and trying to realise what the striking of that hour meant to Britain.

Upon this grave assembly burst Churchill, radiant, smiling, a cigar in his mouth and satisfaction upon his face. 'Well!', he exclaimed, 'the deed is done!' The dream of his life had come to pass. Little he recked of the terrors of war and the price that must be paid. His chance had come![1]

On Friday [26 March] Paderewski[2] lunched among others with C. at Downing St. C. admires him greatly. He says he is passionately devoted to his country, Poland, and his great desire is to see a separate Poland, independent and free. Paderewski asked C. whether he thought Russia would consent to an absolutely independent Poland. C. was forced to say that he did not think so, but thought that Russia would be willing to grant autonomy to Poland.

'I will ask you one question', said Paderewski. 'Of what good was autonomy to Finland?'

Of course there was no reply to this. 'And let me tell you further', went on the Pole. 'When Russian officials were taxed with Russia's perfidy, and Finland insisted that she had the Tsar's word for her freedom. "Ah!" they said, and smiled, "therein lies the secret of Russian greatness. Russia knows when to give her promise, but she knows when to break it!"'

On Friday C. intended to go down to Walton Heath and remain there for the weekend. Presently a message came from Buckingham Palace to ask if C. would go to the Palace on Saturday morning at 11.30, as the King wished to talk to him. 'Damn the King!' exclaimed C. 'Saturday is the only day I have to play golf. I can't play on Sunday for I mustn't shock my Nonconformist friends on too many points at the same time!' After a minute's reflection he said to Hamilton, 'Tell them I was going away for the weekend, but of course if the King wishes an audience of me, I will put it off.' The reply came back that the King certainly did not wish to interfere with the Chancellor of the Exchequer's weekend, and Monday would do just as well. 'God bless His Majesty!' said C.

April 4th 1915

Have been in bed all the weekend with a chill—was just able to summon up enough strength to get to the office on Friday morning [2 April], to see C. who came up for Lord Rothschild's funeral. I was glad to see him, though, for Thursday till Monday is a long time to go, & it made all the difference

---

1. This story, which no doubt came from Lloyd George, has improved in the telling.
2. Ignace Jan Paderewski (1860–1941), pianist, composer, and Polish patriot; Polish premier and foreign minister, 1919.

seeing him yesterday morning. I retired to bed as soon as I returned home
and have only just got up. C. is coming up to town tomorrow, though, having made an appointment with the Archbishop of Canterbury as an excuse
to come up. 'And a very good excuse, too', said C., 'for this purpose!' He
has had Sir John Simon[1] & Mr. McKenna down at Walton Heath for the
weekend, and has been kept occupied with them; so has not been able to
ring me up. I am glad of it, as he might have found out that I was in bed, and
I did not wish him to know, as last time I was ill (only a month ago) he
worried so much that he almost broke down.

C. is steeped in drink, as I tell him.[2] He has been drink mad this last week—
can talk and think of nothing else. I suppose I must put up with it, as it is a
great work, but I tell him that I am very jealous of its occupying his attention
so much. However, we are looking forward to having a little time together
after next week, so it is worth waiting for, and I realise that he must give all
his energies to the drink problem. It must be about the biggest & most
difficult thing he has tackled. He has been seeing people and receiving deputa-
tions all the week, and is receiving encouragement on all sides. He saw the
King last Monday morning [29 March], and suggested that it would be a
good lead if the King set the example, which he did, and it has made a great
impression. When the King wrote to C. & suggested that he was prepared to
set the lead, C. of course wished to publish the letter. He went straight to the
P.M., but found little sympathy in that quarter. 'You'll never do it', said the
P.M. to C., 'the country will never stand total prohibition. It isn't feasible.'
What he really meant was that he himself was not prepared to give up his
wine and his whisky. Later in the day the P.M. sent for C. & said 'About that
King thing—I would not play that card yet if I were you. Of course, I don't
mean to say that it won't have to be played some time, but I wouldn't do it
just yet.' C. then explained—for he saw what was troubling the old boy—
that you would be able to get alcoholic drink if you could produce a doctor's
certificate to the effect that it was necessary for you to have it. At that the
P.M. brightened up. 'Oh, well', he said strutting up & down the room, 'there
will be any amount of doctors' certificates!' He seemed more resigned after
this piece of information, and when the King gave his permission to the
publication of the letter on the condition that the P.M. also gave his, the
latter was quite ready to consent to it.

All this time C. has been rather worried about the Postponement Bill
relating to the Welsh Disestablishment Act. The night the Bill was introduced
it was attacked by the Welsh Members in a very petty spirit, and C. rebuked

1. Sir John Simon (1873–1954); attorney general, 1913–15; home secretary, 1915–16;
resigned in protest against conscription; later opposed Lloyd George and became leader
of the National Liberals.
2. Lloyd George was advocating state purchase of the liquor traffic, in the belief that this
would reduce drunkenness and improve the production of munitions. The proposal was
opposed by the temperance spokesmen, and Lloyd George abandoned it. All that remained was a personal pledge of total abstention by the King—and by Kitchener.

them & spoke out, telling them exactly what he thought of them. The Prime Minister told him when he sat down that it was the best speech he had ever heard him make in the House, and Bob Cecil[1] said afterwards that it was the most courageous speech that had ever been made in the House of Commons. C. must have been extraordinarily excited when he sat down, for when he came to me half an hour later he was still shaking with excitement, & it was a long, long time before he calmed down. When he did become more calm he almost collapsed with exhaustion. He told me of a remark which the P.M. made to him on the Bench—to relieve his excitement, I think—'They call the Archbishop of Canterbury "God's own Butler",' said the P.M. 'but I think those two Welsh Bishops must be God's odd job men—the sort of people who see to the coals, & that sort of thing!'

However, C.'s speech had the effect of rousing the anger of the Welsh N.Cs. who have been holding indignation meetings ever since. They say C. has betrayed Wales. After all, I think it is only anger at losing a little money— only a few thousands. Mrs. Ll.G. has been giving C. a bad time over it. She always wakes up when it is a question of money. As someone once put it, 'As far as she is concerned, she would rather go without food than pay for it.' C. however is not taking any notice of this outburst, though it worried him a little at first.

The casualties of late have been terribly heavy—that is to say at Neuve Chapelle & St. Eloi. Kitchener was discussing Neuve Chapelle with Balfour & C. 'I told French', he said, 'that he had wasted the ammunition. He told me he would want 5,000 shells and he used 10,000. He is far too extravagant.' 'And consider the casualties', said Balfour. 'There must have been nearly 10,000 men lost in these engagements.' 'Eight thousand seven hundred at Neuve Chapelle', said K. 'but it isn't the men I mind. I can replace the men at once, but I can't replace the shells so easily.'

Montagu has been making an analysis of the Cabinet. I loathe Montagu, but he is rather amusing at times. I don't know what class Montagu puts himself in, but I should call him one of the most insignificant but most ambitious of Cabinet Ministers, differing from the majority of the others in that he has in an enormous degree the 'push' which is characteristic of the Jew, & which I am bound to say seems to be an asset where 'getting on' is concerned. However, Montagu divides Cabinet Ministers into 3 classes, those who really count, those who talk & have something to say, and those who don't count at all—though in the latter class some of them talk a good deal. 'People like Jack Pease',[2] C. said to me when telling me of this classification. 'It's exactly

---

1. Lord Robert Cecil (1864–1958): third son of third marquis of Salisbury; Minister of blockade, 1916–18; parliamentary under-secretary, foreign office, 1915–18; cr. Viscount, 1923; high churchman, Unionist, free trader, enthusiast for League of Nations.
2. Joseph Albert Pease (1860–1943), coal and steel magnate, Liberal M.P. 1892–1917; president of board of education, 1911–15, postmaster general, 1916, cr. Baron Gainford, 1917.

as if you asked for a gold collection, and a fellow comes along and puts in a brass farthing. And when you tell him about it, he can't see why you are making a fuss. 'It's the same size as a gold piece', he says to you, 'and it's the same colour, and it makes just as much noise!'

This reminds me that C. has given me an 1872 sovereign, which was sent to France from England in 1872 when France was collecting gold for her indemnity, and subsequently paid by her to Germany. There these sovereigns have remained hoarded up ever since, & some have just reappeared in England from Copenhagen. It would seem as though Germany is disgorging some of her hoarded gold. I have taken the piece to be mounted in a case. I am very proud to have it.

April 8th 1915 (Bedford Hotel—Brighton)
The Russians seem to be having another success. A little while ago everything seemed to be up with them, but they are back again as terrible as ever. C. was at a dinner-party at the Admiralty when things seemed to be going badly with them, & someone remarked that there did not seem to be much of the 'steam-roller' about the Russians, after all the fuss that had been made about it at the beginning of the war. 'Oh, but you are mistaken', said Miss Hozier. 'That is just how a steam-roller works—backwards & forwards!'

The Dardanelles campaign, however, does *not* seem to be the success that was prophesied.[1] Churchill very unwisely boasted at the beginning, when things were going well, that he had undertaken it against the advice of every-one else at the Admiralty—that it was 'entirely his own idea'. And then came the reverse, and now the Admiral says that he cannot carry it through with-out siege operations, and land forces, etc. It will be a long job, & C. says he fears it will add to the length of the war, instead of shortening it. Again, the fact that we are not getting on very quickly tells upon the neutrals who were coming in on our side—Italy who was to come in this month, Greece & Roumania, who were also on the point of coming in. C. says Churchill is very worried about the whole affair, and looking very ill. He is very touchy too. Last Monday C. was discussing the Drink question with Churchill, & Samuel[2] & Montagu were also present. Churchill put on the grand air, and announced that he was not going to be influenced by the King, and refused to give up his liquor—he thought the whole thing was absurd. C. was annoyed, but went on to explain a point that had been brought up. The next minute Churchill interrupted again, 'I don't see—' he was beginning, but C. broke in sharply: 'You will see the point', he rapped out, 'when you begin to understand that conversation is not a monologue!'

---

1. A renewed naval attack failed on 18 March, and it was then decided to call in the army.
2. Herbert Samuel (1870–1963): president of local government board, 1914–15; post-master general, 1915–16; home secretary, 1916, 1931–2; chairman of committee on coal industry, 1925–6; took over leadership of Liberal party from Lloyd George, 1931; knighted, 1920; cr. Viscount, 1937.

Churchill went very red, but did not reply, & C. soon felt rather ashamed of having taken him up so sharply, especially in front of the other two. Later on in the evening C. wrote to apologise but received a note back from Churchill almost immediately, saying that no apology was necessary, 'It was I that was churlish', he wrote, which was generous of him. The two are very fond of each other I believe.

I was with C. on Monday evening [5 April]. I had been in bed all the week-end, & was feeling very seedy, & C. persuaded me to come away here till next Monday. I felt I could not go on any longer, & came here on Tuesday, feeling absolutely lifeless. But I am picking up gradually, & C. writes to cheer me up. We are to be together next week, I believe.

At present C. is still fighting for total prohibition. He writes me today that he has the support of the Unionist leaders. I fear the opposition comes from his own side. He has quite given up his work on the munitions question, as it only meant getting across Kitchener, who is determined to do everything himself. But as Balfour wrote to C. 'he (K.) is quite incapable of grasping the magnitude of the problem'. Kitchener himself on Monday [5 April] acknow-ledged that he ought to have taken C.'s advice months ago, when C. first advised the taking over of factories by the Government. 'But I am a foreigner in England', said Kitchener, in excuse. 'I do not understand the Englishman, nor his ways.' However, that seems to be all the more reason why he should not be pig-headed now, but he is determined that the new Committee shall be controlled by the War Office, which means that the W.O. will muddle along as they have done since the beginning of the war, while people who might have helped will fight shy of it.

C. was also bothered last week by a conspiracy against the P.M. The Tory papers took up gossip that the P.M. was slacking, & the Liberal papers attempted to contradict it. Side by side with this was another tale, that there would be a Coalition Gov., & C.'s name was coupled with Mr. Balfour's in connection with this. C. was very upset, as this was the last thing he would wish for, and also he could see that the P.M. was rather suspicious of him, as the rumour must have come from somewhere. C. went to have a talk with the P.M. about it, & found the old boy in tears.[1] Taken unawares, he confessed that he had doubts about C.'s good faith. C. on the other hand, was pretty sure that it was McKenna who had started the mischief, partly from things he had heard him say, and partly because he is a jealous fellow, never so happy as when he is sowing discord among those who are more influential than himself. C. therefore insisted upon seeing McKenna with the P.M. The P.M. agreed, & it was found that C. was right. C. gave McKenna a good talking to, saying that this was the last time to sow strife in the Cabinet—that the fate of England depended on a united Government at this time, &

---

1. A tearful meeting. According to Asquith it was Ll.G. who wept. Asquith, Jenkins, p. 356.

that if McKenna tried any more of his nonsense, there would be trouble. McKenna's is an extraordinary character—suspicious, jealous, yet with a certain doggedness that keeps him going in the face of any amount of opposition and even ill-will. The impression he gives me is that of always having to excuse himself for something or other. He is summed up in the words— (which I have heard him repeat endless times in the House) 'If you will believe me, it really is not so: you are quite mistaken: it really is not as you think, etc., etc.'

Am reading Meredith's Egoist. C. said he was afraid it would lessen my love for him, as he throws such a clear light on the male character. C. says Meredith has just such an insight on character as the physician has on your body when he puts the electric light arrangement on his forehead. C. says too that Meredith was the first person to conceive the revolt of woman—the revolt against the accepted relations of husband and wife, that is to say, he was the first person to write about it. Though C. says that Ibsen's Doll's House was the work that converted him to woman suffrage, & presented the woman's point of view to him.

April 13th 1915 (Walton Heath)
Returned from Brighton this morning, & came on here this evening. Am waiting for C., who will not be here till late, as he has a dinner. He wrote me that his scheme for Drink was progressing, but that it would be a hard fight, & I am anxious to hear all about it from his own lips.

I had Muriel's[1] company for the weekend, as I got terribly lonely. But it was much brighter after she arrived, & we had a good time together. She was very frightened on Sunday [11 April] by the appearance of an airship, which we both thought was a Zeppelin, but as it went away without doing any damage we concluded we were mistaken.

April 18th 1915 (London)
Returned yesterday from W.H. C. is very tired & has gone for a run to Eastbourne today. He is still busy with drink, but has had to modify his original scheme considerably, as he could not get it through the Cabinet. The P.M. was against total prohibition, & the State purchase of all the public houses. It is a pity, as I very much fear partial measures will do very little good.

The Unionist leaders held a Conference to consider the question, and decided to support the Government. F. E. Smith told C. that Robert Cecil was in favour of their not supporting the Government, on the ground this drink legislation would make the Government unpopular with the working classes, which would be a good opportunity for the Tories at the next General Election. 'If we support the Gov. now', he said, 'we should not be able to take advantage of this at the next General Election.' This is how the

---

1. Frances Stevenson's sister.

man speaks who pretends to be so high-minded and pious, & who always has the interest of morality at heart! However, I would not put too much faith in F. E. Smith. Lord Northcliffe[1] is the latest person to be propitiated. He was annoyed because he had not been consulted, & announced his intention of opposing the action of the Government forthwith. However, C. sent for him and I think has talked him round. Northcliffe pretended that the delay in producing munitions was not due to drink, whereas before his pride was injured he had taken a very different view of the matter.

C. has buried the hatchet with Masterman. The latter, after ten days' seclusion at Selsea, came back & apologised to C. saying that he knew he had treated him badly, and that he was sorry for it. C. said that he was to say no more about it, so they are friends again. C. says he can forgive a man when he apologises so unreservedly as that. 'It isn't the man's fault that he is a failure, & has behaved in that way', said C. to me when telling me about it. 'It's the way he's made. It is just like a shell that has been badly filled, and refuses to go off properly. It isn't the shell's fault that it does not explode. It is the fault of the man who filled it.' C. has acquired the habit of talking in terms of munitions lately. He is very busy on his new munitions Committee.

Sir Edward Grey sent C. a beautiful salmon which he had caught on his holiday. We enjoyed it thoroughly.

April 25th 1915 (London)
C. is coming up from Walton this afternoon & I am to join him at 5. We have had a very happy week, though C. has been very busy. But his spirits have been very good, so that he does not seem to be over-tired.

We managed to spend Monday evening [19 April] together at Downing St. but Tuesday was not successful. On Wednesday C. joined me there after his speech in the House.[2] He was very happy about it, as he thought he had succeeded in satisfying the House on the subject of Munitions. His defence of K. was splendid, I think, considering the fault he has found with him in the Cabinet. It appears that at Monday's Cabinet, K. went for C. because the latter had disclosed to the Munitions Committee, the numbers of men who had been sent to the front. K. said these figures should never have gone beyond the Cabinet. C. said it was impossible for the Munitions Committee to provide Munitions if they did not know how many men they had to provide for. K. thereupon became almost hysterical, said he had only himself to blame for allowing the figures to go beyond the W.O., & concluded by saying that since he had not the confidence of his colleagues there was nothing

1. Alfred Harmsworth (1865–1922), founder of modern journalism; created The Daily Mail; owned The Times; head of British mission to United States, 1917; directed enemy propaganda, 1918; cr. Baron Northcliffe, 1905, Viscount, 1917; Lloyd George's association with Northcliffe, which was often held against him, was by no means serene.
2. Wednesday, 21 April. Motion by Hewins calling for enlistment of all firms capable of producing munitions under a unified administration.

left for him but to resign. Churchill took C.'s side, & went for K., but Grey took K.'s side, whereupon Churchill went for Grey, saying that he was very unfair to C. I gather that there was a general scrimmage, and the Cabinet broke up. On the following Wednesday K. sent a message to C. saying that he would like to see C. if he had time to call in. C. went over, & K. was most pleasant to him, though they had not met since Monday's Cabinet & the row. K. confessed that he did not know what the Gov't. could say to appease the House that day on the subject of Munitions. 'I am afraid there will be a great row about it', he said. 'There is one thing', said C., 'that would satisfy them, and that is the figures you gave me of the men who have gone to the fighting line. If you would only allow me to make public those figures, I think I could make everything all right by showing them how the W.O. has exceeded everything that was expected of them.' K. brightened up. 'Certainly, my dear fellow', he exclaimed, 'you may publish them by all means.' 'I will say then', said C., 'that instead of six divisions, we have sent out more than five times that number.' 'Not five times', said K., 'but six times; & you can add', he continued enthusiastically, 'that every man who has fallen has been replaced.' And these were the very figures the publication of which to a select few K. had deplored almost to the point of tears in Monday's Cabinet. C. was astonished at the change in his point of view and he says he cannot account for it, unless it was that K. saw it was the only way to turn away criticism from the W.O.

However, K. was very pleased with C.'s speech & passed him a note in Thursday's Cabinet to that effect.[1] The two are good friends again.

10 Downing Street
Whitehall, S.W.

Your speech was excellent.

You shall have your man for Welsh division, but would you tell Treasury that certain additional land that can now be bought cheap for the Residency in Cairo, should be agreed to and bought—Grey, Emmot, Montagu, & I, went into it and it was decided to buy the land. The Board of Works will apply to the Treasury to be allowed to purchase. I am only afraid of office people putting up objections. It is absolutely necessary & a good buy—

On Thursday [22 April] we left in the car at 5.0 o'clock & went down to Walton. There was no-one there to prepare a meal, so we collected refreshments of various kinds at Sutton for an impromptu supper. We left the car at Kingswood & went for a long walk on the Heath. C. was quite mad, & improvised mock sermons for my benefit, taking idiotic subjects for his texts. I love to see him in these mad moods; he is like some wild boy broken loose from school. Moreover, I know when he is like that that he has thrown off

---

1. This note of Thursday, 22 April 1915, in Kitchener's handwriting, and on the prime minister's embossed notepaper, has the tribute to the speech scribbled as an afterthought across the top left corner.

all worries and cares for the time being & that his mind is having a rest. It was dark by the time we got to Walton. We passed such a happy evening together.

We drove up to town on Friday morning, C. still as mad as ever, this time composing opera, saying mad things in true recitative style. I helping him with the accompaniment in between. He was so busy all day that I scarcely saw him. In the evening he took Mr. & Mrs. Timothy Davies out to dinner, she being downhearted as she had not seen him for a long while. I think he is very kind & nice to her, and I would not have it otherwise.

C. tells me that Kitchener is furious at the treatment which is being meted out to British prisoners in Germany. He has received a report which tells of horrible & disgusting things, which made him so angry that he announced to the Cabinet his wish of publishing a statement to the effect that the war would not cease until the men who had done these things were handed over to the British Government to deal with. C. & other members of the Cabinet were against this, for they argued that it might prolong a two years' war to a five years' war, for the last thing any country can do is to hand over her own subjects for punishment. She will do anything rather than be humiliated to that extent.

Churchill who has just returned from the front, says that the temper of our men there is becoming frightful. He says they do not care what happens to them so long as they can get at the enemy, & it sometimes leads them to do things which are not quite a credit to the British. He heard a story of a British officer at Neuve Chapelle, who was searching a house that had been taken from the Germans. He came to the cellar, & found the door locked. They forced the door & found Germans inside. The Germans held up their hands, but the British officer cried, 'How many of you are there?' 'Five', came the reply. 'Very well then, divide that between you!' and he threw in a hand grenade, which exploded in their midst!

May 6th 1915
This week and last C. has had a most harassing time—over the drink question, & his troubles are not over yet. The first Drink programme drawn up by him was met with howls of opposition in the Cabinet, so I gather, and he was forced to modify it. It provided for total prohibition of spirits amongst other things. However, he could not get them to accept it, & he & the Attorney General[1] & one or two others set about re-casting it. After this had been done, the Attorney General remarked, 'Well! I think we have removed all the offensive matter from the Bill.' 'My dear Attorney', replied C., 'have you ever seen a pig hanging up in a butcher's shop? Have you noticed how inoffensive & harmless it is?' 'You mean', said the Attorney, 'that it has had all the guts taken out?' 'Exactly', said C. 'that is what has happened to this Bill.'

---

1. Sir John Simon.

C. was very touchy last week, owing to the anxiety caused by the Bill, together with over-work. However, the speech was duly delivered on Thursday [29 April] after much hard work on the part of everyone concerned with it. Was up till 12.0 midnight on Wednesday. But Thursday morning C. & I had a glorious drive up to town through Richmond Park. It was a perfect spring morning, & the foliage was just visible on all the trees. The view over Richmond Valley glorious. There was one enormous fruit tree 'clad in glittering white', that stood out majestically. It was a very happy ride.

C. occupied with Budget over the weekend. Great opposition from every quarter to the taxes. On his way up to town Mr. Bonar Law told him that the Unionists could not possibly support the taxes, which were far too drastic. 'Very well', was C.'s reply. 'If you oppose them, I shall withdraw them. But, remember, the responsibility for dealing with this question will then rest with you!' Bonar Law was rather taken back, not having realised this. In the end he agreed that if the taxes were considerably reduced, his party would support them. C. quite willing to agree to this, having put them up specially high in anticipation of having to reduce them.

Budget speech on Tuesday [4 May]—actual speech went off well, but afterwards drink question raised, although an understanding had been come to with Opposition that it should be reserved. However, once the question was broached, the Irish made themselves particularly unpleasant. C. silenced them in the end by saying that there was no point in discussing the question while he was still carrying on negotiations with persons interested in taxes. This was after people had made their various complaints, & had the effect of squashing the Debate without giving any definite replies or assurances. Governor of the Bank said the performance of C. was the cleverest thing he had ever seen.

C. very bucked with the whole proceedings. Had dinner with him afterwards, before he joined the others at the theatre. He was quite mad—just like a school boy when a prank has succeeded.

Yesterday C. full up with engagements all day, negotiating the Drink question. Fearfully tired when he had finished at eight o'clock, but revived after dinner, & became quite merry, describing to me Tree's effort the night before in The Right to Kill, imitating him in his part as the ardent lover, forgetting his part, & out of reach of the prompter.

Today have been up to the House to hear Second Reading of Drink Bill, but it is adjourned. I really think that for paltry selfishness the House of Commons beats all, & the Irish Party certainly broke the record today. There may be high-flown talk about patriotism & self-abnegation, but it is quite clear that when it comes to a question which touches the pocket, such as the new taxes, every member is for himself. That has been amply shown on Tuesday [4 May] & today & it was even evident when the Drink Bill was brought in last Thursday. One could see from the tone of the House that it was not restriction of areas, or broad policy that the members were interested in, but they wanted to know how far it was going to affect them personally—that was where the interest & excitement came in.

I certainly think that the Irish Party have played up the worst of anyone. Redmond[1] has practically admitted that all they care about is the whisky trade, in so far as it affects their prosperity & profit. One after another the Irish Members got up & said the same things, & I should not have thought it capable for men at this time to give such an exhibition of utter disgusting selfishness. C. had an interview with Redmond & Dillon[2] this morning, & he said it was not very satisfactory. He gave them a piece of his mind. He says they are not out of the wood yet, & if they behave badly over this business, they deserve to pay for it afterwards.

On the whole, however, I do not think C. will be very sorry if he has to drop the taxes altogether. The part of the Bill that he is particularly keen on is State control in certain areas, & this has met with no opposition, much to his surprise, though it is much more far-reaching than the taxes. But of course it does not affect the trade or touch 'vested interests', so will go through quietly.

Good news from Paul from the front. He finds it rather dull at present apparently, but we would rather it remained so as far as he is concerned. But I fear heavy fighting is imminent all along the line in Flanders, if it has not actually begun.

Saw M. Ribot last Thursday [24 April]. He is a dear old man. Sir J. Simon calls him the 'only honest politician in France'.

May 10th 1915

Just returned from Burghclere where I spent the weekend with Mary ——. The country is perfect there, especially at this time of the year. Nothing could be more beautiful or more full of peace. All the family are dears, but the girls are brought up in a strict old-fashioned way. Mary, even though married, being still practically treated as a school-girl. She was telling me of the way in which they have been brought up, in such ignorance of the world, that she on her marriage day knew absolutely nothing of what was expected from a wife to her husband on marriage. The consequence was that she was frightened & unhappy, & the revelations which came to her that day did not tend to make the first 48 hours of their wedding go as smoothly as would have been the case had she been more prepared. The house & gardens are beautiful, however, & one cannot help feeling that one could not live in such a place and not be happy. Little John is a darling, but very self-willed, & will I fear be a dreadful handful later on. Mary herself has not changed an atom since we were at college. It seems only yesterday that we were idling on the river playing the fool or indulging in college gossip. It seemed altogether as though I had been in a pleasant dream for two whole days, & woke up this morning to the realities of things in a train from Newbury to London.

---

1. John Edward Redmond (1856–1918), leader of Irish Nationalist Party, 1900–18.
2. John Dillon (1851–1927), Irish Nationalist M.P.

C. was at the Treasury before me. He had returned from spending the weekend with the P.M. on the River at Sutton Courtney. We motored down together on Saturday [8 May] as far as Reading, & had a glorious time. The day was perfect, though C. was depressed because of the loss of the Lusitania. He said it was the first time that he had really felt angry & a desire for vengeance. He was very tired, too, having had a strenuous weekend. All day Friday he was engaged in negotiations on the Drink questions. He was very sick with the Irish, who he said had done the worst day's work for Ireland that had been done for a long time. He says that if the question of Home Rule ever comes up again—as it might possibly do—he for one will not give the Irish his support. It would mean now, he says, putting Ulster, which is a fairly sober province, under the heel of the rest of Ireland, which has so clearly shown itself to be dominated by the whisky and beer interests. 'My dear fellow', said he to Mr. Acland this morning, 'I've *done* with Ireland!'

May 15th 1915
We have had a strenuous week, & C. & I have seen comparatively little of each other—just enough to keep us going, however, & for him to tell me the news. C. got his Drink Bill & his Budget through on Wednesday [12 May], & was content, but very very tired when I went up to the House to see him on my way home. What occupies most of his attention at present is the Munitions Committee, over which he is having a rare tussle. Sir P. Girouard & Booth are both trying hard to get the control of the output of Munitions to the sphere of the War Office, & are endeavouring to squash the efforts of C. who is doing his level best to extend the works & output generally. Journeys have been arranged for next week to the different centres, in order to incite the engineering works there to increase their energies if possible, & for the purpose of recruiting fresh firms. Girouard & Booth, however, determined that C. should see as little as possible, & tried to arrange that he should visit such places as Elswick, where the work is in full swing, & leave out the places which really need attention. Wolfe, the Sec. to the Committee, has had a rough time the last few days, though he is on the side of the Chancellor. He informed me of what was going on, & I think hoped that C. would get to know. I knew C. had an inkling of what was going on, though he was uncertain whether it was stupidity or malice, so I told him exactly what Wolff had said, as I thought he ought to know. He has now taken steps to ensure that he *shall* see everything that is going on, & has intimated to Girouard & Booth that if they cannot find time to accompany him to all these places, he will take steps to find someone who *will*.

Yesterday at the War Council Kitchener stated that in his opinion we should never get through the Dardanelles.[1] He stated that he had been misled by the Admiralty as to the number of men that would be required for the

---

1. British and Australian troops landed at Gallipoli on 25 April, but failed to break through the Turkish defences.

operations, & that at the rate things were going on it was quite impossible for him to provide the men that would be required for such a campaign. C. himself asked Churchill at the beginning of the campaign whether it would develop into long siege operations. 'Oh no!' was Churchill's reply. 'Nothing of the kind. We shall go through in quite a short time.'

This morning C. met Fisher, who said that he had just sent in his resignation to the Prime Minister, on the ground that he could not countenance what was going on in the Dardanelles. 'It is bleeding the navy white', said Fisher to C. 'And the land operations there are bleeding the army white. We cannot possibly go on with it.'

C. is very disturbed about it. He says if Fisher's resignation is accepted, Churchill will have to go. He will be a ruined man. 'It is the Nemesis', said C. to me, 'of the man who has fought for this war for years. When the war came he saw in it the chance of glory for himself, & has accordingly entered on a risky campaign without caring a straw for the misery and hardship it would bring to thousands, in the hope that he would prove to be the outstanding man in this war.'

C. tells me that when the Cabinet gave their consent to a bombardment of the Dardanelles forts (very unwillingly) it was on the strict understanding that the operations should not be announced in the first place, so as not to commit the Government, & to enable them, if the thing should turn out to be impossible or a more lengthy proceeding than was anticipated, to withdraw from the campaign without any discredit to themselves. This did not suit Churchill, however. On the very first day that the bombardment commenced, he broke faith with his colleagues & caused the announcement to be made in the Press with great eclat that we had begun the bombardment of the Dardanelles forts, & intended to force the Straits. Thenceforth it was of course impossible for the Government to withdraw.

Yesterday C. unveiled the portrait of Hugh Price Hughes,[1] at the Kingsway Hall. He took a lot of trouble in preparing his speech, as he was a great admirer of the man, & I think he thought it an honour to be chosen to pay a tribute to the great Welshman. At any rate, he was glad to do so. He spoke very well, & was very pleased with himself afterwards. He said they had all appreciated it very much. Many of them told him that it was the first time there had been a real appreciation of Hugh Price Hughes. Mrs. Price Hughes was very much touched. 'I do not know how to express my thanks to you,' she said. 'You *understand* him!'

Sunday May 16th 1915
My little god-daughter Nancy is to be christened today. I have undertaken to be her guardian on the strict understanding that it shall not involve any *religious* teaching, but only the responsibility for her moral and material welfare. I scarcely know whether I am fit to undertake even the former of

---

1. Famous Nonconformist preacher.

these two; many people would think I am not. But I do not, oh I do not think that I am wicked & unfit to help in the upbringing of a child. Surely my experiences have made me *more* fit for this: for knowledge is safety.

This evening I am going to keep C. company for supper. He has gone to Woolwich Arsenal—a sort of preliminary for his trip next week. I shall miss him so much, but am glad he is going, for we need the work & courage of every capable man at present.

May 18th 1915
C. had a bomb ready for me yesterday. He had been very busy in the early part of the morning seeing Mr. Balfour, Mr. Bonar Law, the Prime Minister, and others. When I went to him later with some letters, 'Well Pussy', he said to me, 'I'm leaving this place!' I would not believe him, but he assured me it was the truth, & then went on to explain matters: how Fisher was persisting in his resignation, & the Tories demanded a national government—insisting of course on Churchill's dismissal: how Balfour & Bonar Law had suggested that C. should be the next P.M.,[1] but that he had absolutely refused the proposal, as being unfaithful to the present P.M. How the Prime Minister was altogether in favour of a Coalition government: & how—last but not least—the proposal was put forward that C. should go to the War Office, which offer he was quite prepared to accept. Kitchener he said, had misled the Government on the subject of ammunition—chiefly explosives—& was not fit to be in charge of such important work.

We were very excited about it. C. promised to take me with him to the W.O., & we had all sorts of plans. Above all C. was deeply moved by the fact that he had been asked to accept the Premiership, though he does not for one moment regret having refused it. I passed a sleepless night thinking of all the responsibilities that would devolve on C., & all the incidental happenings that would accompany a change of office.

This morning C. was visited *very* early by various Ministers—all very anxious not to be left out! It ended in an enormous breakfast party. I suppose they all know that C.'s word will have a good deal of weight in the formation of the next Cabinet. I am sorry however to hear that Montagu is likely to be included. I do not trust the man, & feel that he is insincere & a hanger-on.

C.'s latest decision is that he will not go to the W.O. He does not want to leave this place, he says. However, I am to dine with him tonight & we shall be able to talk the matter over.

May 19th 1915
Nothing is yet definitely decided. C. is still uncertain whether he wants to go to the W.O., and I think will leave it in the hands of the Prime Minister to decide. At any rate he means to make a fuss over the state of ammunition & high explosives, as he finds that the War Office have been misleading him

---

1. There is no independent evidence for this.

deliberately as to output and contracts, and have kept back reports sent from Headquarters on the subject of the need for high explosives.

C. told me last night that Churchill was taking his defeat very well. 'I feel like a wounded man', he said to C., 'I know I am hurt, but as yet I cannot tell how badly. Later on I shall know the extent to which I am damaged, but now I only feel the shock.' The P.M. told C. that Churchill sent up a note to his bedroom at 8 o'clock in the morning, telling him that he would like to discuss the situation with him. 'Which means', said the P.M. to C., 'the situation as it concerns Churchill personally—how far he is likely to be affected. The situation for Churchill has no other meaning but his own prospects.'

Today, however, Churchill seems to be going to put up a fight. He brought up to show C. & Sir Edward Grey a long letter in justification of his policy against Fisher's, & announced his intention of publishing it. C. showed him that it would be a fatal thing to do. 'There is no public insinuation up to the present', said C. to him, 'that the success of the Dardanelles operations is questioned. If you publish that, you will imply that it is.' Churchill saw that point of view, but later on completely losing his temper when he saw that C. & Grey took it for granted that he was going. 'You don't care', he said to C., 'what becomes of me. You don't care whether I am trampled under foot by my enemies. You don't care for my personal reputation . . .' 'No', said C., 'I don't care for my own at the present moment. The only thing I care about now is that we win this war.'

May 24th 1915

This afternoon the new Coalition Govt. is being decided upon. Up till now certain members have been in the balance, but this afternoon will decide everyone's fate. At the end of last week Churchill was making a big fight to stay at the Admiralty. First of all a letter came from Mrs. Winston C. to the P.M. saying that Winston was the only man for the Admiralty & that if the P.M. listened to those who wished to turn Winston out, he would be showing great weakness. On Friday morning [21 May] a letter came from Winston himself to the P.M., saying that no other man but himself would be able to cope with the naval situation during the war, that the things he had had to endure for the last 10 months were beyond imagination—he did not think it possible for a man to bear such anxiety—and that it would be a poor reward for him to be turned out after what he had done. There was no other man who could do as much. The P.M. became angry at these letters, & wrote him a stern note to say that he 'must make up his mind that he must go'. Winston seems to have seen the futility of pursuing his course & wrote back a very meek note to say that he was prepared to take anything the P.M. would offer him. I understand now that he is to be given the Duchy of Lancaster—the lowest post in the Cabinet. There is no section in the country, as far as I can see, that wishes him to stay at the Admiralty. Masterton-Smith, Winston's own private secretary, told the P.M. that on no account ought Churchill to be allowed to remain at the Admiralty—he was most dangerous there. It seems strange that Churchill should have been in politics all these years, & yet not have won the confidence of a single party in the country, or a single colleague in the Cabinet.

The great difficulty now is what is to become of C. Everyone is keen on his taking up Munitions of War, but many think it would be a pity for him to be Secretary of State for War; on all hands, moreover, he is begged not to give up the Exchequer. It is quite certain that he cannot take on two Departments. The War Office people, however, seem as keen for him to go to the W.O. as the Treasury are for him to stay at the Exchequer. On Thursday morning [20 May] the Governor of the Bank of England called while C. was shaving & asked to see C. C. went down in a hurry, wondering what had happened. The Governor seemed to be very moved. 'I just want to say', he said, speaking with difficulty, 'that I hope you are not going to leave the Exchequer.' He then burst into tears. He was really very distressed at the idea of C. going & when he recovered sufficiently, explained that the City would be very upset if C. went away. 'My dear fellow', said C. laughing, 'a year ago you and the City would have come with a petition for me to leave the Exchequer!' However, C. explained that the decision did not rest with himself, but that the Governor must go to the P.M. about the matter. The P.M. told C. afterwards what had happened. He was much amused. 'I couldn't get anything out of him', said the P.M. to C., 'except "We don't want to lose our man! Don't take our man away from us!"' C. was very much moved at the demonstration of affection on the part of the Governor and the City. He had heard indirectly too that Ribot is very much perturbed at the idea of his leaving the Exchequer. It appears that the whole of France has great confidence in C. since his visit to Paris. Ribot, whom C. is told is rather weak, although a very dear old man, is always very much encouraged after having intercourse with C. & is a different man from what he was before the Paris Conference. He said that he expected to find C. a politician, but discovered that he was a statesman.

However, people admit that there must be a man of great capacity to look after Munitions, & C. would be very glad to stay at the Exchequer & run Munitions as well, which would be quite workable seeing that Treasury matters are fairly quiet now. Bonar Law, however, expressed dissatisfaction with this arrangement. The fact of the matter is that he wants to be at the W.O. himself. Yesterday morning (Sunday) Lord Northcliffe rang up to ask if he might come down to Walton to see C. He arrived soon after 10.0 & discussed the situation with C. He was all for C. taking over Munitions, & not allowing the Tories to get it. He told C. that they had begun intriguing already against the Liberals, and that he was afraid the national Government would not last long. He also told C. that they had been trying to bribe the Harmsworth press, offering to make Lord Northcliffe's brother B. Law's assistant at the War Office if Lord Northcliffe backed B. Law for the W.O. & he succeeded in getting in. Dirty work when the country is in peril!

C. said that he could see on Saturday that there was some intriguing going on, & that B. Law would like to get munitions into his own hands. B. Law's ostensible reason for C. not taking over munitions was that he would not have the time, & that if he remained at the Exchequer as most people wanted him to, he must depute munitions to someone else. Eventually, however, it was settled that he should have the Colonial Office, and Mr. Balfour the Admiralty. The question then came up of Mr. Walter Long.[1] B. Law said there was a very strong feeling in the Tory party that he should become a member of the new Cabinet, & that there would be discord if he did not. Where, then should he go? B. Law said he felt certain he would not accept a minor office—his status was surprisingly high in the party, & he had become rather touchy since his illness. Mr. Balfour then suggested that, in order to arrange matters with as little dissension as possible, he (Balfour) would be quite satisfied with a nominal post in the Cabinet—say Lord President of the Council—which would leave the Admiralty free for Mr. A. Chamberlain, & a vacancy for Long. 'Oh no!' said B. Law instantly. 'I could not have that. It would be putting him above me in status, which could not possibly be allowed!' How this little episode shows the difference between the two men. 'To think', said ——'that they chose this man (Law) for leader in preference to the other!'

However, the matter is still undecided, but we shall soon know, C. had a brilliant inspiration this morning. His idea is that the P.M. should take on the Exchequer temporarily—say for 6 months—& C. should devote his time & energy to munitions. C. went to the P.M. as soon as he came up to town this morning & told him of the plan. The P.M. thoroughly approved, and added that Pitt held both offices during the Napoleonic wars.

C. and I have had a glorious time during the weekend, in spite of worries & uncertainties. On Thursday Mr. Murray asked us to dine at his flat, & took us to see Véronique afterwards—we enjoyed it thoroughly. I think Mr. Murray must know of our relations. C. asked me to broach the subject of a knighthood to him, but he insisted that he wanted no such thing. All he had done was done for the good of his native land & his native city, & love of the Chancellor. He is coming up from Brighton this week to take us out again. He is a dear.

On Friday [21 May] we went down to Walton Heath. I went home to tea first, as it was Muriel's birthday. C. wanted to give her a Persian kitten, but Mamma would not allow her to have another animal. On Saturday we came up, as there was a meeting on the subject of the Coalition. C. took Megan out to tea, & we both motored down to Walton afterwards. Sunday

---

1. Walter Long (1854–1924), president of local government board, 1915–16; colonial secretary, 1916–18; first lord of the Admiralty, 1918–21, a Viscount 1921.

was a glorious day. We started at 11.30 & motored down to Beachy Head & picniced there. Came back through Ashdown Forest & had tea on the common there. It was a perfect day and the sea was motionless.

May 25th 1915
Nothing decided yesterday after all. They could not agree, but by tonight our fates will be settled.

Lloyd George became minister of munitions, and McKenna became chancellor of the exchequer on the understanding that Lloyd George would resume that office later. This was a cheque which Lloyd George never cashed.

June 12th 1915
A year ago today we were down at Christ's Hospital for the last prize-giving that Paul would partake in as a member of the school. We were so proud of him & of all the honours that fell to him. Today we have been taking part in a Memorial Service for him & others of the 23rd London, who have fallen recently in France. Even now it seems incredible that he is dead—that he will never return. It is the first time that I have experienced the death of one who was dear to me, & the hopelessness of it all has thrown a shadow over my life that I do not believe can ever disappear. The nobility of his death takes away some of the bitterness, and the many tributes that we have received from all who ever knew him. But all our hopes and plans have come to nothing, though I know he would have wished for no better end than this. He was so terribly eager to get to the firing line, but I did not worry about him, for it seemed to me that he at least would come safely back, that death at least would spare one so promising & so dear and necessary to us. The shock came cruelly, & has numbed my brain, & the consolation seems to be little for so terrible a loss. They say that time will heal the wounds, & leave only pride instead of grief, but how can we ever do anything but miss him and need him more and more as the years go on?

A further attempt at the Dardanelles failed on 6 August 1915. Bulgaria was now on the point of joining the Central Powers and Lloyd George continued to press for an expedition to Salonika. He also advocated conscription—partly to ensure that workers on munitions were not taken into the army.

September 2nd 1915
It is time to take up my diary again, though I feel it is impossible to fill up the gap. C. has been resting all last week, after a slight breakdown as the result of overwork. I must no longer call him C., but will substitute D., which has the advantage of being permanent.

The Ministry of Munitions is now fairly on its legs, after many stormy passages. The question resolves itself now more or less into a question of labour, which again seems to be resolving itself into a question of conscription. D. is having a rather unpleasant time on account of this, the Northcliffe press by their agitation having put up the backs of the Liberals. The Conservative element of the Cabinet, however, are strong for it, and are looking to D. to lead them through this campaign. This, however, has had the effect of somewhat alienating the Liberals from D. In addition to this, there is considerable feeling in the country against the Prime Minister, who, it is felt, has not coped with the situation with sufficient courage and firmness, (having, in fact, simply allowed things to take their course in the hope that the war would of itself come to a speedy end). Certain mischief-makers, of whom McKenna appears to be the chief, have been trying to foster the impression that D. is responsible, more or less, for the movement against the Prime Minister, coupling this movement with the one which D. does actually represent, i.e. the one that tries to make people see the situation as it really is, in its grave aspect, instead of ignoring the difficulties and dangers.

The P.M. & D. have also come up against each other on the matter of compulsory service. Here again, McKenna has done his best to foment bad feeling & was assisted by an unfortunate incident. D. had advised the members of the Cabinet who were in favour of conscription that the time was not yet quite ripe for making open declarations, but suggested that the question should be approached tentatively. These members ∴ have been meeting and discussing the question, & F. E. Smith sent a note along to D. one evening giving an account of what had happened at one of these meetings. The note, however, was by mistake addressed to the 'Chancellor of the Exchequer', & naturally fell into McKenna's hands. McK. opened it, took it out of the Cabinet box it was in, & two days later returned it to D. with a note to say that he had read it through. Not a word of apology. What had happened during those two days can only be surmised, but D. concludes that the note had been handed about for inspection, as it presented rather a dirty appearance. D. was furious, & wrote a biting letter to McKenna suggesting that the next time a letter came into his hands by mistake, he should put it back into the same box & send it on to the right person *at once*—after he had read it, of course. D. also intimated that had any other of his colleagues done a similar thing, he would have experienced some surprise.

The atmosphere, in fact, has been so unpleasant for some time, and the P.M. so clearly shown to D. that he was not in favour, that D. has said very little at Cabinet meetings, letting the P.M. & his little lap-dogs 'stew in their own juice', as D. expressed it. Things are very ominous on the Eastern front, & no initiative whatever has been taken on the West, & yet there does not seem to be anyone who is able to make any suggestion. When D. makes a proposal it is pooh-poohed by the P.M., who seems to be of the opinion that the war will be over in 3 weeks. The Unionist portion of the Cabinet are simply sick of his 'wait-and-see' methods, and the whole country is getting tired. D. is doing his very best to increase the munitions supply, but is greatly hampered by the Labour question, which he is more and more convinced can only be solved by compulsory service. The South Wales miners have practically intimated that they would be glad of martial law, for then both masters and men would be under control. D. cannot be for ever intervening to settle strikes which have nothing to do with his Department. In both the S. Wales strikes he has been called in at the eleventh hour when Runciman[1] has fanned the discontent into a blaze which he is quite powerless to cope with. D. had a great success at Cardiff, and his name was on everyone's lips. He has been happier since, for the Cabinet have been a little more generous to him since—they have had to, out of sheer decency. He does not say anything, but I know he feels their coldness very much.

We went straight down to W.H. when he returned from Cardiff.

September 15th 1915
Poor D. is very worried. Things are going very very badly with us, and whenever he ventures to call attention to it, he is greeted with a chorus of indignation from Liberals and Liberal journalists. This is not at all what he wants. He hates being praised by the Tories, and made to seem a traitor to his own party. But the fact remains, that Churchill is the only Liberal who is at all friendly to him at this moment.

D.'s opinion is that unless decisive action is taken *at once* we are in danger of disaster. In fact, he says he thinks that even now disaster is inevitable. About a fortnight ago Kitchener saw Joffre and they arranged that a big attack should be made all along the line. Then a few days after the plans were cancelled, and the French offered to send instead 4 Divisions to the Dardanelles, to help our armies there, which have been terribly cut up. Winston was overjoyed at hearing this, & at the Cabinet at which K. announced it passed a note to D. saying: 'I feel like a man who was about to be shot, and who instead is left a large fortune.'

However, the next thing that K. announced to the Cabinet (last Wednesday [8 September]) was that the attack was going to take place, though he did not know when. Moreover, he did not know whether the 4 French Divisions for the Dardanelles would still hold good or not. So there sat K. supposed to be directing the campaign in both theatres of war, with only the haziest notion of what was going to happen in each. Before the French had offered help, the Cabinet had definitely decided that the Dardanelles campaign was a failure, but had no suggestions at all to put forward

1. Walter Runciman (1870–1949): son of a shipowner; Liberal M.P., 1899–1900, 1902–18, 1924–31; Liberal National M.P., 1931–7; succeeded his father as Baron and created Viscount, 1937; president of board of trade, 1914–16, 1931–7; lord president of the council, 1938–9. In July 1915 Runciman proposed to break a strike of South Wales miners by using the government's wartime powers. Lloyd George went down and ended the strike by conceding the miners' demand for a closed shop.

as to the best means of getting out of it or bringing it to an end.

D. said to me on Friday [10 September] that we ought *at* once to make the strongest preparations for a new move on the part of the Germans. He thinks that they will do one of three things:

(1) Break through to Constantinople, in which case the whole of the campaign in the East will come to nothing, & we shall meet with terrible diplomatic difficulties;

(2) March on Italy & overwhelm her, & force her to make peace;

(3) Make an overwhelming attack on the Western Front & break the French line, probably cutting through to Calais.

In none of these cases has any plan of action been thought out, and we are simply proceeding much on the same lines as we were this time last year. The War Office have absolutely no ideas on the subject of any new move. The great attack on the western front is to begin today, but no-one seems very clear as to what we are expected to achieve.

In last Friday's [10 September] Cabinet when the date of the attack was disclosed D. asked whether Sir. J. French had enough ammunition for the purposes of this attack. The P.M. assured him that he had. D. expressed surprise, as according to all previous estimates given by Sir John, D. did not think he could possibly have enough. He suggested that he & French should have an interview on the subject, to clear up matters, & that Mr. Walter Long should also be present to report. This was agreed to, & the interview took place on Friday evening. French said that what he had told the P.M. was that *on a certain estimate* he had enough ammunition—say if the attack lasted six days, & a normal amount was consumed—but that if it lasted longer, & an abnormal amount was consumed, then he certainly would not have sufficient. D. says that is the whole point—that at Neuve Chappelle they had sufficient for a few days, but that the whole thing came to nothing because they were unable to go on for lack of ammunition.

The P.M., who knew very well what the Report would be, refrained from asking for it in the next Cabinet. McKenna, however—not on speaking terms with D. for some time—thinking that as the report was not forthcoming it was unfavourable to D., preened himself up, & asked: 'Are we to have no report on the interview with Sir John French?' 'Oh yes', replied D. 'Mr. Walter Long will read it to the Cabinet.' Imagine the P.M.'s disgust with his henchman!

McKenna put his foot into it again last week. He comes to the Cabinet and makes statements as to Germany being at her last gasp, and the war being over in October. If D. ventures to express the opinion that the war will be a long one, & that we should prepare for it as such, McKenna scoffs and pours contempt upon him. Moreover he (McKenna) has done his best to hinder the output of munitions by stating that the country cannot stand the expense of an unlimited amount of munitions, & that it is unnecessary. He began on this tack last week, & D. turned on him & said: 'You are continually making these statements, but you have never put them into writing. Would you mind doing so?' McKenna hesitated, and then replied: 'Yes, I will do so, if you in return will make a written statement on the working of the Munitions Office.' 'That is exactly what I have wanted to do for some time', said D.

That, however, is exactly what the P.M. does not want him to do, as he knows too well that any such statement must reveal the state of the labour market, and that that in its turn will involve a demand for conscription as the only way out.

On the whole, the Cabinet is divided at present between Pro- and Anti-Conscriptionists. D.'s preface on Monday [13 September] created a great stir, being the first public hint he has given as to his views on conscription. The book[1] is having an enormous sale. Hodder & Stoughton have had orders for over 20,000 already, and we are both very delighted over it. The Liberals, however, are very sick that he should have committed himself to conscription. However, the 'preface' seems to have had the effect of rousing the Cabinet, for both the P.M. & K. made speeches today hinting that at any rate conscription would have to be considered. Last week neither of them would hear of it, and K. on Monday said that the Germans had come to a standstill in Russia, and that the object of the campaign had failed. On Tuesday came the news that the Petrograd railway had been cut, & that the Germans were advancing steadily in the north.

On Tuesday night [14 September] D. dined with Churchill and Curzon. They had a most important talk, and Curzon says the Tories are going to approach the P.M. & say that they cannot proceed any longer under the present state of things. They will demand conscription and the removal of K. from the W.O., as being incompetent and having failed to grasp the military situation. D. & Churchill will throw in their lot with Curzon & his followers, for D. says he cannot possibly be a party any longer to the shameful mismanagement and slackness. He says that things are simply being allowed to slide, and that it is time someone spoke out. As I said before, however, he hates going against his party, & he fears that the Liberals will hate him violently if he goes against them now. He fears Churchill, too. He is not sure whether Churchill will come too, or whether he will remain & get the P.M. to put him into D.'s shoes in the Munitions Office. D. says that Churchill is the only man in the Cabinet who has the power to do him harm, and he does not trust him when it comes to a matter of personal interest. When Churchill left the Admiralty he was sore with D., but soon came round—he could not keep away. However, he simply will not believe that what D. did in May was disinterested. 'You are a clever fellow!' he said once to D., 'You have been scheming for this for months, and have left no stone unturned to get what you wanted.' He simply will not believe that D. did not *want* to become Minister of Munitions, did not *want* to leave the Exchequer. From the same

---

1. Speeches.

principles, he cannot understand why D. did not work to keep him at the Admiralty. 'I have done you many a good turn', he said to D., 'you might have said the word that would have kept me there.' 'But my dear Churchill', said D., 'I have said all along that I did not think you ought to stay there, that the Dardanelles campaign was a great mistake, and that someone else ought to be put into your place.' 'Whatever you thought', was the reply, 'I always thought you would stand by me when it came to the point.' He simply could not believe that a man could be so disinterested as to put the *country* before himself or his personal friends!

Although the past few weeks have not been very pleasant for D. He hates more than anything else that his own friends should be suspicious about him —and suspicious to a great extent without reason, for many mischievous people have insinuated that D. is intriguing against the P.M., whereas D. has always upheld him most loyally, whenever it came to the point. However he will probably win through in the end and by persistence and courage. We hear from all sides that his speech at Bristol last week has strengthened his position in the country enormously. He had a great reception. We prepared the speech in the train going down. I have never seen such a clever perform-ance. The meeting were prepared to be quite hostile and to watch their change of attitude from hostility to interest then to friendliness and admira-tion, until many of them ended in tears—was a sight to remember. We came back the same night, & motored to Walton. Both being very tired, and consequently irritable, we quarrelled, which was a pity. However, we have made up for it this week.

September 17th 1915
The Liberal papers have lost their head. They are gnashing their teeth over Conscription, & can conceal their rage no longer at finding that D. is among the Conscriptionists. Evidently someone has been supplying The Daily News[1] with information, and that someone is no doubt McKenna. He has supplied them with all the particulars on the Cabinet position with regard to Conscription, but to this he has added his old scare—'a plot against the Prime Minister'—suggesting, in a most sinister way, & one which is most difficult to tackle—that the split in the Cabinet over conscription is only designed with a view to getting rid of the Prime Minister. D. has known for some time that McKenna was fomenting mischief against him among the Liberals, but apparently he could restrain himself no longer. However, I think he will soon be sorry he spoke. This outburst, I believe, will do the Prime Minister more harm than good.

The P.M. himself has played a very low trick on D. Mr. Bonar Law had a talk with D. on the situation, & went on to the P.M. afterwards. After this interview D. himself saw the P.M., who then informed him that B. Law had been to him and suggested that he (Bonar Law) should be given the Deputy-

---

1. Radical newspaper, edited by A. G. Gardiner and tepid towards the war.

Leadership of the House of Commons instead of D. D. said that he had nothing to say, if the P.M. thought it advisable to make a change of this kind. He was, however, rather surprised that B. Law should not so much as have mentioned the matter to him, and wrote a note to him to this effect, telling him what had passed between the P.M. and himself. Bonar Law wrote back to the effect that he had never even suggested the matter to the P.M., & that all he had said was when, some weeks ago, he had complained to the P.M. that his name was omitted from a Committee, and that he thought that altogether, as the former leader of the Tory Party—he was not given sufficient responsibility in the Cabinet. That was the only time he had ever hinted at such a thing.

D. was furious with the P.M. & wrote him a sharp note, which brought back a much humbler Document from the P.M., who suggested that the matter should be dropped. D. thinks that the P.M., knowing that the Tories, with D., were in favour of Conscription sought to divide Bonar Law & D., by this means, and get Bonar Law on to his side. He forgets, however, that playing that sort of game with D. is a risky sort of venture.

B. Law, however, does not wish D. to quarrel with the P.M. B. Law says that D. has a great influence over him (the P.M.) in fact, over the whole Cabinet, and that if he takes the trouble he can make them do anything he likes. B. Law says that it was D. who forced the last Cabinet to declare a Coalition Government & that he can force this Cabinet to declare Conscription.

McKenna has outlined his Budget to the Cabinet, with his usual self-complacent manner. The members were for acquiescing in his plan to raise £100,000,000 by taxation, & the rest by loan, but D. made a strong protest.[1] He said that it was absurd, when the war was costing £5,000,000 a day, to only raise 100 millions a year by taxation—that it was sheer cowardice. He said he did not consider it would be too much to ask people to contribute even half their income to the cost of the war, and that we had not attempted to go to the root of the matter in defraying expenditure. The public had not really started to think about economy.

The rest were very much impressed by his earnestness, & as he was very pressing on the subject, the P.M. appointed a Committee to consider the feasibility of his suggestions. He almost went to the point of delaying the Budget, but D. said that he had not meant to suggest that. In fact, McKenna was getting furious, when he saw his Budget on the point of falling to the ground. However, it was decided to proceed with the Budget, on the understanding that it may have to be revised later on.

September 20th 1915
Returned this morning from W.H., where have spent the weekend with D.,

---

1. McKenna's budget was, in fact, a good deal more severe than the two war budgets which Lloyd George introduced.

D. was in high spirits all day—began at breakfast by a wholesale survey of everything almost that the imagination can call up—a fantasy in which potatoes, damson jam, British patriotism (or the lack of it), French courage, pretty women, German tactics & the daily press were all dealt with in a most sweeping fashion. He ended up with a eulogy on love, quoting as the greatest witness St. Paul and the 13th chapter of Corinthians. I gave him my opinion of St. Paul by reading him in turn the 11th chapter, to which he had no answer but that St. Paul must have been badly treated by some woman in order to have obtained that impression.

D. continued to talk nonsense the whole morning, in the intervals of writing a very strong letter to the Press, which has created a great and good impression this morning. 'They think they have got me up against the wall', he said to me, 'and that I am deserted by my own supporters, and then I turn round and give them a knock-out blow. Ah! you thought I was done, you devils, but you will find there is still as much fight in me as ever!' I think he will convince people by his sheer courage and dauntlessness that if they put their trust in him, he will see them through. 'I am fighting for my life', he said to me yesterday, 'But I will win through. I know I am right.'

October 5th 1915
Spent the weekend alone with D. at W.H. He had a perfectly restful Sunday. We went for a long walk on the heath in the morning—a glorious day. D. very much afraid that the attack on the Western front had not come off.[1] The Eastern situation very grave—Buxton[2] had informed D. the previous day that the Germans would be in Constantinople by Xmas. 'But', said I, 'if they once get to Constantinople, our Dardanelles campaign is at an end.' 'My dear Pussy', he replied, 'I am very much afraid that the whole of the Eastern empire is at an end.' He says Grey has lost his nerve. D. protested against the Cabinet separating for the weekend in the face of such a crisis, & urged Grey to say that they should remain in town. Grey completely lost his temper. 'I will consent to holding a Cabinet tomorrow, if I receive a promise that we shall decide to bring the Dardanelles campaign to an end.' Of course, such an undertaking was out of the question, so the Cabinet separated. It shows, however, Grey's views on the Dardanelles campaign. His last tele-gram to Greece has put the backs up of all the Balkan States who were on our side. Things seem to be smoothing out this week, however. The allies are landing at Salonika. This is what D. suggested 9 months ago. Had the Cabinet taken his advice, we might have had a successful campaign in the Balkans instead of a disastrous failure in the Dardanelles. The country is

1. The battle of Loos, which was indeed a failure.
2. Noel Edward Noel-Buxton (1869–1948): Liberal M.P. 1905–6, 1910–18; Labour M.P., 1922–30; cr. Baron, 1930; minister of agriculture, 1924, 1929–30; advocate of compromise peace in both world wars; at this time was anxious to enlist Bulgaria on Allied side.

getting sick of the delay. 'For Heaven's sake', said Crewe[1] in the Cabinet yesterday, 'let us decide *something*. The country is getting impatient: they say we are shilly-shallying.' The P.M. was amazed at this outburst from Crewe, whom he has always regarded as docile and harmless. The Tories in the Cabinet are disgusted with the P.M., & are looking to D. to lead them. Bonar Law, however, advised D. not to quarrel with the P.M., & I think was greatly instrumental in patching up the little estrangement that had occurred between them. D. lunched with the P.M. about a fortnight ago, & they came to a friendly understanding. 'It would be a pity for us to quarrel', said the P.M. to D. in a frank talk. 'I have never believed the stories that have been going round about your intriguing against me. I have always replied to any suggestion of this kind by saying that during all the years we have worked together you have been the most loyal of colleagues. I will be quite frank with you', he continued. 'There are only two men in this Cabinet who count at all, and we are those two. If we quarrel, it will mean disaster.' They parted good friends, D. having persuaded the P.M. to insist on a small Cabinet of 6 or 8 members. This has been since done, though not officially.[2] This smaller Cabinet meets as a Committee, & decides the important matters, while the bigger Cabinet simply talks and wastes time, as far as I can make out. 'Well, what did you decide today?' I said to D. after the big Cabinet meeting yesterday. 'Nothing', he replied—'We never do!'

I discovered later on, however, that D. had wiped the ground with McKenna, whom he loathes heartily. McKenna had complained about the gun programmes that were being laid down, & said that they would involve enormous expenditure that he had never been informed about. D. cut him short in the middle of his complaint. 'Have you ever asked me for any information? Had you sent a polite note—or even an impolite one—I should have had the information supplied to you without delay. You haven't abolished the halfpenny post yet. Send me a post-card & I will see that you get what you ask for.' He went on in this strain for some time, until McKenna began to get rather sorry for himself. 'It is really not fair', continued D., 'to waste the time of the Cabinet like this. Matters should only be brought before the Cabinet when they cannot go any further without discussion. But this is a question that can be approached without bringing it up like this in Cabinet.'

When he saw D. was on the warpath, K. began to get agitated. He had evidently been discussing the big gun programme with McKenna, for he too had made a protest in a letter from the W.O. to D. that too many big guns were being ordered. K. had evidently got something in his mind in the nature

---

1. Robert Offley Crewe-Milnes, second Baron Houghton (1858–1945); cr. Marquis of Crewe, 1911; lord president of the council, 1905–8, 1915–16; lord privy seal, 1908–11, 1912–15; president of board of education, 1916; ambassador in Paris, 1922–8; Asquith's closest associate in the cabinet.
2. This so-called Dardanelles Committee was in fact instituted in June.

of getting up a case against D., but McKenna by being so premature has spoilt K.'s game.

The conscription row has quieted down for the time being. D.'s 'letter to his constituents' pacified people considerably. D. is only waiting, however, to see how this last attack in France has turned out, before returning to the fray. This is a terrible battle. D. says that Joffre is putting his last penny on this fight, for he knows that his position depends upon it. They say he will have to go if it fails, for the French are getting dissatisfied with him. Castelnau, Joffre's second in command, was against a big offensive at the present moment. He spoke for 4 hours against it in the French War Council, but it availed nothing. One of our own generals who ventured to protest against an offensive movement was cashiered on the spot.

M. Thomas[1] and some of the French Generals are over here this week, for a conference with D. They all love him, he gets on so well with Frenchmen— they say he is so unlike the English! M. Paul Mantoux[2] has come over to interpret. He wishes to translate D.'s speeches into French, and I am trying to fix it up with Hodder & Stoughton.

All day long we are getting news of the terrible casualties in this fight. The Welsh Guards have been practically wiped out. In the train on Saturday [2 October] there was a Tommy who had been helping with the wounded at Charing X. He seemed very much affected by what he had seen and heard. He told us how he had said to one poor fellow, 'Well, old chap, we've given them hell this time.' 'Yes', the man answered, 'but, by God, they've given us hell too!'

But we do not *deserve* to win this war. Mrs. Pankhurst has been holding recruiting meetings in S. Wales, and she says there are districts where the people simply don't care whether the Germans are beaten or not. She says they are sulky and difficult to handle, and will not sing the national anthem. And everywhere it seems that the spirit of patriotism is dead in Britain, and that it is each for himself, all the way through. D. has a most difficult task in dealing with the labour part of his Department. From every side comes news of strikes and selfish interests of all kinds at work to hamper in helping the men at the front.

D. has made up his mind that he will not be responsible for cancelling *any* orders for big guns. He says he will bring the matter before the Cabinet, & if they decide that it is to be done, then *he* will not do it. Someone else will have to be responsible.

Now that the winter is coming on it seems all the more horrible to think of Paul lying there in the cold and the rain. During the summer it did not seem so dreadful to think of him resting under a peaceful sky, with the corn-

---

1. Albert Thomas (1878–1932), French Socialist; French minister of munitions, 1916; first director of the International Labour Office.
2. Paul Mantoux (1877–1956), interpreter to supreme war council and at Paris peace conference.

fields smiling around him. But the dreary weather makes one shudder & brings a queer depression, and as time goes on the shock of realising that he will not come back becomes more insistent. It is very difficult to realise that he is dead, and I keep on getting impatient for news of him or for his return.

Mamma, however, has brightened up in making arrangements for our new house at Wallington. I hope she will be happier there. I am going to take a flat in town, so that I need not go home every night.

October 11th 1915

The situation grows daily more grave. The Germans seem to have made up their minds to force their way through to Constantinople. Bulgaria has apparently been pledged to Germany for a long time. Greece, through the treachery of her king, has let us down badly.

D. is terribly anxious, though he says that he fears now that it is too late to do anything. Viviani[1] came over in a hurry last week to discuss the situation, and Kitchener went back with him. K. returned on Saturday [9 October], but instead of summoning the Cabinet on Saturday to discuss the result of K.'s interviews in France, the P.M. insisted on going away for the weekend, postponing the Cabinet meeting till this afternoon. D. however, is all the better for his weekend rest. He was very seedy on Friday and Saturday, and is badly in need of rest. He is very sick with the men who have muddled the Balkan situation. He is sick with Churchill, who will not acknowledge the futility of the Dardanelles campaign. He (Churchill) prevents the Prime Minister from facing the facts, too, by reminding him that he too is implicated in the campaign, & tells him that if the thing is acknowledged to be a failure, he (the P.M.) as well as Churchill will be blamed.

Friday's Cabinet [8 October] was a melancholy affair. No one had anything to suggest, & everyone seemed to be pinning all hope on to K.'s journey to France. Lansdowne ventured the suggestion that we should advise the Serbians to remain on the defensive. 'Yes', said D. bitterly, 'let us give them *advice*! Let us say to them "We cannot offer you anything else, but we can give you *advice*. We have no counsel for ourselves, but such as we have, we send to you!"'

The French Minister for Munitions, M. Thomas, & his retinue were over here at the beginning of the week. They are a most enthusiastic lot, and never seemed to weary of conferences, which continued for practically the whole of three days. On the last day they discussed the question of the employment of women in munition factories, which has been done on a far greater scale in France than in England, & which has been most successful. Thomas was describing the conditions under which the women work. 'In France', he said, 'we put a man to supervise each batch of women: but in England you would have to have a woman.' A rather brutal aspersion upon Englishmen, but one that hit the mark! M. Paul Mantoux, who was interpreting for Thomas, was

---

1. French premier, 1914–15.

speaking to us of the French workmen. 'In time of peace', he said, 'we considered the French workman very difficult to deal with. But we have discovered that when things are at their worst the French workman is at his best.'

The sale of our book has reached 30,000 copies!

The flat is progressing in real earnest. I have already purchased a piano, a chesterfield & an eiderdown, among other things. D. is desperately anxious to get it completed, for he is having a rotten time at home, everyone being against him & making him as miserable as possible.

On Saturday we sent over to the War Office for an up-to-date map of the Balkans, showing us the position of the various armies. They sent us back a map dated 1912, with the boundaries as they were before the Balkan War, & the Rumanian Army on what is now Bulgarian territory. No wonder we have managed the Balkans badly. One would think that the W.O. are pulling our leg, only I do not think they have sufficient sense of humour for that!

October 12th 1915
The situation is desperate, and it seems absolutely impossible to make any headway. One would have thought that Kitchener would have come back from France with a definite plan. The only result of his interviews with the French appears to be that at present Joffre will not allow any forces to go out of France, but promises 64,000 for the East when the offensive is over. The British General Staff have prepared a melancholy memorandum, in which the only definite plan advocated is that we should stick to the offensive in the west. They also suggest that 150,000 men should be sent to Gallipoli: but Carson[1] was told by a member of the General Staff that his plan was not approved of by them, that it was not in the memorandum and that it must therefore have been inserted by the Prime Minister, probably at the instigation of Churchill. At the Cabinet yesterday Kitchener put forward this proposition, & the P.M., Churchill, & others backed it up. It had almost gone through when D. broke in and opposed it most vigorously. He said he thought it was madness to send a force of men to support a hopeless cause, when Serbia was so terribly in need of help. The Prime Minister very much resented this outburst, and kept on interrupting and trying to silence D. until at last D. appealed to the other members that he should have a fair hearing. 'I think I am entitled to express an opinion', he said. 'I know that what I have to say is not in accordance with the Prime Minister's views, but I think that that is all the more reason why I should have a fair hearing.' He was then allowed to give his views. He dictated the substance of what he said to me last night after

1. Edward Henry Carson (1854–1935): Irish Unionist leader; attorney general, 1915; resigned in protest against failure to aid Serbia, 1915; co-operated with Lloyd George and Law in overthrow of Asquith, 1916; first lord of the admiralty, 1916–17; member of war cabinet, 1917–18; resigned again, ostensibly over Ireland, 1918; cr. Lord of Appeal, 1921.

dinner, & has circulated it in the form of a memorandum to the War Council. It seems to me to be the only solution of the difficulty, & even then it must be acted on immediately, or it will be too late.

D.'s statement had the effect of delaying the sending of the troops to Gallipoli for a short time at any rate. They are going instead to send a General to the East to report on the situation! And this when the Germans are hourly penetrating further into Serbia! Colonel Hankey has not long returned from Gallipoli, and has issued a report which makes one weep.[1]

D. said it was pitiable to see the relief of the P.M. when it was decided not to commit the Cabinet to anything definite. D. says that the P.M. has followed the 'wait and see' policy so long that in wartime he cannot be got to understand that it is disastrous. It is all right in peace time, and often answers admirably, but in war it leads straight to disaster. 'It is like a disease', said D. to me, 'you can put off the operation if you like, and you still exist, but it gets worse, and the time comes when it is too late to perform that operation, and then you are done for.' At any rate, the P.M. is still the P.M., & I suppose he feels that he can enjoy a dozen or so more dinners without a split in the Cabinet!

Nevertheless, Carson has resigned today, & D. says he does not think he will stay in many days more. I fear it is too late, as it will seem like the rat leaving the sinking ship, as D. says. I spoke rather harshly last night, for I was feeling very bitter at the delay, I told him he should have resigned a fortnight ago, following up his Preface and letter by speeches over the country, rousing the nation to a sense of danger. He says, however, quite truly, that if he goes out he will be treated as a pariah by the Liberals, and he will not have the advantage of being able to state his case to the country, as that would give us away to the enemy. Whereas if he stays in, he is at least getting munitions for the troops. Perhaps he is right, but I hate him to be associated with a Government that through sheer inefficiency brought Britain to her ruin and humiliated her before the world. He was very sweet to me, though, although I said rather bitter things. But God knows I would not wound him, and I am the first to recognise his courage. He is a little sensible to flattery, though, and it is wretched for him to be cold-shouldered by his colleagues and condemned as a traitor.

D. spoke very strongly in the Cabinet yesterday on the lack of foresight of the War Office. 'We have not a single plan', he said, 'not a single move of the enemy has been prepared for, whereas there is nothing that might not have been foreseen.' They say, too, that there is great discontent in the ranks and among the junior officers on account of the lack of brains in the senior & commanding officers.

Today, in the Cabinet, they have done *nothing*. With the Balkan crisis as it is, and an army sitting doing nothing at Salonika, and Serbia sending tele-

---

1. This report is summarised in Roskill's Hankey, vol. I, pp. 206–8.

grams every few hours for help, the Cabinet *did not even mention* the situation in the East. It is incredible: it would be laughable if it were not so dreadfully tragic. I am afraid I made D. cross again this afternoon, by urging him to make them do *something*. He is the only person of action among them, but he says it is impossible to get the P.M. to do anything. He said if I only saw I would understand. He just sits there and uses the whole of his crafty brain to squash any plan for action that is put forward. D. says that if he were in the pay of the Germans he could not be of more complete use to them. I was in such desperation that I could scarcely keep from crying, & D. was rather upset. I have implored of him to insist on their doing something. Delay is criminal.

Today they discussed *conscription*. Kitchener has at last come forward with a scheme for a quota system for raising men, embodied in a Bill which contains also compulsory powers if enough men are not forthcoming—practically a form of conscription. The P.M. was dead against it, but D., Churchill, Curzon, etc., were supporting K. The P.M. is strongly backed up by McKenna, Simon, Runciman, & that gang. I think, though, that if it comes to a point, the country will stand by K.

8.0 p.m.

Churchill has been to see D. & they have dictated to me a telegram to Roumania & Greece, stating that we will send a force if they will come in—practically embodying the suggestions of D.'s memorandum. They have gone over to the P.M. to ask if it may go. I pray that they may be allowed to send it. Bulgaria has begun her attack upon Serbia. D. has promised to come back to say goodnight. I shall be glad to get home—I was here till nearly midnight last night—back before nine this morning.

October 19th 1915

The telegrams went, but the offer has been refused, on the ground that Greece will not come in, the commanders of her army being convinced that Germany is going to win. That seems to be the general opinion in neutral countries. The Roumanians say that they would only come in on condition we sent 500,000 men and apparently we cannot do that. But meantime nothing has been done—no decision has been come to as to the course we shall take in the Balkans and the Dardanelles, though everyone agrees that delay is criminal.

After D. had interviewed both the P.M. and Kitchener and persuaded them to agree to it, and the telegrams had been despatched to Grey for him to send off, D. took Mr. Davies and me to dinner to the Cecil. After that, we walked down the Strand, down the Waterloo Bridge steps, and home along the Embankment. We had a very pleasant walk, D. being easily able to go unrecognised, as the streets are pitch dark at present.

On Wednesday [13 October] D. & I went down to Walton Heath. I had to go down by train, as D. does not like taking me about in his Gov. car, in case people fix on it for a scandal. I was rather sick about it, as I love driving with him, but D. made me cheer up, saying, 'Never mind! We are "doing" the world in spite of its spitefulness. There is much satisfaction in "doing" the world! I have defied it for 25 years—treated it with contempt, spat upon its tinsel robes, and I have won through. If you pay homage to it in certain things, you can defy it in others as much as you like.' It is very true: he has often said this to me in many different ways. It is perfectly true. If you respect certain forms and conventions, you may break others to your heart's content, and the world will say nothing.

However, I went down by train. When D. arrived he announced that he and Churchill, & 6 of the Tories had made up their minds to resign. The P.M. would not give his consent to any form of conscription, and so D. tendered his resignation, & the others did likewise. The P.M. however would not accept the position, and said that he would resign himself. He asked for 24 hours to consider the whole thing. The Tories were very anxious for him to resign, and for D. to become P.M. But D. will not hear of this: he says he would not think of taking the responsibility at this moment. We are in for a series of disasters, & D. thinks that the P.M. should take the full responsibility for enterprises which he consented should be launched. He has been warned time after time, and has refused to take any definite line of action to save us from disaster. D. says it is too late now for anyone to do anything. He thinks we are done, beaten. I hope he is not right.

On Thursday [14 October] D. stayed down at Walton, suffering from a touch of neuralgia. He won't have the teeth out that give him pain—he is a dreadful coward in that respect. I actually persuaded him to let me telephone for the dentist, & then relented, seeing how miserable the idea made him. I thought, too, that it was just possible that he might feel the effect of it the next day, when there was an important cabinet meeting. So in the end, we decided to put it off.

By Friday [15 October] a new situation had arisen. Lord Derby's[1] recruiting scheme had been hatched, which was to have a six weeks' trial. Moreover, it was not certain that Kitchener would come out on conscription, & in any case I do not see how he can do so until Lord Derby's scheme has been given a trial. It would be quite useless to force a split in the Cabinet on conscription unless K. backed up the Conscriptionists. The P.M. was willing to make some concessions. D. however made a statement to the effect that it was not only upon conscription that the minority which he represented were dissatisfied: it was upon the whole conduct of the war. 'Certain of us are of the opinion that we are about to pass through a most critical and grave period. Next year I believe we shall be fighting for our lives. I know the Prime Minister, Mr.

---

1. Edward George Villiers Stanley, 17th Earl of Derby (1865–1948): under-secretary for war, 1916; supported Lloyd George in crisis of December 1916; secretary for war, 1916–18, 1922–4; ambassador in Paris, 1918–20; the Derby scheme invited men to attest voluntarily their willingness to serve.

Balfour, and others do not take this view. We think, however, that it will be impossible for a Cabinet holding such opposite views to work together.' However no decision was come to then, and the resignations are still pending, it would seem. The 'rebels' have held several meetings, and I think in the end there will be a split.

Yesterday the P.M. was unwell. He came to the Cabinet, but one person after another began to talk about the disasters that were hovering; one talked about the disaster in the Dardanelles; another discussed whether there would be a disaster in Egypt or in India. At last the P.M. could stand it no longer. He passed a note to Lansdowne, got up and went out of the room. Lansdowne informed the Cabinet that the P.M. had been obliged to retire as he was feeling unwell. Today he is confined to his room, and Cabinet discussions have to go on without him, though, of course, nothing can be decided.

Today D. saw Millerand, who says that D. was right after all, and that an expedition in the Balkans should have been undertaken last spring. He is now convinced that the Dardanelles operations are a failure, & though he fears it is too late to render very effective assistance in the Balkans, yet he is in favour of France & England sending troops there. He and D. together drew up a plan upon which France and England are to act for a campaign in the Balkans. D. feels however that it is too late, & that the campaign may prove a forlorn hope.

October 23rd 1915

D. is actually having his teeth out today. I have arranged for the dentist to go down to W.H. All the week he has been suffering from this wretched neuralgia, and I am quite convinced that it will not be cured until he has faced the music. His depression about the situation does not tend to make him more cheerful. Another week has gone, and no real decision has been arrived at. 150,000 troops are being sent by Britain and France to Salonika, but no one knows exactly what they are going to do when they get there. A telegram has just come in to say that Uskub[1] has fallen, so that the Germans will probably be in Constantinople before we even reach Salonika.

Meanwhile, nothing has been done with regard to conscription. The group in the Cabinet who were going to resign on Conscription grounds feel that it would be absolutely futile to go out on that score while Lord Derby's scheme is being tried. It would not be fair to Lord D. to make a split until he has had a fair chance. After all, D. says he *may* get the men that way. But it means six whole weeks delay! I cannot help feeling that in this war first one thing and then another has arisen to give an excuse for taking no decisive action. This week Lord Derby's scheme has delayed any plans being made for raising men; the Prime Minister's illness has prevented any serious decisions being taken by the Cabinet. The fact of the matter is that the P.M. is simply overwhelmed by fear at what is going to happen, & he feels he is now

---

1. Now Skopje.

powerless to avert disaster. The unfortunate part is, that although the North-cliffe press are absolutely right in their estimate of the situation, yet the very mention of Northcliffe makes all the Liberals see red, so that their judgment is absolutely warped by party hatred and jealousy.

The W.O. General Staff have no plan of campaign to recommend. The W.O. itself is hopelessly slow, and Kitchener hopelessly slack. At a Cabinet last week—before the German advance into Serbia had begun, but when news of it was being expected at every moment—D. asked Kitchener in the Cabinet whether there was any news of the Germans having crossed the Danube. K. said that up to the time when he came to the Cabinet he had received no news. D. suggested that the news might have come in since, & said he would get the P.M.'s secretary to telephone to the W.O. & ask if any news had been received. He considered it most important to know when the Germans had begun to cross the Danube. I attach reply which D. received, & which he read out to the Cabinet, to the effect that a telegram had been received in the W.O. *the day before* saying that the Germans had crossed! The extraordinary thing is that K. did not express the least surprise that he had not seen this telegram. Treated it as a matter of course!

'*Late yestdy. afternoon.*' 'Enemy Xd. Danube with one batt. at Raab. Aust. troops Xd. the Slava in 5 difft. places between Sabac & Belgrade. They are so far not in large force. Fight is continuing.'

The Allied armies at Salonika failed to provide any aid for Serbia, which was overrun by German and Bulgarian forces. Kitchener was sent on 4 November to survey the situation in the Near East, in the hope that he would never come back. Asquith set up a war committee originally of five members, which swelled to eleven.

November 15th 1915

I have been very slack in keeping my diary, and a great deal has happened lately, the chief thing being that at the eleventh hour, and only after Mille-rand and Joffre had come over here to confer, we decided to send help to Serbia. There was a great outcry from all quarters at this help being delayed so long, and there were many criticisms of the Government. This resulted in the small War Committee being formed, to deliberate on war matters instead of the whole of the Cabinet. Of course there were many heartburn-ings amongst those who knew that their names were not to be included. The first Committee that the P.M. proposed to appoint consisted of four—him-self, Balfour, Kitchener, and D. But Bonar Law threatened to resign if K. were put on or even if he were retained at the W.O.—he said that all the trouble was due to K., that he was incompetent, and that he had thoroughly mismanaged affairs. D. was also of the same opinion, and wrote a very strong letter to the P.M. on the subject. Previous to this, the P.M. himself had admitted that it was desirable to get rid of K., but did not know how to do it without falling foul of public opinion. It is extraordinary how faithful the public is to K., and how they absolutely refuse to believe any evil of him, in spite of the way things have gone. However, after thinking the matter over during the week-end, the P.M. devised a very crafty way of getting rid of K. —he proposed to send him to the East to take stock of things both in the Balkans, in the Dardanelles, and in Egypt. No sooner thought of than done. K. was told that he was to go to the East; meantime, the P.M. takes charge of the W.O. in his absence; and it is more than probable that K. will eventually take active command of the forces in the East, in which case someone else will be appointed as Secretary of State for War. Many—among them the P.M. & Mr. Bonar Law—are most anxious that D. should go to the W.O. But D. does not want to go, for he has not yet nearly finished his work here. It was D., however, who urged that an expeditionary Force should be sent to the Balkans in Jan. & Feb. last. What was contained in D.'s memo of Feb. is only what they are proposing to do today—if they can! And how much easier would it have been to do it then! But it is singular that the two chief Frenchmen who stood in the way of it then are the ones who are urging it now—Millerand and Joffre. I have just unearthed a copy of a letter from D. to K. in January last, in which D. forecasts the German attack on Serbia.

D. says that K.'s leavetaking was very characteristic, and rather pathetic. On the Thursday after the P.M. decided on his course, K. was to leave for the East. There was a Cabinet in the morning. Just before the end, K. got up, pushed his chair back, inclined his head to the P.M., walked slowly across the room without looking at a single person, and out! Not a word spoken! He might have been going out to lunch. He knew as well as anyone that it was for good he was leaving, but not a sign of his countenance or his demeanour gave evidence of this. D. says that he felt a lump in his throat, and he thinks many other members of the Cabinet were touched also. Crewe passed a rather significant note across to D. Personally, I think it is rather a *cowardly* thing the P.M. has done.

After the decision that K. should *not* be a member of the small Committee, one would have thought that there would be no further fuss. But here McKenna enters upon the scene. Conceited, self-confident, persistent, he cannot conceive of any War Committee upon which he is not represented. The P.M., however, told him at a meeting of the Cabinet, that it was not proposed to put him on it, and McKenna behaved in a very small and childish way. But for a time the P.M. remained obdurate. Unfortunately however, he spent the week-end before the names of the Committee were announced with the McKennas, and when he returned on the Monday, he announced that he had decided to make McKenna a member of the Committee! Mr. Bonar Law would also be put on to balance this, bring the number up to 5.

There was absolutely no reason why McKenna should be on this Committee, and it seems to me that his appointment will destroy the usefulness of it to a large extent. The P.M. had promised to make things easier for D. now that he is at the War Office, by handing over to him the various branches that handicap us now by being in the hands of the W.O. But now it seems that McKenna will nullify all this. For some time past he has been trying to tie D.'s hands by endeavouring to hold up his programme for big guns, and by making wild statements about this Department, intended to do D. harm. Now, on Saturday [13 November], D. discovered by some remarks which McK. let drop at the Committee, that he had been going to the W.O. behind D.'s back and asking them for all sorts of information with regard to our Munitions orders. McK. however, has been misinformed, and D. is going to wipe the floor with him at the next War Council. McK. is evidently, however, out to do D. harm, and will stick at nothing. It is he who has been inspiring various journalists to write articles to the effect that the increase in munitions is not due to D., but to the orders placed by the W.O. before D. came on the scenes. He has also found a hundred & one other little subterranean ways of 'getting at' D., although the ordinary observer would never suspect that it is McKenna who inspires these journalists who go out of their way to throw discredit on the Ministry of Munitions. It is only when one of these journalists, on being pressed, admits that he has written one of these articles 'because McKenna asked him to', that one begins to open one's eyes! However, as I said to D. on Saturday, when, being very tired, he seemed rather depressed about McKenna's attack, I think he is able to deal with McKenna so that he will feel sorry he spoke! But it *is* annoying to be pestered with petty spite and mean intrigues just when you are trying to do your best.

But in the country I don't think there is anyone who is not willing to give D. credit for what he has done. A Monsieur Cruppi, a French Ex-Minister came to call on D. on Saturday, and I had to interpret for him as he could not speak English. He says he was perfectly astounded at what had been done in the way of munitions (he had just been visiting some of the big works). He had expected to see wonderful things, but he was not prepared for what has actually been done. He says that in his opinion in 3 months' time there will be no further need to worry about the production of munitions for the Allies: it will then only be a question of distribution; but he considers it absolutely necessary that D. should take charge of the distribution, which is now in the hands of the War Office. M. Cruppi also told me that he is simply amazed at the work women are doing in England now. He is a keen suffragist, and so is his wife, and he is convinced that after the war the women will have no difficulty in getting the vote, and anything they ask for. I see, too, in today's papers, that the Government are taking up the question of training women for clerical work, in order to fill the places of men who enlist.

Lord Charles Beresford[1] came to D. the other day, and begged him to

---

1. Lord Charles Beresford (1846–1919): admiral; opposed Fisher's naval reforms; Unionist M.P., 1910–16; cr. Baron, 1916.

resign. He says this Government will come a terrible smash when the disasters come, as they inevitably will, and then D. will go down with them. He wants D. to come out, for he says he will have an enormous following, and will be able to rally the country round him. But D. will not hear of this. In the first place, he says he will not leave the sinking ship; in the second place, he says he can do more good by staying where he is and attending to munitions, which are at least a definite asset in the war; and in the third place, he says if he went out he could not state his case, and so would not be able to rally the public round him.

Churchill, however, has at last resigned. He was very sick at not being put on the small War Committee, and at last has definitely made up his mind to go and fight. He wanted to go to East Africa, but the War Office will not let him. I am rather sorry for him, as it must be a terrible experience for one who had so much power in his hands. But all the same, I think he deserves it!

D. & I have been having some glorious times at W.H. at odd moments during the last few weeks. On these occasions he gets right away from politics. Sometimes he will quote reams of Welsh Poetry, explaining and translating it as he goes along, pointing out the characteristic traits or the peculiar style. Sometimes he will discourse on the Welsh preachers, and give a mock sermon in the real Welsh style. Sometimes he will go quite mad, and tease and joke and fool like a ridiculous schoolboy; and sometimes he will tell me all about his childhood's days, or of the earlier days before I knew him. I like him to do this, for I feel that I want to know him as much as I possibly can, so that I can understand him better. He is always very sweet to me on these occasions, and we are so utterly happy. Coming up in the car the other morning he likened them to the oases which one comes to in a journey across the desert, and which even after leaving it keeps one's mind fresh until one comes to the next. We are going down tomorrow night, all being well, to another oasis!

D. was very exercised in his mind as to whether he should or should not go and see the Henrys[1] to show sympathy in the loss of their son. When the blow first fell, Lady H. wrote him some amazing letters because he failed to go round or write at once, and D. felt that if he went round she would only take advantage of his presence to make a scene, and he felt that he could not face it. He went, however, in the end, and it appears that she was very reasonable. I must say I think she deserves a little kindness, for they have both been exceedingly kind to D., only unfortunately at one time he allowed things to go too far, and is now sorry for it. She has written an appreciation of his character, very clever in parts, but failing entirely to realise the deep side of his character. She is quite mad on him, and does not seem to have any pride or self-respect where he is concerned.

---

1. Sir Charles Solomon Henry (1860–1919): Australian millionaire; Liberal M.P., 1900–19; cr. Baronet, 1911.

The other day D. was stopped on his way into the House by a member who asked him why he was going on to the Bench. 'It is the Midwives' Bill on now', said the Member. 'That is nothing to do with you.' 'You are mistaken', retorted D. 'I have everything to do with deliveries!'

November 16th 1915

D. and I were to have gone to W.H. tonight, but at the War Council this morning it was decided that certain members of it should go over to Paris at once to confer with the French Government on the question of Balkan action. So D. has gone over with the P.M., Sir Edward Grey, and Balfour, by the 5.15 from Charing X. He has promised to come back as soon as he possibly can, and I am to get our little home quite ready by the time he comes back. He said that he tried hard to persuade Bonar Law to go instead; but I am glad D. has gone, as I should not have liked to see him left behind. We were all to have gone to see an experiment in liquid fire this afternoon, but that was cancelled at the last moment.

D. discovered this morning that certain officials at Armament Buildings had been discussing Munitions business with people at the Treasury, and that was how McKenna got all his private information! D. had them all up before him, and talked to them quite frankly, and I do not think they will do it again!

The P.M. has promised that now he is at the W.O. the Munitions Dept. shall have a much freer hand. I hope that will be so, for up till the present D. has had to fight every inch of the way, although the work he is doing is vital to the successful prosecution of the war. The War Office are so terribly afraid we shall have too many big guns and too much shell!

One thing I cannot help marvelling at, is the way in which the old P.M. has kept his Cabinet together during all this difficult time. He has done it by pure craft and cunning, propitiating here, or pretending to propitiate, making concessions there, or pretending to make them; giving promises which he never intended to keep, but which were just sufficient to keep the person concerned dangling until something should 'turn up' to alter his frame of mind. Always wait & see! And the extraordinary thing is that this policy seems to work so extraordinarily well, even in war time, from the P.M.'s point of view; though I am afraid the policy of Britain in this war has suffered sadly by it, so that finally nothing but a mad rush over to Paris by four Cabinet Ministers can save the situation! But I do hope D. won't be cold on that wretched destroyer!

November 22nd 1915

They returned from Paris on Thursday night [18 November], and D. drove straight to W.H. I was there waiting for him. D. had brought me a sweet brooch with the Lorraine cross on it; in addition to this he had brought a charming Napoléon premier clock, and two candlesticks of the same period, for our new home. D. has excellent taste in these things, and I can only

wonder that he can bear some of the things which are to be found in his own
houses. He does strike sometimes. I took these things straight to 41a Chester
Square on Friday morning, & in the afternoon D. came to tea with Mr.
Davies, & D. stayed on to dinner. I had to prepare the dinner myself, but
fortunately nothing too dreadful happened and we had a most happy time.
The place is not quite ready yet, but we managed to make ourselves comfortable.

As far as I can make out, nothing very much was settled in Paris. In the
morning there was a Conference with the French War Council, and in the
afternoon a Conference with the whole of the French Cabinet. D. does not
like Galliéni;[1] says he is rather boastful and ostentatious. D. says that at the
War Council in the morning the French tried to cast the blame of the Balkans
disaster upon the English—inferring that the French had been there in time,
but that the English had arrived too late. Hereupon D. interposed 'Let us be
quite frank', he said. 'We were *all* too late. It is true that when it was decided
to send troops there, we both did so as soon as it was possible, and the French
troops arrived first. But even then it was too late. Neither French nor English
troops were in time.' From the turn of events at present in the Balkans, it
would seem as though our troops might never have gone there at all.

Yesterday (Sunday) D. & I escaped to W.H. and Seebohm Rowntree came
to lunch. He had asked to see D. and it appeared that he had come at the
instigation of his father, old Joseph Rowntree,[2] to beg D. not to forsake
democracy, for if he did so, then they could see no hope for democracy in
the future. Rowntree and his party feared that in the midst of this war, and
in view of the work he was doing and the treatment he had received from
his own party, D. might have fallen away from his old convictions and ideals.
They were terribly afraid that he might be spoilt by the adulation of the
Tories, and that he would slip away from the Liberal principles which he
had preached so firmly in the past.

But D. reassured him. 'How can I forsake democracy?' he said. 'It is not
merely that I have taken up the cause of the people, but I am *one of them*. How
could I leave them?' He went on to say that although he was working in
conjunction with Curzon & the others, who were making much of him, yet
he had only once sat at their table, and that was at the request of Bonar Law,
who was also more or less of humble origin. D. explained how he loathed
the Curzon set, and all that they stood for—loathed their mannerisms, their
ideals, their customs, their mode of life. I cannot help feeling that Rowntree
went back with the report that my little man was the same as ever, unspoiled
by flattery as by abuse, still preferring to spend his weekend quietly at W.H.
eating the plainest of fare, and finishing his Sunday by singing Welsh hymns!

---

1. Joseph Simon Galliéni (1849–1916): French general; military governor of Paris, 1914;
French minister of war, October 1915–March 1916.
2. Joseph Rowntree (1836–1925): cocoa magnate and philanthropist, owner of The
Nation.

D. and I spent the rest of the day quietly together. After tea we walked about the garden for over an hour, and we talked about D.'s boyhood. We began by talking of the terrible boredom of childhood: D. said that if he had to choose between dying the next day, and going back to three years of age, he would infinitely prefer death to living his childhood over again. He says he looks upon the years between the age of three and twenty with something akin to horror. There was the terrible struggle with poverty which his mother was forced to undergo, and he remembers the look of despair which would come over her face from time to time when she did not know which way to turn to make both ends meet. He said she was a fine woman, but the awful struggle she went through after the death of her husband must have made her life terribly hard. In a photograph which I have of D. when he was 16 you can see the sad look in his face, & I asked him why there is such a difference in his face now and then. Now it is bright, cheerful, kindly; then it was mournful, reserved, & sad. He answered that he had never seen the brighter side of life until after he was twenty. He was discontented, cramped, and unhappy as a boy. Religion too troubled him. When he was eleven years old, he suddenly came face to face with the fact that religion, as he was taught it, was a mockery & sham. He says he remembers the exact moment—he was in bed—when the whole structure and fabric of religion fell before him with a crash, and nothing remained. The shock to him was so great that he leapt out of bed. From then onwards for years he was in mental distress on the subject of religion—he felt like a man who has been suddenly struck blind, and is groping for the way but can find no support. He says the thought was horrible to him that the universe should be under no direction, with no purpose, no supreme control, and at last he confided to his uncle the state of mind that he was in. Strangely enough, old Richard Lloyd was not in the least shocked, but seemed to understand perfectly well. But D. says that the religious meetings and services were a source of unhappiness to him for years. There was a prayer meeting which was held every week on a Thursday to which D. used to look forward with loathing—the same prayers, the same set phrases, (D. gave me reproductions of some of the happenings at them) the same talk week after week. In fact, it was in the main religion which made his life so hard to bear and so full of boredom. He could not feel that he had a part in it, and yet he was unable to get away from it. This state of mind continued for years & saddened his whole outlook. When he was about 18, however, he read Carlyle's Sartor Resartus, which helped and comforted him, for it describes a man who went through the same phases as he was going through. When he had finished it, he felt strengthened in his mind, for the purpose of things had been revealed to him to some extent, and his vision was cleared. Soon after that, he went to Penrhyndeudraeth to appear in a case there, and stayed with an old Methodist parson, who gave him Renan's Life of Christ to read. He read it with avidity, and it too gave him consolation and peace of mind, for he was able to see things from a broader point of view.

D. says it was a most extraordinary thing that this book should have been put into his hands by a Methodist parson in an out-of-the-way place—the work of an atheist, but the work of a man to whom Christ was a living being, a hero, a perfect *man*. After reading these two books D. felt much happier, but there is no doubt that the mental struggle which he went through during those years left a mark upon him, and helped to form his character.

D. is never tired of sounding the praises of his old Uncle Lloyd, and telling of the wonderful influence which this old man had upon his boyhood. He considers that he owes everything to this old man, who pinched and denied himself in order that D. might continue his education, and staked the last penny of his savings upon the fees for D.'s articles. He is indeed a fine character, almost Christ-like in his gentleness and breadth of mind.

There may be some who, like the Rowntrees, are fearful lest D.'s convictions may be undermined, but as he says himself, these ideals and principles are *part of him*, always have been and always will be. In 1890 he made a speech, right at the beginning of his career, when he had scarcely been outside Wales except for a flying visit to London. In this speech he predicts the great Armageddon which is to be waged against poverty and human suffering. This horror of all the needless suffering which human beings are called upon to endure, is the keynote to his career, and if anyone attempts to portray his character without realising this, then they are ignorant of the man himself and all that he stands for. It is people who do not realise this deeper aim who call him a demagogue, and attribute base motives to all that he does. Those who realise the governing principle, trust him implicitly and have faith in his strength.

He told me the other day that it sometimes comes to him in flashes how far he has come along the political road. He was sitting the other day beside Balfour on the Bench, and a point arose upon which Balfour turned to him and asked him for an opinion. The thought came to him that when he first came to Parliament Balfour was Prime Minister, and D. would have considered a word or a nod from such a great personage as a great event. He would have gone home or written to his uncle (more likely—for his wife never took any interest in his work) saying 'Balfour spoke to me today', or something of that kind. Now here he was sitting by Balfour's side, and Balfour was turning to him for advice! He instinctively turned to his old seat opposite below the gangway, where he sat when he first entered Parliament. He says that he never dreamed then of ever sitting on the Bench as a Cabinet Minister.

November 23rd 1915
International Conference today—French, Russians, Italians, British. They are hard at it now, and will be here again tomorrow. D. very tired yesterday, but looking much better today. It was D. who started the idea of these

Conferences of Allies, and he finds it is the only way of getting any work done.

November 24th 1915

Another Conference all day today, but things are going very well, except that D. persisted in calling the Italian General 'Parafino', until someone passed him a note across to say that it was 'Marafini'. M. Thomas, when he saw this, went into uncontrolled giggles, as he too had been under the impression that it was Parafino. The Conferences continued till late last night, & D. was very tired. He told me as a great secret that we had decided to evacuate Gallipoli. Kitchener, after having refused to take the advice of anyone else, has seen for himself that it is futile to continue there any longer.

In the War Council yesterday they discussed the Serbian retreat, and the apparent impossibility of rendering help to the Serbians. 'This', said Balfour, 'seems to put an end to Lloyd George's plan of campaign in the Balkans.' D. objected. 'Until we recommend abandoning the idea, I think we should wait until we have received the opinion of military experts upon it.' 'What expert opinion', asked McKenna sarcastically, 'has ever been in favour of the scheme.' 'It has never been turned down', retorted D. 'And as the General staff are at this moment considering the advisability of a campaign in the Balkans, I think we ought to postpone discussion until they have pronounced judgment.' The others agreed. But strangely enough before the end of the Conference, the Prime Minister received a communication from the Russian General Staff, saying that they had come to the conclusion that the right thing to do was to give up attempting to advance either on the Western or the Russian front, but to hold these fronts lightly, giving their best energies to a campaign in the Balkans, in order to drive the Germans out of Serbia, & attack Budapest & ultimately Vienna. 'This is rather odd', said the P.M. 'It is exactly L.G.'s scheme.' D. was very pleased, partly because his scheme had found favour, and partly because he had scored off McKenna: for here was an expert military authority deciding in favour of what he had proposed 10 months ago: and if they said it was possible now, when the greater part of Serbia was in the hands of the enemy, how much simpler and better would it have been then, when Serbia was intact, and Germany had not nearly as many troops on that front!

Today we hear that Kitchener is on the way back, & there has been a terrible rush in order to get the matter of the Ordnance Board settled before he returns. We have at last, however, finally taken the Board over, which will make things so much easier for us in every respect. What they are going to do with Kitchener when he comes back, I cannot tell: they intended that he should *not* return, but apparently they have failed to keep him away. Last week they heard that he had left Greece & was on his way to Brindisi, thence home. They wired immediately that he *must* go to Egypt to report. But now he has finished in Egypt, & will be back soon. What will the P.M. do?

D. has just told me that Cabinet Ministers' salaries are to be reduced again by 25%. He will have to economise considerably. I have nearly finished the flat, which will make a considerable hole in my money, but nothing can be too good for D., & I want to make it so comfortable for him.

November 30th 1915

K. comes home today. They have not been able to keep him away. However, in his absence the P.M. has handed us over the Ordnance Board.[1] D. has been fighting for this for months, but the W.O. have dodged him, and by keeping the Ordnance Board have been able to limit very considerably the energies of this Department. Moreover, when anything *was* accomplished, it was only after hard fighting and much unpleasantness, which wears one out in the end. I think they thought they would break D. as they have broken other people, but they did not know with whom they were dealing. When once D. fastens his teeth, he never lets go. He made up his mind that he would get rid of Von Donop, and Von Donop is now without a job. It has been a silent duel between these two for months, the W.O. on their side continually trying to discredit our Dept. in petty little ways. During the Conference last week we announced our intention of sending a message to the Press to say that the International Conference between the Allies was being held. The W.O. sent a minute across to say that the Russian Admiral had expressed a wish that no announcement should be made about the visit of the Russians to England. D. seeing that this was only a move on the part of the W.O. to prevent publicity being given to the fact that the Ministry of Munitions had summoned an International Conference, & thus obtain the credit for it, had the Admiral rung up, & asked him what his views were upon the subject. The Admiral replied that he had no objection whatever to the announcement being made, so that the W.O. had the lie direct.

The great value of D. having got his way is that the W.O. will understand that he is a person to be *feared*. Up till now in this war the W.O. have had it all their own way, & anyone who has come up against them has fallen. Now they see that he has the power to 'down' them, & they will respect him none the less for that. D. has appointed General DuCane[2] as Master of Ordnance instead of Von Donop, and V.D. can now go back to the Germans for all anyone cares.

---

1. The Ordnance Board was in fact suspended for the duration of the war. Other changes, more momentous for Lloyd George's future, are not recorded here. Sir Douglas Haig succeeded Sir John French as commander-in-chief of the British Expeditionary Force. Sir William Robertson became chief of the imperial general staff. He laid down that he alone was to advise the government on strategy and issue orders to the commanders in the field. The secretary for war had no function beyond 'feeding and clothing of the army'. These rules were directed against Kitchener, but they restricted Lloyd George just as much when he became secretary for war in 1916 and were equally harassing when he became prime minister.
2. Sir John Ducane (1865–1947): general; special appointment at ministry of munitions, 1916; British representative with Foch, 1918; master-general of ordnance, 1920–3.

One typical instance of the way in which the War Office have been trying to undermine the success of the Department was a case which occurred last week. The Ministry have made a point of concentrating a great part of their energies upon the manufacture of *heavy* guns, which D. is convinced are more necessary to us than anything else. The Conference last week was convened partly in order to discuss with the Russians what we could spare for them in the way of munitions, & what they were specially in need of. At the last moment before the Conference began D. discovered that the W.O. without consulting our Department, had agreed to give away to the Russians one-sixth of the whole of our output of heavy guns. D. says this was done partly in order to defeat the object of the Conference, and chiefly so that when the big attack comes next spring, there will not be so many big guns to show for our own army, & consequently not so much credit for the Ministry of Munitions. This may seem an amazing charge to bring against our Department, but in view of what the War Office has done in the past, it is quite likely to be true.

D. found in discussion with the Russians afterwards, that what they were most in want of was lighter artillery, quickly moved about, and this D. was only too glad to give them, on condition that they should forego the big guns promised by the W.O. This they were quite willing to do, so that D. had his own way after all.

D. told me a funny story about Clemenceau. The French Cabinet at present consists of very old men—some of them over 80, one of them I believe verging on 90. This is because all the previous premiers were asked to belong. Clemenceau who is 75, was invited among others. 'No', he replied, 'I am too young!'

D. is having a wooden fence put in the garden at W.H. to shelter some particularly choice roses that are being planted. I remarked that the fence was an improvement. 'I hate fences', replied D. 'I always feel like knocking down every fence I come across!'

D. & I spent a very happy weekend together, but came up on Sunday night [28 November] as Mrs. Ll. George was ill, and all alone. The boys are going away to France this week, and both she & D. are feeling rather miserable about it. I believe D. would be heartbroken if anything happened to Gwilym, to whom he is devoted.

D. was jubilant on Friday evening [26 November], on the result of the Merthyr election.[1] It was a great triumph for the pro-War party, in a place which was supposed to have been left almost pro-German by Keir Hardie. It was a blow too to the Trades Unions, as Stanton, the successful candidate, had been slashing at them right and left in his speeches. Thomas,[2] the cham-

---

1. Caused by the death of Keir Hardie.
2. James Henry Thomas (1874–1949); general secretary N.U.R., 1917–31; Labour M.P., 1910–31; National Labour M.P., 1931–6; opposed conscription, 1915; refused to join Lloyd George's government, 1916; led railway strike, 1919; colonial secretary, 1924, 1935–6; lord privy seal, 1929–30; dominions secretary, 1930–5.

pion of the Trades Unions and the non-Conscription party, had gone down to defend the Official Labour candidate, who was beaten. Stanton had said that he would advocate conscription if it would help us to win the war.

Evidently Thomas was a little sobered by the defeat of his party; and it was indeed rather a come-down after the violent speech which he made recently in the House of Commons on the workers and Conscription. Early on Saturday morning [27 November] he rang D. up, saying that he thoroughly approved of the new Drink Order for London, & he hoped D. would not give way. There was really nothing in the workers' protests. He would support D., and intended in fact to make a speech that night in support of the new order. D. was very nice & courteous to him, as it was really a great score, D. having made a point of cutting him in the House after his last speech.

December 3rd 1915

The General Staff have reported in favour of the evacuation of Salonika. There is a great row going on between the British and French Governments. The latter are simply furious at the proposal, considering it to be a sign of weakness and irresolution. They say, moreover that it will drive Greece and Roumania into the arms of Germany. Meanwhile Germany has finished the crushing of Serbia, and is preparing for some fresh enterprise, while we are still hesitating at Salonika not knowing whether to advance or retire. The impression in France seems to be that we have broken faith, and that Kitchener has gone back on his word to send help to the Balkans, having been talked over by the King of Greece. The French are beginning to get very sick with us. Things seem to be in a very critical position, and we are unable to make up our minds on any single point. Serbia has gone. What shall we do now. Withdraw from Salonika & Gallipoli and defend Egypt. That is the only advice the General Staff can give. But do not imagine we have made up our minds on this point! Discussions are still going on in the Cabinet, and decisions are postponed from one meeting to another. D. thinks the Government will come down in disgrace very soon. A message from Lord Bertie[1] from Paris stated that Lord Kitchener was in a very pessimistic mood when he visited the French Govt. on his way home from the East. The only thing that can save us now is a shortage of something—food or munitions—in Germany. The Russians, too, are making a little progress, and we have given them a good quantity of munitions lately, & the Italians have given them rifles. D. has got a bet on with Lord Reading that the war will still be going on *next* winter. Lord Reading says it will be over by then. D. says it will be a great pleasure to him (D.) to lose the bet.

I cannot understand why the English people do not realise the awful misery that is going on, say, in Serbia and parts of Russia. Here we seem to have got used to streams of khaki in the streets, & the frequent sight of people in mourning. We seem to forget the dreadful suffering which war is bringing.

---

1. Lord Bertie of Thame (1844–1919): ambassador in Paris, 1905–18.

Sometimes one sees a woman sobbing, coming from the War Office, and then one realises with a pang what war means. But the dreadful scenes of desolation, the homes wrecked and pillaged, the dead men & women and children lying by the roadside, the streams of starving and diseased refugees— these it has not been our lot to witness, & so the grimness of war in its reality has passed us by.

M. Mantoux, M. Thomas' interpreter, met Mr. Rowntree in this Office the other day. Both are earnest Socialists, but it was strange to see the differ- ence in the attitude of the French & the British Socialist. Rowntree cannot tolerate the idea of war, and I think would be glad to see it brought to an end on any terms. Mantoux would not have it cease until the Germans are beaten. 'We must make them understand', he said, 'that it cannot happen again.'

D. & I are off shortly to W.H. till Sunday evening [5 December]. D. has had a slight cold, & has been kept indoors for the last two days. But I have managed to get over to see him.

December 6th 1915
Returned yesterday evening from W.H. where we had been since Friday evening. Saturday & Sunday mornings John,[1] the artist, came to paint D.'s portrait. Up to the present D. does not like the painting, and is inclined to be querulous on the subject. 'Do you notice what John says about pictures which he does not like?' said D. to me. '"Very pleasant!" He seems to think that because a thing is pleasant to look at, it is not worth anything; and I feel that he is going to make this an *unpleasant* picture!' D. is rather upset at the pros- pect, for he likes to look nice in his portraits! This portrait will certainly be uncommon, for John is an uncommon person. He seems extraordinarily conceited, but is nevertheless a very fascinating person. I suppose a great many artists are conceited, for they need confidence in their own powers more than anything. D. is sitting again early on Wednesday morning, & we are going down there tomorrow night.

Megan came from school to spend Saturday afternoon with us. She is a dear child, and very sweet when she is away from the other female members of her family. D. was telling me of the extraordinary insight which she had when she was a young child. Once, when only about 5 years of age, she said to him suddenly. 'Father; what's the use of living?' Another time, when about the same age, they were talking together. D. remarked that there was a Welsh saying that there were two bad payings—to pay in advance and not to pay at all. 'There is a third, father', said Megan. 'What is it?' he asked. 'To pay back', she replied.

D. told me again about his childhood on Friday night. He told me how he used to wander alone for hours through the countryside; he told me of the joys of nutting, of the exultation of finding a new nut tree. 'My dear Pussy', he said, 'the thrill of making a successful speech is nothing to that which you

---

1. Augustus John (1878–1961).

experience when you discover a new nut tree, its branches weighed down with ripe nuts, or a new cherry tree, black with cherries!' He told me of how he went upon a search for a rare fern, the Frono regalis, of which there were but few specimens; how he made up his mind that he would get one, and tramped miles day after day, searching the marshes and bogs and woods and streams. How one day, on a precipice by the river, he saw at last one of these ferns over-hanging, quite out of reach, but yet it was there. He set about to find a means of obtaining it. He climbed up, but the rock was almost sheer, & when he had gone as far as he could possibly reach, he was still unable to touch it with his hand. He climbed down again, & procured a long branch of a tree, & found that with this at arm's length he could just touch the fern. But the plant was firmly fixed in between the rocks! Then began a slow and arduous pushing of the branch among the roots of the fern. How long it took him to dislodge it, he does not know, but the sweat was standing on his brow and his breath was coming in gasps, before the thing gave way—and tumbled into the rushing stream below. However, its rescue from the river was comparatively easy, and D. carried it home triumphant, the beautiful rare fern. D. himself was muddy and torn and wet and exhausted, but his purpose was achieved. The fern is still there in the old cottage garden, and a clump of it has been planted at Brynawelon. D. is going to bring me a root of it when next he goes to Criccieth.

On Saturday morning [4 December] D. discovered that the French had sent an urgent telegram requesting members of the British Government to meet them at Calais that day. The P.M., Balfour, and Kitchener had already started. D. had not been asked, either because he was not available, or (which is more likely) because he held different views from the others on the question of Salonika. All last week D. strongly opposed our leaving the Balkans, and on Friday came an angry telegram from France, complaining of our shilly shallying, of our decision to leave Salonika, and of our lack of firmness in handling Greece. They complained bitterly that we had gone back on our decision of the Paris Council the week before, and that Kitchener had evidently been talked over by the King of Greece, and had made arrangements with him which were quite outside the intentions of the French. They said moreover that we were creating a very bad impression and were playing the German game.

Then came the flying visit on Saturday. The result of the meeting was given out as being that the French had come round to our way of thinking, and had agreed to evacuate. They insisted however that we should take the whole responsibility for the move. By the telegrams this morning, however, D. could see that the French are still very dissatisfied, and that no satisfactory arrangement had really been arrived at on Saturday. For instance, what about Greece? Had any agreement been come to with her as to evacuation? Would she cover our departure, & protect us from the enemy? Pending a decision on this point, it could not be said that anything had been decided upon.

While everything was in this state of chaos, a telegram comes from Paris from Thomas to say that he is on the way over to talk with D. on the subject of the Calais conference, and to explain to him the real opinions of the French. He was due to arrive about three. Perhaps he & D. together will be able to clear up things a little. The other members of the Cabinet seem to be paralysed. Bonar Law is the only one who agrees with D.; all the others are for evacuating at top speed.

Meanwhile, at the War Council this morning, the question was discussed. Kitchener read a telegram received from Greece, saying that the *Germans* demanded the evacuation of the Balkans by the Allied troops, and were willing to allow the Greeks to cover the re-embarkation. Then D. started. 'It is a good thing', he said, 'that the British and the Germans have found something to agree upon at last! Here are the Germans asking for our withdrawal, and here are we replying that it is the thing we wish most to do at present! It is a long time since the British and Germans have been so unanimous upon any point! Surely this must be the beginning of concord between us and the enemy!' He lashed with his tongue right and left, sparing none, and laying bare before them the whole of their impotent cowardice. Kitchener's face grew dark. 'It is not so!' he said. 'I beg your pardon', retorted D. 'It is what you have been reading from that telegram. The Germans advise the Greeks that we must go, and we are advising the French that we must go. Is not that so?' The Prime Minister grew pale and speechless—he had no words to aid him. 'The French', continued D., 'do *not* want to go out of the Balkans. The French are a proud race, and it hurts their pride to have to withdraw under the protection of the miserable little traitor, Greece.'

In the end, it was decided to wait until it was known what Thomas had to say. D. has taken the matter into his hands, and we must perforce come to a decision soon. In the meantime, after a majority of our Cabinet have decided in favour of evacuation, we are still disembarking troops at Salonika!

It is the same thing in the case of Gallipoli. Everyone has decided in favour of evacuation, but no one has the courage to carry the move out. Meantime our men there are dying in hundreds owing to the severe weather conditions, no provision having been made for a winter campaign. The Prime Minister, after pooh-poohing the idea that the Turks would be able to bring up more guns and ammunition to the Peninsula, now learns that there is a road *beneath* a ridge over which they can move in absolute freedom, and which our shells cannot touch. He tells this to his colleagues with an injured air, as though saying 'What *business* had the Turks to conceal this from us!'

Meanwhile affairs at the Treasury are none too promising. Lord Reading told D. today that things were in such a hopeless muddle that the Governor of the Bank of England was obliged to go to the Prime Minister and demand that Lord Reading should be installed at the Treasury to straighten out things a little, and to advise, and Sir Robert Chalmers recalled from India to replace Sir John Bradbury. It seems as though all the men in whose hands the direction of the war lies—military and otherwise—are absolutely incompetent. Where will it all end?

December 29th 1915

And so M. Albert Thomas had his way. He explained to D. how it was that he had come over. When the members of the Calais Conference returned to Paris & explained to the Cabinet there the following day what decision had been arrived at, viz, to evacuate the Balkans, great dissatisfaction was expressed by the rest of the Cabinet. The members of the Cabinet persisted in declaring that that was the view taken by the British Govt. and that in those circumstances they had been forced to acquiesce. Whereupon M. Thomas interposed that he knew that that was not the view of the whole of the British Cabinet, that Mr. Lloyd George had told him when he was last in London that he (Ll.G.) was entirely opposed to evacuating the Balkans, and was very much in favour of following up the idea of a Balkan campaign, either this year or next. As the French think much more of D.'s opinion than any other member of the Cabinet, the French became again undecided, and in fact the Cabinet refused to accept the decision arrived at the day before by the Calais meeting. Thomas thereupon offered to come over to London again & see D. & endeavour to obtain a reconsideration of the decision. There were prolonged Cabinet meetings on the Tuesday, at which Thomas set forward very passionately the desire of the French to remain at Salonika. In the course of the discussion, the Prime Minister expressed the opinion that there would be a great deal of danger to risk if the Allies remained at Salonika. 'Danger!' retorted Thomas. 'Mais il y a de danger *maintenant*!' 'Yes', said the P.M. 'But we have an assurance from the Greeks that they will protect our armies from any attack by the Bulgars, if we withdraw.' Thomas turned a look of contempt and scorn upon him. The Prime Minister commented upon it afterwards to D. 'The French are too proud', said D., 'to accept any protection or assistance from a rascally traitor.' 'Yes', said the P.M. greatly moved, 'They would rather that the whole of the 60,000 men should perish than suffer a humiliation of that kind.'

The result of these deliberations was that Kitchener was to go over to Paris to consult with the French cabinet, with full powers to make any arrangements that should be arrived at. This was D.'s suggestion. He knew that once K. got over there he would be entirely in the hands of the French, who would make things so hot for him that he would be obliged to give way. The French will never forgive K. for the promise that he made to Greece to withdraw from Salonika. K. did not relish the idea of going. 'The French are not very keen on me at present, for some reason', he said. However, he went; and the result is that the Allies remain at Salonika, to fortify it for a campaign in the Balkans, next year. There will doubtless be complications with Greece before then. But for the moment that crisis, at any rate, is passed. What would have happened if Thomas had not come over, it is best not to imagine.

D.'s 'Too late' speech in the House of Commons created a sensation. I went up to the House to hear it. The whole House was thrilled at the ending. His words seemed like those of a prophet, and the warning did not fall upon deaf ears. The W.O. people however, were furious at the charges which he was unable to help bringing against them, and the next day I heard that Tennant and Von Donop were to be seen poring over the report of the speech, taking it line by line, in the hope that they might find something which they could challenge. Later Von Donop decided that he would postpone his justification until after the war!

On Wednesday last [22 December] D. went up to Newcastle, and thence to Glasgow. He had a fearfully tough time, and I am very anxious for his safety.[1] Mr. Davies says that he was very doubtful as to whether they would return alive. D. says that the men up there are ripe for revolution, that they are completely out of hand. They have been told that the war is Labour's chance. But D. is convinced that there is German money up there. The men are certainly misled, for they say that the war has been engineered by the capitalists in order to enthrall the working classes, and that the war for them is not against Germany, but against the capitalist. D. seems to think there will be serious trouble before things are settled, but nevertheless he came back from Glasgow quite cheery, & nothing daunted. He gave a Xmas dinner coming back on the train, & after dinner a concert was held, D. being the Chairman. Everyone had to take his turn—reporters, messengers, anyone who was capable of doing anything to entertain. Mr. Davies says D. was quite mad, and they had a rollicking time. I was waiting for him at W.H. where he arrived about 10.30 & we spent the next day, Sunday [26 December], together very happily. D. brought me a most handsome dressing-gown, which Mr. D. was sent to purchase in Glasgow—and had plenty of fun out of it, I believe. I gave D. my photograph for a Xmas present, & we have devised a skilful way of disguising it so that the case looks like a pocket book & he can carry it about in his pocket.

---

1. Lloyd George was shouted down when he addressed a mass meeting of shop stewards in Glasgow.

Diary 1916

January 21st 1916
Have been too busy to keep a diary lately—very long hours, and lots to do,
& things very worrying on the whole. The suppression of the Forward[1]
caused trouble. It was done in a hurry, because the excitable Labour branch
of our Department were scared at the vivid accounts given of the Glasgow
meeting, & D. had to work up a case afterwards to justify himself. It would
have been far better not to have suppressed the paper, but D. has not time to
attend to everything himself, and the Labour Dept. are continually letting
him down, and I have constantly urged him to make a clearance. The difficulty is that it is almost impossible to find anyone who is really competent to
deal with the situation. D. thought Lord Murray[2] was, but after hopelessly
muddling the visit to the Clyde, and realising as he had not done before what
fearful difficulties he had to grapple with, he collapsed, and has not appeared
at the Office since. They say it is a heart attack, but I am quite certain that it
was brought on at any rate by funk, and that he will try & shake off the
responsibility for the whole matter. I never did trust the man: he is too
smooth and oily, and too bent on manoeuvring an advantage for himself out
of anything that he undertakes. D. thinks he is a good friend, but I doubt it.
At any rate, he would always put himself first, and has absolutely no courage.

However injudicious the suppression of the Forward was, D. made a very
good case for himself, & his speech went down very well. I went up to the
House to hear it, though I always mean to keep away when he makes a
speech I get so dreadfully nervous when the time draws near for him to get
up, and the suspense does not go until he sits down. Sometimes the tension is
so great that I feel that I must scream, and I regularly make up my mind that
I will keep away the next time he makes a speech. However, when the next
time comes, I am just as keen as ever to be a witness of the performance!

January 31st 1916
The Conscription Bill is practically through. At one time it looked as though

---

1. Glasgow Socialist weekly, suppressed for reporting Lloyd George's meeting.
2. Lord Murray of Elibank, formerly Liberal chief whip.

there would be a nasty smash in the Liberal Party. The P.M. was in the hands of McKenna, Simon, & Co., who vowed they would resign if the Conscription Bill was brought in. Although the Derby figures justified the bringing in of compulsion for the single men, yet this section of the Cabinet wished to quibble over the exact meaning of the P.M.'s pledge.[1] They brought forward a plan for examining each case of the single men, & finding out whether the majority of them had not some good excuse for holding back. Meanwhile conscription was to be delayed until all the single unenlisted men had come before a tribunal, & made out a case. Of course the country would not have stood this, but the P.M. was still wobbling dangerously between Simon & McKenna on the one hand, & D. on the other. When he had been with D. he was in favour of declaring for conscription; when he had been with the others he was in favour of going back upon his pledge, or of putting off the evil day. Meanwhile you had the whole country speculating as to whether the First Minister of the Kingdom would keep his word, or whether he would break it! Rather an undignified position for anyone to be put into!

The eventful Cabinet which was to decide the fate of conscription was held on a Monday afternoon. The P.M. had spent the weekend under the baneful influence of McKenna, and on Monday morning D. heard through Lord Reading that the P.M. was leaning towards putting off declaring for compulsion, & thus breaking his pledge. D. thereupon sent a message through Lord Reading (who was lunching at No. 10) to the P.M., saying that if the P.M. kept his promise to the compulsionists, he (D.) would stand by him through thick and thin; that if there were a general election, he (D.) would do all the dirty work up & down the country—speaking & the like and would work for him like a nigger. If however the P.M. did not see his way to keep his promise, he (D.) would be obliged to send in his resignation; but whatever happened, D. made it quite clear to the P.M. that under no circumstances would he take office in a Tory Government. This was a very happy statement, as insidious rumours were going round that D. was out to throw over the Liberals & would be received with open arms by the Tories.

Lord Reading delivered D.'s message to the P.M.; and the result was that when the Cabinet began, & everyone was waiting anxiously for the discussion on compulsion to begin, the P.M. raised the question instead of the evacuation of Helles. The discussion dragged on and on, and when every member of the Cabinet had expressed his opinion at least twice upon the subject, the P.M. declared the meeting to be at a close, saying that it was now nearly five o'clock and that there was not time to raise the question of compulsion that day. Whereupon Lord Curzon lost his temper, and protested that the P.M. was simply wasting time deliberately, and in order to avoid giving a decision. In reality he (the P.M.) was endeavouring to gain time to reconsider his decision in the light of D.'s message. He gained his point. Lord

1. Asquith promised that no attested married men should be called up until all single men had been taken.

Reading told D. that the P.M. was much touched by his promise of loyalty and help, and the message had in fact the effect of deciding the P.M. to declare at once for compulsion. A meeting was summoned for the following morning, & the P.M. announced his intention of redeeming the undertaking which he had given with regard to compulsion. Whereupon McKenna broke in with the objection that there was no definite undertaking for compulsion contained in the P.M.'s pledge. The P.M. turned on him quite roughly. 'What do you mean?' he asked. 'I think there is a very definite undertaking, & I am prepared to carry it out to the full.'

It was not certain then whether the Simonites would carry out their threat of resignation. It was pretty sure that Simon would go, for a man cannot resign twice & still stay in the Cabinet.[1] I asked D. whether McKenna would go. 'I don't care whether he does or not', was the reply. 'He will either have to resign or eat mud, & one is as galling as the other.'

The anti-compulsionists in the Cabinet have tried several means of making the P.M.'s decision non-effective—such as reducing the size of the army, etc. But they have not been very successful. If a general election were fought now on the question of conscription, the conscriptionists would sweep the country. And although a certain section of the Liberal party look askance at D., and call him a traitor (behind his back, of course) yet in the country everyone is convinced that he has a larger following than ever. I happened to hear however that the chief thing which these Liberals objected to was D.'s associations with Lord Northcliffe. Of course Northcliffe's few harmless visits to D. have been magnified in the City into endless secret conclaves, & I must say I think this has done D. a little harm with his Liberal friends, for Northcliffe is not trusted, nor does he deserve to be. I mentioned to D. therefore what some Liberals were saying. 'Let them wait!' was all the reply I got, in rather a savage tone. 'I'll teach them to decry me behind my back! I'll give them something to be annoyed at!' Some of the Members, Welsh ones, even went a little further, & went down to their constituencies with the idea of running an anti-Lloyd George campaign. (Mrs. Llewellyn Williams[2] went so far as to say that she was afraid L.G. had done for himself: she was *so* sorry for him!) The result of the meetings summoned in these constituencies by the intrepid M.P.s was that votes of confidence were passed in the Minister of Munitions, and the Members were summarily told by their constituents to 'follow Lloyd George'. D. was greatly amused and encouraged when this was related to him. He really is working frightfully hard, and leaves no stone unturned to make his work a success. There is some talk of his going to the War Office. Everyone admits that Kitchener is a failure there. He has lost heart, and they

---

1. Sir John Simon was the only cabinet minister to resign in protest against conscription.
2. Wife of Llewelyn Williams, a Welsh M.P. and for many years a great friend of Lloyd George's. He quarrelled with Lloyd George, however, at this time and he and Lloyd George ceased to see each other.

say that he never puts in any work. 'We wonder', said one prominent man at the W.O. to D., 'what he does with his time. He is never there, and he never knows what is going on. He does not even read the telegrams.'

D. was asked to a dinner about a fortnight ago—Lord Reading, Montagu, & McKenna. D. could not make out at first what the object of the dinner was, but he soon discovered that it was to discuss the question of K.'s successor at the W.O. Lord Reading had apparently been asked by the P.M. to sound D.'s views. D. expressed an impartial view, when questioned, as to who should succeed K., but was very emphatic on the point that he *should* be succeeded. 'Anyone', he said, 'would fill the post better than K.—even Jack Pease!' They agreed, but did not seem to have got what they wanted out of him. However D. pretended not to understand what they were driving at. At last Montagu could stand it no longer. 'Well', he said, 'I am going to be the "enfant terrible" of the party and ask you if *you* would consent to take the post if you were offered it?' Then they began to weigh the pros and cons. D. admitted that he had done most of the hard work at the Ministry of Munitions, and that he was quite ready to seek fresh fields. But he said that whoever went to the W.O. would have a frightfully difficult task, for D. considers that disasters are still to come. However, they promised D. full support if he should go there, McKenna suggested *en passant* that they (he and D.) should bury the hatchet. 'Let us be quite frank', he said, 'you & I make a pretty strong team both pulling together: but pulling different ways we have several times risked overturning the cart altogether. The P.M. too', he added, 'is very disturbed at the continuous quarrels between the two of us. Surely it would be better if we patched up our differences and agreed to work together!' D. agreed, & they parted very good friends. How long it will last I do not know. The matter of the W.O. remains at that. K. is supposed to have a command in the East in the near future, but how soon this will occur depends on many things. K. continues to attend War Council and expound his policy. He was dilating on the iniquities of the Russians the other day at the War Council. Someone asked whether it would not be possible to ask them to give detailed statistics of their resources, in order that we might be better able to judge what to expect of them. 'It would be no use', said K. 'Their figures are never reliable.' Whereupon the company smiled. K. talking of the Russian figures as unreliable was humorous. Practically all the figures which the W.O. have supplied to the War Committee have been incorrect.

D. & I manage to spend a good deal of time together now that the flat is in existence. He comes along there to dinner from the House of Commons, and walks home across the Park. I gave him a birthday dinner on his birthday [17 January], & we managed by dint of manoeuvring to spend the following weekend together. On the Sunday [23 January] we motored down to Eastbourne, & I stayed on the pier while D. went to see Lord Murray, who was staying down there recovering from various heart attacks.

Last Thursday D. spent the evening with me, as he was off to France the following day. I was very depressed, as D. had had a communication from some psychic individual telling him to beware of the 28th & 29th of January, & I never can quite bring myself to disbelieve in these psychic people. D. too loathed going away, though I think he always itches for an exciting time when there is one coming. He says though that he could face disgrace with me now, and still be quite happy. 'I can understand Parnell now for the first time',[1] he said to me on Thursday night. Although it would be bitter grief for me were I to be the cause of his disgrace, yet it is comforting to know that he feels like that. 'I shall love you the whole time I am away, Pussy', were his parting words to me. 'And I shall long to get back again to you.' Oh, how I long to see him back again safely. I spoke to Mr. Davies at G.H.Q. (France) on the telephone this morning, & he said they would be in London tonight at 11.0. I am to go straight to Walton Heath & wait for D. there.

February 1st 1916

D. returned very late last night from France. They were delayed in crossing the Channel owing to mines which had been laid everywhere and which necessitated their waiting till high tide in order that the mines should be deeper in the water, and therefore more harmless. The destroyer which had convoyed them across on Friday [28 January] was torpedoed on Saturday while convoying transports across. They left Paris on Saturday half an hour before the Zeppelins arrived there—the reward of virtue, D. says, as F. E. Smith had wanted D. to join him at a dinner in Paris with some lady friends of his; but D. refused, wishing to get back as soon as possible; & left for Boulogne on Saturday night immediately after the Conference.

On Sunday the party visited headquarters at St. Omer, & left there at 4.0 yesterday. In crossing the Channel they had to take a zig-zag and roundabout course, in order to avoid the mines if possible, & from all accounts the crossing was rather a strain on the nerves.

D.'s face was care-worn and drawn when he arrived in London, & I could see that the visit had told on his nerves. 'You must take my mind off it all, Pussy', were almost his first words to me. 'I feel I shall break down if I do not get right away from it all. The horror of what I have seen has burnt into

---

1. Charles Stewart Parnell (1846–91): leader of the Irish Home Rule party, 1877–90. In 1889 Captain O'Shea, a former Liberal M.P., sought a divorce on the grounds of Mrs. O'Shea's adultery with Parnell. Parnell and Mrs. O'Shea had in fact been lovers for years past, and she had borne him three children. They offered no defence. The divorce went through, and in June 1891 Parnell and Mrs. O'Shea were married. In November 1890, after the hearing of the divorce case, the Irish parliamentary party re-elected Parnell as its leader. Gladstone then issued a letter, stating that Parnell's continuance in the leadership of the Irish party would make his own leadership of the Liberal party 'almost a nullity'. Members of the Irish party demanded Parnell's resignation. He refused. After a prolonged debate, 45 members of the Home Rule party repudiated Parnell's leadership, 26 remained with him. Parnell fought to retain his position until his death on 6 October 1891. The split in the party was not ended until 1900. In a larger sense, the triumphant position to which Parnell had raised the Home Rule party was never recovered. Parnell had sacrificed a great public cause for the sake of a woman's love.

my soul, and has almost unnerved me for my work.' He had been to see the son of John Hinds, M.P. lying wounded in the hospital at the Welsh head-quarters over there. The poor boy had been shot through the head, & the bullet had torn through part of his brain. He was in dreadful agony, & was paralysed all down one side. D. insisted upon fetching two more doctors to the hospital to see if they could not do anything for him, though everyone said his case was hopeless. D. later on spoke to the Commander-in-Chief, who promised that the best doctor out there should be with the boy by 5.0 yesterday afternoon. Since he has been home, D. has managed to send a brain specialist from Etaples to see him, & still hopes that it may be possible to save the boy's life. But the incident had quite unnerved him. 'I wish I had not seen him', he kept on saying to me. 'I ought not to have seen him. I feel that I cannot go on with my work, now that the grim horror of the reality has been brought home to me so terribly. I was not made to deal with things of war. I am too sensitive to pain & suffering, & this visit has almost broken me down.'

However, I did my best to take his mind completely away, and this evening he tells me that I just saved him from a complete collapse.

Mr. Davies says that the Military Staff out there are fearfully insolent and over-bearing. The Prussian is not in it, says he. We hear that from all sides, & they say that the rank and file and the junior officers are getting fed up with them. D. says however, that there is much more energy & more grip at G.H.Q. since Haig has been there. When French was in command it had the air of a picnic, but now they mean business.

Today the men from Lang's on the Clyde are out on strike, owing to the introduction of women into the works. Mrs. Drummond (W.S.P.U.) came to see me yesterday on the subject of holding meetings up there to try & make the men see the criminality of their actions. She is a dear motherly soul, with a bewitching Scotch accent, & quite the right way of touching people in their kindliest spot. A great sense of humour, too.

D. brought me the most wonderful blouse from Paris. I don't know when he found time to buy it, but he is most wonderfully pleased with his selection, and so am I.

D. came to dinner. D. was continually harping on poor young Hinds, although we did our best to keep him off it. Eventually we got him on to the subject of Criccieth & the days when he was a boy, & he cheered up consider-ably. He told us how he used to go to Criccieth from Llanystumdwy with a tin can for two pennyworth of treacle, & of the delight of the anticipation of treacle on his bread for tea. 'What a fearful temptation it was', he said, 'to keep your fingers out of the tin on the way home!' 'I am quite sure', I said, 'that you very rarely managed to keep *yours* out and what is more, I can guarantee that you managed to escape being discovered!' He laughed & said I was quite right!

February 2nd 1916

In bed with a bad cold on the chest. D. came to me in the evening, & we had dinner together off cold pheasant & cheese. D. had been in the afternoon to see an experiment with an enormous caterpillar machine, which can crawl over the enemy's trenches while the men inside are quite free from harm, as it is bullet-proof. D. still very tired and suffering from the strain of his journey.

February 3rd 1916

D. spoke at Ponders' End, at a meeting organised by Mrs. Churchill to open a Munition Workers' Canteen at the factory there. D. had very little time to prepare a speech—went over it with me in the afternoon before starting, but had very few notes. He always delivers a lot better when he has no notes, & this was an instance bearing out the theory. They made him stand up on the table, so that the men could see him better, & he was in fine form. The audience was first rate—the men were keen workers, and sympathetic to him, & helped him along with their witty remarks & keen appreciation. It was an excellent little speech, & I was so proud of him. D. talks of my being a flirt, but I have never seen anyone to equal *him* in the way he flirts with an audience. With look, & gesture, & smile, & with his seductive voice, he wins them to him, & can do anything with them. Mrs. Churchill made a very nice little speech. She is a very charming person, & no wonder 'Winston' is fond of her. Much to everyone's surprise, Mrs. Bonham Carter (Miss Asquith) turned up, though as far as we can make out, she had not been invited.[1] D. is of the opinion that she turned up expecting to see a row. It appears that even Mrs. Churchill was uneasy as to how the meeting would go off, as many of the workers are hostile to him at the present moment. The Asquith clique are rather gloating over the Glasgow row, & probably Mrs. Bonham Carter expected a similar performance here. 'The Asquiths and their friends are boasting', said D. to me, 'that Lloyd George cannot hold a meeting with the workers now.' However, she was unpleasantly surprised if she came with this object. One of the speakers referred to D. as the man of the moment, & one of the audience shouted: 'Put him in Asquith's place!'

Dillon informed D. that the French were absolutely sick of the Prime Minister. They are convinced that we shall never get on with the war as we ought while he is at Downing Street. However, Mrs. A. herself has been heard to declare that 'Nothing but God Almighty himself will drive Herbert out of Downing Street.'

We heard that poor young Hinds died yesterday. Col. Lee[2] says it is better so, for he would most probably have been an imbecile if he had lived, & D.

---

1. (Lady) Violet Bonham Carter (1887–1969): Asquith's only daughter by his first wife; m. Maurice Bonham Carter, 1915; cr. life peeress as Baroness Asquith of Yarnbury, 1964.
2. Lord Lee of Fareham who later presented his house at Chequers to the nation.

says the scene of pain for his father & mother would have been greater in the end. Col. Lee says he knows many such fine handsome young fellows who have become gibbering idiots from the terrible wounds they have received. D. still very tired, & went off to Walton Heath for a rest. I went down in the afternoon, and we spent the evening getting out figures of ammunition required & available for the next big offensive, taking different dates as a basis for the estimates. D. finds he will be able to come up to all the requirements of the Commander-in-Chief, and is very pleased with the result of the computation. We spent a most happy evening together.

February 7th 1916

The public are enraged at the damage that the Zeppelins were allowed to do last week, and cannot understand why we do not do *something* to prevent their doing such extensive harm. This time they even got as far as Wales, & the Midland towns were of course quite unprepared for them, and in many cases the authorities seem to have lost their head.

Today, after more than 18 months of war, the Commander of the Royal Flying Corps has issued a minute to the Cabinet in which he states that no definite instructions have ever been issued to the R.F.C., and suggests that it should be clearly defined what the R.F.C. are supposed to do in the event of an air raid, etc., etc. It seems to be an unholy muddle at present between the W.O. & the Admiralty, each Department putting the onus of attacking the enemy upon the other; consequently nothing happens. One hears the most appalling tales of the unpreparedness of our air service, & according to the Memo. issued to the Cabinet, there seems to be very good reason for complaint. It does seem extraordinary that we allow things to slide along for all these months, until some big disaster happens. The public *know* nothing: they can only guess from stray gossip at what is going on, and they wander in bewilderment, not knowing what is the best thing to do for the good of the country.

The latest phase is that Germans, *at large in this country*, are writing insulting letters to the Government, boasting that, *though naturalised*, they are still Germans & can help their country; or that though they were born in England & we treat them as British subjects, yet *they are Germans*, & count themselves as such. But *we*, poor trusting fools, keep them at large in our midst! Surely we are asking for defeat.

McLean,[1] an arch-plotter in Glasgow among the workers, has at last been deported, and his paper suppressed. This looks a little more like business.

February 8th 1916

D. had Gwynne,[2] the Editor of The Morning Post to lunch. 'Since all the

---

1. John MacLean (?–1923), Glasgow revolutionary leader; nominated by Lenin as Russian consul and prospective head of British Soviet government.
2. Howell Arthur Gwynne (1865–1950): editor of Morning Post and keen tariff reformer.

Liberal papers are attacking me', he said. 'I must keep someone on my side.' Gwynne told him: 'There are only two men in the country whom I believe in at the present time—yourself and Carson.' D. referred to Carson's disappearance for the time on the grounds of ill-health. 'Ah', said D., 'he has married a young wife and it is telling upon him.'

D. dined with me and told me of the above conversation. He said he has been thinking, all the way to Chester Square, of how he wished he could marry me. But we both agreed that we must put that thought out of our minds, for it only leads to bitterness and discontent, and sometimes to injustice and folly. However, he has sworn to marry me if he ever finds himself in a position to do so, & I am content with that. Not that I wished him to promise it, for I am happy as we are—we have our little home now, where we can spend many evenings together in solitude—and how sweet the evenings are! The only thing we lack is children, but I often think that if I were married & had children, then I should not be able to keep in touch with D.'s work to the extent that I do now, & perhaps should be less happy. At present all our interests lie together; he does nothing but what I know of it; I almost know his very thoughts. I don't suppose I should see nearly as much of him if I were married to him.

I asked D. if *he* believed in Carson. 'Yes', he said. 'He is a great man: he has courage, he has determination; he has judgment.' I questioned whether he had judgment. 'Oh, yes', was D.'s reply. 'He was extraordinarily clever over the Ulster business: his calculations were almost unerring.'

D. *was* to have dined with the Governor of the Bank of England, but remembered a 'previous engagement', & came to me instead. He said the thought of our little room compared with a formal dinner was too much for him. 'The Governor would not understand it if I got up & went to lie on the sofa when I had had enough to eat', he said. He certainly did need a rest.

February 9th 1916
Had a terribly busy day—all of us hard at it from morning till night. D. managed to find time, however, to go to tea with Mrs. Timothy Davies. He does not go there often, but he says she has been a good friend to him, and he does not wish to appear to neglect her. He always tells me when he is going, so I don't mind so much. I don't care for her so much—she is too pretentious, & I don't think she is very sincere. However, I don't like to think badly of D.'s friends, as I like to think that he has good taste!

D. went in the morning to Russell Rea's funeral. They played Chopin's funeral march. D. says he prefers Handel, but that neither of them end up rightly, as the former ends up in a strain of passionate grief, and the latter on a note of triumph. Neither is true to nature. D. says that the true funeral march should end up in a passage of calm resignation. Nature, he says, cannot sustain the passionate grief, but neither does she ever quite reach the point of triumphing over bereavement; but she gradually gets more & more resigned to the loss.

February 10th 1916

D. had a very busy day, & was very tired at the end of it. We did not have much time for gossip.

Sutherland[1] says that a friend of his has just come back from France, & he reports that the difference between London & Paris at the present time is simply amazing. At the Savoy, here, things seem to be as gay as ever—you see the same crowds of showily-dressed, painted women, the same dancing, the same band—which still wears the costume of a Hungarian band! In Paris they say there is nothing of this now. The same man told a story of how he visited an inn at Rheims—the only inn that is now open & which caters for the officers there. He saw a piano in one of the rooms, & asked one of the daughters of the inn whether she would play something. She shook her head. 'No', she said. 'There is no music in France now.'

They say that the French are pained at the two Asquith marriages which have recently taken place—Miss Asquith to Bonham Carter & Miss Tennant to Lord Granby—because of the show and display at both of them. The French cannot understand the attitude of a Prime Minister who allows such a display in his family at a time when everyone is preaching economy & sacrifice & the necessity of abandoning everything to get on with the war.

A War Council was held this morning to discuss Air Defence. We are now getting down to hard facts with regard to the 'air'. We now learn that apart from the aeroplanes charged with the defence of London (24 in number) there are *two* for the defence of the rest of the interior of England. No wonder the Zeppelins were able to cruise about for twelve hours unharmed in England last week.

D. impressed upon them the necessity of defending Woolwich against air raids at all costs. 'The destruction of Woolwich', he insisted, 'would be a worse piece of news to us than the loss of two Army Corps. Never mind about the rest of London! Let them destroy the remainder of London, if only Woolwich is safe!'

February 11th 1916

General Lord French came to the Office today, to discuss Air Defence with D. French is being made primarily responsible for the Air arrangements, much to the annoyance of the Harmsworth Press. I must say that the Government do seem to be very wobbly on the subject of the organisation of the air service, and don't seem to have any definite plans in view.

Roumania seems to be wobbling badly. I do not blame her if she decides to safeguard herself against a fate such as Serbia and Montenegro have experienced, and comes in with Germany against us. Our policy in the

---

1. Sir William Sutherland (1880–1949): private secretary to Lloyd George, 1915–18; parliamentary secretary to Lloyd George, 1918–20; lord of the treasury, 1920–2; chancellor of the duchy of Lancaster, 1922; acted principally as Lloyd George's press officer.

Balkans has been disastrous from the beginning. They say the Greeks are very angry at the way we have behaved towards them. Our diplomats over there blunder all along the line. Someone asked the German Ambassador there what he was doing to bring Greece in on his side. 'Sitting still', he replied, 'the English are doing my work very well for me!'

D. dined with Lord Reading to meet Colonel House,[1] who has just come from Berlin.

February 12th 1916
This morning we had a dreadful rush, & I went home with a frightful headache.

Sir G. Riddell came into the office this morning; he was in a great state lest anything should come of the hint that Lord Northcliffe should be made Minister of the Air. 'Trade jealousy', said someone. But I think it is more than that. Sir G. says that if Lord N. once gets a footing inside the Government, he will not rest until he is made Dictator. I think there is something in it. Lord N. is unscrupulous, & a dangerous man, in spite of, or perhaps because of, his very smooth exterior. I do feel that D. should not have too much to do with him. N. will use him for his own ends, & throw him over when he has no further use for him.

D. went off with Sir George to play golf.

February 13th 1916
Entertained a wounded soldier at 41a Chester Square. D. lent me the car to fetch him and take him back. The poor fellow has lost his left arm & leg, & is now at a home set apart for soldiers who have lost their limbs. He says the home is full, & there are 2,000 applicants waiting for admission. At this home they provide them with new limbs, & teach them how to use them. This man had already got a new leg, & was shortly going to get another arm.

He was wounded last June, & he told us how disheartening it was then at the front for our men to find that they could not reply to the enemy's fire. They dared not send a shell over to the German trenches, for they got back 20 or 30 to every one that they sent. And they could not reply when the Germans shelled. They would telephone back to our artillery, asking whether we could not fire; but the gunners would reply that we had no ammunition. Things are reversed now.

February 14th 1916
Another frightfully busy day—full from morning till after eight in the evening, when D. went to dine with Lord Reading & Col. House, the Prime Minister, Grey, & one or two others. They were to discuss points of policy between England & U.S.A. & D. at first said he could not go, as he had another dinner engagement. But they insisted it would be no use having the discussion unless D. was there & D. had to put off his other engagement. He

---

1. President Wilson's personal representative.

has promised to tell me what happened, but has not had time to do so yet.[1]

February 15th 1916

Cabinet held, at which they discussed Air Service again. In spite of the amount of talk there has been on the subject, they don't seem any nearer a decision on the subject. The present Government do not seem to be *capable* of making up their minds about *anything*. Curzon is in favour of making an Air Ministry (of which he would be the head) and set forth plans for the creation of the same. D. said 'I should like to know what sort of a Department it would be. Would it have the power to make its own plans, fashion its own policy, & be absolutely independent, like the War Office, or the Foreign Office? Or would it be a Department like the Ministry of Munitions? For instance, I have no initiative—the War Office orders so many guns—I produce them. I do not question: I do as I am told.' Kitchener thereupon threw up his hands in dismay & roared with laughter & the others did the same. 'Well!' said Curzon, 'all I can say is that the Ministry of Air would be about as much like the latter description as the Ministry of Munitions itself is!'

D. has refused to attend a Mansion House meeting to inaugurate a 'Thrift Campaign', though most other Cabinet Ministers are going. D., however, said frankly that he does not approve of these 'Thrift Campaigns'. He says the people will never save unless they are made to. He is for a policy of bold and heavy direct taxation, & for *forced* loans or savings. They say the Treasury is in a fearful muddle, & that they do not know where they are.

The Italian Liaison Officer, General Delmé Radcliffe, called on D., & urged on him the wisdom of a journey to Italy. He says that no one would have such an impression upon the Italians as D., that a visit by him to Rome would produce an extraordinarily good effect. Delmé Radcliffe had just been to Grey, & had been urging him to take D. with him when he goes in a fortnight's time. D. is inclined to go. Though I know he would do a lot of good, yet I dread these journeys to the Continent, they are so full of anxiety. But still, the anxiety that I have to endure then can be nothing to what others have to go through who have their dear ones in the firing line.

February 16th 1916

General French came to see D. this morning—still on the subject of air!— D. says he is very pessimistic about the state of affairs. D. asked me what I thought of him. I said I was rather disappointed: there is something in his face expressive of weakness. D. says he is really a most courageous man—never downhearted & depressed—always cheerful, & never losing his head.

D. refused absolutely to go to the Cabinet. He says they never decide anything, and he is absolutely sick of it. He says he is in a good mind to chuck

---

1. In fact they discussed peace terms which President Wilson might be persuaded to support. Nothing came of the idea.

the whole thing, but I know he will not. Apart from everything else, it would be a cowardly thing to do—like running away.

D. had to give a man 'the sack' today for doing an indiscreet thing. The poor fellow was frightfully cut up, and that upset D. very much, though he could not go back on it, as the man had committed a gross breach of discipline. 'But it was only because he was an ass', said D. 'He never meant any harm. And I could see the pain in his face—and I *loathed* myself for causing it.' The incident upset D. for the rest of the morning.

February 17th 1916
D. not at all well. I think he is really very depressed about things in general, & is rather pessimistic about us ever pulling it off. He says that Colonel House, when over in Germany, was not received by any of the military authorities, nor by the Kaiser. They absolutely refused to have any discussion about anything. Thus House concludes that they are not thinking about coming to terms, and are confident of victory. House thinks they are preparing for a great offensive on the western front, & told us to beware. From all he said, it does not appear that Germany is by any means coming to the end of her resources. House says that the United States will intervene soon, either peaceably, to treat for terms of peace between belligerents, or, if Germany refuses to come to terms, then U.S.A. will take up arms on our side. How far this is true, one can only surmise, but it seemed to me that U.S. were not quite disinterested, for House intimated that meanwhile it would be unwise for England to press the blockade!

An important Cabinet meeting on the Navy. D. would not go, until they sent for him, & practically demanded that he should appear. He said nothing would be decided, & he was quite right. He told me afterwards that Balfour sat with a look of boredom on his face, occasionally vouchsafing a remark, but with the air of one who is thinking: 'Well, this is a great nuisance, but I suppose, as the Navy is my job, I had better say something now and again.' Bonar Law passed D. a note: 'Balfour always looks as though he were fighting in the air.' D. replied 'Yes—except when we are discussing aeroplanes!'

February 18th 1916
I persuaded D. to go down to Walton Heath for the day, as he was feeling so tired & done up. He went after having met the officials of the Labour Department on the subject of the impending strike at Woolwich. The President of the A.S.E. has been prosecuted for urging some members of his Union to strike, and for fining them for refusing to do so. The members at Woolwich have threatened to strike wholesale unless the prosecution is withdrawn, & all the officials of this Department to a man are urging D. not to prosecute. They are afraid of a row. Bodkin, too, who is prosecuting, wishes to withdraw, but D. will not hear of it. 'There is only one alternative', he said to them. 'And that is for Mr. Asquith to go to the King and tell him that we

cannot govern England, & that he suggests that Rhys should be made Prime Minister, & the A.S.E. should govern in our stead.' So, having decided that the prosecution must go on, D. departed cheerfully for Walton Heath. 'I shan't worry', he said to me, 'now that I have made up my mind. It is only when I am uncertain what course to take that I am worried.'

The Woolwich men are expected to strike on Monday [21 February].

February 19th 1916
D. had another quiet day at Walton Heath, & I kept him company.

February 20th 1916
A very dull day.

February 21st 1916
D. remained at Walton Heath, but could not keep his mind off work. He is preparing a Memorandum to show that the Germans have *not* yet come to the end of their resources and that we cannot count on being superior to them either in men or material. Kitchener wrote a memorandum at the beginning of last year to show that the Germans had come to the end of their resources! D. says that no figures produced by the W.O. are ever right. Kitchener will say anything to carry his point. 'He lies blatantly', said D. 'And everyone knows now that he is lying.'

D. says that unless the U.S.A. come in to help us, we cannot hope for victory.

February 22nd 1916
Nothing of importance occurred, but D. was hard at work all day, and looked very tired and poorly by the evening.

February 23rd 1916
D. had McKenna & Grey to lunch, & they discussed the prospects of the war. Grey is frankly pessimistic, and is for making peace at once. D. expressed amazement. 'On what terms?' he asked. Grey replied 'On the status quo.' D. reminded him that there are our Allies to be dealt with, and that France will never make peace until Alsace & Lorraine are restored to her. McKenna was for treating for peace now—getting President Wilson to intervene & mediate. D. took him up sharply. 'Public opinion would not stand it', he said. 'Well', said McKenna, who rarely has the courage of his opinions. 'Perhaps not just *now*—not on the 23rd of February; but let us say in June or July, perhaps.' 'What does the Prime Minister say?', inquired D. 'He says there will be peace within the year', said McKenna. But they went on to say that he was being filled with Kitchener's stories of a wonderful offensive in July & August, which would drive the Germans back into Germany and break them altogether. The P.M. will accept *anything* which will lull his conscience, and allow him—as D. puts it—to enjoy his dinner. Meantime there is *not a single definite plan* for the spring campaign, but the Germans, on

the other hand, are giving the French a terrible time round Verdun.[1] I believe it is touch and go whether they break through.

D. had an interview with 'H.M.' The King pressed him to go to Italy—said it would do an immense amount of good. D. was very elated at the request but it appears that the question was raised at the Cabinet in the morning (which D. by the way refused to attend) and the P.M. showed considerable heat when it was suggested that D. should go. 'The French *Prime Minister* went', he said. So the matter was not pressed.

I do not think D. is as ill as he thinks he is. He always thinks he is dying if he has a bilious attack. But I think men are mostly like that. He is very tired & overworked, but I think a rest would put him right. Unfortunately it is very difficult for him to take a holiday. He talks of resigning when he has settled the question of the filling factories, but something else is sure to turn up before then. D. is heartily sick of the present Government. He says it would be laughable if it were not tragic.

February 24th 1916
D. & I drove up from W.H. in the snow. It was a glorious morning—everything dazzlingly white. D. loves the snow: he says it thrills him.

March 11th 1916
Nothing of great moment has happened lately. D. has quite recovered from his indisposition, after knocking off a good deal of his work & resting at Walton Heath. He is now full of energy again, but very depressed at the way we do *not* 'get on with the war'. Everyone tells the same tale—that the country is sick of the present Government & loathes & despises Asquith. And yet, now that there is no Opposition, it is very difficult to turn them out. There are signs, however, of a row in the country. The married men say that they have been tricked by the Government, & they say that many of them will refuse to come when they are called. Many people are asking: Why does not Lloyd George make a stand & turn the rotters out? I asked D. this morning why he did not. He replied that it was a very difficult thing to do; that it would immediately be put down to personal motives. 'It would be much easier', he said, 'were I not in the running for the Premiership—if I could point to someone else and say: Put *that* man in Asquith's place. But who is there who would make a fitting Prime Minister? Bonar Law is limp and lifeless; Balfour can never make up his mind about anything. There *is* no one.' He had just been for a walk with Lord St. Davids, who had been questioning him on the issues of the war. 'Shall we win?' he asked D., 'or will it end in a bad peace?' 'I will tell you', D. replied. 'I do not boast; I am not a braggart. But I will tell you this: if I were put in charge of this war, I would see the thing through; as I shall not be, it will end in a bad peace. I have never said this before, but that is my opinion on the matter.' Lord St. Davids urged him to come out

---

1. The German offensive against Verdun began on 21 February 1916.

and lead the country; but D. says there are all manner of subtle influences at work, which would make a venture of that kind a hazardous thing, & might end in his ruin. I do not believe it: I think D. would have the country solid at his back. And in any event, even if it is risky, I think he ought to speak his mind. Otherwise, I tell him, he will be classed with the rest of the Cabinet as a body of failures, & when the country *turns* them out, he will be disgraced with the others. I think he is pondering over it, and should not be surprised if he takes action soon.

March 12th 1916
D. went to dinner with the Lord Chief Justice one evening, to meet Oppenheimer, the famous Consul.[1] D. says he thinks Oppenheimer is not to be trusted, and that he is in the pay of Germany. D. therefore talked with a purpose, as it was probable that everything that he said would be carried back to German ears. Oppenheimer expressed the view that the war would end this year. D. flatly contradicted him. 'It will not end until 1918', he said. 'We are going to see this thing through, and the war cannot be brought to a successful conclusion for us until then.'

Carmen Sylva[2] died last week, & D. told me an interesting tale about her. She was admitted as a Bard at the Welsh Eisteddfod, and D. was asked to propose the vote of thanks to the Chairman of the meeting. Now D.'s political opponent was the Chairman, & D. was the Member for Carnarvon Boroughs, & the whole thing was done with the idea of be-littling D. before his constituents. However, D. refused to be humiliated. He accepted the invitation & got a wonderful reception at the meeting. The people stood up & cheered & waved, & Carmen Sylva stood up with the rest; but she was a little puzzled as to the meaning of the demonstration. D.'s speech to the Chairman was everything that it should be, without a hostile or jarring note; and the tables were turned on the Chairman, who had thought to 'do down' the Member by asking him to propose a vote of thanks to his opponent. By accepting the invitation D. showed that he was above petty rivalries, and his action was much appreciated by his constituents. (D.'s political judgment is very shrewd!)

This morning we went to see the portrait of D. which has been painted by Augustus John. I have seen it while it was being painted, & hoped all along that some finishing touch would redeem it. But alas! I was disappointed. It is a hard, determined, almost cruel face, with nothing of the tenderness & charm of the D. of every day life. It is true that it was painted when the Germans were slowly overcoming Serbia, & the British Government failed to come to the aid of the desperate Serbians; day after day D. urged that

1. Sir Francis Oppenheimer (1870–1961): consul-general at Frankfurt, 1910–11; commercial attaché at The Hague, 1914–18; attacked by The Daily Mail in 1916 on grounds that his father was a German Jew and his brother the solicitor for Dutch firms in blockade cases.
2. Pen-name of Queen Elizabeth of Rumania.

something should be done, that we should not dishonour ourselves by allowing this thing to happen. But nothing was done, and the disgrace which the
others did not feel was manifest in D.'s expression & the tragedy of it all told
keenly upon him. He himself suggested that the picture should be called
'Salonika', but unless this were done I do not consider it a good portrait. One
critic remarked that it is a remote likeness, but full of temperament and
character. That may be so, but it is only one phase of a very complex character. The rest of John's drawings & paintings are coarse to the last degree,
in my opinion. If John does not approve of a picture, he says 'Yes—very
pleasant.'

Mr. Hughes, the Prime Minister of Australia, came to see D. yesterday.[1]
He is a very able little man, but very plain. Someone, referring to a portrait
of him, said, 'But it does not do you justice, Mr. Hughes.' Hughes promptly
replied, 'It is not justice that I want: what I need is mercy!'

D. & I are very, very happy. I do not know what I should do if anything
happened to him. D. got into trouble the other day at W.H. Mrs. Ll. G. was
outside the door while he was talking to me on the telephone, & took him
severely to task. 'I know very well whom you would marry if anything
happened to me', she said. D. tried to laugh it off, but he says she knows very
well that his affection for me is real.

March 27th 1916
4.0 o'clock. Just returned from a delightful weekend. I was to go to Dover
with Major Collard & Mrs. Collard & one or two others for the weekend in
order to see the Inland Water Transport activities at Sandwich. They were
going by train at mid-day on Saturday [25 March]. Late on Saturday morning D. heard that he was to go to Paris with the P.M., Kitchener, & Grey.
I therefore persuaded him to come down to Dover with us on Saturday, as
the boat was starting from there on the Sunday. He agreed to do this & he
& I & Mr. Davies motored down to Dover on Saturday afternoon & joined
the others there at dinner. It was a simply perfect afternoon, & a simply
perfect run. On Sunday morning we motored over to Sandwich all together
& went on to Canterbury. In the afternoon we went on to the pier to see
them all off. I was very anxious until I heard in the evening that he had arrived
safely. The previous day the Sussex had been torpedoed while crossing the
Channel, & nearly 100 lives had been lost. It is only a chance now whether a
vessel reaches the other side safely.

This morning we got up early and motored into Canterbury for breakfast.
After breakfast we went over the Cathedral. Everything looked so beautiful
and peaceful in the sunshine, and we were loth to leave it. We motored in to
Maidstone for lunch, & arrived in London for tea.

D.'s visit to Paris was quite unexpected. He was not invited to go with the
others—that is to say, the P.M. did not invite him to go; he suggested that

---

1. William Morris Hughes (1864–1952), Australian prime minister, 1915–23.

D. should meet them in Rome, since everyone was insisting on his going there. D., however refused to do this, seeing no profit in a visit to Rome with the P.M. However, on Thursday night [23 March] we had a wire to say that M. Thomas was coming over from Paris. He did not state his object, but when he arrived on Friday it was pretty obvious that he had come to insist that D. should come over with the others to the Conference. He tackled D. first, but D. absolutely refused to go, whereupon Thomas went to the P.M., with the result that D. was sent for and told that he must go. It seems disgraceful that they should have tried to keep him out of it simply from mere jealousy. D. will not forget the incident however. He bides his time, but when he does hit, he hits hard. He has been very quiet lately, but he says he will not stand it much longer. The country is sick to death of Asquith, & would welcome a change. They only want a leader to step forward. Thomas told D. that a party is forming in France to turn out the Government & 'get on with the war'; and in Italy the same thing is happening: and it is suggested that these three progressive factions should join up & form an international 'get-on-with-the-war' party. Whether anything will come of this I do not know, but D. & Thomas are going to Italy together later on.

March 28th 1916
Have wired to D. to tell him to come back at once. Strikes on the Clyde are assuming alarming proportions, and no-one will take any responsibility for drastic action. It is clearly a move financed by the Germans, & not a trade dispute at all. They will probably have to declare martial law.

March 29th 1916
D. returns tonight, late. There was a terrible storm yesterday all over the country, so that I am very glad they did not return last night. I shall not be at ease, however, until they arrive in London. Crossing the Channel is full of peril nowadays.

April 17th 1916
Another great crisis—the greatest since the Coalition Government was formed, and greater than that. Things have come to a head over general compulsion. D. has for some time been very sick at the way the war was being tackled, but a favourable opportunity did not present itself for forcing an issue. Now, however, the question of men must be settled one way or another, & the Cabinet is divided. D. was the first to take the stand of general compulsion, & it was naturally thought that he would be backed by the Unionists in the Cabinet. They have, however, ratted almost to a man (F. E. Smith being the exception) being afraid of losing office apparently. When this happened D. was torn between inclination & expediency. Fortunately the Army Council took the same view as D., & they are making a firm stand. If Asquith will not accept compulsion whole-heartedly, then they will resign, & D. with them. The doubtful point is whether the Unionists, or which of

the Unionists will resign. D. came up to town last night and dined with Bonar Law & he says he has never seen anyone in such a state of abject funk. He (B.L.) does not know which way to turn or what to do. If D. goes out, it is almost impossible for B.L. to stay in without becoming an object of contempt; & yet he is very loth to resign.

Last night also the King sent Lord Stamfordham to reason with D., & to beg him not to resign but to give in to the Prime Minister. D. replied: 'I have sworn an oath of allegiance to His Majesty, and for that reason I cannot give in. If I had not taken that oath, I might.' Sir W. Robertson told D. afterwards that Stamfordham had gone away a different man.

D. was convinced that he would have to resign, as he thought it was most unlikely that the P.M. would climb down all that way. But as he (D.) has the Army Council and Kitchener behind him, he is not afraid. He thinks a lot of Sir William Robertson, who has written a very able memorandum on the need for men, and saying that nothing but compulsion for all will be of any use; and D. feels that with this document behind them they can make a firm stand.

There has been a lot of rushing to and fro during the last week, one person seeing another and ascertaining the latest views on the situation, and seeing whether Asquith has changed his attitude, or whether Bonar Law is funking. Today things have reached a head. Something must be decided at this Cabinet one way or another.

April 18th 1916

Nothing conclusive happened. D. & I dined together last night, and D. told me what had taken place. The P.M. had started off by expounding the theory upon which the non-compulsionists based their attitude. D. expounded the views of the compulsionists. Apparently, however, everyone was most eager to find a solution to the deadlock, if it was to be found. The members seemed to realise that if D. resigned there would be a great commotion, and when D. suggested that a new Committee should be formed to confer with the Army Council and endeavour to find an alternative, it was easy to get their consent. McKenna was the only dissentient, and he was punished by being left out of the new Committee, whereas he had been on the old one. As a matter of fact, D. already had an alternative scheme.

The new Committee met this morning, & D. unfolded his scheme. It amounted to exactly the same thing as compulsion, giving full compulsory powers, i.e. the men were to be taken as they were wanted, & not all together in a lump. D. calls it the 'American system', 'because', he informed me, 'I want the P.M. to think that he has a *precedent*!' D. unfolded his plan at great length, & talked them round gradually to his way of thinking. The P.M. is only too glad to find something which he can adopt as an alternative and must avert a smash, and the others are also willing to make a bargain. D. himself is most anxious to avoid a break, for he says that Asquith himself is the only man who can get Compulsion through the *House of Commons* at present. D. moreover is not anxious to leave the Ministry of Munitions at present. He says if another man came in there now, he would find lots of things not running quite smoothly, & some of the biggest factories not yet working. He would take all the credit himself for putting these things right. Whereas in 6 weeks time the place will be quite in order—D. will get the credit for the big things that have been done & the concern can be handed over safely to someone else. That is the reason that D. is working so hard to avoid a smash. Many think however that nothing real will be effected until Asquith goes. He is the cog in the whole concern, & those who think he should be dispensed with are becoming more & more numerous in all parties.

D. is much more cheerful yesterday & today. Last week he worked himself up until he was nearly ill.

April 19th 1916
D. sent a message to me last night to say that the King approved of his proposals, so that everything looked hopeful. This morning, however, things looked bad again. D. had heard that the P.M. had gone back, & was going to oppose D.'s proposals again. However, when the Cabinet met it appeared that it was Henderson[1] who was making the trouble, on the ground that Labour would not accept compulsion. Bonar Law has intimated to D., that if D. resigns, he (B.L.) will resign also, so that it is now all the more difficult to reject D.'s proposals. Nothing was decided at the Cabinet, & it was arranged that Henderson should confer with the Army people this afternoon. D. sent a message across to Sir William Robertson in the middle of the meeting that he should not accept less than 50,000 men in the first month, & make Henderson agree to that. Sir William Robertson went one better, & it was agreed that the demand should be for 60,000 men in the first month, and 15,000 *per week* afterwards. The minute this fails, compulsion to be applied by a resolution in Parliament. Henderson agreed to this, and D. is once more reassured. He thinks the matter will go through now without further opposition.

Churchill is very sick at the idea of the thing going through quietly. He is all for a split, and for the forming of a vigorous opposition, in which he would take an active part. Some other people are annoyed too at D.'s success in bringing round the Cabinet—but they are for the most part people who wished a split for their own ends. I am glad that for the present there will be no break. It is not an opportune time for D. to resign. He is convinced that the men will not be forthcoming, & that in another 5 or 6 weeks there will be another opportunity. Many Liberals are convinced that Asquith must

---

1. Arthur Henderson (1863–1935): leader of Labour party, 1914–18, 1931; president of board of education, 1915; member of war cabinet, 1916–17; resigned over Stockholm conference, 1917; home secretary, 1924; foreign secretary, 1929–31; led opposition to economy cuts, 1931; president of world disarmament conference, 1932–5.

go, but D. thinks that at any rate the section of the Liberals who were angry with D. before and talked about 'plots' and 'intrigues' will realise that he is not out to wreck the Government, & must give him credit for having done his best to preserve unity in the Cabinet.

April 20th 1916

The matter is quite settled, & D. is 'satisfied', to use the expression which he gave to the newspaper people. In the Cabinet D. raised the question of giving secret Cabinet information to reporters, as some of the daily papers had had the Cabinet discussions reproduced almost word for word. It is now proposed to make it an offence to divulge any information of this kind. D. also raised the question of barges for the transport of munitions across the Channel, & this will probably give a leg up to the Inland Water Transport department, much to the satisfaction of Major Collard.

This afternoon D. was very distressed at the tone taken by The Manchester Guardian in describing the situation. They suggested that D. had done his level best to break up the Cabinet, but that even if he had resigned he would not have been missed, as he had lost his following in the country. D. wired to The M.G. to contradict the 'infamous lie', & wrote a very stinging letter to C. P. Scott,[1] who had been staying during the week at Downing St. C.P. had urged D. to resign, on the grounds that as long as Asquith remained Prime Minister nothing would be done, and he was disappointed at hearing that a settlement had been arrived at, & that A. would stay in office. To have allowed this statement to appear in his paper then was nothing short of infamous: but of course it must have been put in without his knowledge, & someone will have to pay for it.

The Westminister Gazette also have taken the same line, but then they are very angry with D. for his attitude on compulsion, & will have nothing to do with him.

D. intends to make a speech next week to justify his position, & has gone away to Criccieth for the weekend to think about it. It makes my heart ache to see him during a crisis of this kind; he is quite knocked up, & not looking or feeling at all well. One also needs a lot of patience, as he is rather trying when these worries are on. Still he has many good friends.

On 25 April 1916 there was a republican rising in Dublin which was crushed after five days of fighting. Lloyd George was commissioned to seek a solution of the Irish question. He negotiated with Redmond and Carson and reached agreement with them on the basis of Home Rule at once for twenty-six counties, while six counties of Ulster were to remain part of the United Kingdom until after the war. Lloyd George

---

1. Charles Prestwich Scott (1846–1932): editor of Radical Manchester Guardian, 1872–1929, and its proprietor after 1905; Liberal M.P., 1895–1905; always placed great faith in Lloyd George despite differences over policy.

*told Redmond that he had placed his life upon the table and would stand or fall by
the agreement come to. Lansdowne and other Unionists raised objections and demanded
amendments which Redmond refused. Asquith lost his nerve and the proposals were
abandoned. Lloyd George did not keep his promise to resign.*

*On 5 June 1916 Kitchener was drowned on his way to Russia. Lloyd George
succeeded him on 4 July as secretary of state for war. The British offensive on the
Somme began on 1 July.*

July 26th 1916

The Irish negotiations have fallen through, & D. is depressed and worried
about the situation. The Irish are angry with him: they think he should have
upheld the original terms of the agreement, & I think they have reason to be
angry. A large section of people think that D. should have resigned when he
failed to carry those original terms in the Cabinet: he himself told me that he
would do so if the Unionists refused them. Now, however, he upholds the
P.M. and says the Irish are unreasonable. I think he has done himself harm by
his present attitude: he would have done himself less harm by leaving the
Government, but it is too late now, as he has openly upheld Asquith in the
House of Commons. I think he feels that he is in an awkward position, & I
do not know what to say to him, as I don't agree with what he has done.
I don't think he has quite played the game, but on the other hand I feel that
I must help him in every way that I can. Perhaps he has good cause for doing
what he has done. I hope it will not do him harm. His reputation in the
country was so high that it would be a pity if it were spoilt by this wretched
Irish business.

It is a long time since I kept a record. I lost heart after being ill: was very
depressed and rundown for a long time, & D. & I had constant quarrels, &
got out of tune with each other. I was sick at heart and had no courage to face
the future—the result of my illness—& D. sent me down to Walton Heath to
recuperate. I was feeling very bitter & sore with things in general, when one
night I had a dream. I dreamed that D. had been killed, & the horror that that
filled me with drove out every other feeling. I knew then that I loved him
better than anything in the world, & that if he were dead nothing else would
matter. It is extraordinary what a difference this dream made to my mental
attitude. That is all past, however, & we are now just as we always were, &
he says if I had not come to the War Office he would not have come. But
here we are, and D. seems to be getting on very well with everyone. It was
rather depressing at first, until we got into things—we felt just like children
going to a new school, & D. knew he would have great difficulties to cope
with. But everyone here seems very pleasant and anxious to help, & D. is
tackling things with great vigour. They seem to rely on him to put everything right, in spite of the fact that some of his colleagues in the Cabinet do
their best to undermine his influence secretly. Of all the Cabinet worms, I

think Montagu is the wormiest. He writes the soapiest & most grovelling letters to D., but all the time is doing his best to secure D.'s downfall. So we discovered from a Memorandum to the P.M. which he inadvertently gave Mr. Davies with some other papers. However, I think it will take a cleverer man than Montagu, with all his cunning, to ruin D. And at any rate, D. now knows what his methods are.

The Russians are very keen on D. They come and pour out all their troubles to him, believing implicitly that he can put everything right for them. Two Russian Generals came over recently to discuss the Russian difficulties in the way of munitions. They were given instructions to 'see Lloyd George', as he would be certain to help Russia. They said that over there everyone looks to him & he is the only man that counts. So they say it is in France and in Italy.

I am sharing some of the reflected glory. People have just woken up to the fact that Ll.G. has a lady Secretary, or rather, that the Sec. of State for War has a lady Secretary. I have people calling to interview me, & I have my photograph in the papers!

We spent a very pleasant weekend with Major Stern,[1] at a beautiful house which he has near Worthing—just D., Mr. Davies & I. Major S. is very entertaining, & D. was at his best too. He told us some very interesting yarns. He related to us how he met von Bethmann Hollweg at dinner the year before the war & they discussed military matters. D. mentioned the growing size of the German Army & said: 'You know, if the Germans continue to increase the size of their army, you will drive us into introducing Conscription into England.' 'Never fear', was the reply, 'we should not wait for that. The moment we thought there was the least likelihood of conscription being introduced into England, Germany would declare war on you. We could not afford to wait any longer.'

July 28th 1916
Sir George Riddell came in today. He says the Asquithites are still plotting to get D. out of power. McKenna & the rest of them (including Montagu) would stoop to the lowest means in order to get rid of him. 'They would put poison in his cup', said Sir George: 'they would stoop to the trick that was played on Parnell if they thought they would get rid of him that way. The divorce in that case was only brought about from political motives, because Parnell's opponents thought that was the way to crush him. McKenna and these others would resort to those very means if they thought it would bring Ll.G. down.' I think Sir G. was giving me a hint to be very careful, as D.'s enemies are always on the watch; and the publicity that has been given to my appointment will make it still more necessary for us to be wary.

I think perhaps D. is right after all in the course he is taking with regard

---

1. Sir Albert Stern (1878–1966). The house at Worthing (Highdown) belonged to his brother, who was on military service in the East.

to the Irish. If he were to resign now, the Asquithites might be able to exclude him from the Cabinet altogether, & thus rob him of a great part of his power. For however dear a man may be to the people, his power is insignificant to effect anything if he is not in the Cabinet. Whereas if D. remains where he is, he retains his power, & when this Government falls, he will be as powerful as any of them. 'Let him remain where he is', said a man to me today; 'and before Xmas your office will be in Downing St.'

August 2nd 1916
The Irish are clearly not going to rest until the Government is out. The P.M. seems to be a little nervous, & there is some talk of his resignation. D. says however that he thinks this is only a move to rally the Liberals to him. At present their faith in him is somewhat shaken, & he is being attacked on all sides. Mrs. A. is very alarmed at the idea of being driven from 10 Downing St., and today has written D. a very urgent letter, begging him to use his influence to send the Wimbornes[1] back to Ireland, her way of pacifying Ireland, whence danger threatens the Premiership. She does not hesitate to seek D.'s aid to keep her husband in power, but never misses an opportunity I believe of stooping to slander & intrigue to damage D. However D. treats all these letters with contempt. Society women do not appeal to him, & have never had any influence over his actions.

There is in formation at the W.O. a first-class scandal. Mrs. Cornwallis West has been using her influence with some of the Generals to get sent to the front a boy whom she had made love to, but who had apparently scorned her advances. The boy was sent to France as a result of her manoeuvres & is now in the firing line.[2] Sir A. Markham has taken up his case, & insists on an enquiry into the action of the Generals concerned. A Bill is to be passed in order to keep the thing secret, but it is gradually leaking out and rousing people's curiosity. MacLean, an M.P. was asked to sit on the enquiry. 'But I have no idea what it is all about', he said to D. 'How can I say I will sit on the Committee when I know nothing of the case it is to consider.' 'Go home', said D. to him, 'get your Bible, & read the stories of Potiphar's wife and Uriah the Hittite, & they will give you the case in a nutshell!'

D. dined last night with Sir Max Aitken,[3] & Gen. Sam Hughes[4] & other Canadians were there; also some of the W.O. generals, & also Lord Rother-

1. Lord Wimborne had been Viceroy of Ireland.
2. Mrs. Cornwallis-West, aged 63, patronised Sergeant Patrick Barrett, aged 26, and obtained a commission for him. When he rebuffed her advances, she used her influence with Sir John Cowans to have him sent to France. He was in fact merely transferred to another unit.
3. William Maxwell Aitken (1879–1964): self-made millionaire; Unionist M.P., 1910–16; cr. Baron Beaverbrook, 1917; Canadian military representative, 1915–16; minister of information, 1918; minister of aircraft production, 1940–1; member of war cabinet. 1940–2; lord privy seal, 1943–5; proprietor of Daily Express, Sunday Express, and Evening Standard; his books are a principal source for Lloyd George's political career.
4. Sir Sam Hughes (1853–1921): Canadian minister of militia and defence, 1911–16.

mere,[1] Northcliffe's brother. D. says he does not know whether Rothermere had drunk too much, & whether he was merely excited; but he suddenly started an attack on the British Army officials. The last offensive had been a failure, he said: 'The communiqués are full of lies. They are merely for the purpose of deluding the public. They are full of lies, lies, lies! I *know* it', he said. 'I know it from information which I have received from the spot! Your officials at the W.O.', he continued, turning to D., 'they are trying to mislead you. They, too, are feeding you with lies.' D. let him go on, & when his excitement had calmed down, put the other side of the case, & turned the thing off. D. says there was something in what Rothermere said, but nevertheless it created a very unpleasant scene, especially as there were officials from the War Office there. It was unfortunate, too, that the Canadians were present.

Northcliffe himself, however, writes from the front in praise of everything which he has seen. D. proposes to go over there himself next week, & then I suppose there will be a few reforms in some quarters. He has already taken up the question of transport very vigorously.

August 3rd 1916
Had a most exciting night. D. rang up about one o'clock, saying I had better go down to the cellar, as there was going to be an air raid on London. I asked him if he were going down too: he said yes. I put on some clothes & went out to see if there were anything to be seen, then sat & watched at the window for sometime on the chance of anything happening. About 2 D. rang up again to say it was all right, & I could go back to bed. 'Where have *you* been?' I asked. 'On the roof', he replied, 'but there was nothing to be seen!'

August 4th 1916
We went on Wednesday night [2 August] to a private view of the 'Somme Films', i.e. the pictures taken during the recent fighting. To say that one enjoyed them would be untrue; but I am glad I went. I am glad I have seen the sort of thing our men have to go through, even to the sortie from the trench, and the falling in the barbed wire. There were pictures too of the battlefield after the fight, & of our gallant men lying all crumpled up & helpless. There were pictures of men mortally wounded being carried out of the communication trenches, with the look of agony on their faces. It reminded me of what Paul's last hours were: I have often tried to imagine to myself what he went through, but now I *know*: and I shall never forget. It was like going through a tragedy. I felt something of what the Greeks must have felt when they went in their crowds to witness those grand old plays—to be purged in their minds through pity and terror.

1. Harold Sidney Harmsworth (1868–1940): younger brother of Lord Northcliffe; cr. Baron Rothermere, 1914, Viscount, 1919; air minister, 1917–18; after Northcliffe's death, proprietor of The Daily Mail, Evening News, Sunday Dispatch, etc.

There were few people there, most of them well known people. Most of them exceedingly kind and nice: all except Mrs. Masterman, whom D. & I both thought rather aloof and cold. Probably she disapproves of our relations, for she most surely knows, & what would be winked at between a celebrity & a society woman must not be tolerated between D. & his private secretary! However, I like Mrs. Masterman. I think she is sincere, & she is certainly very pretty, though D. says not.

August 8th 1916

Spent a very quiet and happy weekend alone with D. at W.H., marred only by the fact that on Sunday morning [6 August] we received the news of Sir Arthur Markham's death. D. was deeply upset, though he knew that Markham had not long to live. About 6 months ago D. dined with him & one or two other faithful followers, when the Liberals were all turning on him because he advocated conscription, Markham had just come from the doctor, who had told him that he had not long to live. But he was entirely unconcerned, his main theme being that he had 'done' the insurance company. They had found nothing wrong with him, & he had insured himself heavily. He probably killed himself over the Barrett-Cornwallis West affair, which he had taken up so vigorously. He was determined to go to the bottom of the matter, & D. promised him that if he did not raise the matter in the House publicly, he (D.) would get an Inquiry, & thrash the matter out. Together with the news of Markham's death came a note suggesting that the inquiry should be dropped. 'No!' said D. 'I must keep my promise to the dead.'

Markham's death upset D. for days. He cannot get it out of his mind. He was a good friend to D. & in 1911, when D.'s throat was so bad, it was Markham who pressed him to take a rest, & in his gruff way put his house at Beechboro' at D.'s disposal. 'You need a rest', said M. to D. 'You are much worse than you think you are.' 'Probably', said D. to me in telling me about it today, 'he stood much more in need of rest at that very moment than I did.' D. says Markham must have known he was near the end, for before he left the House last Thursday [3 August] he came to D.'s room & took him by the hand. 'You're a white man, George', he said & turned & went away. D. never saw or spoke to him again.

The King sent for D. to hear the details of the case, & D. explained things to him. When he told the King about Cowans,[1] the King roared with laughter. 'They tell me that he is a trifle fond of the ladies', he said. 'Yes, your Majesty', replied D., 'and I believe the ladies are very fond of him!' Speaking of Mrs. Cornwallis West, the King said: 'My father often told me that she was the most beautiful girl he had ever met.'

I heard an amusing tale about Sir W. Robertson. It appears that when excited he sometimes drops his aitches. He was asked to break the news gently to Sir Horace Smith Dorrien that his services were no longer required at the

---

1. Sir John Steven Cowans (1862–1921): quartermaster-general, 1912–19.

French front. He sent for Smith-Dorrien, and 'Well, 'Orace', he said, 'I'm afraid you'll 'ave to 'op it.'[1]

Speaking about someone who wasn't a lady, but tried to give herself the airs of one, & in doing so showed plainly that she wasn't, D. said to me: 'In order to prove that she is what she isn't, she has to be what she is!'

Montagu still writes letters every day to D. in a crawling style, ending up nearly every time with 'God bless you'; and this when we certainly know that he is intriguing the whole time behind D's back. But D. says he does not trust one of them. 'There was never a truer thing said', said D. to me, 'than Lord Rendel's advice to me when he congratulated me on becoming a Cabinet Minister. "But remember", were his words, "there is no friendship at the top."'

August 10th 1916

People are very pleased with D.'s speech to the Canadians last Monday [7 August]. He himself is rather attracted by Sir Sam Hughes, who he says is a courageous and powerful man in spite of his somewhat blustering style. 'I looked at him in the Cabinet today', said D., 'and then I looked round at the others; but Hughes was the only man there with fire in his eyes.'

September 30th 1916

Letters of congratulation on D.'s interview with American journalists are pouring in.[2] Grey felt himself bound to write a letter of protest, saying that it was an unfortunate thing to have done: D. in reply sent him a copy of a secret message intercepted from von Bethmann Hollweg to America asking them to propose a peace conference. We have discovered a wireless installation, & are intercepting all their messages, but they do not know it. This is a great find. Had not D. given his interview, Wilson would most probably have made the proposal to us, & it would have been difficult for us to refuse to discuss terms. This would spoil all chances of a great decisive victory for us. Now D.'s interview has made peace proposals impossible for some time to come. The enemy are furious, and are gnashing their teeth with rage.

On every hand we hear that D. never stood so high in the eyes of the nation. The French adore him. They say he is the one man in England who counts. He loves the French too.

Someone has just grown a new seedling saxifrage, & he wishes to call it the 'Lloyd George Saxifrage'. The plant will not be ready for division for another year. 'Tell him', said D., 'not to be too much in a hurry to call it after me. In another year the mob will probably be howling at me, & he will want to call it the "McKenna Saxifrage" or some such name!'

1. Another version is ''Orace, you're for 'ome'. Smith-Dorrien had protested against counter-attacks during the second battle of Ypres.
2. Lloyd George had made a speech advocating 'the knockout blow'. Bethmann Hollweg issued a Peace Note on 12 December, making a vague offer for negotiations with the Allies. On 18 December 1916 President Wilson invited the belligerents to state their respective aims; perhaps 'they would not prove irreconcilable'.

October 12th 1916

Lord Northcliffe paid a frenzied visit to the W.O. yesterday—D. happened to be away—& unburdened himself on Mr. Davies. D., he said, was interfering with the Army—he (Northcliffe) had heard from a friend of Sir William Robertson's that he (the C.I.G.S.) could not sleep at night because of the interference of politicians. If this sort of thing went on, Northcliffe would feel it his duty to expose it, both in the House of Lords and in his own newspapers. He wished to warn D. of this.

The fact of the matter is that Northcliffe is furious because D. does not take his advice. N. went to the front & was informed by people at G.H.Q. that everything was perfect. Naturally that is what they would tell a newspaper man. They told N. they did not want any interference from anyone— naturally. As a matter of fact they *were* rather afraid at first that D. would interfere in strategy & that sort of thing. Northcliffe evidently said to them: I will see that that is all right. I will manage that for you: leave it to me, etc., etc. He came home & told D. that everything was perfect. D. went to the front, & did not like the appearance of the *transport* question over there. In a friendly way he made inquiries on the subject: said he only wanted to be of help, & if there was anything they wanted done he would see that it was done. They admitted to him that the transport was their great stumbling block— that any minute the whole of the transport arrangements might break down, and that they would be very glad of any assistance in the matter. D. picked out a good man—Sir Eric Geddes[1]—& sent him over to discuss matters with Haig. Haig was very impressed with Geddes—confided to him everything and begged him to see to the transport arrangements at once. Thereupon a new Department was formed—a section of the Q.M.G. Department was transferred to Geddes, & the whole of the transport handed over to him. At the same time other little scandals arose in the Dept. of the Q.M.G. with the result that some officials in the Army Clothing Dept. were told to resign, & Lord Rothermere, Lord N.'s brother, appointed head of that Dept. Thereupon Northcliffe lost his head, especially as D. chaffed him on the subject of his being hoodwinked at the front over transport. Nasty paragraphs began to appear in the papers about politicians interfering with the Army. D. discovered—at least I discovered in one case, that certain generals at the front were ventilating their reactionary views to the Press, & certain officials at home—those with whose work fault had been found—were also airing their grievances to newspaper proprietors.

This week the question of Roumania has come up.[2] D. is very strong in

---

1. Eric Campbell Geddes (1875-1937): general manager designate of North Eastern railway; made a major general when he directed railway transport in France, and an admiral when he organised naval supply; first lord of admiralty, 1917-19; member of war cabinet, 1919; minister of transport, 1919-22.
2. Rumania entered the war on the Allied side on 27 August 1916. Her territories were overrun by German and Austrian armies after a short campaign.

urging that pressure should be brought to bear in the Balkans to assist Roumania and to prevent her suffering the same fate as Serbia. Robertson on the other hand wishes all our strength to remain on the Western front; being a soldier he does not look at the political side, nor does he realise what loss of our prestige following upon such a catastrophe would mean to the conduct of the war. Evidently he had been brooding over the difference of opinion between himself & D. & evidently either he or one of his staff had been talking to Northcliffe about it. Hence Northcliffe's visit, which was very opportune as it happened, for it gave D. a grievance to bring up against Robertson as a counter stroke to Robertson's grievance against him. That is always D.'s method: when you are attacked, do not stand on the defensive, but *attack yourself*! Therefore when D. received a letter of complaint this morning on the ground that D. did not back him up in his policy, D. wrote this reply.[1]

Robertson came to him almost in tears this morning, very upset by D.'s letter. However, they made it up & compromised on the subject of the Balkans, D. assuring Robertson that he did not wish to hinder him in his work, & Robertson promising to send two divisions to the Balkans to help to keep the pressure off Roumania.

However, D. does not intend to let the opportunity pass for dealing with the subject of Officials and the Press. No one who has not worked *inside* the W.O. can realise what a hotbed of intrigue and jealousy it is. The officials are powerful, especially in society and at Court, & I realise now what people meant when they talked of the danger of attempting to touch the Army or reform the W.O. At the least grievance the head of a Dept. will go to Buckingham Palace, or to the Press, & supply them with official information which should only be kept in the W.O. They will stop at nothing if they think their prestige or their standing is being menaced. I never realised what an all-powerful thing a General is—until he is out-done by another General. It is tragic—it is wicked. But I will back D. up against them in a fight. He has already won over the Transport—he beat them over the Army Clothing affair: now he is going to insure himself against being stabbed in the back, by raising the question of Officials divulging Departmental Secrets to the Press. He intends to bring it up at the War Committee next sitting. This will make it a breach of discipline for officials here to communicate anything of a confidential nature to the Press; and at any rate it will make it impossible for the Press to repeat it.

D. has one great asset on his side in this fight: i.e. he does not have any truck with society people. He neither cares for their opinion nor curries for their favour. That is the great curse of this Department. The business which it conducts can never be straight so long as this sort of thing is allowed to go on.

---

1. No letter is attached, though the marks of a paperclip remain on the original. Most of the letter is reproduced in Frank Owen, Tempestuous Journey, pp. 324–5.

As for Northcliffe, everyone says he has gone mad—suffering from a too-swelled head. He is very jealous, too, of his brother's appointment. However, he too will find that it does not pay to quarrel with D.

October 16th 1916

We were at Walton Heath yesterday—D. examining the Dardanelles papers, & trying to make up his mind as to what line he would take in giving evidence before the Inquiry.[1] We did not do much work, however, & as a matter of fact the evidence has been postponed till next week. Sir G. Riddell came in to dinner. He keeps D. informed as to all the gossip that goes on in newspaper circles, & his latest piece of information is that there is a conspiracy between Northcliffe and certain members of the Army in high offices to get rid of Ll.G. Everything which has been happening lately points to this. Northcliffe is evidently out for mischief & the matter will have to be thrashed out. Unfortunately D. can only defend himself against the charges of 'interfering with the Army' by publishing information which would be useful to the enemy; so that if N. makes public statements, as he threatens to do, a very serious state of things will have arisen. However, D. intends to call a meeting of the Army Council, at which he is going to discuss the question of information being conveyed to the Press by members of the Army Council or their immediate staff.

D. was in great spirits this morning on the way up. Nothing pleases him better than the prospect of a fight. He had an amusing dream. The French revolution was being discussed, and someone said that the movement was 'irreligious'. 'Not at all!' was D.'s retort. 'Only God had taken the wrong side in politics, and they were pulling him by the ear over to the right side!'

Lord Grey told D. of a dream which he had last week. He got on top of a bus, where he met D. who informed him that he had just seen Joe Chamberlain. 'He tells me', said D. to Grey, 'that there will be three great instances of Members of the Government being howled down in the House of Commons. The first, the time when Alfred Lyttelton was howled down when he was put up to speak instead of Balfour; the second when the Prime Minister was howled down over the Parliament Bill; the third will be when you (Grey) are howled down after Bucharest has been laid in ashes!' For Roumania's sake, let us hope there is nothing in it. But D. is pessimistic. He cannot stir them up to do anything to help in the Balkans. D. is passionately in favour of saving Roumania at all costs, but the great Generals cannot take their minds off the Western Front.

October 18th 1916

D. leaves for France tomorrow, to attend a Conference at Boulogne with

---

1. In July 1916 the government agreed to select committees of inquiry into the Mesopotamia and Dardanelles campaigns. The committees did not report until 1917. Much of the material relating to the Dardanelles was not made public.

French Ministers on the subject of Policy in the Balkans. The Prime Minister, Balfour and Grey are also going. D. did not want to go, & out of devilment suggested that McKenna should go instead. McKenna thought that there must be some ulterior reason for the suggestion (probably imagined that D. would arrange to have them all torpedoed) and insisted therefore that D. should make one of the party. 'If I had insisted on going', said D. to me, 'he would have tried to prevent it.'

October 23rd 1916
D. returned from France very disappointed with the whole proceedings. Briand, whom D. had relied upon to give him a firm backing to the policy of vigorous action in the Balkans, failed to insist upon the plans, although he outlined them clearly enough. D. said he was afraid to oppose the rest of his and our people, who were against it, except M. Thomas. So that D. stood alone, and nothing definite was decided upon in the way of helping Roumania.

D. called for me at Brighton on Sat. [21 October] where I had been staying since Thursday, and we went on to Colonel Stern's house near Goring, where we spent the weekend & returned this morning. D. & I went for a long walk yesterday morning. D. was thinking more about the speech at Cardiff on Friday than about the war. I think he has given up as hopeless the idea of sending any definite and immediate help to Roumania. He is very depressed about it however.

I forgot to record a touching story which D. heard when he was in Paris last time. General Gouraud, a chevalier of the old type, wears the military cross, the French V.C., & someone complimented him upon the honour which he had attained. 'It must be a very difficult honour to win', said his admirer. 'Monsieur', was the reply, 'it is much more difficult to live worthy of.'

Another tale which is illustrative of the splendid spirit of the French in this war is this: a young Frenchman had also won the croix de guerre for his bravery in remaining 26 hours in no man's land trying to obtain some important military information. He had three children, & someone remarked that he should not have done it, risking his life in this way when he had his children to think of. 'It was for them I did it', was the simple reply.

D. was very much taken with a remark of Briand's to the effect that 'This war is too important to be left to military men'. It is exactly D.'s view, but unfortunately he never thought of putting it quite in that way. I like D. to be the person to put things in a particularly clever way. Briand, however, seems to have the knack. He likes too to be associated with D. The other day he alluded to himself and D. as 'we two Bretons'. D. however is rather disappointed in Briand. He finds that he gives ground when attacked and cannot be relied upon to stand firm. Thomas is much more a man of D.'s calibre but has not D.'s vivacity nor brains.

October 24th 1916

M. Thomas came over to London yesterday with an urgent message to D. from the French extreme Liberals to continue to press for a vigorous Balkan campaign. This backing bucked D. up, & he went to the War Committee this morning 'full of beans', but in a most Machiavellian state of mind. He began by saying that Thomas had come over to him to impart to him the serious view his party took of the fact that nothing was to be done in the Balkans: that the English Gov. were impairing their reputation in France by the attitude they were taking up. 'And not only in France', said D., 'but in England too we shall be discredited. There will be a repetition of what happened in Serbia: we shall have to confess that there is still one more small nation that we were powerless to help. But the people will not suffer this as they suffered the fall of Serbia. They are beginning to complain, & they are asking themselves whether the present government are capable of carrying this war to a successful conclusion. You cannot say that we were not warned in time. *Two months* ago I called attention to the fact that Roumania was threatened & that something should be done *at all costs* to save her. If Roumania is overrun, the Germans have the supremacy in the Balkans. They can replenish their store of wheat and oil, they have the road to the East: what is there to hinder them from continuing the war indefinitely? I do not know that even now we have not lost the war by our fatal policy of drift in the Balkans. But of course it is too late now to do anything. Two months ago it might have been useful: now it will be of no avail. But the people will want to know why: they will want an explanation from a Gov. which has failed to help the small nations & so lost the war.'

When D. begins to talk in this strain they get frightened of him. He becomes prophetic, & his prophecies have generally come true. There is not a single thing that he has foretold that has not turned out exactly as he predicted: and they are beginning to realise it. This outburst had the effect therefore of making them wonder whether there was really not time to do something in the Balkans; & they proceeded to reverse the decisions which had been come to at the Boulogne Conference. They decided then & there to send 2 divisions to Roumania & to send a message to the French to inform them of the change of plan, & to urge them to help also. D. still pretended that it was too late, but the more he pretended the more anxious they became to prove that it was not, & they ended up by becoming quite enthusiastic about the Balkan expedition. A similar thing happened over the expedition to Salonika, when the Conference was held at Calais, & the decisions come to there were reversed the following week through the instrumentality of Thomas and D.

D.'s chief source of happiness, however, lies in the fact that he has triumphed over the 'soldiers'. He says it would have done him no end of harm for the soldiers to realise that he was not backed either by the English or the French Cabinet in his policy. Whereas now they will see that he had been able to enforce his will upon the rest of the Cabinet, & that he has a way of getting what he wants in the end. They will feel, he says, that he is a man to be reckoned with. The soldiers, he says, respect nothing so much as power, & this incident will considerably strengthen his influence & his prestige among them.

October 31st 1916

A War Committee held, at which D. brought up the point of sending some-one of influence to Russia to consult chiefly upon *military* matters. He has urged this for some time, as things are not going well between us and Russia. The Russians are dissatisfied with & mistrustful of us. They think we are selfish: that we only act for our own advantage. The changes in their Govern-ment have left us few friends there in high places. D. has constantly urged that someone should be sent to fulfil the mission upon which Lord Kitchener was bound. Today he persuaded the War Committee that Sir W. Robertson should go, & they agreed that he should be sent by the Gov. with full powers.[1] Sir W. Robertson was absent, & no protest was made on his behalf. McKenna, who would undoubtedly have opposed the matter, since it ema-nated from D., had gone to the front to see Sir Douglas Haig. He is apparently intriguing against D. behind his back, persuading Sir D. Haig and Sir W. Robertson that D. is interfering in their province & that they must get rid of him, and making bad blood between them in that way. However McKenna defeated his purpose by being absent at this point, for his protégé (Sir W.R.) is being sent away on a long voyage & will be off the scenes here for a little while. I think McKenna is the only person whom D. really detests. He does not dislike an enemy when that enemy plays the game and fights in the open, but no one could help despising and detesting a man who has given him so many thrusts from behind as McKenna has.

It is true that D. does not agree with Robertson's strategy, & that he thinks the Somme offensive is a ghastly failure: but he has made no secret of it; he tells them his views openly. And while admitting to Robertson that he (D.) has no right to interfere in the strategy of the General Staff, he contends that at the same time he cannot pretend to acquiesce when he disapproves, and that he must put his views on record. Robertson thinks that D. ought to back him up in everything: D. does not think so.

November 4th 1916

D. has succeeded in getting through a proposal for a great conference to be held in Paris with representatives of all the Allied countries, to discuss the war policy for 1917. He contended that such a conference is necessary for the successful pursuit of the war. He suggested that two representatives should be summoned from each country, & that it should be purely political, i.e. that no experts should be present. The Committee agreed. D. suggested that the

---

1. Robertson did not go to Russia.

Prime Minister should be one of our delegates: Grey suggested that D. was inevitably the second, as representing most clearly the feeling of the country. Balfour agreed, & it was determined that these two should be present at the Allied Conference to be held in Paris next week. D.'s great contention was that all the representatives should be invested with full powers to make decisions of great moment on behalf of their respective countries.

D. put his proposal at the end of an exposition which the Prime Minister said was the most logical statement he had ever heard. It was however a very damning statement, for it showed how our conduct of the war had met with failure at every turn—that everywhere we had been too late—that everywhere the enemy had gained his object. Every word of it was true, but it was put simply without any elaborate phrasing. I think it must have frightened them: at any rate it has stirred them to action in the form of agreeing to summon this big conference to examine the conduct of the war.

D. wants the political conference to be before the Chantilly Conference, which is a military conference and which is held on the 15th. He thinks that the decisions arrived at at the political conference will probably upset the applecart of the military people.

November 10th 1916
D. tabled a proposal at the War Committee for taking drastic measures with regard to the food supply of the country, which is getting serious. He suggested a shipping dictator and a food dictator, much to the disgust of Runciman & Curzon who were highly indignant. McKenna of course expressed contempt of his proposal, but D. nevertheless insisted upon putting his motion on record, a proceeding which the others dislike very much as D. can always point to it when they have failed to do anything and it is too late.

As a matter of fact, D. is feeling very sick with everything and talks of resigning & taking on the food job outside the Cabinet. He says they have made a muddle of the whole war, & he fears it is too late to do anything. He says the soldiers are quite right in resenting his interference—that he has no right to dabble in strategy—all the same, he feels certain that they are running the country on the rocks. I tell him that if he resigns he will simply be playing into their hands: but he says: no, he will simply be letting them go to hell by themselves, for that is where they will be in two years' time. All the same they want to get him out of things, & will crow if he does resign. But he will not: he is getting the upper hand of them even now: he has beaten them on every point & they are afraid of him. He has not been sleeping the last few nights, & this has added to his depression. But he will recover & be his old self again.

Haig has written him a very nice letter, inviting him to G.H.Q. when he goes over to France. D. has replied very diplomatically suggesting that Robertson should go too!

The conference has been delayed till next week. They will probably cross on Tuesday [14 November].

November 11th 1916

Col. Stern drove D. & me & Grace Stonedale down to college[1] for the afternoon. It was very jolly, & D. was very merry. It quite took him out of himself and away from all his troubles and probably did him good, as the war is beginning to prey upon his mind. We were very busy all the morning with a statement which he is preparing on the Situation for the Paris Conference, & which is a very gloomy & threatening document, & an indictment of the whole policy of the war. Grace remained at college, and Col. Stern drove D. & me back to Walton Heath, where we finished the Document, which was to be submitted to the Prime Minister before being translated into French. Little Miss Davies—typist—was also there, & D. & I tried to make her feel at home, as Mrs. Ll.G. had been rude to her in the morning, & she had been very upset by it. It is extraordinary how everyone dislikes Mrs. Ll.G. Mr. J. T. Davies was talking to me about her this morning: he says that sometimes when he is feeling particularly unfriendly to her, he tries to find some redeeming feature about her which will compensate for all her unlovely qualities. But it is impossible to find one. I have often felt the same too. She is simply a lump of flesh, possessing, like the jellyfish, the power of irritating. But I am being very nasty. I try as much as possible to refrain from commenting upon her, as she has good reason to dislike me. But she has no pride. D. has told her time & again that he does not want her in London, that he would much prefer her to live at Criccieth—when she has been making a fuss about me. I am sure I would not remain with a man who showed so plainly that my presence was not wanted.

Little Miss Davies was telling me how everyone worships D. in Wales. She says that she is quite sure they would not mind if they were told to worship him in the Chapels, instead of the Almighty!

November 13th 1916

D. still depressed: says that everything is in a muddle. He tells me there is likely to be a break in the Unionist Party. Bonar Law is very dissatisfied with the conduct of the war, and although he has not much courage with which to come to a definite split, yet he is very near to the end of his tether. Then there is D.'s quarrel with Robertson & the rest. D. says he sees no way out of it. It is too late to do anything. The Germans are cleverer than us, he says, and they deserve to win. (Very broadminded, of course, but not very helpful.) I think D. is over-anxious about the coming Conference. I think he really does consider that it will be the turning point, and that everything will depend upon the decisions that are taken there. He is determined to frighten Briand and the rest of them. I only hope that he will not be disappointed, for I feel that his resignation would mean ruin to himself and to the nation. Northcliffe has been bragging that the War Office has broken everyone who went there, & that D. will be no exception to the rule. If it were only for the sake of

---

1. Royal Holloway College, at Englefield Green.

defeating that man, I hope that D. will remain & make a fight of it. N. certainly has a swelled head, & I wonder the public stand him as they do.

As a matter of fact, the general opinion is that D. has done remarkably well with the W.O. He has carried the day on every occasion where there has been a trial of strength, & there is certainly much more evidence of energy & 'push and go' than when we came. Of course we know that there are certain people who are doing their best to plot against him & bring him down, but then there always have been people doing that sort of thing, & D. has always had to guard himself from attacks from the rear as well as frontal attacks, & the military are not nearly as skilled as he is in games of craft, nor do they possess one-half the courage that D. has in a fight. In fact, my opinion is that they are more cowardly than even the ordinary run of men, and ten times as vain.

I wanted D. to let me go to France with him tomorrow on account of my aunt's death at Versailles. My cousin is quite alone, & I wanted to go to her; but after reflection he said no: people would throw it up against him & there would be a scandal. It is a great crisis of the war, he says, & he must be very careful, for he is fighting for his life single-handed & his enemies would use this as an additional weapon against him.

November 14th 1916

Had breakfast with D. before he started. He told me that Max Aitken & Carson had been to him yesterday.[1] Bonar Law thinks of resigning, & they came to ask him if, in the event of this, he would be willing to form a Ministry. He flatly declined. He said he wouldn't think of being responsible for a Ministry to run the war at this stage. There is nothing but disaster ahead. Had they asked him, some months ago, he said, it would have been a different matter: but now, he would simply get blamed for losing the war, & have the negotiating of an unfavourable peace. Nevertheless I pointed out to him that in the event of his being offered the Premiership he would be bound to accept —he could not refuse to do his best to save the country, whatever the odds against it. But he persists in saying that he would decline. The Unionists, although they would agree to his becoming Premier, would still be distrustful of him; and rightly, too, he says, for his ideals are not theirs, & he hates their régime & their policy, & always will. The Liberals, too, in such an event, would revert to their old cry of his trying to oust the P.M., & would dislike him for having done so. However, we shall see.

D. says the Cabinet have consented to appoint a Food Dictator, who will be announced next week. It is time. D. says also that we may get conscription of women in the near future. I think it is very necessary.

---

1. Aitken's account is in Beaverbrook's Politicians and the War, vol. II, pp. 110–22; one-vol. edition, pp. 312–24. According to this, Lloyd George asked to see Aitken, not the other way round. Nor was the idea of Lloyd George's becoming prime minister discussed.

November 15th 1916

Col. Stern took a party including Mr. Davies & me to dine & to a concert last night. Very amusing. Up till now we have seen only the official side of Col. Stern—his 'Tank' side, occasionally playing the rôle of host on very respectable lines. We had heard rumours of another side. Last night we had a glimpse of it—of 'Bertie Stern', of the Smart Set. I enjoyed it, though, though I'm glad I don't belong to them. Am beginning to feel, however, that I can deal with them effectively. They are very entertaining, & I like the glitter & light and laughing, but I'm glad I don't *go home* to it! However, Col. Stern is one of the least frivolous of them, though he seems to have a considerable reputation! He is not quite sure how much I know about him!

November 18th 1916

D. returned safely last night from Paris, & we went straight down to W.H. It is a dreadful anxiety on these occasions until we hear from the Admiralty that the boat has crossed safely. The weather was very cold & the sea very rough, & D. had been rather ill, so that he was quite done up on his arrival at W.H. However, he had recovered by this morning. He says the Conference at Paris was very satisfactory in the decisions which they came to. They decided that large numbers of troops must be sent to the Balkans & every encouragement and help given to Russia in her policy. As the policy of General Alexaeff[1] is that the war will be won in the Balkans, it was tantamount to the acceptance of that theory by the Conference. Sir W. Robertson has therefore been beaten in his strategy. D. however, though pleased at having carried the point, feels that the decisions come to at these Conferences are never acted upon with sufficient vigour, and in any case he feels that it is too late now to do much in regard to saving Roumania. That is his chief anxiety at present. He feels that we have lost our chance, and he is very, very depressed at the outlook. He says he would like to resign & be made instead President of the War Committee. I feel however that his resignation would be a disaster & would be misunderstood by the public. It would be too much like 'running away'.

D. was to have dined with Bonar Law last night to talk things over, but B.L. is evidently in a wobbly state of mind and did not want to see D.[2] He is very jealous of his position as leader of the Unionist Party, & does not want to play second fiddle to anyone, even D. Max Aitken acts as the go-between between these two. He is a very good friend to D. though he confesses quite frankly that he is first, second, & third 'a Bonar Law man'. But apart from that, he is all for Ll.G. I think he is quite loyal & very patriotic, & simply wants an arrangement whereby we may obtain victory by the surest &

---

1. Chief of Russian general staff.
2. According to Politicians and the War, vol. II, p. 135; one-vol. edition, p. 337, Aitken prevented Lloyd George from dining with Law because Sir Henry Wilson would also have been present.

quickest means. He is very anxious for D. & B.L. to join forces & 'get on with the war'.

Max Aitken told Mr. Davies how Northcliffe had been to him & told him that he was out to destroy Ll.G. 'I want your help, too', he said. 'I am going to get as many newspapers as possible to help me.' Max Aitken refused. He said there was a war on & Ll.G. was the only man in the country who knew how to carry it to a successful conclusion. Therefore he (Max) would be a traitor to his country if he tried to injure him at the present moment.

November 19th 1916

D. & I went down to W.H. last night. It was very cold & cheerless down there when we arrived. The old woman who looks after the house, though a very good sort, does not know how to make the place comfortable, & Mrs. Ll.G. does not bother, or else does not know how either. There was not a scrap in the house to eat when we got down there, but fortunately we had taken a tongue & some cheese & fruit down with us, so we managed to get together some sort of a supper. D. was very rattled, but managed to cheer up eventually, & he was looking quite well & cheerful this morning when I left. He certainly does need all the love and care one can give him in the job which he has now before him.

November 20th 1916

D. informed me that he proposed to make an extensive tour of the Empire in order to rouse people to further action. As a matter of fact, it had been discussed by the Paris Conference and was now before the Cabinet. If approved, D. would go first to Russia, then to India, Greece, the Balkans, Egypt, Mesopotamia, & he might possibly go to Canada. I was very upset when he told me, knowing the dangers that would accompany such an expedition, & thinking of the lonely time I would have, though of course it would be no worse than for thousands of other women whose husbands have gone to the front. But D. then revealed the fact that he intended to take me too. He said if there were two women it would not matter, & he intended to take one other girl as a typist. At any rate, he has promised that he will not go without me.

The Report on the Barrett v. Cornwallis-West case is finished, & things look black for Sir John Cowans. It shows clearly that he used his influence to grant the request of this society woman to gratify her anger against an innocent boy whom she had wronged. D. says that it will not be possible to keep him. He says it cannot be tolerated that a Member of the Army Council should use his position in this way & allow himself to come under the influence of such a woman for the purpose of interfering with the career of 'the man at the bottom' as D. expresses it. I feel sorry for Cowans, as he seems to have been bothered & pestered by this woman until he got sick of the whole thing and wanted to finish it. How he will hate & despise

Mrs. C.-W. in future. It is she who will have ruined his career & good name.[1]

November 21st 1916

D. had a great row in the Cabinet with McKenna today. The question of Sir W. Robertson going to Russia was discussed. D. said that he left the decision in the hands of the Cabinet, that he did not wish to press for it, but that what he objected to was the impression that one of his colleagues in the Cabinet was trying to give Sir W. Robertson that D. was urging the proposal in order to get rid of Robertson. Immediately all the others demanded to know the name of the person he was alluding to. D. demurred and said that he would prefer to disclose it to the P.M. alone. But the others would not have it: several of them, they said, had been in Robertson's company, & it was only fair to them that they should be absolved from the accusation. 'Very well', said D., 'then I will tell you. It is the Chancellor of the Exchequer!' Of course McKenna denied it flatly, but D. insisted, saying,—'one of two people then is lying, and I think I know which to believe'. Eventually D. wrung it out of him in the end that 'perhaps he had not denied the suggestion that Robertson was being sent because D. wanted to get him out of the way'. That was enough for the others. The prestige of McKenna is now lower than it was before. D. literally hates him, & I do not think he will rest till he has utterly broken him.

I said to D. 'Who was it who actually told you that McKenna had said this to Robertson?' 'No one', he said; 'but I guessed that he had said it.' 'Then whom did you mean when you said that one of two people was lying? Who was the second person?' 'That was pure bluff', said D. laughing, 'but I was right, and that was how I got it out of him!'

On 20 November Lloyd George, Law, and Carson met together for the first time. Lloyd George put forward his plan for a war council of three. At a second meeting on 22 November he revealed that the prime minister was not to be a member of the war council. Law did not look kindly on this idea.

November 22nd 1916

D. dined with me last night, very weary & preoccupied. He has a big scheme on now. He wants to get Carson back again to help in the conduct of the war. Carson says he is too tired, & is sick of the whole thing, but D. tells him it is his duty to come in and help him. At present D. has to fight single-handed: it is like wielding a battle-axe, he says, against the rest of the Cabinet, in order to achieve every mortal thing that wants doing. But the effort tires him out, he says, & his energy will not last for ever. He feels that he must have some-

---

1. Cowans became quartermaster general in France.

one to support him, & less opposition to face. He thinks that if Carson came in, he, Bonar Law & D. could arrange to run the War Committee & leave the P.M. to run 'his show', i.e. the Cabinet which would not then count for much. The thing was discussed yesterday at the Cabinet, & nothing was decided, but D. thinks that if he presses hard enough he can get his way, if only the other two will back him. He is dining tonight again with Carson & Bonar Law. I hope they will soon take action. D. says that the P.M. is absolutely hopeless. He cannot make up his mind about anything, & seems to have lost all will-power.

The Empire Tour is off, for which I am not sorry. There would only have been endless plots against D., while he was away. ('There will be that, any-how', said D. when I told him.) But it does not matter so much when he is here to defend himself. Sir W. Robertson is supposed to be going to Russia, but is very sulky about it. Meanwhile the Pro-Germans in the Russian Gov. have succeeded in turning out Gen. Alexaeff, the one hope of the Russian Army. They are one by one getting rid of all the good men in Russia and putting rotters or Pro-Germans in their places.

Lord Lansdowne has issued a Memo. in which he asks for Peace. It was discussed at this morning's Cabinet. D. said that it was a very serious docu-ment, upon which the Cabinet must have an absolutely clear decision: the views of the Cabinet must be obtained upon it, & a definite understanding reached. He (D.) was one of those who would not think of peace at the present moment. He believed in the knock-out blow. He urged that the views of the Cabinet should be definitely ascertained. It was agreed that there should be time given for the consideration of the Document & the matter brought up again. It looks as though if Lansdowne is outvoted he will have to resign. You cannot have a man in a War Cabinet who thinks we ought to make peace.

November 23rd 1916

D. lunched today with Lord Derby, & Sir Douglas Haig and Lord Cavan[1] were present. D. said he talked to Haig as a father to a child, and as he has never been talked to before. D. said Haig listened to him all the more because he had seen D. fighting alone for the Army at the Cabinet this morning. But at lunch he gave Haig his frank opinion. He said that there was a feeling of uneasiness in the country about our military operations. We have been talk-ing of 'great victories' for the last few months, but in the end it only means that we have advanced five or six miles. We have been using up all our splendid men and our hoarded munitions, & what has it resulted in: six miles at the most. The people know that this is not victory. The Germans take 250,000 men and they capture vast cornfields and valuable oil-wells. Hinden-

---

1. Frederick Rudolph Lambart, 10th Earl of Cavan (1865–1946): field marshal; com-manded XIV corps in France, 1916–17; commanded British troops in Italy, 1918; C.I.G.S., 1922–6.

burg[1] is full of agility & resource. He is like a well-trained pugilist, not hitting doggedly at one & the same place all the time, but skipping about and hitting his enemy where he perceives him to be weakest. He does not go on punching, punching at the same place when he sees that he is not gaining a clear advantage by this process. The people here feel that with us there is no ingenuity. They would like to see a little more imagination, a little inventiveness, a little originality. They feel that at present there is none of this, and they are getting a little impatient. D. said that Haig listened very attentively to what he said, & Lord Derby told him afterwards that he and the others were most impressed by what he said. Lord Derby is quite devoted to D. He has unbounded admiration for him, & I know is absolutely loyal. He is a true patriot and a thorough gentleman, & D. has great need of people such as this to serve him at present.

November 25th 1916
D. lunched with Bonar Law & Carson, & Bonar Law afterwards went straight to the P.M. to put his ultimatum to him, i.e. that Bonar, Carson & D. should form a Committee of three to run the war, otherwise he—Bonar Law— would resign. The P.M. of course put the matter off, saying that McKenna would fight very hard against it, and he must be given time. That means that Mrs. McKenna will oppose it, & that is what will weigh with the P.M. No one else attaches any importance to McKenna & what he says and thinks. It is intolerable that things like that should be allowed to weigh with the P.M. while we are in such grave danger of losing the war. [2]

    Mrs. Asquith too is using all her arts to prevent a smash. She insisted upon D. going with her yesterday to the Abbey to hear the Elijah—called for him at the W.O. and drove with him there. One can always read the signs of the times when Mrs. A. pays attention to D. It means that she knows that the position of the P.M. is wobbling, & that it lies in D.'s power to save or smash him. However, though things like that may have weighed with D. formerly, I do not think that he will allow such considerations to weigh under the present circumstances.

    I drove down to Sutton with D. this afternoon. He was terribly tired. I told him that I do not think that the Committee of three idea is a good one. It would be much better to smash up the Government & get rid of the P.M. altogether. D. says that Derby is of the same opinion. I think D. has his doubts about it too.

November 27th 1916
The P.M. has refused B. Law's ultimatum, & D. says he will resign. He is

1. Chief of German general staff.
2. The so-called ultimatum was a memorandum drafted by Aitken and approved by Carson, Law, and Lloyd George at lunch on 25 November. Law took the memorandum to Asquith but, according to Politicians and the War, vol. II, pp. 149–50; one-vol. edition, pp. 351–2, did not threaten to resign. Asquith did not refer to opposition from McKenna.

waiting to see what Bonar will do. Bonar says the P.M. practically wept to him, telling him how great an affection he had for him & how much he relied upon his help in this great struggle. This has made B. waver. D. says he wishes he could tell him what the P.M. really thinks of him, how when D. suggested that he should be included in the dinner at Downing St., a few weeks ago, the P.M. refused, saying that Bonar 'had not the brains of a Glasgow baillie'. The P.M. will cry to anyone if it serves his purpose. But D. has practically made up his mind to go out of the Government. He says that incidentally it will save his life. But I am perfectly certain that if anything there will be more work for him to do outside than in. He cannot slacken his efforts to try & bring the country round & make a last attempt to win the war. When Bucharest falls will be his time. The people are getting furious & the House of Commons exasperated, & I cannot help feeling that if they would only summon up courage to turn the Government out this would be a solution of the present stalemate. D. would then get his chance. I know the country would back him solid.

They say that a German aeroplane has just been dropping bombs in Sloane Square. But we brought down two Zeppelins last night.

November 30th 1916
B. Law, Carson & D. have drawn up a memo on the reconstitution of the War Committee & its new powers, & a copy of it has been sent to the P.M.[1] If the P.M. refuses to accept it, then there will be a smash. The only weak spot is Bonar Law, who cannot make up his mind to strike. If D. strikes alone, it will mean his forming an opposition, but if he & Bonar strike together it will mean the smashing up of the Government. Asquith has great influence over Bonar, & is using it to his full advantage. D. says that the P.M. is absolutely devoid of all principles except one—that of retaining his position as Prime Minister. He will sacrifice everything except No. 10 Downing St. D. says he is for all the world like a Sultan with his harem of 23, using all his skill and wiles to prevent one of them from eloping. However the whole country is pretty sick of him. We are receiving countless anxious letters from all parts of the country, urging D. to take over affairs. He seems to be the only one in whom the people have any confidence, & I am certain that if he were to resign now he would have the backing of the whole country.

Von Donop has received notice to quit. Since before the formation of the Ministry of Munitions, D. has been suspicious of him. On every possible occasion he has done his best to obstruct the output of munitions for the Allies. D. says that either he is deliberately trying to help the enemy, or else it is his German blood unconsciously asserting itself. He could not have helped

1. This was in fact the memorandum drawn up on 25 November and communicated to Asquith by Law. Asquith more or less rejected it on 26 November. Lloyd George had an inconclusive conversation with Asquith on 27 November. Lloyd George presented a memorandum of his own to Asquith on 1 December, and Asquith rejected it the same day. (Politicians and the War, vol. II, pp. 185–7; one-vol. edition, pp. 387–9.)

the Germans more if he had been in their pay. Moreover he has always sided with McKenna in his attacks on D. and has never missed an opportunity of opposing D., & trying to thwart him. D. vowed he would get rid of him before he went, and I am surprised he has left it as long as he has. The old man has taken it very well however—simply sent a note to ask D. when he should go.

Cowans also has got to disappear, though I think D. is rather sorry for this. The King, however, ventured to send a message to say that in his opinion Cowans had done nothing to justify being dismissed, which made D. very angry, as he said the King had no right to try & use his influence in that way. So that for this reason, D. is not so sorry that Cowans is going. It will show the King, he says, that his words have no weight in matters of this kind. I am sorry for Cowans, but he is being made Q.M.G. in France. D. says that these dismissals will make the soldiers more afraid of him. It will show them that he has power to enforce his will.

December 1st 1916

D. went to see the P.M., who as usual would not give a definite answer to the Memo. He says he will see D. tomorrow & tell him his decision. D. will be well backed up if he resigns. Northcliffe has turned up again, grovelling, and trying to be friends with D. again. He sees that the other game will not work and if there is anything big happening Northcliffe would hate to be out of the know. But D. has beaten him once again. He (N.) acknowledges that D. is the only man who can save the country, & N. will back him. D. does not think that the P.M. will accept the terms. He is rallying all his forces round him, and will make a supreme effort to retain his position.

December 2nd 1916

The P.M. has sent a reply to D.'s Memo, but it simply proposes an alternative which is if anything worse than the old régime. Moreover he insists on being Chairman of the new Committee, & the vital point of D.'s proposal was that the P.M. should have no part in it at all. The P.M. also insists that the Cabinet shall have the final word in all matters, which of course nullifies everything which might be achieved by the setting up of a new Committee. D. was to have seen the P.M. at eleven this morning, but when he received the P.M.'s letter he refused to go across, as he said there was no point in his going as the P.M. would not agree to his proposals. D. has this afternoon written a letter of resignation, which he intends to hand in at 12 o'clock tomorrow.[1] He is giving Bonar Law till then to make up his mind definitely, but has informed him that he (D.) will go out whether Bonar does or not. Max Aitken is doing his best to persuade Bonar to come out, but has told Bonar that he (Max Aitken) is going to put his money on Ll.G., and will give

---

1. There is no other evidence that Lloyd George wrote a letter of resignation this day. He was in fact waiting for the result of Law's meeting with the Unionist ministers on 3 December.

him the backing of The Express.[1] This will be a great asset to D., even if Bonar refuses to come out. Bonar is insisting upon putting personal considerations before national—says he cannot secede from Lansdowne and Chamberlain—they have been so good to him! Bob Cecil they say is furious at the idea of D.'s proposals even being considered. 'This means', he said to Bonar, bursting with rage, 'that George is practically dictator!' 'So it does!' said D. to me when he was relating the story. And so it does! But I feel that as long as Asquith is there it will be impossible to get a move on.

D. sent for Montagu this afternoon & showed him his letter of resignation. He says he knows that anything he shows or tells Montagu will go straight to the Prime Minister! And sure enough, this evening a message came through that the P.M. is coming up to town tomorrow. D. is quite firm that unless the P.M. agrees to his proposal re the War Committee, he will resign.

December 3rd 1916
D. & I motored down this morning, I to Wallington, & he to Walton Heath. The Unionists held a meeting in which they called upon the P.M. to resign.

This afternoon D. went to see the P.M. They thrashed the matter out, & the outcome of it is that the P.M. has agreed to D.'s terms contained in his Memo, & D. expects things to turn out all right. All the newspapers are wildly excited. Rumours are abroad of D.'s resignation. I cannot help wishing that Asquith would *not* agree, & then there would be a smash, & things would be thoroughly cleaned up. Things are very, very bad all round. However, it seems that D. has persuaded the P.M., who told Bonar Law that 'he *would not* resign'. Which shows that that is really the only thing that he cares about.

December 4th 1916
Things seemed more settled this morning, & the P.M. has permission from the King to reconstruct the Cabinet. D. was angry with me this morning because I told him he would disappoint everyone unless he went the whole hog. We have had endless letters & telegrams assuring him that the country will back him up in any steps that he takes for the more vigorous prosecution of the war. He has the country solid behind him, & I feel certain he could turn Asquith out easily. It is just a group of politicians who are rallying round Asquith & allowing him to live in a fool's paradise. McKenna is going about saying that Ll.G. is doing this simply to get rid of him. 'He must think I am a very small man', was D.'s reply when he was told of this. Austen Chamberlain is furious with Bonar Law for 'selling his colleagues', as he calls it.

We are now given to understand that the Tory meeting yesterday was *hostile* to D., & that the reason for their demanding the resignation of the P.M. was that they thought it would cut the ground from under D.'s feet; for if the P.M. resigned (so they argue) D. would be called upon to form a new Ministry, & would fail, owing to the fact that these Unionists would fail

---

1. Aitken had just acquired the controlling shares in The Daily Express.

to back him up.[1] The King would then send for the P.M. again to form a Ministry, & then his position would be stronger than ever. They forget the fact that D. is not bound to form a Ministry from among the same people as before. As a matter of fact he would, if called upon, be able to form a very much stronger Cabinet from among his own supporters than the one which now exists.

It now remains to be seen whether the P.M. will adhere to the proposals which he accepted yesterday, or whether he will go back on them. I think it most likely that he will try and wriggle out of them.

December 5th 1916

The P.M. has this morning written to D. to tell him that he cannot accept the proposals. He must be Chairman himself, & he must have Balfour as First Lord. This of course is impossible for D. to accept, & he has therefore sent in his resignation. The P.M. was evidently encouraged by his reception by a section of the Liberals at the House yesterday, & also by the explanation conveyed to him by the Unionists of their resolution on Sunday [3 December].[2] D. is much happier now that the course is clear. We had dinner together last night, & he told me that when once his mind was clear as to the best course to take, he was never unhappy as to the consequences of his action. He was willing to accept the result, whether unpleasant or pleasant. He is now willing to suffer loss of Office, comparative poverty, or whatever comes to him, for it is quite clear that the step he is taking is the right one. I cannot think that the people will suffer him to be out of power for long. Already they say there are disturbances in the streets at the rumour of D.'s resignation. They say the soldiers especially are alarmed at the idea of his going out of Office. Even the soldiers at the Head here are on his side now, & Sir William Robertson has informed him that they will back him up. 'Stick to it', he said to D., 'you are all right!' D. is quite happy. He says he would not be sorry to be out of Office, so that he could have a rest. But I tell him that he must not think of taking a rest until the War is over. Everyone is looking to him, and to him alone, to pull us through, and he must not disappoint them. It is the greatest moment of his life. All classes seem ready to accept him as Dictator & to leave the direction of the War to him. Some of the messages he has received are very touching & bring a lump to one's throat.

They say Mrs. Asquith has gone quite mad & is rushing all over the place

1. This is the most controversial point in the affair. Aitken certainly thought that the Unionist decision was hostile to Lloyd George, and the information here probably came from him. The Unionist ministers later claimed that they had merely wanted an end to the crisis and did not take sides between Asquith and Lloyd George.
2. How did this explanation reach Asquith? Beaverbrook, (Politicians and the War, vol. II, pp. 239–40; one-vol. edition, pp. 441–2), alleged that the leading Unionists visited Asquith on 4 December. Austen Chamberlain, who was one of them, asserted that they did not meet Asquith until 5 December, after the decision to fight had been taken, and Chamberlain was undoubtedly right. What communications, if any, passed previously between Asquith and the Unionist ministers will remain for ever unknown.

sending messages to people. She is most abusive about D., & cannot think of things bad enough to say about him.

D. has just been in to tell me that the P.M. has resigned. The Unionists informed him that the situation was too critical for any other course, but they have promised to make it as difficult as they can for D. to form a Cabinet. The P.M. on his part is trying to extract promises from the Liberals that they will not serve under D. What will happen? I am glad it has come to an open fight, for in a fight I would back D. against anyone. The P.M. wanted to stick to his position, & fight, but they would not let him. 'He won't fight the Germans', said D., 'but he will fight for Office.' My opinion is that as soon as he is out of office, & the power is in D.'s hands, the whole crowd will begin to toady to D., & will be only too glad to serve under him.

December 6th 1916

A *terrible* day—we were all nearly sick with excitement and suspense. In the morning B. Law was sent for by the King to form a Cabinet. D. urged him to do it, but B.L. was very afraid. In the afternoon Ministers, including the P.M. were sent for to the Palace, in order that things might be 'talked over', with a view apparently to reconciling the differences between the Ministers. It seemed likely that after all the P.M. would come in in some capacity, & even that he might agree to D.'s original terms. But it seems that the others would not agree to his coming in as P.M., & they separated with a view to the P.M. considering whether he would consent to serving under another P.M. i.e. Bonar Law, Balfour, or Ll.G. He went away—Northcliffe says to consult McKenna as to what he should do. Northcliffe apparently has the wires tapped, & knows the innermost secrets of everything that has been going on. However that may be, he swears that in every step the P.M. has taken in this crisis he has acted on McKenna's instructions as to what he should do. In this case McKenna told him most emphatically—according to Northcliffe—that he was not to accept a subordinate position, McKenna no doubt being aware that his own chances of a job were nil under any other P.M.

Therefore a message was soon received to the effect that Asquith refused to serve. Bonar Law we heard a little later, has informed the King that he could not undertake to form a Cabinet. He felt no doubt that he would not get the support of either Liberal or Labour, & so would be totally unable to form a Coalition Gov. Accordingly D. was sent for about 7.0 o'clock & was asked to form a Gov. & he said he would. I saw him directly he returned & he was very pale & said he would like to run away to the mountains. 'I'm not at all sure that I can do it', he said. 'It is a very big task.' However we were at the W.O. till after midnight, D. conferring with B. Law, Carson, & others. It was agreed that D. should meet Labour & see what he could do with them. The hostile section of the Unionist party, including Cecil, Chamberlain, Curzon & one or two others, were to be interviewed by B. Law who should try to gain their support. By this time a message had been received from the

P.M. to the effect that his Liberal colleagues had refused in a body to serve under D. Such patriotism! However, I think he can do without them! We all went home very tired & excited, but happy. There was the light of battle in D.'s eyes for the Liberals had deliberately challenged him. But I think he was confident of victory, though he would not own it. 'I'm not Prime Minister yet', he said to me. 'Oh yes you are', I replied. I know he will not fail.

December 7th 1916
The Labour meeting this morning was a great success. Everything depended on it, and D. was at his craftiest. They asked him awkward questions, & he put them off with chaff. The majority of them came there sulky, hostile, and they went away laughing and friendly. They adjourned to consider whether they would give him their support, but D. had no doubt as to what their answer would be. Later on in the day they sent word that they would support him. This was a great victory, & a great set-back to the Asquithites, who in the meantime are rallying their forces to try and bring D. down, but their supporters are ratting from hour to hour. We hear today that there are 40 odd Liberal members who will support D. through thick and thin, & 129 who will support him if he forms a Government. These with the Labour people & a considerable number of Unionists will form a formidable backing, & D.'s hopes rose. This morning before the Labour meeting things were rather gloomy, for Edmund Talbot[1] came & said he could not rally the hostile group of Unionists, who might if they held out make things very awkward in the House. However B. Law was able during the day to bring them round—but at a price! By taking Balfour at the Foreign Office with Lord Robert Cecil as Chief of the Blockade, & Chamberlain at the India Office. I am sorry, for I feel it is a blunder to have those two at the F.O. I wish D. could make some other arrangement. We do not want Bob Cecil in the Government at all. He is spiteful & malicious & will do D. no good. It was very amusing to see them tonight when they came to see D. & confer with him. They were actually kept waiting ten minutes or $\frac{1}{4}$ of an hour— all these great Tories—Curzon, Cecil & the rest, who a few years ago would not have shaken hands with him & who could find no words strong enough to express their bitterness & hatred—now waiting to be granted an audience of the little Welsh attorney!

B. Law is helping D. all he can. After the Labour meeting he said to D. 'Well, you've courage, George! You've courage!'

In the afternoon D. was in high spirits. 'I think I shall be Prime Minister before 7.0 o'clock', he said to me. And he was.

---

1. Lord Edmund Talbot (1855–1947): Unionist chief whip, 1913–21; viceroy of Ireland, 1921–2; cr. Viscount FitzAlan, 1921.

Diary 1917

Lloyd George was duly established as prime minister. His projected war committee of three became a war cabinet of five (the other original members were Lord Curzon, Arthur Henderson, Bonar Law, and Lord Milner, with Maurice Hankey as secretary). The traditional cabinet disappeared. Carson, the third conspirator, was not included in the war cabinet. He became first lord of the admiralty. Balfour became foreign secretary. Lord Derby, previously under-secretary, became secretary of state for war and was soon under the spell of Sir William Robertson, who remained C.I.G.S.

Lloyd George believed that a greater measure of Allied cooperation was needed in order to win the war. An Allied conference for this purpose was held at Rome in the first days of January 1917. It achieved little. Lloyd George wished to shift the main offensive to the Italian front. The British and French generals opposed this and, to Lloyd George's discomfiture, Cadorna, the Italian chief of staff, opposed it also. No strategic decision was taken at Rome. The conference had however a surprising strategical outcome. Lloyd George was much impressed by General Nivelle, who had just succeeded Joffre as French commander-in-chief, and accepted Nivelle's plan for a new offensive on the western front. Thus, a conference promoted to prevent a western offensive turned the principal opponent of such an offensive into its advocate.

January 9th 1917

Just waiting for D. to return from Rome. I shall breathe again when he arrives. I have not been able to sleep while he was away, owing to anxiety. I felt certain the Germans would try to get at him in some way or other, & we have had many warnings. To increase my fears, the portrait of Bacon in the Cabinet room fell down a night or two ago, smashing the big clock on the mantelpiece in its fall. This of course was a bad omen, & depressed me very much. Then came the news of Mr. Selous' death in East Africa. It seems that no-one, old or young, is to be spared in this terrible war. Mr. Selous was a dear old man. He took me over his museum himself, telling me thrilling stories connected with the hunting of this or that animal. I loved him at first sight & indeed we seemed greatly drawn to each other, judging from a remark which I heard he made to Mrs. Selous. Altogether, I have felt perfectly miserable since D. went. We had a supremely happy week before he left, & saw the New Year in together. We have both recovered from the strain of the crisis, which had made us both very bad-tempered & irritable, specially with each other. The incessant work & worry & excitement, together with the late nights and irregular hours & meals, got on our nerves. D. developed a cold & so, having retired to bed, obtained relief in that way. I, not being ill, merely became more grumpy, until Xmas weekend, when we took a rest. The rest of D.'s family went off to Criccieth, so that he & I were able to go down to W.H. for a few days, & by the time we returned to town we had recovered our normal state of health.

The day of D.'s speech in the House was the worst. Apart from having been ill, he had worked himself up into a perfect fever, for, after all, such a lot depended on his statement. As the time drew near for the delivery of the speech he was quite pitiful, & almost ill with fright. Of course it was a great ordeal for him, his position being a most extraordinary one, with nearly all the Tories backing him, a large number of the Liberals in Opposition, & his late Chief sitting on the Bench opposite! But he delivered it magnificently, & was splendidly received. It was a great speech, & I was proud of him, though it was impossible for a long time to realise that he was really Prime Minister.

January 10th 1917
D. returned safely, after a dreadful crossing. Owing to a blunder on the part of the Foreign Office, there was no packet boat ready for the party at Calais, & they had to cross in a destroyer that happened to be there. They had a frightful journey as the weather was dreadful.

D. very pleased indeed with the trip. He was given a right royal welcome in Rome, & held the Conference in his grip, according to all accounts. By sheer persistence he got Sarrail[1] there, though the Italians did their level best to prevent it, as they do not approve of Sarrail. D. says he is a remarkable, fascinating character, handsome, impulsive, full of fire. The situation became rather acute when the Balkan question came up for discussion, D. & the Italians siding against the French and Russians. The sitting that day terminated without an agreement having been arrived at, & D. was at a loss to know what to do. In the evening a message came up to him that Sarrail was waiting below and wanted to see him alone. He came up, & begged D. to agree to giving him a free hand in the Balkans. His idea was to march into Greece, & shoot every man who attempted to stop his army. D. said he could not possibly agree to it. 'If you march into a country that is not defended & start shooting down the peasants', he said. 'It is simply a repetition of what

1. Maurice Paul Emmanuel Sarrail (1856–1929): French general; commanded French 3rd Army, 1914; commander-in-chief of Allied Forces in the Orient, 1915–17; the only Republican general.

happened in Belgium, & the Germans would always hold it up against us.' 'Well, but you need not know anything about it. I will take the whole of the responsibility, if only I have your approval of the idea.' D. said he could not possibly agree to this. However, they talked a little, & then D. said: 'Look here: I promise you that whatever happens in the Balkans, I & my colleagues will see that you get fair play.' 'Done!' said Sarrail. 'Here's my hand upon it.' They shook hands, & Sarrail went away satisfied, & intimated to his Gov. representatives that he had come to an agreement with Lloyd George. They were very much upset & could not understand it. 'We parted from the Conference & things looked as though they could not be settled. Then Sarrail comes to us & says he has been to see you, & is prepared to agree to your propositions.' They did not understand the sympathy between the temperaments of two men like Ll.G. & Sarrail. The latter knew that Ll.G. would not let him down, & was prepared to leave the whole of his fortune in D.'s hands.

D. also had an interview with the Queen of Italy. He says she is a nice gentle creature, bound up in her children, her husband & her home. She gave him a book of pictures of her hospital, which he has given me to keep. He brought me home too an exquisite little marble model of the child taking a thorn out of his foot; & also a beautiful necklace of corals.

I am so happy now he is back. I did not realise how much I had worried until the relief came. The Italians said they quite expected the train to be blown up. Rome is infested with Germanophils. I am to go with D. next time. D. made a fuss because there was no-one in the party who could write & translate French, so that Col. Hankey has told me that I must be ready to go next time there is a journey.

The following entry illustrates the original notes from which Frances Stevenson usually wrote up her diary.

January 12th 1917

> Speech.
> Greatness of a P.M.
> Altered constitution of Gov.
> Mrs. Asquith—back in 6 weeks.

January 15th 1917

D. returned from W.H. very fit after weekend, though we had both been very miserable without each other. D. said he would have sent for me, only that he felt it would not quite be playing the game with Mrs. Ll.G. 'She is very tolerant', he said, 'considering that she knows everything that is going on. It is not right to try her too far.'

D. had an important conference today. General Nivelle[1] & Haig were over, on the question of the next offensive. D. first of all met the English generals this morning, & a trial of strength arose between him and Haig. D. asked as to the length of the line which it had been suggested should be taken over from the French by the British. This had already been discussed in Rome, but nothing decided. 'Oh', said Haig, 'that has already been decided by Nivelle & myself: no further discussion is needed.'

D. turned on him. 'That is a question', he said swiftly, 'to be decided by the War Cabinet; and it will be discussed by the War Cabinet.' The discussion then proceeded.

D. then raised the question of officers. 'The French', he said, 'have of course a much higher percentage of trained officers. What is our percentage?' 'Oh, that is not to the point', said Haig. 'I wish to know', insisted D., 'what percentage of trained officers we have! Is it ten percent?' 'Well', said Haig, insolently, 'supposing it is ten percent?' 'There is no "supposing" about it', said D. turning on him angrily. 'I ask you for a definite statement. I have a right to know & I *will* know.'

Sir William Robertson & the others were getting frightened, expecting a row. But Haig saw that he must give in & supplied the figures. He proceeded, however, to run down the French. They had no infantry, he said: their officers were just fat tavern-keepers, no good at anything. 'Well, all I can say', broke in D. sharply, 'is that with no infantry & fat tavern-keepers for officers they have taken more guns and more ground than the British with half the casualties. And in that case their generals must be wonderful men.' This was a nasty one for Haig, for everyone knows that the French generals are simply splendid, much better than the British, but of course that was the last thing Haig would care to admit. However, he had just let himself in for it!

This afternoon D. met the whole lot together—French and English & another trial of strength arose. The French want us to take over 15 miles of their line, which means that we must put 4 divisions more into the field. Of course Haig opposed this. D. backed up the French. 'If we take over that line', he said, 'it means that the French will have four more divisions to put into their manoeuvring army. If we do not, we shall simply take a trench or two with these four divisions & the French will not be able to complete their manoeuvre. Moreover, their soldiers have been fighting $2\frac{1}{2}$ years—ours only 6 months. It stands to reason that men with $2\frac{1}{2}$ years training must be far better than men with only 6 months.' Haig disagreed. 'Well then', retorted D., 'all I can say is that if $2\frac{1}{2}$ years is not better than six months to a soldier, it is the biggest condemnation of military training I have ever heard! If we lend them the men, they will take twice as much ground with half the loss.

1. Robert George Nivelle (1856–1924): French general; succeeded Pétain in command of 2nd Army at Verdun, May 1916; succeeded Joffre as commander-in-chief of French armies in north and north-east France, December 1916; superseded by Pétain, April 1917.

This has been proved. Therefore it seems best to me that we should take over their line, so that they may have the extra men.'

'You rubbed it in well', I said, 'that the French have fewer casualties than we do.'

'Yes', he replied, 'and I mean to. Haig does not care how many men he loses. He just squanders the lives of these boys. I mean to save some of them in the future. He seems to think they are his property. I am their trustee. I will never let him rest. I will raise the subject again & again until I *nag* him out of it—until he knows that as soon as the casualty lists get large he will get nothing but black looks and scowls and awkward questions.'

The question then arose of the *time* of the offensive. Nivelle wanted it next month—February. Haig wanted to wait until May. D. was inclined to hesitate until Nivelle told him the reason—because he said, the Germans had not realised until the Somme what an enormous amount of munitions we had. Now they are putting forth an immense effort to raise a quantity for the next push. So that the sooner our offensive begins the better. 'But in any case', said D., 'I should have backed Nivelle against Haig. Nivelle has proved himself to be a Man at Verdun; & when you get a Man against one who has not proved himself, why, you back the Man!'

I hope D. will not go too far in this backing of the French against the English, otherwise our generals will get vicious. But I think he is perfectly right in all his theories as to the respective worth of the generals. All our men who came back from the front express the same wish—that the French would lend us some of their generals.

February 1st 1917

D. has been preparing for his great speech on Saturday [3 February] at Carnarvon & has not been able to make up his mind whether to attack the Asquithians who are secretly plotting against him with great energy. Someone advised him to see Asquith & have a frank talk on the subject but he eventually decided not to. He thinks he will leave them to work out their own ruin. Meanwhile they are still holding on to the party funds, have set up an organisation of their own in Abingdon Street, but sent a message to us that our Whips were too active & that we were breaking the observance of the no-party agreement!

Personally I hate the idea of Montagu hanging round. He is not to be trusted & I feel sure he is a spy. I spoke to D. about it but he said: 'Don't you worry: I know my Montagu; I only tell him things that I want Asquith to know!' I think D. knows what he is about, too, but you cannot be too careful of these people.

Hankey, Secretary to the Cabinet, is full of admiration for D. He is amazed at the amount of work that is being got through now. He says that two years ago he warned Asquith: 'We shall win on land & be beaten at sea unless proper precautions were taken.' In spite of this, nothing was done & everything has been left to D. to do in the six weeks he has been in Office. D. in telling me this, finished up by saying: 'I wonder whether I have come into this show in time!' At any rate he is doing as much as any human being possible could to inspire the people with courage, to see that the necessary emergency measures are passed, and to tackle every difficulty bravely. He is very fit & in very good form, though I have to remind him to take exercise or else he forgets & then gets a little sluggish. We went for a two hours' walk on Walton Heath last Sunday [28 January] & talked the speech over. His courage and good spirits are amazing. I cannot help wondering sometimes how he keeps up, with so many things to worry him. He tells me that he could not go on without me, & I like to believe that that is true, for I love to think that I am helping him a little.

I wanted to go to Carnarvon with him but he will not take me to North Wales. He says his old uncle would see at once what our relations were, & it would upset him. I always feel nervous and unhappy too, when he is making a speech, in case something should go wrong.

D. has been very unhappy this week owing to the change from No. 11 to No. 10. They did not bother to get a comfortable room ready for him & the first night he came down to my office to work after dinner. The second night he did not go up to dinner at all as he & Mrs. Ll.G. were not on speaking terms. She had closed the bedroom windows on the quiet, thinking that the room was cold, but knowing that he always gets a headache when he sleeps with closed windows. He was furious when he found out, as it made him feel seedy all day. She does not study him in the least—has hung up some hideous family portraits painted by some cheap artist, though he has had them taken down more than once before. In fact, the whole house is hideously uncomfortable at the present moment, quite unworthy of a Prime Minister & very irritating to him, for he has a keen sense of what is beautiful & artistic & what is not.

Mr. Bonar Law came in during lunch today & D.'s speech was discussed. B.L. said he hoped D. would not get into the habit of *reading* his speeches as it took away so much of the effect. 'Well', said D., 'I always feel inclined to throw away my notes but I find that if one trusts to the audience one is apt to be led away to say foolish things on the spur of the moment.' 'If you don't mind my saying so', was Bonar's reply, with a twinkle in his eye, 'I think that fact has contributed in a large measure to the success of your speeches!'

As a matter of fact, nowadays D. has to think more of what the effect will be on the *reader* than on the *listener* of his speeches. They are circulated all over the world as soon as ever they are uttered, so that there is no time to correct a slip or indiscretion, and therefore it is of the utmost importance that everything that he says should be prepared beforehand & he does not always have time to commit it to memory.

February 3rd 1917

The Derby poisoning trial came on today.[1] D. was not in the least upset when the facts were made known to him—rather amused than otherwise.

Spoke to D. at Criccieth on the phone this morning. He seemed quite cheerful. Returns tomorrow night. Very dull & depressing without him.

William Watson has written a beautiful poem about him in The Manchester Guardian. It brought tears to my eyes & a lump in my throat.

February 5th 1917

D.'s speech a great success. He returned last night looking very fit in spite of long & cold journey. Some say it is the greatest speech ever made. F. S. Oliver wrote to Carson today saying that the peroration was the greatest utterance since Lincoln's Gettysburg speech. That is rather extraordinary, as D. was reading that very speech to me last week at Walton Heath, & he said he thought it was the greatest thing that Lincoln ever uttered.

On 31 January 1917 the German government announced the opening of unrestricted submarine warfare. On 2 February President Wilson broke off relations with Germany, though without declaring war.

D. has been working like a Trojan all day & is quite done up. There is an acute crisis between America & Germany and it may end in war between them. D. saw the American Ambassador today. The latter says that D. has no idea how much the Americans think of him. Everything he says is read with greediness & his actions are followed with intense interest.

February 7th 1917

Opening of Parliament today by the King. D. returned here after the opening ceremony & did not go back to the House for the afternoon's business. This very much offended the bad-tempered section of the house, i.e. the hostile Liberals. They tried to make things as unpleasant as they could and will continue to do so whatever anyone may say about the No-Party agreement during the war. When D. heard of what had passed in the House, he said: 'I think I shall have to get rid of this Parliament. It is an Asquith Parliament and I want a Parliament of my own.' I should not be surprised if we had a general election before the summer. That, however, is what the pacifist members are afraid of, for they know the majority of them would not have an earthly chance of getting back.

I think D. is working too hard. He has people to breakfast, meetings all the morning, a business lunch, meetings all the afternoon and evening up till dinner-time, then more often than not a business dinner. But besides the work,

---

1. A crazy scheme to poison Lloyd George.

he has all the worry & the awful responsibility for the whole conduct of the war. I am afraid he will break down under the strain. However, I have succeeded in persuading him to take a short walk every day. Last week he scarcely took any exercise at all, and became quite fagged out. He is looking much better for the little exercise he is taking.

The tension still remains acute between America and Germany. D. hopes America will declare war, as he thinks it would bring peace nearer our grasp. 'It will be very lucky for me', he said to me, 'if they do so, for it will help me in my job. The people too will be convinced of my good luck & it is a very good thing for them to believe in your luck. It gives them added confidence in you!'

Lunched today with Col. Stern and Conan Doyle. The latter is a nice old gentleman, very courteous and interesting. We wanted him to write a biography of D. It is much needed, specially in the States, whence we have repeated inquiries. Conan Doyle would not do it, as he has never before written a biography & also he is full up with his history of the war which he is writing. He is absorbed in this, but is having a good deal of difficulty in getting material & facts. I could see, moreover, that they are only giving him what they want him to know. Stern & I told him one or two things that opened his eyes. He has a childlike idea of the infallibility of the W.O. officials.

February 9th 1917

T. P. O'Connor has written an article on D. in The Strand Magazine. I wonder whether these people, when they write these articles, really believe what they say, or are simply writing what they think they *ought* to say? T.P. talks about the beauty of D.'s family life! T.P. must know D. well enough to realise the conditions of his home life. Of course D. is fond of his children, but as he himself said to me when I made the same remark in defence of someone else: 'Every animal is fond of its young.' As a matter of fact, he & Olwen are continually at loggerheads & yet he is always pleased when the papers make a fuss of her, simply because she is his child. Of course D. is very clever in the way he *pretends* at being the happy family man when people visit him at home. He makes me very angry sometimes, but he tells me that it is necessary—it is very useful to him in his public life. I do not believe it is as necessary as all that. Everyone knows that Sir Edward Carson did not get on with his late wife, and he made no pretence of it, but for all that he was not less popular with his own party. I think it is a good deal the result of D.'s kindly nature too, & the fact that he wants to play the game by his wife & not to hurt her feelings in public. I can understand that, but I think he rather overdoes it, & it hurts me when I read articles like T.P.'s where they hold him up to be a model family man. It amounts to hypocrisy.

T.P. calls him a mystic. If there ever was a realist, it is D. He may possess qualities which appear to be those of a mystic, but his desires and ambitions are those of the realist every time. He must have the concrete, though by the very fact that he is willing to wait patiently for it a very long time if necessary, might lead one to believe that he is satisfied with the abstract. What religion he has is purely emotional, and not spiritual. He reminds me more & more of the characters in some of Anatole France's novels & he is much more a Frenchman even than a Welshman. But was there ever a Welshman who was a true mystic?

Mr. Hodder Williams asked me if I would not write the biography but I am afraid that my book would not pass the censor. Will anyone ever write The *Real* Lloyd George?

February 10th 1917
Went with Sir James Murray to Orpen's studio to see his portrait of Lord Bryce which is to be exhibited in the Academy in May. It is a fine study. There were also portraits there of Mr. Churchill & Violet Asquith, but the latter is not such a good likeness. Churchill's is a speaking likeness. Sir James is very anxious to get D. to sit for Orpen & has asked me to sound him & find out whether he would do so. Sir James will buy the picture & leave it in the Aberdeen Gallery during his life time, & at his death leave it to whomsoever D. would name.

February 14th 1917
D. & I went down to W.H. yesterday evening & had a very happy time. These times are all the more precious now, as D. is so busy all day long & we see comparatively little of each other.

Carson had been unburdening his mind to D. on the subject of Mr. Asquith. He loathes him, and thinks he is a complete hypocrite. Carson said that before the crisis, when Bonar Law was completely taken in by Asquith, Bonar said to him (Carson) 'I can't think why you prefer Lloyd George to Asquith. Asquith is so straight forward & simple: you always know where you are with him.' 'The reason that I like Lloyd George', was Carson's reply, 'is that he always puts his cards on the table. Then you know exactly what he is playing.' 'That is all very well', was my remark when D. told me this: 'You may put your cards on the table, but you take care to keep one or two up your sleeve in case of emergency.' D. laughed. 'You give me credit for a great deal more craft than I am capable of.' 'I think you are a past master in craft', I replied, laughing. And D. knows he is, too.

Carson also said that Mrs. Asquith is still beside herself with rage at D.'s accession to the Premiership. Mrs. Lowther told Carson that she receives long letters from her simply bubbling over with hatred of D. 'If he had been supplanted by a big outstanding figure', says Mrs. A., 'it would have been understandable and bearable: but to be ousted by that little . . .', etc., etc. I know the kind of letters Mrs. A. writes. I have her letters to D. filled with abuse first of all of one member of the Cabinet, then of another. It is quite sufficient that one never, never by any chance hears any one, rich or poor, small or great speak of her with anything but dislike and contempt. She and McKenna between them were the ruin of the late P.M.

D. was very pleased last night, for he had given the soldiers a dressing-down in the morning. He was dealing with Haig's demand for more men & informed them that Haig would get no more than had already been decided upon. 'He does not make the best use of his men. Let him learn to make better use of them. There is no danger now on land. The danger is on sea.' That was D.'s reply.

We talked of what would happen after the war. 'I should like to have a hand in the peace settlement', said D. 'And then I should like to be Prime Minister for 4 years after the war. There will be a lot to do then & I should like to be the one to do it.' 'I wonder', he said presently, 'whether, if I went out now, I should live to be a great figure in history. I doubt it.' Personally, I have no doubts at all on the subject. It is D. who has saved England from being beaten in this war. He has supplied the country with Money, Munitions, & Men, & now he is trying to retrieve victory from among the wreckage of the last government.

He told me how Lord Shaughnessy has prophecied that D. would be the Prime Minister of the Unionist Party. 'But you couldn't do that?', I asked. 'My dear Pussy', was his reply, 'the thing is done. The Unionists have adopted me, and after the war it will be more and more difficult for the Liberals to receive me back.' He hinted at Tariff reform. It is an extraordinary thing, but I have always felt convinced even before the war, that D. would eventually become an advocate of Tariff reform.

February 17th 1917

D. was worried last night. His Unionist colleagues have been causing him trouble. I felt certain that sooner or later they would come to blows about the land, the old bone of contention. It had already been agreed that food *prices* should be fixed. They all agreed to that. Henderson argued that if prices were to be fixed, you must guarantee the *wages* of the agricultural labourer. *That* was agreed to. 'Very well', said D., 'but if you guarantee that to the labourer, you must also guarantee to the farmer that his rents shall not be raised.' At this there was an outburst from Curzon & Long—What! interfere with their rents? Preposterous! Interfere with the rights of the English land-lord? They had never heard of such a thing! D. was furious with them, & turned on them fiercely, & cowed them for the moment. But he summoned a meeting for this morning—it is proceeding at the present moment—to thrash the whole matter out. He says he is not going to be made the tool of the landlords, & if he has any bother he will go straight down to the House and tell them that he cannot work with the Tories: that he undertook the Premiership thinking that the patriotism of the Tories was beyond question: that they are all right so long as it is only the rights of the workmen & the middle classes that are being interfered with: they are quite willing for them to make sacrifices: but as soon as the suggestion is made that their rents should be controlled, they say 'Perish the British Empire! We will not have our rents touched!'

Another bitter grievance arose from the statement by Mr. Bathurst that farmers were going to be allowed to shoot pheasants over their land. This was too much. The Tories know that there is a shortage of food, that it is even yet doubtful whether this vital problem can be dealt with effectively: they do not mind being put on short rations of meat and bread. But directly the word 'pheasant' was mentioned—'The air was filled with the cries of the sacred bird', said D. in recounting the scene to me. 'Its feathers were ruffled & the safety of the British Empire was imperilled!'

D. is sick of Long & says he thinks he will have to get rid of him. Long is disgruntled & wants to be included in the War Cabinet.[1] This is impossible but he will not take 'no' for an answer.

I am glad D. has come to grips with them on the land question—and game! It is the old quarrel of the land campaign but D. is fighting them on better ground this time. He will not hesitate to ask for a dissolution if things become impossible, but he says he will state his reasons publicly first.

Yesterday they also decided to make further drastic restrictions with regard to drink. Bonar Law, who is very timid where bold measures are concerned, passed D. a note saying that after this the Gov. would be out in a month. D. replied that he did not think so and wanted to bet on it.

February 24th 1917
D. has been very worried all the week about his old uncle, who is very ill and not expected to live. I think D. will be very upset when the end comes, for he often says that he owes everything to him & that it is he who has kept him up to the mark during the whole of his career, writing him every day a letter of encouragement. D. says that often in the early days of his Parliamentary career he spoke in the House simply because he knew it would please the old man to see his name in the newspapers the next morning. Uncle Lloyd's interest in D. never flags nor does his enthusiasm diminish, & it must have been a wonderful thing for the old man to see his boy Prime Minister. D. showed me a picture of the cottage at Llanystumdwy & told me how he remembered the old man standing in front of the gate one day when he (D.) returned from school. Uncle Lloyd looked at him for a long time & then said: 'I wonder what will become of this lad!'

It was thought that he was failing now simply because he had nothing left to live for & they begged him to try & keep his strength & pull himself together, for Dai's sake. 'Never fear', he said. 'There are some men who are too small for their job, & some who are equal to their job. D. is a man who is bigger than his job, and I want to see him do big things.' All the same, they say now it is merely a question of how long it will be before he dies.

---

1. Walter Long had become colonial secretary in Lloyd George's government.

D.'s speech yesterday seems to have made an enormous impression. He himself was very pleased with it, but was very tired afterwards. We both went down to W.H. after it, but were both too tired to enjoy each other's company, as I had been up till 2 the night before over the speech. However, we are going down again today for a quiet weekend.

D. goes to Calais on Monday to meet the French. 'It is a very ticklish corner that I have to turn. It practically means putting Haig under Nivelle, & it will be a hard fight, but I mean to have my way', said D.

Asquith sent a message, when it was announced that D.'s speech was to be postponed from Thursday to Friday, asking that it might be further postponed till Monday. D. refused, as for one thing it meant a waste of time, & another thing it would interfere with his plans for going to France. Whereupon it was announced in the papers that 'Mr. Asquith would not be able to be in his place in the House owing to a chill!' No war measures, however urgent, must be allowed to interfere with Mr. Asquith's weekend!

February 26th 1917
D. & I had a sweet weekend, & he is off to Calais today. I hope he will return safely tomorrow.

Lloyd George secretly drew up with the French a plan for putting the British expeditionary force under Nivelle's command. Nivelle produced this plan at the Calais conference with some embarrassment, and Lloyd George pretended to be surprised. After protests from Haig and Robertson, the arrangement was limited to the coming offensive, and Haig was given the right of appeal to the British government.

February 28th 1917
D. returned safely from France, where a very stormy Conference had taken place. Briand & Nivelle could not arrange between them beforehand who was to put the plans for the coming campaign before Haig—plans which would put Nivelle in virtual command of British and French troops. When the time arrived it was left to Nivelle to break the news, but D. says he was in a very awkward position as the new proposals concerned himself. He floundered about most hopelessly & had to be helped out in the end. Of course Haig objected, but D. remained firm. After the Conference it was arranged that Haig should sign an agreement putting himself under Nivelle, but Haig would not. Robertson suggested that D. & Haig & himself should confer on the subject. 'No', said D., 'there will be no Conference until that document is signed. Either Haig signs it, or he goes—or I go.' He signed it in the end, very unwillingly, but D. said that at one time it looked very much as though he or Haig would have had to resign. But D. says he was prepared to take the risk.

The perfect secretary: Frances Stevenson at work in her Whitehall office

The photograph case made 'like a pocket book' so that Lloyd George could carry it without comment

Frances Stevenson and Lloyd George's daughter, Megan, in Paris during the Peace Conference

A doodle by Lloyd George during strike negotiations.
The drawing, made in the red and blue crayons he liked to use,
incorporates the details of Welsh pithead structure

One of the little notes Frances Stevenson used to leave on Lloyd George's table at the House of Commons after he had delivered a speech

A note to Bonar Law in 1918: Lloyd George writes of Hayes Fisher—'The P.M. doesn't mind if he is drowned in malmsey wine, but he must be a dead chicken by tonight.'

September 2nd. 1915

It is time to take up my diary again, though I feel it is impossible to fill up the gap. C. has been resting all last week, after a slight breakdown as the result of overwork. I must now longer call him C., but will substitute D., which has the advantage of being permanent.

The Ministry of Munitions is now fairly on its legs, after many stormy passages. The question resolves itself now more or less into a question of labour, which again seems to be resolving itself into a question of conscription. D. is having a rather unpleasant time on account of this, the Northcliffe press by their agitation having put up the backs of the Liberals. The Conservative element of the Cabinet, however, are strong for it, and are looking to D. to lead them through this campaign. This, however, has had the effect of somewhat alienating the Liberals from D. In addition to

One of the loose sheets from the Diary

APRIL, 1916.

4th Month.

30 Days.

APRIL, 1916.

Pages from the more formal bound volumes in the collection

A friendly occasion: (from left to right) the Duchess of Hamilton, Lloyd George, Lord Fisher and Frances Stevenson

The Cannes Conference, 1922:
A rare photograph showing Frances Stevenson and Lloyd George together in public: front row (left to right) Lady Curzon, Lloyd George, Lady Markham, and, Lord Curzon; and, behind, Tom Jones, Lord Riddell, Sir Albert Stern and Frances Stevenson

BEAUVAIS, le 3 Avril 1918.

Le Général FOCH est chargé par les Gouvernements Britannique , Français et Américain de coordonner l'action des
Armées Alliées sur le front occidental; il lui est conféré
à cet effet tous les pouvoirs nécessaires en vue d'une réali-
sation effective. Dans ce but, les Gouvernements Britannique,
Français et Américain confient au Général FOCH la direction
stratégique des opérations militaires.

Les Commandants en Chef des Armées Britannique, Française
et Américaine exercent dans sa plénitude la conduite tactique
de leur Armée. Chaque Commandant en Chef aura le droit d'en
appeler à son Gouvernement, si dans son opinion, son Armée
se trouve mise en danger par toute instruction reçue du Général FOCH.

The Beauvais document of 1918 by which the British, French and
American governments empowered Foch to co-ordinate the action of the
Allied armies on the Western Front: this is the only surviving copy

Lyautey[1] was commenting to D. afterwards on Nivelle's difficulty in not getting to the point. 'He was walking round and round the porridge and not sticking the spoon in', he said.

March 1st 1917

Old Uncle Lloyd died last night. D. is very upset and will be until after the funeral has taken place. It is a great strain for him, coming at this time. He will miss the old man very much, and he says I am his only devoted friend now—that I shall have to fill the old man's place. God knows I shall try. D. needs so much someone who will not hesitate to give him everything, & if necessary to give up everything, & whose sole thought & occupation is for him. Without that it is hopeless to try and serve him.

March 10th 1917

D. has been very depressed all the week, partly owing to the fact that he was still feeling his uncle's death very much. Also Megan developed measles, and had a very bad time, as they were afraid it would go to her head, & D. immediately felt convinced that she would have meningitis. However, she is better again now, but what with these worries and the worries of his work, poor D. has had rather a bad time. He is working too hard into the bargain, but I am persuading him to take a little walk every day, weather permitting, & he is also taking a wonderful concoction of egg, port wine, honey & cream every morning, which seems to buck him up a lot.

March 16th 1917

D. has again had a very trying and anxious week. The question of giving General Nivelle the supreme command over British & French Armies had to be settled and naturally led to a good deal of unpleasantness. D. had to be very firm. Robertson tried to wriggle out of the agreement of the Conference at Calais last month, & to pretend that no real decision had been arrived at. Nivelle on the other hand had been proceeding on the lines of the instructions he had received at that Conference, & the whole thing resulted in a first-class row. Robertson tried to get Derby to take his side against D. while Haig it seems had approached the King for sympathy. D. tackled Robertson in front of Derby, & made him own up that the thing had been definitely decided at Calais, but D. got very angry over the whole thing, & even lost his temper with H.M. when the latter suggested that no interference should occur in Haig's position: that after all he was a great British soldier, & his position & prestige was the first thing to be considered. Then D. turned on him. 'I do not agree with Your Majesty', he said hotly. 'The most important thing seems to me that the lives of our gallant soldiers should not be squandered as they were last summer, but that they should be used to the best advantage. It seems to me that General Haig's prestige is a very minor consideration

---

1. French minister of war.

compared with this!' The King was rather upset at this outburst. 'Well, well, perhaps you are right there', was all he could say.

The outcome of these meetings was, however, that Nivelle was told that he must treat Haig with a little more respect, and not write him insolent letters as he had been doing. The whole thing was settled once more & it is hoped that things will proceed a little more amicably.

Nevertheless the whole business was a source of worry to D. & coming at the same time as the fuss over the Indian cotton duties, gave D. rather a bad time. D. took a very firm stand over these duties, which was the only thing he could do after Austen Chamberlain[1] had committed him, but it made a section of the Liberals very angry, & rather worried D. He hates to feel that the Liberals are unfriendly to him, for he knows he can never go over to the Tories—indeed the Tories themselves do not want him for good—they will throw him over as soon as he has served their purpose.

April 2nd 1917

Last week was a good week for D. His speech on the Electoral Reform Programme[2] was simply magnificent, and he surpassed himself in persuasiveness and eloquence. He had a tough fight in the Cabinet to get the thing through, as it deals a blow at the Tories. But he and Henderson arranged things between them before the Cabinet meeting. 'You do the heavy truculent working man', said D. to Henderson, '& then I will do my bit & we will see if we cannot manage it together.' And Henderson did. While the meeting was going on, I was sitting in my room, when suddenly I heard someone shouting & banging their fist on the Cabinet Room table. This went on for a long time & there was no doubt it was someone in a great rage. I thought D. was having a bad time & that his Tory colleagues were going to resign in a body. Not at all. It was Henderson putting his case, as D. told me afterwards. Then D. put the case in a very forceful and persuasive way, & the result was that the Cabinet agreed to accept the Speaker's Report, leaving Proportional Representation and Women's Votes to the House to decide. Thus D. was able to face the House on Wednesday [28 March] with a clear brief, not having conceded anything to the Tories, but with a progressive programme. This pleased the Liberals mightily—in fact some of them sent him a message—those who had repudiated him as a turncoat—to say that he had brought them round to himself again with a sweep. The reaction among the Liberals is almost touching: they can see that 'their old girl', as D. puts it, 'is not faithless to them as they thought she was, but was true to them all the time.' It has done D. an immense amount of good & he never was so strong as now. The

---

1. Secretary of state for India.
2. The Speaker's conference had recommended universal suffrage for men at the age of 21, and this was supported by the government. Household suffrage for women at the age of 30, which was also recommended by the conference, was left to the house of commons which accepted it after a free vote. Proportional representation was not achieved, owing to differences with the house of lords.

danger that seemed apparent at one time of his falling between 2 stools has been averted, and his position is very secure.

He had a talk with B. Law on Saturday [31 March], & Bonar accidentally let out that if there was a general election, the Tories expected to come back again with a swing. But if he thinks that, he has miscalculated. At any rate since last Wednesday all their chances in that direction have been knocked on the head, & The Observer pointed that out very clearly yesterday. D. has the country solid behind him, & what is more, he is the *only* man they will rally to. But it shows what was in the minds of the Tories all the time, & what D. suspected.

D. & I had hardly seen each other last week, so we drove down to Walton on Saturday to lunch, & had two hours of bliss together. D. saw I was rather down & lonely, & it was sweet of him to suggest it, for he was very tender & kind & bucked me up again. I feel as though I ought not to mind when he is busy & cannot pay me very much attention, but I suppose I am only human and I get depressed. But he soon puts me right again.

The United States declared war against Germany on 1 April 1917.

April 9th 1917

D. has had another good week. America has decided to come in & D. feels that it is a piece of good luck, for it will solve some of our greatest difficulties, including the shipping difficulty. The Americans adore D. He is speaking at the American Luncheon Club on Thursday [12 April] to celebrate the entry of America into the war. We lunched with some members of the management on Saturday [7 April] to fix things up. They were full of excitement at the fact that D. was going to be their guest. 'Lloyd George has a bigger sound in America than "Prime Minister"', one of them said. 'For Lloyd George is the man who does things, and that means everything to America.'

Richard Lloyd George was married on Saturday [7 April], & D. went down to Bath for the wedding. He tried to get up enthusiasm about it but I think he was rather sad in his heart, for Dick did not show up very well over his first engagement, & his wife is not such a sweet girl as Dilys Roberts.[1] Moreover she has all the money & the Welsh people are saying that Dick has been 'bought over'. It will not be a very popular marriage in Wales. It is too like a piece of business, & the North Wales people especially will not forgive him for giving up a Welsh girl. Strangely enough, her father, Sir John Roberts died on Saturday. They said the breaking off of the engagement had preyed on his mind, & he had been ill for some time. It was a curious coincidence that he should have died the very day of the wedding.

---

1. A Welsh girl to whom Dick had been engaged, but who herself broke off the engagement.

The French government and most of the French generals now had doubts about Nivelle's projected offensive. Lloyd George insisted, and largely thanks to him it took place. It was a complete failure.

Charles, the new Emperor of Austria, put out feelers for peace to the French government through Prince Sixte of Bourbon. Lloyd George supposed that this was an offer for a separate peace and was very excited. However the Italians, who were the only ones actually fighting Austria-Hungary, refused to consider the idea. Negotiations between British and Austrian representatives continued fruitlessly until March 1918.

April 10th 1917

Painlevé, the new French Minister for war, came over to consult D. about the military operations. It appears that the new Fr. Gov. have their doubts about Nivelle, as to whether his plans are sound. I do hope he will not fail, for D. has backed him up against Haig, & it will rather let D. down if he proves to be a failure.

April 11th 1917

D. went down to Folkestone to meet M. Ribot, & he returned very excited. Ribot had shown him a letter written by the Emperor of Austria, to his cousin a Bourbon Prince, asking him to approach the French President with the idea of proposing a separate peace for Austria. Only the President & Ribot had seen the letter, and the latter had come over to ask D. to approach the King on the subject.

D. & I had an impromptu dinner in my room, & then set to prepare D.'s speech for tomorrow. I think he has a good speech, & he is very fit.

April 12th 1917

D. made a magnificent speech at the American Luncheon Club. I heard the speeches tucked away behind a screen on the orchestra platform, with some of the wives of the American members. It was a great meeting, & they were most enthusiastic. I fear however that he will get another little note from the King on the undignified tone in which he spoke of 'kings & their tricks!'

After the speech D. & I drove down to Windsor as D. had to see H.M. about the Emperor of Austria's letter. I had tea in the town while D. was at the Castle & then we drove back again together to Walton Heath. We were very happy. D. was in excellent spirits & very pleased with his speech.

April 13th 1917

D.'s speech yesterday has been received with great applause—specially by the Liberals. This has pleased him very much. He goes off North tonight to see the Grand Fleet, & will not be back till Monday [16 April]. I hate his going away. I can never rest till he returns, in case some harm may happen to him.

Next week he is going to Paris, & I am trying to persuade him to take me this time.

April 14th 1917
D. went to see the Grand Fleet—left last night and will not return till Monday. Am taking the opportunity of having a thorough rest—am going with Margie to Colonel Stern's house at Goring-by-Sea till Monday. Col. Stern is away in France and has lent us his house. It is a beautiful place—right on the top of the downs, with a beautiful garden, & inside, every comfort one can desire. Mamma told me that she had heard that I should marry Colonel Stern. Was never more surprised in my life. I hope he does not want anything of the sort, as he is quite a good pal, and besides I am quite sure he knows of the relations between D. & me. He has several times invited us down to his house together. I like him, though he has an unloveable side, but he is most kind and considerate. But it is always a question of how deeply these qualities penetrate—whether they are merely on the surface and displayed from a point of view of diplomacy, or whether they are genuinely spontaneous and natural. I have never found Col. Stern lacking for one moment in them so, unless he is extraordinarily clever, I am inclined to assume that they are natural—and indeed I prefer to do so, for it is bad for me to be continually looking for a hidden motive in every kind action, though public life rather tends towards fostering this attitude. In any case, Colonel Stern is interesting by reason of his 'Tanks', & he is an extraordinarily good business man.

April 18th 1917
D. left this morning for St. Jean de Maurienne, near the Italian frontier, where he & Ribot are to meet the Italian Prime Minister to discuss the question of a separate peace with Austria. I wish it had not been necessary to announce his departure for the Continent before he left, but apparently it had to be done to avoid any misunderstanding as to his absence from the House when the American Debate came on. I cannot help feeling that the Germans will not miss a chance of doing him harm. However, I must possess my soul in patience till he returns on Saturday [21 April].

April 21st 1917
Lunched with a very nondescript party at the Automobile Club, among them Matthew Keating, M.P., a funny little man with a sad look in his eyes. They say he drinks tremendously. I asked him if the Irish still wanted to cut the Prime Minister's throat. 'No', he said, 'but we were very sad at the tone of his speech on Ireland in the House. He seemed to throw all his old principles overboard, & it was as though he were trying to test the strength of the Irish party against his own.' I suggested that he was trying to provoke a demonstration of the strength of the Irish Party in order to convince Carson of its power. Keating was rather pleased at the suggestion. Apparently it had never occurred to the Irish before, nor had it to me, as a matter of fact until that moment. But I fancy he will convey it to his colleagues, & it may inspire them with a little friendlier feeling towards D. In any case, I think they are anxious to welcome him back as a potential peace-maker, & it is not unlikely

that D. will be able to make some settlement possible between the two sections. D. has done many things which seemed impossible. I hope for his sake he will be able to surmount this obstacle.

Sir Vincent Evans[1] was lunching at the Automobile Club. I think he is one of the greatest humbugs I know. He loses no opportunity of advertising himself, chiefly through the reflected glory of the Lloyd George family, attaching himself to them in public whenever possible. He knows all about D. & me, & aids & abets us whenever necessary, & for this he knows that he is on D.'s right side, & it gives him extra chances of being in D.'s company—which fact (being in D.'s company) he never omits to make public. On the other hand, he trundles Mrs. Ll.G. about to all sorts of functions, and gets himself photographed & talked about in connection with her. He makes flowery speeches about her virtues, & assiduously makes a fuss of her, knowing that by this means he gets on *her* right side, which is also useful on occasions. He makes a great pretence of being a scholar, & yet is as coarse-minded as it is possible for any man to be. I don't believe he is even kind, but should rather imagine him to be vindictive. D. is nice to him because he is an old friend and for D.'s sake I have to be nice to him too, otherwise I could not be civil to such a repulsive personality.

April 23rd 1917

D. returned on Saturday afternoon. As I thought, the Germans tried their best to get him. He ought, upon an ordinary calculation, to have returned by the midnight tide on Friday night, & there were 5 destroyers waiting to catch him in the Straits. The boat that he should have crossed on, & one other, attacked them, & accounted for three. But fortunately D. elected to cross by day on Saturday, & so avoided them. Everyone however thinks it is high time he should stay at home, & I have been rubbing this in, as it is foolish that he should take risks that can be avoided.

Nothing came of the Conference. The Italians are dead against it. They wanted pieces of Austria for themselves, & are not disposed to make peace, & of course we can do nothing without them. But D. talked to them pretty strongly. They wanted us to promise them Asia Minor at the end of the war, & to guarantee them compensation in case we did not get it. 'First of all', said D. to them, 'I should like to know what contribution you are going to make to the conquest of Asia Minor?' They replied that they could not send a force there. 'Very well', said D., 'can you send a force to Salonika? If you can release our men at Salonika, we can send our men to Asia Minor to conquer it for you.' No, they could not possibly spare a man. Then D. flashed on them. 'What you are doing at present, is simply to defend your own frontiers. You want us to conquer Asia Minor *for you* and hand it over to you at

---

1. Sir Vincent Evans (1851–1934), leading Welsh journalist in London and ubiquitous promoter of Welsh culture; secretary of National Eisteddfod Association, 1881–1934; governor, museum, library, and university of Wales; C.H., 1922.

the end of the war, or else to guarantee you compensation!' I think the Italians saw their dream shattered. After all, as D. says, we are giving them guns, coal, money, & they are simply defending their own country. 'Let me tell you', was D.'s parting remark to them, 'we can make peace with Austria *tomorrow*!' 'I thought I would just let them know', he said to me, in telling me of the meeting, 'how little they really count.'

Apparently D. was recognised & welcomed everywhere he went. At St. Jean du Maurienne a little girl came up with flowers for him & Ribot. The latter offered her money, whereupon she was very distressed. D. kissed her on both cheeks, & she went away very happy. I have got the tricolor ribbon that the flowers were tied up with. D. brought me back such a beautiful blouse which he had chosen himself. He was as pleased with the purchase as I was.

We went down to Walton H. on Saturday afternoon [21 April], & had a perfect weekend. I do not think we have ever loved each other so much. D. says that ours is a love that comes to very few people and I wonder more & more at the beauty & happiness of it. It is a thing that nothing but death can harm, and even death has no terrors for me now, for D. asked me yesterday if I would come with him when he went. He begged me not to stay behind, but for both of us to go together, and I promised him to do so, unless I have any children of his to claim me. So, I am not afraid now of the misery if D. is taken away, for then I shall go too & his end will be my end, and until then everything is happiness, if our love stays. I hope by any chance I shall not go first, for I know his misery would be great, and he could not leave his work, which is a great one. I am so happy now that we have decided this, for sometimes my heart would stop beating with terror at the thought of life without D.

Yesterday morning D. & I drove to Windsor. I lunched in the town while D. went to the Castle & had lunch *en famille* with the King and Queen & children. He enjoyed it thoroughly. He said it was all so homely & was much amused at the Queen's account of little Prince John, who was losing weight because he did not like the porridge & suet pudding they gave him at Osborne. 'What's the matter with the pudding, John?' she said. 'It's lumpy', was his reply. This incident tickled D. immensely—the King's son complaining of the lumpy suet pudding he was obliged to eat! D. thinks the Royal Family are beginning to like him a little better lately. He stayed there quite a long time, & the Queen was specially nice to him, he said. The King also seemed glad to talk with him. 'I must say I did treat him abominably at first!' And so he did. Many a letter from G.R. he never even answered, and once he even forgot an appointment with him!

We then drove on to Lord Derby's house at Sunningdale, and D. went in to have a little talk with him while I had tea at the Wheatsheaf. D. wanted to talk to Derby about recalling General Murray from Palestine.[1] He does

---

1. Sir Archibald James Murray (1860–1945): general; C.I.G.S., September–December 1915; commanded forces in Egypt, January 1916–June 1917; recalled after battle of Gaza.

not think Murray is any good & has advocated his recall for some time. He wanted to get Derby on his side in the matter, & I think he succeeded in persuading him. The suggestion is that Smuts[1] should go in his place.

D. did not stay very long & we drove back to W.H. & had a peaceful evening together.

D. & I had a discussion about General Collard, who has been to the fore lately. I was talking to D. about him, & D. admitted that, although he considered him to be very efficient, yet he did not like him much. 'He is not *quite* a gentleman', he said to me. And then he told me about Henry James,[2] whom Coleridge had described as 'almost a scholar, almost a statesman, almost a gentleman'. This led to another amusing story about Balfour & the gentleman in question. Henry James had been writing articles criticising the administration of Ireland, & the Secretary for Ireland (I forget who he was) wrote to Balfour complaining about this. Balfour absent-mindedly put the letter in his pocket & did not read it through, but meeting James a little later on, remembered it, & handed it to James, saying, 'Here is a letter I have had about you. You had better read it.' James read it, & handed it back to Balfour without a word, but with a very annoyed expression on his face. Then Balfour read the letter, & found at the end a P.S. consisting of the quotation from Coleridge 'Almost a scholar, etc. . . .'

But the funniest story I have heard for a long time is about a friend of Max Aitken's, who paid him a surprise visit on the subject of the horrors of the war. Max Aitken had not been talking to him very long before he found out that the man's mind had become unhinged & he made for the bell to ring it. But the man—Robertson Lawson by name—stopped him. 'None of that!' he said. 'There is one man who can put a stop to the war, & that is yourself. But before you can do so you must be purified. Get down on your knees & repeat the Lord's Prayer!' Aitken, seeing him fumbling with his pockets, & fearing that he had a revolver concealed about him, thought the wisest plan was to obey. He dropped on his knees & began saying the Lord's Prayer, quickly, in order to get the ordeal over. 'Stop!' said the man. 'You must say it with much more fervour than that!' And he had to begin all over again. The man kept him there for two hours, & then consented to leave him. 'There is one other man who can help', he said to M.A. as he was leaving, 'And that is Donald of the Chronicle. I am just off to see him.' But as soon as he had gone, Aitken —Lord Beaverbrook, rather—got on the telephone to Donald and warned him of what was about to happen. Whereupon Donald fled to Walton Heath.

The number of madmen seems to be increasing. We have any amount of

---

1. Jan Christian Smuts (1870–1950): Boer general, British field marshal; South African minister of defence, 1910–19; prime minister of South Africa, 1919–29, 1939–48; member of war cabinet, 1917–19; did not take command in Palestine; in 1918 wished Lloyd George to propose him as commander-in-chief of the American armies in France.
2. Henry James, Lord James of Hereford (1828–1911): Unionist politician, not Henry James the novelist. Coleridge is the lord chief justice, not the poet.

letters from these men, thinking that they can stop the war if only they can get the P.M.'s ear. One of these men who wrote demanding to see D., & followed the letter up with a call, signed himself 'Rabbi Ben Ezra' and stated that he had been a caterpillar until 11.30 a.m. Easter Monday, at which time he had emerged from the chrysalis!

April 25th 1917
D. went down to W.H. yesterday early in the afternoon to try & prepare his speech for Friday [27 April], when he is to be given the Freedom of the City of London. I went down in the evening, & we walked about the garden & talked it over. I think it will be a very good speech.

D. also talked to me of his hopes on the Irish question. He had had a long talk with Carson about it, & he is trying to persuade Carson to make concessions. He put it to him on imperial grounds. 'At every stage', he said to him, 'the Irish question is a stumbling-block in the conduct of the war. It ought to have been settled last year. I feel that I was a coward then not to insist upon a settlement then. It has done much harm in Australia. Hughes begged me last year to settle it for the sake of Australia, but I failed to do so. Twice since then he has sent me messages saying that it is essential that the matter should be settled. I have refrained from pressing the question, knowing your difficulties. But I feel that it can remain in abeyance no longer. Now that America has come in I get the same representations from that side. If we had settled it last year, we should have had many hundreds of thousands of recruits from Australia. If we do not settle it now, this government will not be able to continue. There is only one way it can be settled, and that is by county option. It is up to you and your party to agree to this, for the sake of the Empire.'

Carson said he would see MacDowell on the matter, & consider whether it would be possible to do anything in the matter. D. has sent a message through Dr. Page, the American Ambassador, to President Wilson (secretly) asking him to send a message urging that the Irish question should be settled. He thinks if he can get this it will be a very great help, & will influence Carson. 'I think I see my way out of it', he said to me. 'I want to get it settled now, and then my way is clear. I should then have the vote of the Irish & could defeat the Asquithites. I can see what the game of those devils is. They [the Asquithites] will support the Franchise Bill & get it through, but there will be a period of 6 months between the time of passing the Bill & the time when it comes into operation. During that time the Asquithites will try & vote the Government out—probably on the Irish question, & in any case if they have the Irish votes they may be able to do it—*but*, having turned the Gov. out they will say—'You cannot have a general election, for the new register does not come into operation till the end of the six months, and now there is no register for an election.' Therefore it will follow that an Asquith Gov. will be set up *without* an election, & we shall not get a chance of going to the country. The Asquith Gov. will then pass a Bill prolonging the life of Parl., & thus further put off going to the country. In the meantime they will take the credit for all the measures I have taken for the prosecution of the war. *But*, if I settle the Irish question now, this will knock all their plans on the head, & my course will be clear in front of me. So I do not propose to bring the Franchise Bill forward until the Irish question is settled, & I have great hopes!' Then, speaking of the Asquithites, 'I'll let them see what I am made of before I have finished', he said, fiercely, 'I'll give them hell! It will take more than they are made of to down me!'

D. also told me that he had come to an agreement with the Imperial Cabinet on the subject of Preference for the Colonies. He suggested his scheme which he had put forward as far back as 1907—a scheme whereby the colonies are assisted by shipping subsidies, which avoids taxation & therefore does not increase the price of the commodities. D. put this forward & Borden,[1] to the surprise of everyone, backed it up & spoke convincingly in favour of it. 'I did not tell them', said D. to me, 'that I had talked with him for an hour on the subject yesterday!' The scheme was adopted, and it will, D. thinks, clear the atmosphere for the settlement of the Irish question, for it pleases Tories and Colonials alike very much.

D. certainly is going ahead. He says no one can conceive the gulf that lies between an ordinary member of the Cabinet & the Prime Minister. I think he himself is amazed at the power that now lies between his hands, and he is certainly losing no time in using this power beneficently. If only he can settle the Irish question! I feel that everything hangs on that.

It is only this week that the trees are beginning to bud. Spring is very late this year, & the weather is still very cold. Even yet there is not a leaf to be seen anywhere.

Poor Mr. Bonar Law's son is missing. He is feeling the blow very keenly.

April 26th 1917
D. had another long talk with Carson & MacDowell this morning, and seems very confident. 'I think I am going to settle the Irish question, Pussy', he said to me joyfully. He is seeing the Nationalists on Sunday [29 April]—the first time since last year. He has not yet received the message from President Wilson, but he received a letter from Lord Bryce this morning which was very useful. He sent it over at once to Carson with a note. D. is very good when he tries 'encircling' tactics, gradually surrounding his opponent until he is forced to capitulate without any direct assault!

April 29th 1917
Yesterday was glorious! D.'s speech was wonderful, & he delivered it splendidly. The whole proceedings were full of enthusiasm, & a high enthusiasm which thrilled & inspired. I have never seen D. in better form, & I loved to

---

1. Sir Robert Laird Borden (1854–1937): prime minister of Canada, 1911–20.

see him the centre of praise and admiration. The speech will stand out as one of his greatest, certainly one of his most significant speeches. The reception he got too, has encouraged him, for the responsibility is a heavy one on his shoulders. He was rather depressed the night before, for Northcliffe had been to him the night before & told him that this Gov. is even more unpopular than the last! The truth is, that D. is doing things without consulting or paying any heed to Northcliffe, and this rather riles the great man. Churchill was present at the Guildhall strange to say, but looking very sulky. D. says he cannot understand why he came there. Someone asked him afterwards what he thought of the speech & he replied: 'Events will show.' Everyone remarked how surly he was looking, & he left quite alone. Everyone else was full of admiration.

D. is very happy & fit this morning, & has gone off to play golf. It will do him good, & he has a very heavy week next week. The events of the next few days will probably show whether he can solve the Irish question or not.

Sat next to Megan at the Mansion House Lunch. She is an amusing little person, but is getting rather artificial. D. thinks she is growing selfish, but that is not her fault, for she has not been taught to be unselfish. I think she is wonderfully unspoilt, considering the way she has been brought up. Many children would have been unbearable. She informed me that her mother 'reminded her of a character out of Dickens'. 'But this is only for your ear!' she added.

May 12th 1917
D. very pleased with his performance at the Secret Session. He explained to the House the real position as regards food, & said that he had no real anxiety as to the food question. 'Why then', he was asked, 'were we told in January that we were approaching a famine, & that we might starve before the summer?' 'Because I wanted the people to cultivate!' D. retorted. The House roared with laughter & appeared quite ready to forgive his Machiavellian tricks.

In the meantime, Nivelle has fallen into disgrace, & let D. down badly after the way D. had backed him up at the beginning of the year. Sir Douglas Haig has come out on top in this fight between the two Chiefs, & I fear D. will have to be very careful in future as to his backings of the French against the English. However D. appears to take it as the fortunes of war, and has accepted his defeat cheerfully, though he was very sick as it gradually became apparent that the French were failing hopelessly in the offensive.

Lloyd George tried to revive the scheme for settling Ireland which he had put forward in June 1916. The Irish Nationalists refused to accept this. Lloyd George therefore took up a suggestion from Smuts that the Irish should settle their own affairs in a Convention. Though this Convention failed to reach agreement, it took the Irish problem out of politics for the next twelve months.

May 19th 1917

Saw Lord Northcliffe this week—he sat in my room before going in to see D. He is an extraordinarily commonplace man, with a very good brain for business. He is rather dull to talk to, very vain, but kindhearted I should say. Nothing original. Those are the men that get on.

The Irish question has suddenly taken a turn for the better, & D. is very bucked. The Irish, too, are very pleased with the proposal for a Convention, and D. is hopeful that peace may reign for a few months at least in that quarter, though I do not know whether he has any hopes of the Convention ultimately solving the Irish puzzle. He has had a very pleasant interview with Redmond & with an effort hopes to pull the thing off.

Meanwhile D. is seriously contemplating some changes in his Ministry. He says he wants someone in who will cheer him up and help & encourage him, & who will not be continually coming to him with a long face and telling him that everything is going wrong. At present, he says, he has to carry the whole of his colleagues on his back. They all come to him with their troubles and trials, instead of trying to relieve him of anxiety. D. feels that he must have someone a little more cheerful to help him to cope with all these mournful faces—Bonar Law not the least of them. I think D. is thinking of getting Winston in in some capacity. He has an intense admiration for his cleverness, & at any rate he is energetic and forceful. D. has seen him once or twice lately & I think they have talked things over. Churchill is very loath to associate with the Asquithites. He hates McKenna & was telling D. that McKenna simply gloated when the submarine losses were high. Much as D. loathes McKenna, however, he did him a good turn the other day. A big banker—Sir Edward Holden I think it was—came to D. & said that it was proposed to make McK. a director of their bank. They wished however first to ask D. if he approved of the appointment, as if he had any objection the appointment would not be made. If D. had had any malice in him, he could have withheld his approval, but as it was he knew that it would make a financial difference to McK. & so endorsed the appointment. I think McK. hates D. too much, however, even to be grateful to him, if he knew what he had done. I don't know whether D. is seriously thinking of taking Churchill on, as he knows his limitations and realises that he is eaten up with conceit. 'He has spoilt himself by reading about Napoleon', said D. to me.

Harold Spender is writing a book about D., & I am looking out some material for him. I do not know what the book will be like. Personally I think Harold Spender himself is a frightful bore, & D. himself, though he likes him, says he is one of the most tactless persons he has ever come across. His latest example of tactlessness, though perhaps he is not to blame for it, has been to ask me if I would get Mrs. Lloyd George to dictate to me anecdotes about D.!!! I hope he will suggest the same thing to Mrs. Ll.G.

May 26th 1917

D. has been very, very tired this week—more tired I think than I have ever seen him before, and he has been working unceasingly from morning till night. What with the strikes, the submarines, the food difficulties, besides the general conduct of the war, he has had a strenuous time. However, the strikes have been settled for the time being, the submarines have caught far fewer ships, & Lord Devonport[1] is resigning, which will enable D. to deal drastically with the food question. So that at any rate a few difficulties have been overcome. D. went down to the House yesterday and made a very good little speech & the House was immensely pleased & encouraged, & sobered by it. They broke up for the adjournment very quietly. D. has appointed a Commission to enquire into the industrial unrest. That is the most sinister thing at present, & is simply being engineered by German agents and Pacifists who are trying to corrupt the workers. However, if they get hold of the right people and deal with them the trouble will subside. And I feel sure that D. will now deal with the whole thing with a firm hand. A letter has just been intercepted from C. P. Trevelyan[2] to a friend in Petrograd—a most malicious document—gloating over the fact that the poor would soon be hungry, & that then would be the time to bring about a revolution. What they expect to gain by a revolution here, I do not know. These, however, are the sort of people who must be watched. We hear on all sides that the country itself is solid for D. and that they realise that he is the only man who can pull them through the difficult time after the war. But it is the C. P. Trevelyans & the German agents who are trying to stab him in the back, to say nothing of the Asquithites.

D. saw a Deputation from the Miners this week, & explained to them all the difficulties of the food problem. Incidentally, he offered the post of Food Controller to Smillie[3] as a gift, telling him chaffingly that Lord Devonport would be very pleased to change places with him. Nothing has yet been decided as to who will take Lord Devonport's place, but D. is trying to get a Labour man in, and to show the working classes that he is trying to settle their troubles with good will, or at least to give them every chance of being settled.

There is a very disquieting movement going on in certain quarters to insinuate that it would be an excellent combination if Asquith were to unite with D. & there were to be a joint Premiership. It is a most pernicious movement, engineered undoubtedly by Asquith & his followers, because they see it is their last chance of avoiding the 'wilderness' for an indefinite space of

---

1. Food controller, 1916–17.
2. Sir Charles Phillips Trevelyan (1870–1958); 3rd Barone; Liberal M.P., 1899–1918; Labour M.P., 1922–31; parliamentary secretary to board of education, 1908–14; resigned in protest against declaration of war, 1914; a founder of the Union of Democratic Control, 1914; president of board of education, 1924, 1929–31.
3. Robert Smillie (1857–1940), miners' leader. Lord Rhondda became minister of food.

time. They pretend that it is for D.'s good—that the work of running the war is too much for one man, & that for his health's sake it would be good for him to have a partner. I think it would be fatal to take Asquith back in any position. It would be a tacit acknowledgement at least, so it would strike people, that the Government could not get on without him, and that he was indispensable. The extraordinary thing is that people like Lord Murray of Elibank are keen about it, but I do hope D. will be quite resolute in sticking out against it. Poor D.! He needs all his energy and strength of will to fight against all these forces, & I hope he is going to have a good rest during the weekend. The last two weekends he has been down at W.H. enjoying what he calls 'domestic bliss', & has come back looking twice as tired as when he went down. This week I am going to try my hand & see what I can do!

Montagu is doing his level best to get into the Government by hook or crook, but D. says he will not have him. D. says he does not like his readiness to turn his back on Asquith. He says that if it had not been for Asquith Montagu would have never been heard of—that he is purely a man who has been made by Asquith. But Montagu has no scruples in deserting his bene-factor and going over to the other side as soon as it suits his interests to do so. He is as treacherous as a man can be.

May 28th 1917
A most amusing day yesterday. Grace Stonedale & I went down on Saturday [26 May] to look after D. during the weekend. (Mrs. Ll.G. being at Criccieth.) He wanted absolute rest, & arranged that Olwen & a friend who was staying with her should remain at Downing Street. However, his family with their usual consideration for him (!) wished otherwise. Dick & his wife arrived without any warning to lunch on Sunday morning, having borrowed the official car for the purpose of motoring down. Then they got on the tele-phone with Olwen & arranged that she & her friend should come down in the afternoon. The whole thing was done without D. being consulted as to what he would like or what he intended to do. He was perfectly furious, for not only did it disturb the whole of his Sunday's rest, but as he said, they never think about him or consider him in any way, but simply use his house & garden & car when they think they will. I saw he was very upset by the whole thing, & tried to soothe him by saying that it was most natural for them to come & pay their father a visit on the spur of the moment; but I honestly think the whole thing was engineered & done a good deal out of spite, as they knew pretty well that he would not be there alone. However, they all cleared off after tea, & we had the rest of the day to ourselves. We went for a jolly walk in the woods after tea, & I found 3 four-leafed clovers, all of which I presented to D., as he needs luck at present more than anyone! The country is just beautiful the last few days—all the spring flowers in their full beauty, & nature more than lovely after the hard winter. In the woods there was a carpet of bluebells under the green canopy of trees. D. certainly

looks much, much better today for the rest & is in much better spirits. I got quite alarmed about him last week, especially as he was not at all nice to me, which is always a sign that he is overworked or very worried.

Mr. Davies had an amusing morning on Saturday going through the Birthday Honours List with Lord Stamfordham.[1] He says Lord Stamfordham is very pro-Asquithian. He wanted to take William Watson's name out because he had written 'The Woman with the Serpent's Tongue'. However, D. insists on having him in (because he wrote 'The Man Who Saw'!).

Today the French are over, to discuss the military situation in the Balkans. The French want to turn Tino[2] off the throne and set up a republic in Greece under Venizelos. D. I think is inclined to take sides with the French, but our military advisers are dead against the plan, & are even on the point of removing troops from Salonika. A good deal depends on the outcome of this conference, not only from a military, but I think also from a political point of view.

May 29th 1917
The French departed today, & D. is very pleased with the result of the Conference. They have decided to depose Tino, & establish a republic in Greece— this much against the will of our military people, but D. overruled them. Robertson was inclined to be nasty, but D. turned on him roughly. 'We are entitled to your military advice, General Robertson', he said sternly, 'which you have not yet given. The *policy* is ours.' D. said he crumpled up, & was as meek as a lamb for the rest of the Conference.

The French are delighted with D. They quote him in France as 'the last word' on the war. Painlevé told D. that in Paris last week, some politicians who tried to detract from Ribot's speech in the House, used as their most forcible argument the fact that Lloyd George (so they said) had expressed dissatisfaction at it! And Painlevé said that this argument carried a good deal of weight with it! In the same way the London correspondent of a Paris paper has been writing to Paris to say that Lloyd George thinks the Russians have played a low-down game & is privately saying very strong things about the way they have let the French down.

I forgot to write last week of how D. has seen Prince Sixte, brother or brother-in-law of the

The diary breaks off here. In the interval before it is resumed, there had been a bloody and unsuccessful British offensive in Flanders. The submarine menace was largely overcome. Churchill joined the government as minister of munitions, and Montagu as secretary for India. On 24 October the Italians were heavily defeated at Caporetto and retreated to the Piave. Lloyd George seized the opportunity to propose an Allied

1. George V's private secretary.
2. King Constantine.

conference at Rapallo. He intended to set up a Supreme War Council, which would have the additional advantage of reducing Robertson's powers as C.I.G.S.

On 7 November the Bolsheviks seized power in Petrograd and established a Soviet government.

November 5th 1917 (In the train to Rapallo)

On Friday last [2 November] D. received a message from the French & American Govts. asking him to go to Italy in order to use his influence to stop the Italian rout. The Germans were advancing rapidly into Italy, & the Italian Army was completely demoralised. It was feared that they would not attempt to make a stand unless outside influence was brought to bear. Sir W. Robertson left for Italy last Monday [29 October], & French & British troops are already on the way to the Italian front, but they cannot reach there for some days. D. decided to leave on Sat. morning [3 November], & I persuaded him to take me with him—indeed, he did not need much persuading, for I think he had already made up his mind before I asked him. We left London on Saturday morning, crossed in a destroyer, which was most thrilling. We crossed in $\frac{3}{4}$ of an hour, tearing through the water. We were escorted by another destroyer, & passed destroyers & transports on the way, but no submarines! Arrived in Paris about 10 at night. With us were Sir Henry Wilson,[1] Gen. Smuts, Gen. Maurice,[2] Col. Hankey & their respective A.D.C.'s, Mr. Davies and myself. We stayed the night at the Hotel Crillon, on the Place de la Concorde.

Paris is a very sad city, but it was nice to be there once more. The hotel was full of soldiers—Americans, French, English, & everywhere you see in the Paris streets the blue of the French uniform. Many of the women are in black. The little theatres & cafés in the Champs Elysées are many of them closed, or being used for war work.

We stayed the day in Paris, D. conferring with various people all day. He had General Pershing[3] to breakfast, & Briand visited him in the afternoon. Briand showed him a copy of a letter which he had written to Ribot, stating that he had been approached by the Germans with an offer of peace terms, the Germans offering to give up Alsace-Lorraine & Belgium.[4] Ribot had

1. Sir Henry Hughes Wilson (1864–1922): director of military operations, 1910–14; C.I.G.S., 1918–22; assassinated by members of I.R.A., 1922.
2. Sir Frederick Maurice (1871–1951): general director of military operations, 1915–18; in May 1918 wrote letter to The Times, accusing Lloyd George of misstating the number of British troops in France.
3. General John Joseph Pershing (1860–1948): commanded American expeditionary force to Europe, 1917–19; given rank of General of the Armies by Congress, 1919; American chief of staff, 1921.
4. This was a considerable exaggeration of the offer which an unofficial German representative had made. Germany would only have given up a portion of Alsace, and Belgium would not have recovered complete independence. The Briand-Lancken negotiations were of no real importance.

never taken any action on that letter, & now of course the Germans would demand more after the Italian disaster. Probably the suggestion would not then have been accepted by the Allies, but D. thinks he should have communicated it to the British Gov. D. also saw Gen. Haig, & had a very serious talk with him. He made it quite plain that the time had come when he was going to assert himself, & if necessary let the public know the truth about the soldiers & their strategy.

I sought Suzanne [my cousin] out during the day, & luckily found her at Mdme. Debray's flat. She quite broke down when she saw me, the surprise was too much for her. We spent a great part of the day together. She is very lonely, but will not come to England. Her mother's death has aged her a lot, & I have not seen her since Paul died, so that many things have changed since we saw each other the Xmas before the war. The world is much sadder.

We left Paris at 8 o'clock in the evening, M. Painlevé, M. Franklin-Bouillon[1] & two French officers accompanying us. We slept in the train and I woke at 8 o'clock this morning to find myself amidst the most wonderful scenery of Savoie. We were approaching the Alps, & the day was perfect. As we went on the scenery became more & more wonderful. The sky was deep blue, the mountains were capped with snow, & all up the sides were the autumn tints of the trees—from bright yellow to golden brown, & then the deep green of the firs. Lower down the slopes were the vineyards, also with their autumn tints, and here & there the Italian villages nestled among the mountains. We reached Modane about 10.0 o'clock & stayed there about an hour, owing to a breakdown in the tunnel. We went for a walk through the little town. It was a beautiful morning & the sun was shining brightly.

After passing through the Mt. Cenis tunnel, I think the scenery if possible was more beautiful. We were right in amongst the mountains, & it was a superb panorama. On one road winding down over the mountains we watched the huge motor caissons on their way to the Italian front, taking up supplies and ammunition. The train has been going slowly, as the route is crowded with troop trains taking British and French troops to the front. They are passing along the line at the rate of 40 a day, & all the villages we passed turned out to see if we were a troop train.

We arrived at Turin just before lunch, but the crowd on the platform was surly and hostile, looking at the train with sulky faces. Turin is full of Germans, & there were pro-German riots there a short time ago. The place is full of spies, & as everything passing to the front goes through Turin, it is a dangerous place. The whole thing left a very nasty impression upon us.

We gradually left the mountains & got into the plains, & are now approaching the coast, where it is a little more hilly.

---

1. Henri Franklin-Bouillon (1870–1937): French politician; a French representative at first session of supreme war council at Rapallo, 1917; negotiated with Turks, 1921–2; known by the British as 'Boiling Frankie'.

November 6th 1917

Arrived in Rapallo about 7.30 last night. There were cheering crowds at the station. The Italians—Orlando—The Prime Minister—Sonnino[1] & others were there to meet us. A Conference was held before dinner. D. says the Italians seem stunned, & are quite helpless. They have no suggestions to make. Orlando keeps on assuring the French & the English that the Italians will never give in, even if they are driven to Sicily! But that is not very satisfactory. They still talk of the 20,000 men of the 2nd Army, when that army is practically nonexistent. They acknowledge, however, that the arrival of the French & British troops in Italy, or at least the knowledge that they were on the way, has saved Italy from utter disaster—which shows to what an extent they had become demoralised. The Italians, however, are still retreating, & it seems now that only a miracle can save the northern provinces of Italy.

D. & Mr. Davies & I got up early this morning & went for a walk before breakfast. It was a beautiful morning, & the view across the bay was wonderful. For the first time in my life I have seen olives & oranges growing in the open. I am thrilled with all the surroundings, but it is a place where one wants to be lazy.

The Ministers had another conference after breakfast, & some of us went to explore the town. We bought lace made by the women in Rapallo; we saw fugitives from the invaded parts who had just arrived, sitting huddled in the square, their faces drawn with fatigue and terror. Coming back, we met D. & Gen. Smuts, & joined them in their walk. The Conference had not been very satisfactory, the Italians having no fixed plans, & yet not seeming very keen on anything we propose. D. says he will not leave until Cadorna has been replaced.

But apart from dealing with the immediate situation, D. has a great plan which he intends to carry through immediately. He has made up his mind that Gen. Robertson has got to have his power taken away from him. Had it not been for him, & his Western front policy, British Divisions & guns would have been sent long ago to reinforce the Italians; & the whole aspect of the war would have been changed. D. has urged this all the summer, but Robertson insisted that Divisions must be kept on the Western front, & that the autumn attack there would be decisive. No real effect, however, has been produced by our last attack, enormous losses have occurred & the Italians have suffered a disastrous defeat. D. therefore has conceived an ingenious device for depriving Robertson of his power. There is to be an inter-Allied Military Council established at Versailles, with Gen. Sir Henry Wilson at the head of the British representatives. Any decision on strategy will be taken by this Council, on which there will be representatives of all the Allied powers, & the decision will then be communicated to the War Office, who will carry

---

1. Italian foreign minister.

it out. All the allied fronts will thus be under common direction, & all the campaigns will be undertaken by common consent. Thus a victory in one part would be a common victory, & a defeat would be a common defeat, for which all would be responsible.

This plan had been communicated to Gen. Robertson before our arrival, & he was here when we arrived. D. says he is frightened by the Italian disaster, which D. foretold in a memo. circulated at the Rome Conference last Jan., if we failed to help them. D. thinks Robertson will consent to anything now, though of course he will not be pleased at the idea of losing his power. But I feel certain D. will not give way on this point—it is the only chance of winning the war. D. has been fighting the soldiers all the year on this point, & this resulted in the attacks on him in The Globe, The Morning Post & other papers. The Italian defeat, however, proved that he was right, & when it happened he sent for Gwynne, the Editor of The M. Post & said to him: 'If I have any more of these attacks, I will publish the whole facts. You ask me not to publish, because it would undermine the confidence of the people in their leaders. Do you realise that the object of these attacks is to undermine confidence in me? I too have an army—the people. It is most necessary that that army should retain its confidence in me, in order that we may win the war. You do not think this is of account, but I know it, & if necessary I shall take steps to inform them of the facts in order to defend myself & to win the war.' But I think D. has won this time.

I do not like Franklin-Bouillon. He is a shifty individual, & runs Painlevé. He also talks far too much.

I feel rather out of place here, being the only woman. But everyone is very nice & being able to talk French I get along well with the French people.

November 8th 1917 (Peschiera, nr. Lake Garda in the train)
We left Rapallo last night after dinner, the Conference having been success-fully terminated. The First meeting of the Supreme Allied War Council was held yesterday in the hotel. Everyone agrees that it is the most momentous decision of the war. D. is very pleased with the results. He has also succeeded in getting rid of Cadorna.[1] The Italians jibbed a good deal when it was suggested. But D. insisted. 'No one denies', he said, 'that the Italian troops are brave. Even the bravest troops suffer defeat sometimes. But you must admit also that even the bravest troops will not achieve victory if they are badly led. We cannot consent to imperil our troops under an inferior com-mand.' In the end, they gave way, and Cadorna is to be given a post on the Supreme War Council! General Wilson is our representative—indeed, I believe he put the idea into D.'s mind in the first place. The Council is to have its headquarters at Versailles. I have no doubt that it will have far-reaching effects, even after the war. It will certainly have a very great bearing upon the conduct of the war henceforth.

---

1. Italian commander-in-chief.

Robertson takes his defeat very quietly. One can see he is sick about it, but I think he must be agitated about the general situation.[1]

The whole company is heartily sick of Franklin-Bouillon. It appears that he shouts everyone down at the Conferences, & gets his own way by a process of sheer exhaustion. Painlevé is entirely in his hands. I am sorry for the little man, as he seems a nice man, but Bouillon is a mountebank. D. is thoroughly sick of him, & so is everyone else. I think he is dangerous. For some reason, he was most anxious that the Council should sit in Paris, & D. thinks there must be something behind it. He did not get his way in this, however. He gives one the impression of being insincere and crafty.

Yesterday afternoon D. & Gen. Smuts & Mr. Davies & I, went for a lovely drive, in between two conferences. We went first of all to Porto Fino, a lovely little place nestling on a hill overlooking the bay. Then we returned & went in the other direction along the coast towards Spezzia. The ride was perfectly beautiful, the sea was calm and blue, but a little misty, the hills are still clad in their autumn tints. The road winds along up and down the cliffs, & you come out upon one glorious view after another. When high up you can see the Appenines all round, with the little white villas dotted in among the vine-yards & groves. Here & there the cypress trees stand out black above the autumn tints of the chestnuts and birches & the green of the holm oaks and oranges.

The Italian situation itself however seems almost hopeless. To begin with, those responsible do not seem to realise the urgency of coping with it—'what must be, must be', said Orlando.—And when they do grasp it, they seem quite incapable of deciding what is to be done. Everything seems disorganised, the soldiers seem incapable of making a stand. Since yesterday they appear to have lost another army corps, if not two, and the Germans have already crossed the Piave at one point, though the Italians vowed they would never retreat from that line. What is to be done? Is it any use our sending help if it is to be thrown away? There seems to be no organisation, no discipline. Everywhere you see bands of soldiers loafing about, doing nothing appar-ently, many of them men who have run away from the front. Just now two trains have passed each other, one full of Italian soldiers coming away from the front, the other full of French soldiers going towards the front! Trains full of refugees—old women, young women & children & even strapping young men—are continually passing, but no one seems to know exactly what is going to be done. Everything is in confusion. The King asked D. to come here to meet him to discuss the situation. We arrived here at 9.0 as arranged, and waited an hour in the train before any definite message was received as to what was expected of us. There was no one whose duty it was to meet us,

---

1. Robertson was not in fact defeated. When the question of the supreme war council was raised in the house of commons, Lloyd George explained that it had no powers; it could only advise and discuss. Robertson remained supreme until February 1918 when he was finally dislodged.

there were no cars to take the Ministers & Generals to the rendezvous. Fortunately General Delmé Radcliffe turned up with two cars of his own, & they served the purpose. But that is an indication of the state of things throughout. It does not seem to be anybody's business to take charge of matters, & so nothing is done. Worst of all, nobody seems to realise the urgency of time in the present matter. Tomorrow seems to do as well as today. Meantime the Germans are pressing on & it seems doubtful whether our troops will arrive in time. They may eventually stem the tide of the invasion, but the Italians will never recover all they have lost during the last three weeks. From one point of view it will be an advantage as far as peace terms are concerned, as the Italians will no longer be able to talk about Trieste and Smyrna with the same determination as before!

D. & the other ministers & generals are at present at a Conference with the King, who is supposed to be a man of action. Perhaps something more satisfactory may come of this talk. It is a very wet day, & one can scarcely see the lake & nothing of the surrounding scenery.

November 9th 1917 (Aix-les-Bains)
Arrived here early this morning & had breakfast at the hotel. We had a most varied journey yesterday. After lunching in the train at Peschiera General Wilson left with General Foch to visit the Italian front, with full powers to make arrangements as to the disposition of the French and English troops. They were all unanimously of the opinion that the King of Italy is a great-hearted little man, & a thorough patriot. The difficulty is, said General Wilson, to find out exactly what the number of forces is which the Germans are opposing to the Italians. The King says 21 Divisions, but we can only trace 6, & the French 9 at the most. However, perhaps General Wilson will be able to clear up things a little. 'Success to you', said D. when he was saying goodbye to them. 'It is to save Europe that you are going—the fate of Europe depends upon what you are able to do now.'

General Delmé Radcliffe drew a horrible picture of the Italian retreat. He says the soldiers stampeded and trampled the civilian refugees under foot. Hundreds met their death in this way. The confusion on the roads was indescribable. He himself at one point took 4 hours to go 400 yards in a car, and at one time he despaired of crossing the Tagliamento in time.

In the afternoon we stopped for an hour at Brescia, and saw many trains of refugees passing through the station. The whole scene was very sad, & a downpour of rain added to the gloom. D. went for a stroll in the town, and came back followed by a crowd—it seems impossible for him to go into a remote town like that without being recognised. We parted from the French Ministers here, as they went to see their troops on the Italian front—D. very relieved at getting rid of Franklin-Bouillon.

We then proceeded to Milan, where we spent another hour. We visited the cathedral, but it was dark & we could scarcely see any details. But we could just discern the wonder of that magnificent piece of architecture, & it filled us with awe.

We parted here from the Italian Ministers, who proceeded to Rome. We left them much more cheerful than we had found them—my heart bled for their grief—there was tragedy written on the face of Orlando, & when at Brescia an old general came up with the news that the snow had fallen heavily & blocked up the Silvio, thus relieving them of the menace from that quarter, their relief was pathetic. However, they were quite cheerful when we left them, and I think D. has performed a service to Europe by visiting them so promptly in their hour of need.

Today we started after breakfast, & went for a long run through the mountains to A....... The scenery was most wonderful—mountains on each side, their tops snow-clad, the fir trees lower down powdered with snow, & lower down still the autumn tints—yellow & burnished gold—of the beeches and chestnuts. It is a wonderful country, & its dignified beauty pleased me more than the caressing grace of Rapallo.

D. is now preparing his speech for Monday [12 November].

Diary 1919

No diary has been preserved for 1918. During that year Lloyd George and Frances Stevenson were both struck by the influenza epidemic and saw little of each other. Germany concluded an armistice on 11 November 1918. Austria-Hungary disintegrated. The Lloyd George Coalition won a general election, but the Unionists were now in a great majority. Churchill became secretary for war, and Austen Chamberlain chancellor of the exchequer. The peace conference opened at Paris on 12 January 1919. It made little progress during its first two months. The Big Four (Lloyd George, Clemenceau, Orlando, and President Wilson) then took matters into their own hands and conducted all the important negotiations themselves. Though the war cabinet continued to meet in London, it made few decisions, with Lloyd George, and often other members, absent in Paris.

March 5th 1919

Arrived in Paris, P.M. having spent a most successful month in London, settling the Miners' dispute, & getting the new House of Commons to work. Everyone congratulates him most heartily on the way in which he seems to have brought comparative peace into the industrial world. On our arrival in London at the beginning of February there was an atmosphere of gloom & pessimism. But the P.M. soon dispelled this by his clever negotiations, & also by his speeches on the industrial situation. He has certainly put every ounce of energy into the job, but in spite of this he is very cheerful & in the best of spirits.

The Tories—at least the more difficult of them, such as Long & Curzon— have got their tails up as the result of their success at the Election. 'George thinks he won the election', said Walter Long to his neighbour at a dinner the other night. 'Well he didn't. It was the Tories that won the election, *and he will soon begin to find that out.*' But the P.M. swears he will go to the country again if they try any of their obstructing tricks. They are already trying to prevent his schemes for Land Acquisition & Land Settlement, & there was a great row in the Cabinet on Monday [3 March]. 'If this goes on', said D. to the others, 'hell will be cut loose in this country and I will tell you who will unlock the door—*I* will!'

Austen Chamberlain seems to have made rather a muddle of things already, & everyone's voice is raised against him. He was very independent, too, when the post of Chancellor was offered to him—complained that he had not been sent for by the P.M., but that the Office had just been thrown at him—like a bone at a dog. 'Stop a minute, Austen', said the P.M. to him, 'there is a good deal of meat on that bone.'

The P.M. is rather glad, I think, that the Ministers who are getting all the criticism are the old Conservative clique, & not the new blood that he has introduced.

The King was very anxious for D. to come back as soon as possible—at any rate by the 21st March. 'Everything gets hung up while you are away', said H.M. to D., 'no-one seems capable of taking any decision.' But when we arrive in Paris everyone says 'It is a good thing you are back. No decisions have been taken since you left!'

The Duke of Connaught travelled across with us. He & D. & Sir Henry Wilson[1] had a merry lunch together.

March 7th 1919
D. plunged into hard work at once. Today he had a set-to in the council with Foch,[2] who had advised a standing conscript army in Germany. D. foresaw that if Germany maintained a conscript army, it would be an argument in favour of all the other European countries maintaining conscript armies—in fact, it would be impossible for them to do otherwise. D. got his way, for he had talked the whole thing over with Clemenceau in the morning, & the latter promised to back him up. 'What I proposed practically amounts to the abolition of conscription in Europe', said D. when telling me about it.

March 8th 1919
Churchill arrived late last night from London, & breakfasted with the P.M. this morning. Full of his speech in the House on the Military Service Bill. He certainly does not lack self-confidence—in fact if he had a little less he might think a little more before he acts & speaks. One cannot help being fascinated by him, although I *cannot* bring myself to like him.

March 9th 1919
Went to see Tales of Hoffman with Captain Harmsworth. I like him, though he is not very popular with the other young people of the party, partly I think because he is so serious & does not like playing the fool. I think he feels his responsibilities, owing to the death of his two elder brothers in the war, & the fact that he will have to take on his father's businesses.

Churchill came to lunch, & as usual was quite interesting. He is taking Foch's side in the question of disarmament, being in favour of keeping up big

---

1. Sir Henry Wilson had succeeded Robertson as C.I.G.S.
2. Marshal Foch had been made Allied commander-in-chief in April 1918. He was now in theory chief military adviser to the supreme war council, but often used his position to defend French interests.

armies in Europe. Churchill, being S. of S. for War, wants a big army. P.M. is determined to stick to his proposal, carried in the week, of a voluntary army in Germany. Foch is rather sulky as a result.

P.M. had a little dinner-party in the evening. He is not feeling very fit, however, & still looks very tired and pale.

March 10th 1919

P.M. lunched at Mr. Balfour's flat to meet with Queen of Rumania, & according to everybody, was in his best form. D. says she is very naughty, but a very clever woman, though on the whole he does not like her. She gave a lengthy description of her purchases in Paris, which included a pink silk chemise. She spoke of meeting President Wilson on his arrival. 'What shall I talk to him about?' she asked. 'The League of Nations or my pink chemise?' 'Begin with the League of Nations', said Mr. Balfour, 'and finish up with the pink chemise. If you were talking to Mr. Lloyd George, you could begin with the pink chemise!'

March 11th 1919

P.M. lunched at the Embassy, & had Montagu & Mr. & Mrs. Jimmy Rothschild to dinner.

D. annoyed because the French are proving difficult over the question of indemnities. The French want reparation to be the primary charge, & if that were so, we should come in for a very small share, right at the end. D. will not agree to it, so told Montagu to break off negotiations with them at once. He also told Kerr,[1] who is in charge of the question of fixing the boundaries on the Western front, that he was not to come to any arrangement at all with the French. D. hopes by this means to make the French strike a bargain with him. 'I am making a good fight for the old country', said D. to me, '& there is no one but me who could do it.' It is perfectly true, & D. is not boasting when he says it, though I don't think he would say it to anyone else but me.

Went to see Carmen with Captain Harmsworth—an excellent performance, & I thoroughly enjoyed it.

March 12th 1919

Sir Rosslyn Wemyss[2] came to breakfast. He is on his way to Brussels to confer with the Germans, & after having come to terms with them, to offer them food. He may not promise them food, however, until they have agreed to our terms. 'I only hope', said the P.M. to him, 'that the Germans will realise that the pistol you are pointing at their heads is stuffed with sausages, & not with bullets!'

Lady Rothermere came to lunch—a very lively person & extraordinarily young for her age. I can understand, however, why she & her husband do not

---

1. Philip Kerr (1882–1940): Lloyd George's private secretary, 1916–21; succeeded cousin as 11th Marquis of Lothian 1930.
2. First sea lord.

live together, & I should not imagine that the fault is altogether on his side. However, she is very fascinating, which makes up for a great deal. Her son is not the least bit like her, but is far nicer than his father—a much nicer nature I should imagine, but still rather cold & calculating. But he is extraordinarily handsome, & I like him.

March 13th 1919

P.M. still not feeling at all well, & rested in the morning. In the afternoon we went for a run to Fontainebleau. It was a delicious, springlike afternoon, & the Chateau looked beautiful. We took along one of the girls from the Majestic, 'the Peach', & D. flirted with her to his heart's content. However, he was quite open about it & I think it did him good, so that I did not mind.

In the evening we all went to see Figaro at the Opéra Comique. It was an excellent performance, but the people recognised D. in the first interval, & gave him a wonderful ovation. It was rather embarrassing, & of course for the rest of the evening he was the centre of all eyes, so that it rather spoilt the performance for him. He says it is the last time he will go to a theatre. It really is hard lines that he should not be able to enjoy himself quietly without becoming the centre of attraction.

March 14th 1919

President Wilson arrived, & D. says he can think & talk of nothing else but his League of Nations. D. says that everything must hang on to that for him to take any interest in it. I fear it will be very slow work now that he has come back. He has started to annoy D. already by talking of matters that have already been settled as though they were still open for discussion & as though he intended to reopen them. I am very glad he has started to annoy D. as I think the latter was rather too prone to encourage & agree with him while he was here before. I do not think they will ever get a move on until President Wilson has been put in his place, & D. is the only person who can do it. Clemenceau cannot tolerate him at any price. If it were not for D. who acts as a sort of intermediary between their two minds, things would be impossible.

The French are still haggling about the right bank of the Rhine.[1] But D. attacked Clemenceau on his practical side 'You speak as though that would afford you security', he said. 'Can you name a single river in this war that stopped an advance?' Clemenceau was forced to admit that this was true.

March 15th 1919

D. talked to Clemenceau about his wound, & C. described the incident.[2] 'There were nine shots', said the old man to D., 'and oh! it did seem such a long time.'

---

1. The French were seeking to establish a separate republic under their control on the left bank of the Rhine, with bridgeheads on the right bank.
2. An attempted assassination.

D. is furious with Wilson. The meeting of the Peace Conference had to be adjourned this afternoon because Wilson said he had not read the papers, & therefore could not discuss them. This is the sort of thing that will make D. very angry. Moreover, Wilson insists on re-opening questions that have been settled so it looks as though there will be a row.

March 16th 1919
We went on an excursion to the devastated area around Soissons. Soissons itself is in a terrible state, the principal streets being altogether destroyed. We were lucky in coming across there a French Colonel, who volunteered to conduct us over the Chemin des Dames, where he himself fought for seven months last year. The place is a desolation, simply a series of shell-holes—how men could have lived in it passes the imagination. He showed us heaps of stones which had once been farms or mills. We had to walk warily, because of the unexploded grenades and shells which were lying about everywhere.

We lunched in the woods beyond Senlis, where the ground was carpeted with daffodils & primroses. D. was in his best form, as he always is on these occasions.

We had Megan Jones (Leila Mégane) to dinner, & Mr. Balfour & others. Afterwards went up to Mr. Balfour's flat & had some music. Megan Jones has a wonderful voice & ought to do well, but like all artists, is very self-centred.

March 18th 1919
J. H. Thomas[1] flew over from London to see the P.M. about the Labour situation. He is an amusing creature, not very reliable & very open to flattery & coaxing. However he is playing our game at the moment. At present it is in the balance whether there will be a strike of the Triple Alliance or not, but in any case D. is preparing to take action in case there should be. The Miners however are likely to get a good part of their demands conceded as a result of this Commission. 'The trouble is', said Thomas very wisely, 'they are trying to get the grievances of a century righted in five minutes, and they won't give you five and a 'arf.' D. however is going to take a firm hand. He says if he has to choose between the Peace Conference & London he must choose the Conference, 'for the sake of the world', as President Wilson would say. Both Wilson & Clemenceau are insistent that he should stay here until the preliminary terms are signed.

Thomas cannot speak without swearing (though he moderates himself before ladies). The P.M. laughingly said that Thomas' first words on arrival would be, 'Christ, isn't it b..... cold.' What he actually said was: 'Is that you Davies? Well, I've b..... well arrived.'

---

1. J. H. Thomas was secretary of the National Union of Railwaymen. The railwaymen, miners, and transport workers, had formed a triple alliance for joint industrial alliance. In fact the railwaymen struck alone in September 1919, and the miners struck alone later.

March 19th 1919

Went with D. to St. Cloud to play golf. D. very cheerful, but very jealous because he says I walked with Esmond Harmsworth all the time, & he took me there to walk with him. Told me a funny story about Clemenceau & Klotz.[1] The latter is very unpopular, & a deputation of ministers waited upon C. asking that he should be removed as he was not playing the game. Clem. explained that he did not wish to dismiss him now, as it would unstabilise the Government. 'Very well, we must shut our eyes', said they. 'Yes', said Clemenceau, 'one always shuts one's eyes at the most delicious moment.' It was Clemenceau who also said that 'all the great pleasures of life are silent.'

General Allenby[2] came to lunch. He is a fine-looking man, & one I imagine who would stand no nonsense. D. was urging him to give the French the facts about Syria, that the French would not be tolerated there. I believe he did at a subsequent meeting between P.M., Clemenceau & Wilson.

The French are very obstinate about Syria & are trying to take the line that the English want it for themselves & are stirring up Arabs against the French. They are also making impossible demands with regard to indemnities, & on the whole are behaving rather unreasonably. 'France is a poor winner', said D. 'She does not take her victories well.' The real reason, I think, is that the French are terrified at a repetition of 1914. They cannot believe that Germany is defeated, & feel that they cannot have enough guarantees for the future.

Clemenceau, Wilson & Orlando have addressed a joint letter to D. urging him to stay in Paris until the preliminary terms are signed, & D. has decided to stay.

March 21st 1919

D. promised to go to dinner with the Count de Castellane, thinking it was only a small men's dinner. On finding it was a big affair with lots of women he absolutely refused to go, declaring that he had been tricked into it, & that he was not going to be run in that way. Nothing would move him & he dined by himself.

The situation in England seems better, though still anxious, & D. will probably stay here for another fortnight. Everyone is chafing at the delay in the decisions of the Peace Conference. The fact of the matter is that President Wilson can think of nothing but his League of Nations, & that poor old Clemenceau is not the man he was. D. says that he is breaking up, & that the old Clemenceau was killed by Cottin.[3] It is very pathetic. D. says he just comes to the Conferences & has not the energy to take part in the Debates or to give any decisions. I think D. would be glad if Briand came back as Prime Minister, though that is unlikely as long as Clemenceau is alive. The French

---

1. French minister of finance.
2. Edmund Henry Hynman Allenby (1861–1936): field marshal; cr. Viscount Allenby of Megiddo, 1919; commander-in-chief, Egypt and Palestine, 1917–19; special high commissioner for Egypt, 1919–25.
3. Cottin had attempted to assassinate Clemenceau.

themselves though are beginning to perceive the difference & to understand that France is not pulling her full weight in the Conference. The only two things that have been decided since our return to London—the disarmament of Germany & the resolution to send food there—have been put through & originated by D. The French press seem to realise this & there is a laudatory article on D. in today's Figaro. He is very pleased with it. He is determined too to take the bull by the horns & to force decisions on the vital points during the coming week. He has gone down to Fontainebleau today for a complete rest & a hard think. When he withdraws from the world in that way even for 24 hours something is bound to happen afterwards! Once his mind is made up President Wilson's typewriter will prove a very inadequate weapon with which to defend his nebulous doctrines.

D. is also very annoyed with the American attempt to increase their army & double their navy, while preaching the gospel of the League of Nations. By the way it is a pity that history has been deprived of Wilson's first speech on this subject—when opening the discussion on it at the Quai D'Orsay. He explained in this speech how Christianity had failed in its purpose after 2,000 years. But the League of Nations was going to go one better than Christianity & would supply all defects. This speech was afterwards cut out of the procès verbal.

March 23rd 1919
Yesterday morning a man called Millard came to breakfast—an American journalist who has been in Germany lately. He says the conditions in Germany are terrible—the rations allowed for a whole day are not enough to make what we should consider a decent breakfast. The people have practically no clothes, & their mental capacity has decreased by 60% owing to privation. They have money, but cannot buy food. They are looking to the Allies for salvation. They do not mind the armies of occupation, in fact they are glad to have them there to preserve order. They curse the Kaiser, & will hear nothing against the Allies. They blame their own government which led them into this war. They describe themselves as a 'betrayed people'.

The dance at the Majestic last night was an amazing affair—a most cosmopolitan crowd—the last touch was put on it when Lord Wimborne arrived with a crowd of wonderful ladies. People rather resent this invasion of the Majestic on Saturday nights, & steps are to be taken to put a stop to it, otherwise the thing will become a scandal.

March 24th 1919
D. arrived back from Fontainebleau with his plans all made. He means business this week, & will sweep all before him. He will stand no more nonsense either from French or Americans. He is taking the long view about the Peace, & insists that it should be one that will not leave bitterness for years to come, & probably lead to another war.

Lunched at Mr. Balfour's flat today. D. was very pleased that he had asked me. Lord & Lady Cranborne were also there, the latter a really nice girl. Mr. Balfour very much occupied with a very charming French lady, who was there, but whose name I did not discover. I do not care much for General Sackville West, who seems to me to be a very second-rate individual.

We had a very jolly little dinner—some young people up from the Majestic & D. was in very good form—absolutely mad. When he gets to the point of trying on other people's hats he is always most amusing. He tried on a Staff officer's hat & someone said he looked like Lord French. 'Oh no, that can't be', said D. 'Lord French is *naughty!*'

March 25th 1919
The fruits of D.'s weekend already beginning to mature. The great topic is Poland—Poland at breakfast, lunch & dinner, & I presume at the meetings too. D. is dead against the 'corridor' system, under which a large slice of Germany containing 3 million Germans is lopped off & put under the Poles. D. says it will simply mean another war. The French are furious with him for opposing the idea. D. says the peace must be a just peace, & we must prepare such terms for the Germans to sign that we shall feel justified in insisting upon them, & if the Germans refuse to sign them, then the people—our people— will back us up. To add this corridor to Poland is simply to create another Alsace Lorraine. In the same way, D. is against the French retaining the left Bank of the Rhine. He says the French are opening their mouths too wide & is preparing for a row on the subject.

The French were in difficulties about Odessa. D. proposed a military plan to relieve the situation there. Foch was sent for, & approved entirely of the plan. 'Mais vous êtes un grand général', said Clemenceau to D.

March 26th 1919
The Times & Daily Mail attacking D. for his Polish policy but he means to stick to it, though he is in conflict with the experts on the subject. He is bring-ing Wilson round to his point of view, in fact, already has succeeded in doing so, & Wilson is now almost as enthusiastic as D. himself. The French do not particularly mind—it does not concern them very much.

Tonight D. & I had dinner quietly together. He was very tired after a very hard day's work, but I think is satisfied at the way things are going. The Press are furious with him because he protested against the leakages which were occurring as to what passed at the Conferences, & now the 'Four' are sitting from day to day in secret, & no bulletin is issued. As a result the French papers are being very vigorously censored, & The Times & Daily Mail are taking up the attack on their behalf.

March 27th 1919
D. very eloquent again on the subject of Poland, about which there is still very stiff opposition. He is certainly taking the most impartial view of the whole situation, & is looking very far ahead in the making of this peace.

'Supposing you were Germany', he said to Sir Eyre Crowe,[1] who was at dinner & who took the view of the experts on the Polish question: 'Here she is, with no food, no raw material, stripped of her colonies, stripped of Alsace Lorraine, stripped of a large portion of her coal and iron,—it is just a bleeding torso of the Germany that was—and you come . . .

The rest of the entry for this day is lost.

March 28th 1919
A most unpleasant scene between Wilson & Clemenceau.

March 30th 1919
Went for a picnic in St. Germain woods. D. had a complete day of rest, & badly needed it.

April 1st 1919
Dined with Evan Morgan at the Majestic. Seely asked us to join his party (which included D.), but D. thinks it better that I should not be seen dining with him in public. I think he is right. We joined the party afterwards for some music. Mr. Webber played Wagner, & it was all 'very pleasant', as Augustus John would say.

The Conferences proceed morning & afternoon & evening, & D. very busy & preoccupied.

April 2nd 1919
D. received a most unpleasant document from Clemenceau, attacking the English for their claims in the East.

There is no doubt that D. is getting unpopular among the French just at present. They say that he is being won over by Wilson to pro-Bosch tendencies. I suppose it cannot be helped, if the French prove themselves as greedy as they are doing.

Sat for my portrait for Orpen. He is a charming little man & not so terrifying as John.

April 3rd 1919
D. very pleased because he has got his way over Poland. He won Wilson round, & has persuaded him that the plan was really his, in order to make him the more keen about it. Paderewski has announced his intention of coming from Poland to challenge the decision.

Sat for Orpen again this afternoon. He showed me some of his sketches of Peace Conference delegates. C.I.G.S. & Reading are wonderfully good, specially the latter.

---

1. Permanent foreign under-secretary, 1920–5.

April 4th 1919

C.I.G.S. & Mrs. —— came to dinner. The former rather quieter than usual. Very eloquent on the subject of his portrait. 'That picture', he said, 'is going to fetch the biggest price any portrait ever fetched. There are going to be two bidders—one is Scotland Yard; the other is Madame Tussaud's.'

Mrs. —— is one of these rather vain women, who have been very beautiful & still expect a lot of attention. She made a great fuss of C.I.G.S., trying to give the impression that he was fond of her—as he may be—but was very annoyed when he refused her invitation to spend Sunday with him. He turned to me & said under his breath: 'You see, I like to start the week fresh.'

April 5th 1919

P.M. not feeling very well, & President Wilson in bed, but the meetings went on just the same. Clemenceau was very pleased at Wilson's absence, & could not conceal his joy. 'He is *worse* today', he said to D., & doubled up with laughter. 'Do you know his doctor? Couldn't you get round him & bribe him?...' The old man did not attempt to conceal his feelings on the subject.

D. came back from the morning meeting very pleased. 'We are making headway', he said to me, 'which means that I am getting my own way!' Anyway, by the evening they had reached an agreement on reparation & indemnities & D. *had* got his own way, after having fought the matter for over a fortnight. Baruch, the American, went up to him after the meeting & said to him, 'Now I understand why you are Prime Minister. You are far & away ahead of the whole lot.'

April 6th 1919

D. stayed in bed with a cold & a bit of a temperature, & I stayed in to nurse him. He was quite happy, & it was a rest for him, though it was a pity it happened today, for the weather was beautifully warm & really springlike. However he will probably be well enough to get up tomorrow, & the day in bed will have made all the difference to him.

April 10th 1919

General Smuts came to breakfast, on his return from Vienna. He gave a most eloquently depressing account of the conditions there. It is a world that we cannot imagine, he said—a world completely gone to pieces. There is no authority—no business. Every shop is closed, & an inventory is being taken of everything, in order that everything may be nationalised. Even the houses are nationalised, & families have just enough rooms given to them for their use. (This certainly seems to be a solution of the housing problem, & might be tried in London at the present time!) There is scarcely any food there & everyone is starving. Smuts's batman & another soldier were walking in the streets of Vienna when a child came up & asked for food. One of the soldiers gave him a biscuit. Instantly the two men were set upon by a swarm of children, who seemed to come from no-where, & they were almost torn to pieces as the children fought to get to their pockets to see if there were any more food anywhere.

It was a horrible description of a famine-stricken country & represents a terribly difficult problem to deal with. Nothing is moving. The only people from whom they seem to expect any help are the British. The French are worse than useless. Smuts says they are insolent & cruel to the populace, & that the resignation of Karolyi[1] was due to the fact that he could no longer tolerate their treatment of him & his government.

Paderewski came to lunch, with his story of Poland's woes. There are very few people who have ever impressed me as much as he did. I could have listened to him for hours. More often one is disappointed when one meets great men who have been greatly praised, but this time the fulfilment was greater than the expectation. He is a really remarkable man. He told us some of the history of the Poles, and left one with the impression that they had been a greatly under-estimated nation! He traced back the history of some of the other Balkan races—& told us for instance of the origin of the Bulgarians, who originally came from the Volga (Volgarians). The Armenians he said were the oldest race, as they trace their descent from the Hittites. 'It just shows you', said the P.M., 'how difficult is our present task. We are digging up the foundations of a very old world.'

April 13th 1919
We went for a short run round St. Germain & Versailles, picnicking in the woods at the former place. Lord Rothermere came too. He is terrified that the working classes may gain in power & take the money away from the rich, & is backing D. simply because he feels that he is the one strong man in Britain who can guard it against Bolshevism. He is no better than Northcliffe himself really, & not as human; but it suits D.'s purpose to play the brothers off against each other at the present moment, now that The Daily Mail & The Times are becoming so violent against D. Rothermere told us that Churchill was in touch with Wickham Steed,[2] which is just what one would expect, knowing how disloyal & ambitious Churchill is & always will be. He is giving D. great trouble just at present, as being Secretary of State for War, he is anxious that the world should not be at peace, & is therefore planning a great war in Russia.

Dined at the Majestic with Mrs. Astor & Sir R. Borden & some others; & had some music afterwards which D. much enjoyed.

April 14th 1919
D. left for London in excellent spirits.[3] He has made up his mind to attack

---

1. Michael Karolyi, president of Hungary, 1918–19.
2. Editor of The Times, February 1919–November 1922.
3. Over 200 Unionist M.P.s sent Lloyd George a telegram protesting against his leniency towards Germany. Lloyd George returned to Westminster and routed his critics by lumping them with Northcliffe, whom nearly all M.P.s disliked.

Northcliffe & declare war to the knife. He says that N. is intent on trying to oust him, so he (D.) is going to attack him now in order that people may know that N.'s motives are purely personal, & that he may be discredited from the outset. He told me part of his speech before he left, & I must say it is very clever & amusing, & will make N. very sorry for himself.

Left for Bethune with Mrs. Astor, who was going to Ypres. We started about 5 & spent the night at Amiens. Weather terribly wet & stormy. D. must have had a very bad crossing.

April 15th 1919

Left soon after nine & arrived at Bethune soon after 12, passing along the Vimy Ridge & through Arras & Lens—a region of horror and devastation. Annezin is just beyond Bethune, & we found the cemetery quite easily, & also the old woman who has been looking after Paul's grave. She took me to it: it is beautifully kept, but it was a terrible moment to see it for the first time. The pathos of it all swept over me, & the regret that his young life should have been cut off before it was scarcely begun—for he went straight from the schoolroom to the battlefield. Nevertheless, I was glad to have seen the place where his body lies, & to think of it as something that I have seen; though as I stood there I knew it was not *he* that lay there, but only so to speak a relic or memorial of him. Indeed, I have often felt him close beside me, especially in times of trial when a difficulty or a danger has been overcome. Still, the wave of regret sweeps over one from time to time, that he is not here to enjoy the good things of the world, & to live his life to the full.

Returned to Paris about 10 at night.

April 16th 1919

The P.M.'s speech was delivered in the House today—got a garbled report through late this evening, but spoke to J.T. on the telephone who says it was a wonderful performance—one of his very best. I am glad D. is coming back tomorrow—it is desolate without him, & I don't enjoy my freedom a bit.

April 17th 1919

D. returned, in the highest of spirits, & very pleased with himself. He had a wonderful reception, & gained complete mastery of the House, while telling them absolutely nothing about the peace conference. But he treated them to an amusing skit on Northcliffe, which pleased them hugely, & which will make N. squirm. D. is determined to fight him tooth and nail, to hold him up to ridicule & to discredit his papers. Lord Rothermere, who came in tonight was not quite sure how to take it, but young Harmsworth did not like it at all, & has gone to London. I doubt if he will return. He hopes I think to inherit The Times one day, & therefore will not wish to incur his uncle's displeasure.

D. was very sick that I was not in the House yesterday, and said he missed my note which I always send him directly after a speech. Nevertheless, I think it was wise for me not to travel backwards & forwards with him, as he was away such a short time. It is jolly, too, to meet again after even a short parting.

April 19th 1919
We intended to go for a tour round the devastated areas, starting this afternoon & spending the night at Amiens, & returning to Paris tomorrow night. At lunch time, however, D. returned & said it would be impossible as there would have to be a meeting this afternoon & tomorrow morning. Very disappointed, but still, 'duty first'. Perhaps we shall be able to go for a short run tomorrow.

D. very tired after a heavy day & we dined very quietly & went to bed early. The Italian claims are giving a certain amount of trouble, the Italians being very obstinate. It is a difficult position, as we must stand by them & the Pact of London, though D. says they are making a mistake in pressing it. They on the other hand say that Germany promised them more than this if they remained neutral, & Orlando naturally feels that he cannot go back to Italy empty handed.

By the secret treaty of London in 1915 Great Britain and France promised that Italy should receive south Tyrol, Istria and the northern part of Dalmatia. Fiume was not included. At the end of the war the Italians claimed Fiume also. President Wilson resisted the Italian claims to Fiume and northern Dalmatia. Lloyd George and Clemenceau recognised that they were bound by the treaty of London. If the Italians took their stand on the treaty, Great Britain and France would back their claim to Dalmatia; but in that case they could not have Fiume. If they claimed Fiume, this was an abandonment of the treaty of London, and all their claims would have to be considered on the basis of nationality. Orlando withdrew from the peace conference, but returned in order to be present when the peace terms were presented to the Germans. President Wilson appealed to the Italians over the head of their government. This move was unsuccessful. The peace conference never settled the question of Fiume.

April 20th 1919
D. arranged for the meeting to be at 10, so that we could start before lunch for a run, & picnic out of doors. About 11.30 I went to the salon window, from where one can see the Conference room in President Wilson's house, to see if there were any signs of the meeting breaking up. Suddenly Orlando appeared at the window, leaned on the bar which runs across it, & put his head in his hands. I thought it looked as though he was crying, but could not believe it possible until I saw him take out his handkerchief & wipe his eyes and cheeks. I was sorry for the old man, & thought someone had been treat-

ing him badly, but D. told me afterwards that he broke down during a speech which he (D.) made on behalf of Italy's claims, in which he extolled the Italian people & the part they had played in the war. Orlando was overcome & began to sob, & then got up & went to the window.

We had a glorious day—went to Noyon & Lassigny & surrounding places —most interesting. D. so sweet & in such good spirits. Auckland Geddes[1] & Guest[2] came with us, & also Sir George Riddell.

April 21st 1919

D. came to meet me on my way up to breakfast, & we went for a short sharp walk up to the Arc de Triomphe. Who would have thought when I made the same visit with Suzanne [my French cousin] one morning before breakfast 14 years ago, that I should one day be coming there with the Prime Minister of England, after a terrible war! There is nothing to compare with these little walks with D., when we unburden our hearts to each other & feel that we are about 10 years old!

In the evening we dined with Sir George Riddell at Fouquet's & D. enjoyed himself immensely. He has very little opportunities for these little pleasures, as he cannot go about very much, but he thoroughly enjoys it when he does. Before leaving he asked the orchestra to play Sambre et Meuse which they did with great zest.

May 5th 1919

The big four decided to take strong measures with the Italians, who have been waiting in Rome expecting to get a message from Paris imploring them to return. D. today sent for Imperiali, the Italian ambassador in England, & told him that if the Italian delegates had not returned to Paris by Wednesday morning, the Four would consider the Treaty of London as null and void. 'Would you mind repeating that?' said Imperiali, with a scared face. D. repeated it. Imperiali hurried away. Clemenceau sent for the Italian ambassador in Paris, & gave him the same intimation. I do not think D. cares much if the Italians don't come back, as he never was in favour of the Treaty of London & would be glad of an opportunity of cancelling it.

May 6th 1919

The Italians are returning in a hurry with their tails between their legs—as someone suggested 'fiuming'—in order, it is presumed, to be in at the finish. The Peace Treaty has already been printed, & Italy's name has to be put in in writing. The whole proceeding has been undignified & unfortunate, and nobody has come out of it very well—neither Orlando nor Wilson—if anything, I should say that the prestige of the latter has suffered most.

---

1. Auckland Geddes (1879–1954): director of national service, 1917–19; president of board of trade, 1919–20; ambassador to United States, 1920–4; cr. Baron, 1942.
2. Frederick Edward Guest (1875–1937): Liberal M.P., 1910–22, 1923–9; Conservative M.P., 1931–7; chief whip of Lloyd George Liberals, 1916–21.

May 7th 1919
P.M. went down to Versailles to present the Peace terms to the German
delegates—a most beautiful spring day. I do not think D. realised before he
went what an exciting event it would be, but he came back quite exhausted
with emotion—ill, in fact, & it was some time before he became himself
again. The Germans were very arrogant & insolent, & Brockdorff-Rantzau
did not even stand up to make his speech.[1] This infuriated the allied delegates,
& Hughes got up in a passion & came to the P.M. & said: 'Is Clemenceau
going to allow this fellow to go on like this?' D. said that he felt he could get
up & hit him, & he had the greatest difficulty in sitting still. He says it has
made him more angry than any incident of the war, & if the Germans do not
sign, he will have no mercy on them. He says for the first time he has felt the
same hatred for them that the French feel. I am rather glad that they have
stirred him up, so that he may keep stern with them to the very end. If they
had been submissive & cowed he might have been sorry for them.

May 8th 1919
Went down to St. Cloud with D. for golf & stayed there to tea. A perfect
afternoon, & D. in very good spirits, though he did not play golf well. He
was thinking about a speech he has to deliver in the evening at a complimentary dinner to Sir George Riddell. He prepared rather an amusing speech,
but when the time came changed his mind & instead delivered a serious
speech, paying a great tribute to France & the part she had played during
the war.
    Everyone seems delighted with the peace terms, & there is no fault to find
with them on the ground that they are not severe enough. Someone described
it as 'a peace with a vengeance'.

May 9th 1919
D. dined with Venizelos.[2] The two have a great admiration for each other,
& D. is trying to get Smyrna for the Greeks, though he is having trouble with
the Italians over it.

May 10th 1919
Pashitch[3] came to lunch—a fine dignified old man, with a beautiful kindly
eye. There is no love lost between the Serbians & the Italians. D. asked the
number of Italians who had perished in the war. Pashitch replied about half
a million. 'But', he added, 'you can lose very heavily in retreating.' The Serbs
are willing to give up Fiume if they can have the islands off the Dalmatian
coast. They are very wise in their choice. As D. said, 'It is like giving up
Portsmouth, so long as you can retain the Isle of Wight.'
    After tea we motored to Barbizon near Fontainebleau for the weekend. A

---

1. It was later explained that when suffering from emotion his legs became powerless.
2. Greek prime minister.
3. Yugoslav prime minister.

lovely spot, ideal for lovers, & specially beautiful at this time of the year. The lilac & fruit trees are all in blossom, & the woods are wonderful.

May 11th 1919

Spent a very happy day wandering about the woods, though was annoyed by Mrs. ——, who expected D. to pay a lot of attention to her, & I was cross in consequence. She is a most self-satisfied person, talks a lot & loves the sound of her own voice. Of course all women are fascinated by D. & he in turn is nice to most of them, & once having started they expect him to go on. The silly ones get their heads turned immediately & there is no doing anything with them. It is most amusing to watch. But I got rather angry with Mrs. —— having had rather too much of that sort of thing lately. However D. & I made it up in the evening.

Mr. Balfour came down to tea, & stayed to dinner. He was most entertaining, being in a jovial mood, & reminisced freely. D. told him of the first time he heard him (Balfour) in the House, during an Irish Debate, and chaffed him on his insolence to the Irish members who were attacking him about one of their party who was said to be wasting away in prison. For answer Mr. Balfour simply pulled a paper out of his pocket, & read a record of the man's daily increase in weight since he had been in prison.

May 14th 1919

Painlevé came to dinner, & was in very good form. He went through the whole of the story of the German advance on Paris in 1914—how when the Germans got nearer & nearer & it seemed inevitable that they should reach Paris, the French authorities thought that the best plan would be that the citizens of Paris should be placed under the care of the American Embassy, & that the city itself should be delivered up to the Germans without a fight. By this means the city would not be destroyed, at any rate. But the Chambre des Deputés refuted this proposal indignantly 'For', they said, 'if Paris is surrendered, France will perish: but if Paris is destroyed, France may still live.'

After dinner we all went up to Mr. Balfour's flat, where a young Russian pianist played the most wonderful things.

May 15th 1919

D. has just gone off to visit the Welsh division on the Ancre. They are going back to England on Saturday [17 May] to be disbanded, & he has promised to go & bid them farewell. It was the Division that he had helped to raise in 1914, & both his boys were in it at first, so that D. has a special interest in it.

Everything seems desperately lonely when he has gone.

May 16th 1919

Went to lunch at Armenonville with Bertie Stern, who has just come to Paris & says he is going to have a good time, which means he is going to give other people a good time. He is a most generous & thoughtful person & the best host I have ever met. One of his friends asked me the other day why I did not marry him. 'One excellent reason', I replied, 'is that he has never asked me.' But all the same I think he might ask me if he did not know perfectly well that I would not leave D.

May 17th 1919

Lady Curzon & her step-daughter Cynthia[1] came to lunch. I rather like them both, especially the former. They say she is completely 'fed up' with George Nathaniel, & I am not surprised.

Dined at the Pré Catelan, Evelyn Fitzgerald being the host. D. & Churchill & C.I.G.S. & others were there also, & we had a very merry time. D. thoroughly enjoys dining out like this, & loved the dancing. He is a thorough Bohemian. We stayed till quite late, & some of us went on to the Majestic to dance. The Saturday evening dances there are great fun, but I do not say much to D. about it, as he gets rather jealous.

May 18th 1919

Had a most enjoyable day. D. went to hear Dr. Black preach in the morning & then we went on to lunch with Bertie Stern at the Pré Catelan in the Bois. A perfectly delightful warm spring day, & the Bois looking absolutely perfect. Lord Fisher & the Duchess of Hamilton joined us also, & after lunch the former entertained us for nearly an hour with the most humorous anecdotes. He gave us many of his experiences with beautiful ladies, interspersing his stories with philosophic maxims on life in general. 'The Saints', he said, 'were all sinners to begin with. Therefore I say: "Sin like blazes!"' And again: 'The three holiest men I know of all had nagging wives. They were driven from home for this reason & went round the country preaching. That was the cause of their holiness.' He went on & on, until our sides ached with laughter. No one would credit that the old man is nearly 80. The Duchess sits by his side & prompts him from time to time. She does not impress me very much. I should think she is rather a stupid woman, but evidently he thinks a lot of her.

May 21st 1919

Winston came to breakfast & was in great form. He is flying every day & loves it. He spoke of Hawker & his cross-Atlantic flight. 'The Daily Mail are making great copy out of it', he said, 'dwelling on the feelings of his wife "the poor little woman who is now a widow...".' 'Yes—but who made her a widow?' asked D. angrily. He is very angry about the whole thing, & thinks it ought to be stopped. It was simply a Daily Mail stunt to increase its circulation.

Played tennis this afternoon & dined with Bertie Stern & Major Crankshaw & others at the Ambassadeurs. Thoroughly enjoyed it. Major C. is quite one of the nicest people I have ever met. Danced afterwards at the Majestic.

---

1. Later married Oswald Mosley.

May 23rd 1919

D. & I had a long talk. I know Stern would marry me if I gave him the slightest encouragement & if he thought I would leave D. It is a great temptation in a way for although I don't love him we are good friends & I know he would be very kind to me. It would mean a title & wealth, whereas now I may find myself old & friendless & having to earn my own living, if anything should happen to D. People will not be so anxious to marry me in 10 years' time. On the other hand I know I should not be happy now away from D. & no-one else in the world could give me the intense & wonderful love that he showers on me. He was very sweet about it, & says he wants to do what is best for me. But I can see that he would be unhappy if I left him, so I promised him I would not.

May 25th 1919

D. told me this morning that he had definitely made up his mind that he could not let me leave him. So that is final, & I am very glad. I need not worry about it any more. It would be very foolish to spoil for material prospects the most wonderful love which ever happened.

We picnicked near Fontainebleau in the woods, Mr. & Mrs. Churchill & others coming with us. The day was spoiled for us, however, by a terrible accident which we saw on the way back. We had stopped to mend a burst in a little French village when a lorry & a motorcycle, both going at top speed, collided. Of course the man on the bike was killed, though not outright, but the whole thing happened under our eyes, & we could not help seeing it. It is the first time I have ever seen a man killed. It is the anniversary of Paul's death, too. It upset us all very much. The French driving is much too reckless. There is no speed limit, & little regard for human life. I suppose this is the result of the war.

June 14th 1919

D. returned from the meeting of the Four rather excited, having had a great battle with President Wilson over Silesia. D. wants to make concessions to the Germans over this, as he feels they are being unfairly dealt with in this matter. President Wilson suggested a plebiscite which D. hotly repudiated. It was a monstrous proposition he said. 'It is loading the dice!'[1] Pres. W. was very angry & strongly resented D.'s remark, & asked him to take back his words. D. refused, repeating that what he said was true. They parted without having 'made it up', but D. got his way, which was all he wanted! He & the President have had some rather warm passages on the League of Nations. D. contended that the annexation of Silesia was not in accordance with the principles of the League. 'But Mr. Lord[2] says so-&-so', said the President in defence. 'Mr. Lord!', exclaimed D., 'Mr. Lord! When I agreed to the 14

1. In fact a plebiscite was held in upper Silesia, largely on Lloyd George's prompting.
2. R. H. Lord, American historian.

points I did so because I thought they expressed the wishes of the American people, & not because Mr. Lord wanted them!'

June 28th 1919

Went to Versailles for the signature of the Peace. Though I am glad I was there, yet the thing as a whole was rather disappointing. It was very badly stage-managed by the French, the peace delegates (including D.) having to push their way into the Salle des Glaces, along with the visitors. Almost half the room was taken up with representatives of the Press. The Press is reducing everything that is noblest and impressive in modern life into terms of Press photographs and Press interviews. In fact they try to dominate everything. How can you concentrate on the solemnity of a scene when you have men with cameras in every direction, whose sole object is to get as near as they can to the central figures? How can you be impressed as much as you would like to be by what is said, when you know that all round you are people taking notes, and that the people who are speaking *know* that they are taking notes. One or two reporters, for the sake of preserving a record, would not be so bad. But they have to be dealt with in armies nowadays. The Press is destroying all romance, all solemnity, all majesty. They are as unscrupulous as they are vulgar.

June 29th 1919

We said goodbye to Paris, & returned home. We have had a wonderful time there, & we left with many regrets. D. hates returning home. He has been well looked after in Paris—has had every comfort—the best food—the best attendance. He has been able to entertain at will. When at Downing St., or Walton Heath it is another matter. There is never enough to go round & what there is, is very inferior. I have never seen anyone with such a capacity for making a place uncomfortable as Mrs. Lloyd George. Her meanness forces the household to economise in coal & food, & everything that makes for comfort. The servants would be a disgrace to any house, & the P.M. is rightly ashamed of them. But it is no use his protesting—he says he gave that up long ago, because it had no effect & only caused unpleasantness.

D. had a wonderful reception at the station. I think he had an idea that his reception would be rather a wash-out, as he knew that Winston had turned down the idea of getting troops to line the streets. But the welcome he had was far more spontaneous than any organisation could have made it, & to crown all, the King himself, with the Prince of Wales, came to the station to meet him. The people at the court tried to dissuade him from doing so, saying that there was 'no precedent for it'. 'Very well', replied the King, 'I will make a precedent.' And everyone seems to have appreciated his action. Everyone threw flowers at D. & a laurel wreath was thrown into the Royal carriage. It fell on the King's lap but he handed it to D. 'This is for you', he said. D. has given it to me, & though it will fade, I will keep it all my life.[1] I know

1. The wreath is now in the Lloyd George Memorial Museum, at Llanystumdwy.

better than anyone how well he deserves the laurels he has won. He is very tired however & will go away to Criccieth as soon as he can for a little rest.

June 30th 1919
D. went up to the House & had a wonderful reception.

July 3rd 1919
D. made an excellent speech in the House, & it was very well received. He has complete authority over this House. Carson made a very graceful speech & paid some fine tributes to D., who was very tired afterwards. We were going to have dinner alone together, but family manoeuvres made it impossible.

July 5th 1919
D. left for Criccieth for a fortnight. He needs the rest dreadfully badly, so I cannot grudge him his holiday, though everything is so dreary when he is not here, & time hangs so heavily. However, I must bear up for a fortnight, & just look forward to the time when he comes back again.

July 12th 1919
D. comes back next Friday [18 July]. It seems months since he went. Talked to him over the telephone, which cannot often be managed. He says he is much better. I have been down to Cobham to see how the new house is getting on, & trying to make things as comfortable as possible for D. Stopped them hanging a picture of Mrs. R. Ll.G. in the Front Hall, which I think was great cheek. How everyone dislikes her! I have never heard a single person say a good word for her, not even D., who usually finds *some* good points about everyone.

July 14th 1919
Had a darling letter from D. which makes me want to see him more than ever. But it is not very long till Friday now—and then. . . . He is much better, it seems. All he needed was a little rest. Unfortunately the family are coming back with him. We had hoped to have the weekend together.

July 18th 1919
D. has returned—Oh! what joy! He says the last few days have been terrible to go through. I thought they would never end, & that his return was too wonderful a thing ever to come true. But here he is, back again, & as loving as ever. Tomorrow we have a great plan. I hope it will come off.

July 19th 1919
The procession was a great success, & everyone was very happy. D. went to Buckingham Palace & got a great cheer as he drove up. The people *love* him, & he will do his best for them. I think there are very few statesmen who have been as *near* to them as he is.

D. says the King made a great mistake in having the ex-King of Portugal on his right hand to take the salute as the troops marched past.

The people thronged into Downing St. in the afternoon & stayed there for hours in the pouring rain. They refused to go away until D. had made them a little speech.

July 20th 1919

Our plan came off, & we are so happy. D. is going down to Cobham to join Mrs. Ll.G. there today. He is speaking in the House tomorrow. D. is not looking forward to his work this week, but still he says he thinks he sees his way at present to deal with things.

D. & I watched the fireworks together last night. They were wonderful. It is sweet to be with him again.

July 21st 1919

D. came up from Cobham yesterday evening, as the Prince of Wales had telephoned inviting him to a dinner he was giving to the Allied Generals. I came up from Wallington too. We were very lucky.

D.'s first impressions of the Cobham house were not very good. It was wet & cold & they had not even bothered to light a fire for him, & even when he asked for one they were hours making it—& when they had made it it was not worth looking at. That is how he is always served. So that he is not very favourably impressed. However, I think it will be very nice, *if only* they make it warm. He would not even have had a room of his own if J.T.D. & I had not insisted on the billiard room being turned into a dining-room, & the latter being made into a study for D.

November 26th 1919

We had a perfectly wonderful day yesterday. Went down to Cobham Tuesday evening, & played golf at Burhill yesterday morning. It is a beautiful course & it was a lovely sunny morning. The pro & I beat D. & Ernie[1] hollow, so I am rather pleased with myself. I want to be really good at golf as D. has been so sweet about my learning & takes such a patient interest in my progress. Came up in the evening in time for dinner. Dined at the Cazalets—Mrs. C. & Thelma are both sweet—kind and sincere. But it is extraordinary how not one of these women wants Nancy Astor to get in. They all dislike her.

November 28th 1919

Dined at Sir Philip Sassoon's[2] last night. D. & Sir Eric Geddes & others there too. Miss Ruth Draper recited. She is wonderful, & D. enjoyed himself

---

1. Ernie Evans, another of Lloyd George's secretaries.
2. Sir Philip Sassoon (1888–1939), 3rd Baronet: private secretary to Haig, 1915–18; to Eric Geddes, 1919–20, to Lloyd George, 1920–2; under secretary of state for air, 1924–9; had a house in Park Lane and country houses at Trent and Lympne.

immensely. He had previously been rather upset, having been to visit Sir Charles Henry who is dying. Lady Henry has been complaining to everyone that D. had not been to see her husband, in spite of all their past kindness to him (D.). The fact is that every time that D. has been there Lady H. has got him by himself & made a scene, she being perfectly mad about him. Last night he took Macpherson with him, so that this should not occur, but she took him aside & showed him a letter Clark (D.'s secretary at the time) had written to her on the very day D.'s little girl had died in 1907, asking her to lend D. her car, as he had not one of his own then. She showed him this to remind him of her kindness to him, knowing well that it breaks D.'s heart to think about that terrible time or to have it referred to. D. says he thinks she is the most selfish woman he knows of. She is constantly asking people to dinner to meet D., & D. consistently refuses. She then tells the people who turn up expecting to meet the P.M., that he *was* coming but he preferred dining alone with her.

November 29th 1919
Nancy Astor elected the first woman M.P. I am beginning to understand why she has so few friends. I used to think it was jealousy, but I know now that it was true when they told me she was treacherous & not to be trusted. In spite of her repeated protestations of friendship & goodwill to me, I find that she takes every opportunity of saying spiteful things about D. & myself. It is almost incredible, but it is true. Anyhow, she will get her reward in the House of Commons! I do not think any *wise* woman would choose to sit in the House!

D. & Mrs. Ll.G. on very bad terms. D. is giving a big weekend party at Cobham, including the American Ambassador & Mrs. Davies, and Mrs. Ll.G., instead of helping, is doing all she can to *hinder* D.'s arrangements. She simply hates him to enjoy himself & will not lift a finger to make the Cobham house comfortable.

Sir James Guthrie has painted a wonderful likeness of D. He had the last sitting this morning. Mrs. Ll.G. went up to look at it, & when D. asked her what she thought of it she said—'I can't lay my finger on anything bad in it!'

December 1st 1919
Went to see the first lady M.P. take her place in the House. It really was a thrilling moment, not from the personal point of view, but from the fact that after all these hundreds of years, this was the first time that a woman had set foot upon that floor to represent the people—or a certain number of them. I had a lump in my throat as I saw her come in at the far end—a very graceful, neat figure—& wait for her turn to walk up the floor. The P.M. was very self-conscious & nervous & made a false start in his anxiety to get it over. He was obviously relieved when he reached his seat, & the House was much amused.

December 5th 1919

D. has left for Manchester, & I think his speech ought to be a rattling good one. He will have rather a difficult job, but he will call up all his powers of persuasion & is bound to succeed. He has rehearsed most of the speech to me, and is not going to prepare it too fully, which is much better. When he has masses of notes, he never delivers so well.

December 6th 1919

Danced at the Grafton Galleries last night. Carpentier[1] was there, so there was great excitement. He is a wonderfully good looking man, but very modest. Everyone made a great fuss of him, & he had to spend nearly all his time giving autographs. That is a thing I have never been able to do—bother people for autographs. I think it is unkind & embarrassing.

Went to see Abraham Lincoln at the Lyric Theatre, Hammersmith. A wonderful play & wonderfully acted. You feel that you really have seen & heard Abraham Lincoln himself. Mrs. Lincoln appears to have been rather a tiresome woman, though!

December 7th 1919

D. returned from Manchester late last night, well satisfied with his speech. It was an enormous success, & I am told one of his best. It will do a great deal of good in that part of the world, especially in view of the Spen Valley election. We do not want Simon[2] to beat the Coalition man, Fairfax. The former behaved disgracefully to D. over the libel action a couple of years ago, when some evening papers accused D. of running away during an air raid. Simon accepted the brief for D., came to lunch the day before the action came on to talk over all the details, stayed for some time while D. went over the whole thing with him & then about 6 o'clock in the evening sent word to D. that he had thought the matter over & had come to the conclusion that seeing that The Westminster Gazette was supporting the Asquithians he (Simon) did not feel justified in appearing for D. This at the eleventh hour, after having had weeks to think about it, & when it was extremely difficult to find a substitute who could master the case in so short a time. He is indeed as someone said: 'A big man on a small point, & a small man on a big point.'

December 8th 1919

D. dined with me at the flat last night. We had a jolly little party to celebrate the third anniversary of his becoming Prime Minister. Sir George Riddell came, & it was all a great success.

---

1. Georges Carpentier, heavyweight boxer.
2. Sir John Simon was running as an independent Liberal against a Coalition Liberal who was defending the seat. Tom Myers, a Labour man, got in.

*An Allied conference was held in London in an attempt to settle problems of the Near
East, especially Syria and Mosul. According to Lloyd George, agreement would have
followed if Clemenceau had remained in office.*

December 11th 1919
M. Clemenceau arrived & conferences proceeded all day long. D. brought
them in to my room for tea, & Clemenceau thoroughly enjoyed his cake. He
has a great love for sweet cakes—almost like a child. He was in great form &
ragged everyone, from D. to Philip Kerr. Talking of what they should discuss
tomorrow when Scialoja, the Italian Foreign minister was to be present.
Clemenceau said: 'It doesn't much matter what you tell him so long as it is
not the truth!' He has a wholesome contempt for the Italians. 'Qu'est-ce que
vous voulez?' he exclaimed. 'There you have a country where the King
counts for nothing, where the army does not obey orders, where you have
180 Socialists on one side, & 120 men belonging to the Pope on the other!'
'But what shall we tell him!' said D. 'Nothing', was Clemenceau's reply.
'We will ask him a few questions instead.'

D. says Clemenceau has definitely made up his mind to be President of the
Republic, & will continue in Office probably till February next. 'I have
become a fetish with the French', said Clemenceau to D. 'Like the little gold
pigs that the ladies put between their bosoms. They think I can do no harm
& so they will keep me there!' Mrs. Ll.G. went to Spen Valley to speak & D.
& I spent the evening together.

December 12th 1919
Conferences continued today, Clemenceau just as high-spirited as ever. They
all adjourned to Lord Curzon's for lunch. Clemenceau in a discussion about
the League of Nations, said: 'I have come to the conclusion that *force* is right.
Why is this chicken here? (pointing to his plate). Because it was not strong
enough to resist those who wanted to kill it. And a very good thing too!'

Speaking of President Wilson, he said: 'I do not think he is a *bad* man, but
I have not yet made up my mind as to how much of him is *good*!'

Speaking of Gladstone, he said: 'Ah! there you have a great man.' Someone remarked that he was a humbug. 'But is it not true that every great man
has to be a great humbug? Nevertheless he (Gladstone) lived his own life.'

D. is very pleased because Balfour told him that Clemenceau has said that
he thought D. had beautiful eyes and beautiful hands (which he has!).

Philip Sassoon has just dropped in for a chat. He has been very attentive
lately, I think probably because he wants to get an Under-Secretaryship, or
something of the kind. Nevertheless he is an amusing person, & as clever as
a cartload of monkeys.

December 13th 1919
D. brought Clemenceau & the others in to tea with me again today. Clemen-

ceau had slipped on the boat coming over, & had hurt himself, & though it
was not noticeable the first day, he was obviously in pain today & could not
sit still. He was as lively as ever, though, & chaffed Mr. Balfour, who had had
a difference of opinion with him in the meeting. Clemenceau had in fact
reproved him for going back on his word. 'Take this', he said to Balfour,
handing him some iced cake. 'It is good for perfidy.'

I asked M. Clemenceau's secretary to get me his autograph for a friend, as
I dislike asking people myself. The Sec. has just rung up to say that 'M. le
President' has consented to let me have his autograph on condition that I sent
him one of my own for his grandson. Imagine the joy of the grandson on
receiving my autograph!

They go back tomorrow. I hope the old man's injury does not get any
worse.

D. refuses to go down to Cobham tonight. He can't bear the idea of a
family tête-à-tête. It is a pity, as it simply means that he stays here working or
at any rate, in the atmosphere of work, instead of going off & getting a rest.

December 16th 1919

Have persuaded D. to cut work this afternoon & come down to Cobham for
a rest & fresh air. He has a very hard week in front of him, & is beginning to
worry a little about things, which he always does when he gets tired. He is
annoyed at having to go down to Criccieth for Xmas, but as Mrs. Ll.G.
announces her intention of staying here if he does not go, he thinks it best at
any rate to make sure of getting her down there! But he is coming back
directly after Xmas & then we hope to go to Paris for a meeting & then
perhaps go on for a short holiday somewhere.

December 17th 1919

We went down to Cobham & had a quiet & restful afternoon & evening. We
went for a walk in Richmond Park on our way, as it would have been too
late for a walk when we arrived there, though we did walk again in the
garden after dinner. D. cheered up wonderfully, & he talked to me about his
early speeches, including Limehouse. He says I cannot imagine the impression
that the Limehouse speech had had not only upon the Tories, but on the
Liberals themselves. D.'s colleagues were astounded & afraid at it. He dined
with some of them after the speech, & Sydney Buxton sat like a man in a
dream, not saying a single word. Some of those so-called Liberals were as
Conservative as the worst of the Tories.

We talked about the new Land Bills, & the fact that so many of the big
estates are being sold up. D. says it is a good thing, for the land cannot afford
to keep the man who actually farms it plus the landowner, who usually does
nothing for a living except take his rents. 'I sometimes wish', said D. to me,
'that I were in the Labour Party. I would tear down all these institutions!'
He says the great landlord was all right in mediaeval times, when he was a
sort of local king, & in time of war led his men into battle, & provided his

quota for the King's army. But now he has no raison d'être, & must go. I
wonder what old Lord Cholmondeley would say if I told him that!

D. very anxious that his speech at the Mansion House should be a success.
He is very fond of the Prince of Wales, & for that reason will find an increased
difficulty in speaking about him. At least, that is what he *says*, but I think he
has got a splendid little speech. He is specially anxious to make cordial references to the King & Queen, as he thinks the King will get a little jealous of
the fuss that is being made about the Prince. He is to be at Mrs. Rupert
Beckett's dance tonight, to which I am going. I have never actually spoken
to him & don't suppose I shall tonight for that matter. But it will be interesting to see him there.

December 19th 1919

Was introduced to the Prince, who was very charming & said he was glad to
meet me as he had heard such a lot about me! I wanted to ask him what he
had heard. I congratulated him on his speech in the afternoon, and he told
me he would never get used to speaking in public—he was far too nervous.
'My trouble is that I have not a ready pen', he said. 'I find it so difficult even
to prepare a speech.' I was terribly nervous, & I felt I was trembling all over,
& I hardly know what I said, but I hope he did not think I was a perfect fool.
He is a dear thing, with beautiful eyes, but such a boy.

December 20th 1919

P. Sassoon came down to Cobham with D. & Sir George Riddell & me today
& we played golf at St. George's Hill. Had a very jolly day. He is quite good
company. Very ambitious though, which he admits. D. has asked him to
come to Paris with us after Xmas purely D. says because he has been nice to
me! He certainly has, & very attentive—almost embarrassing, in fact. He
seems to be fabulously rich, but is clever also, & can be most amusing. But
one of the worst gossips I have ever come across. D. & I drove back to
Cobham & had tea there, but P. Sassoon & Sir George came straight up to
town. We came up later on & went to dinner with Oliver Locker-Lampson.
A very amusing party—P.M. & Mr. Birrell, the Austen Chamberlains &
some others. After dinner we listened to the Black Syncopated Orchestra.
They were amazing—all the semi-religious songs of the negroes. D. says it is
very significant—their songs about the oppressed people. He says a race who
can sing these songs like that will cause trouble one of these days.

December 23rd 1919

D. has gone away today, & it *is* wretched without him. I get such a terrible
feeling of loneliness when he goes, & feel almost frightened at his being so far
away. However, as D. says, we have not done badly this year. We had all
that time at Paris together, & then a month at Deauville, & as he says, we see
each other every day & almost every hour of the day. But I suppose that only
makes it all the more hard when he does go away.

He made an extraordinarily good speech in the House last night. I behaved very badly. I was feeling very tired & had a splitting headache, & D. had annoyed me over a trifling little thing, & I quite forgot to say anything to him about his speech, or to compliment him on it. I usually leave a little note on his table in the House in case I don't see him at once, & so that he may get it directly. But this time he didn't. And when he came back to Downing St. after 11.0 he came up to me & said: 'You haven't said a word to me about my speech—not a word. And you know how I count on your words to me after my speeches.' I felt a perfect pig at once, & did my best to make up for it, & it ended quite happily. But I hate myself for having behaved like that.

December 24th 1919
Just off down to Wallington for a family party at Xmas. Have been simply overwhelmed with presents, until I feel quite ashamed of myself. Have had some most beautiful things, & people have been so kind.

Diary 1920

January 17th 1920 (Paris)

D.'s birthday. I gave him a watch-chain, with which he was very pleased. None of his family have bothered to write him. A scrappy wire from Megan, with whom however he is exceedingly annoyed, as she promised to return to school here yesterday, & failed to do so. He will not easily forgive her for this breach of faith. He hates a broken promise, & he did not think she would break her word.

D. exercised in his mind as to whether or not he should go to the elections at Versailles. He was going, if Clemenceau had been elected, but after the turn things have taken does not know whether to do so or not.[1] I persuaded him not to under the circumstances. One of the French papers—L'Œuvre—had actually put in big letters in its first edition, 'Oui, mais Lloyd George est un peu là.' What it means no-one knows; but they are evidently trying to create the impression that in some way D. is responsible for the volte-face. However the heading was withdrawn in the Second edition.

D. did not go. We went to St. Cloud to play golf after lunch. A most amusing meal, at which Winston waxed very eloquent on the subject of the old world & the new, taking arms in defence of the former. He has arrived simply *raving* because of the decision of the Peace Conference with regard to trading with Russia, which absolutely & finally ruins his hopes of a possible war in the East. At times he became almost like a madman. Sir George Riddell happened to ask him who it was at the War Office that has issued a communiqué of an alarmist character, bidding people prepare for a new war. Winston glared at him, & almost shouted 'You are trying to make mischief.' Someone happily turned the conversation to other matters or it looked as though there might have been bloodshed.

Dined with the Montagus at Ciro's. Sat next to Mr. Bonar Law & Jimmy Rothschild. The former says he does not mind sitting next to me, as he knows I do not expect him to talk! Winston still raving on the subject of the Bolsheviks, & ragging D. about the New World. 'Don't you make any mistake',

---

1. Clemenceau had been defeated in the Presidential election by Paul Deschanel.

he said to D. 'You're not going to get your new world. The old world is a good enough place for me, & there's life in the old dog yet. It's going to sit up & wag its tail.' 'Winston', said the P.M., 'is the only remaining specimen of a real Tory.' 'Never mind', laughed Winston, 'if you are going to include all parties, you will have to have me in your new National Party.' 'Oh no!' was D.'s retort, 'To be a party you must have at least one follower. *You* have none.'

January 19th 1920

D. went to the Quai-D'Orsay, where there was a final meeting with Clemen-ceau to clear up a few outstanding matters prior to Clemenceau's departure. D. returned very upset. He said he had been shocked at the way the old boy had been treated by the officials at this meeting. Foch had been openly rude to him, & D. was annoyed with Henry Wilson who had answered Clemen-ceau very sharply. It seems almost incredible that the old man should be treated thus when he is down, & I think D. has taken it to heart very much. He thinks people might one day treat him in the same manner. Clemenceau, however, has never ruled by love, but by fear, so that he has many enemies. The French are vindictive, & will not spare a fallen foe. Already the man in the street is saying that perhaps it is just as well for France that Clemenceau is not President. Various reasons are given, but there seems to be little or no regret for the turn things have taken. Sic transit gloria mundi! The old man is frightfully hurt at the insult he has suffered, but as always, puts a brave proud face upon it. D. has been consoling him with stories of Gladstone, who was Prime Minister when he was well over eighty & brought in his Home Rule Bill when he was 83. Clemenceau brightened up considerably at this story—'Really?' he asked. D. could see that it called up possibilities to the old man—As he himself puts it: 'I still have my teeth!' D. thinks after a short rest he will come back into politics and make havoc of his opponents.

January 20th 1920

This is rather a dreary & depressing week. Each day we have been going home the next day. We really leave tomorrow. Nitti[1] goes tonight, back to a general railway strike. The new French Government is not ready to go on with the Conference. It looks from the French papers (a great many of which are inspired) as though the new Gov. would try & repudiate some of Clemen-ceau's decisions. D. says if they do that he will refuse to go on negotiating. D. is now the doyen of Prime Ministers—in other words, he is the Dictator of Europe as far as treaties are concerned. It is not surprising that his word should carry weight, since he alone of all the European Ministers has survived the war & the peace. Even Winston, who has been fuming all the week about Russia, said to D. yesterday. 'Well you have downed me & my policy, but I can't help admiring you for the way you have gone about it. Your strategy

---

1. Italian prime minister.

is masterly. You saw me going in one direction & you blocked the way. I tried another & found it blocked too. You have gone on consistently, never varying, but always with the same fixed idea. I fought you, & you have beaten me, yet I cannot help admiring you for it.' 'The worst feature of Winston', said D.—& I believe he said it to Winston himself—'is his vanity! Everything that he does points to one thing—self.'

January 21st 1920

Returned from Paris. Clemenceau was at the Gard du Nord to say goodbye to D., & it was a pathetic farewell. The old man was evidently cut up at parting with D.—for a close friendship has sprung up during the past year between them—and D. on the other hand is genuinely distressed at the way the old man has been treated. He tried to cheer C. up. 'I envy you', he said. 'You are going off to rest and quiet & freedom from worry, whereas I am going back to the same old attacks, which will probably succeed eventually in downing me, as they have you.' 'Ah', said Clemenceau, 'but your people will do it in a cleaner way!' 'That is quite true', said D. to me on telling me of the incident 'And what is more', he added, 'I don't mind falling in a straight fight. A good rapier-thrust is an honourable ending. Clemenceau has been stabbed in the back.'

The crossing was very fine. We—D. & I—went on to the upper deck to get the benefit of the breeze. I am sorry to leave Paris, but I don't mind where I go so long as I am with D. D. swears that this is the last Paris will see of him as far as the Peace Conference is concerned. P. Kerr says this is the end of the Peace Conference—in fact, if not in theory.

January 22nd 1920

D. went to lunch with the King & returned in great distress because H.M., thinking to do him a special honour, asked him to carry the state sword in front of him (H.M.) when he goes in State to the House of Lords. D. says he won't do it. 'I won't be a flunkey', he said to me. The thing is, how to get out of it without offending H.M.? One thing D. is quite determined on—that he *will not* do it. He suggested to the King that the Peer whose business it is to do the thing would be offended if he were supplanted. D. came back & went straight to Bonar Law & told him it was *he* who was to carry the sword. Bonar was frightfully agitated, & has sent for Lord Edmund Talbot, who is going to represent to the King that it really ought to be a peer! D. thinks this will help him out of it; but unless I am much mistaken the King will find out D.'s little ruse, as Edmund Talbot is sure to give it away.

D. says there has been a quarrel between Grigg[1] & Halsey who went to Canada with the Prince, & the Prince has taken Halsey's part. D. says this is

---

1. Sir Edward Grigg, later Lord Altrincham. He succeeded Philip Kerr in 1921 as Lloyd George's private secretary. In 1935, when a Conservative M.P., he acted as intermediary between Lloyd George and Baldwin.

a great pity, as Halsey lets the Prince do as he likes, while Grigg is far the abler man. They are all three coming here tomorrow morning.

January 23rd 1920

D. very busy on the political situation. Asquith is standing for Paisley, & if he gets in, it will be a great blow to the Coalition. Unfortunately our Whips are not first-rate, & the Unionist Coalition Whips do not always play a straight game. They are not wholeheartily for D., & are always watching for their chance of putting the Unionist Party back into power again. I should not be at all surprised if they did not even at this moment rather hope that Asquith will get in, in the hope that he will take away Liberal support from D., whereupon the Unionists would reap the advantage. D. at present is very silent, which means that he does not quite see his way. But I know he is weighing up the situation. Some are anxious for him to come out & lead a party of his own, but the difficulty there is Bonar Law. My only hope is that he will not have F.E. & Winston as his lieutenants in forming such a party. They may be brilliant, but they don't do him any good.

D. & I went down to Cobham & had a quiet evening. Was going to the theatre with Lord Cholmondeley, but saw D. wanted to go down, so put it off. Lord Cholmondeley is a good natured, dear old thing, & never gets put out at anything.

D. had a tough time with the Prince today. The latter was determined to have his way about giving Halsey political authority during the tour. The P.M. was as equally determined that Grigg should have this authority, & eventually had to insist as Prime Minister that the Prince should agree to it. Eventually he did, but objected that the question of where he should go to was not a political matter & that therefore it could be left to Halsey. The P.M. had to point out that it was essentially a political matter.

January 24th 1920

Played golf with Lord Riddell against D. & Mrs. Carey Evans.[1] We beat them.

February 2nd 1920

D. & I had a perfectly divine weekend at Cobham—all alone. Played golf on Saturday with Lord Riddell & Philip Sassoon. The time simply fled. It is our last weekend for some time, I am afraid, as Mrs. Ll.G. returns soon & will be in London some time.

February 8th 1920

D. just returned from Cliveden, completely exhausted. He went there yesterday for the weekend, but could not stand it any longer. Nancy Astor had asked a crowd of people to meet him, & instead of seeing that he had a rest, they crowded round him & bothered him with questions. Garvin[2] was also

1. Lloyd George's elder daughter.
2. J. L. Garvin, editor of The Observer.

there, very disgruntled, & he groused about the Peace Treaty & other things until D. turned on him & pulled him to pieces. However he did not see the fun of staying there under those conditions, so fled after tea. I got a telephone message to say he was returning, & he arrived just a few minutes after I reached No. 10.

D. rather worried about Paisley. People are saying that Asquith ought to get in.

February 10th 1920
D. made a splendid speech—one of the best I have ever heard—quite in his old form. Simply wiped the floor with the Opposition bench, one member after another, until they sat squirming in their seats. It was a great effort, & the House was immensely appreciative. It is a very good omen for the beginning of the Session. If only Asquith does not get in! Unionists simply furious about Lord R. Cecil's letter.[1] D. rather glad, as now he can go for him as much as he likes.

February 11th 1920
D. excelled himself in the House today. Last night he was wondering how in the world he should make a speech on nationalisation, but a revolutionary member, speaking after Brace, gave him his chance, and he was not slow to take it. The House was thrilled & when he had finished they cheered & cheered. It is a wonderful rally to the Coalition, & indeed to the House of Commons in general. It was so essential that he should make his power felt just at this moment, when people are seeking in all sorts of quarters to try & weaken the Government. 'I think I am forming my party, Pussy', he said to me afterwards. Still these two days have taken it out of him, and he is still worrying about Paisley. He has got these Foreign Ministers over too, for the end of the Peace Conference, so that he has his hands full. Nitti was in the Strangers' Gallery to hear D. speak & I was so glad for this reason that he made a good performance.

February 12th 1920
Dined last night at Philip Sassoon's. Did not know till I got there that the Prince of Wales was to be there. Just 8 of us. I sat between the Prince & Sir Robert Horne.[2] Was simply shaking with fright at first, but that soon vanished, & we got on quite well. He is really a nice boy, & most amusing when his shyness wears off. He must know about D. & me, because he said: 'Mrs. Lloyd George does not spend much time in London, does she?' with a meaning look. I said: 'No; she preferred being in Criccieth', & let him infer what he liked. He is very sick at having to go off on another tour, & when I said

---

1. Lord Robert Cecil, an Independent Unionist, sent a letter of support to Asquith at Paisley.
2. Sir Robert Stevenson Horne (1871–1940): Unionist M.P., 1918–37; minister of labour, 1919–20; president of board of trade, 1920–1; chancellor of exchequer, 1921–2; cr. Viscount, 1937.

it was hard luck, said: 'Well, you tell the P.M. that!' He evidently thinks D. is largely responsible for it. I said it was most important that he should be in India to inaugurate the reforms, & of course they could not be delayed. He said: 'Well; I hope it will do some good.' I still don't like his voice very much. It is rather hard. Still, I suppose after D.'s, anyone's would sound poor.

February 14th 1920

D. dined with me last night—we had a very happy time, though he was tired with the heavy work of the week. He rang me up this morning to say that on his return he found the American Ambassador had been ringing up asking to see him urgently. He came round at once, with a long dispatch from Wilson. 'That fellow is going to make mischief again', said D. to me. I found when I got to the Office that Wilson had once more put in his oar in the Fiume question, & said that if the arrangement arrived at this week in the Conferences is carried into effect, America will withdraw the guarantees she gave in the peace treaty with regard to the protection of France! D. is simply furious. J.T. says he was simply mad last night. But we have sent Wilson a reply today that will give him something to think about. The funny thing was that nobody knew where to find D. when the American Ambassador rang up; & when J.T. went to find Nitti at his hotel, no-one knew were to find *him*. He did not turn up till nearly one o'clock, & was overcome with confusion and altogether very ashamed of himself! D. has a good opinion of Nitti—thinks he is the best thing Italy has produced during the Peace Conference.

Just off to Trent for the weekend. D. says I can ask Sassoon if he would like to be his Parliamentary Secretary. William Sutherland is going to be Scottish Whip.

February 16th 1920

Returned from Trent this morning—after a most interesting & enjoyable weekend. The P. of W. & his two brothers were there. Played tennis with Prince Henry. Prince Albert is great fun.

After dinner last night we danced & were very merry. Sir Robert Horne was there, very exercised in his mind as to whether he should accept the P.M.'s offer of becoming a Minister without a portfolio, in order to help D. generally. I tried to persuade him to do it, because I know it would relieve D. enormously. I think Horne is inclined to accept. He suggests that Macnamara should take his place at the Ministry of Labour. It ought to be a good appointment. Lunched today with Sydney Walton & Charles Garvice—the latter very interesting & charming. I had to confess that I had never read one of his books, so he is sending me one.

February 18th 1920

D. & I went down to Cobham last night, & had a very happy time. After dinner D. sang Welsh songs, as I have never heard him sing them before. He told me afterwards that Mair used to play them for him to sing, & that it is only now that he can bear to sing them again. We went for a beautiful walk this morning. It was like a warm spring day. D. very fit, in spite of his strenuous work lately. Yesterday there was a heated discussion in the Conference, because the French wished to have the guardianship of the Holy Sepulchre at Jerusalem. D. was furious, & asked whether the British were not good enough to guard it. They were good enough, he said, to protect travellers on their way to it, & to see that the streets leading up to it were kept clean. But when it came to entering the place & guarding it—no! the French must do that. 'What claim has France to do it, even from a religious point of view? Is France a Catholic power?' The French dared not answer yes. D. got his way, as usual.

February 19th 1920
The agitators are getting busy with regard to the decision about Constantinople. D. promised Lord Robert Cecil today that there should be a debate on the subject, & suggested March 1st. He did this on purpose, because he knows he has got a good case against Lord Robert & his crowd (though they don't realise it) and I think he wants them to work up a crisis, in which Asquith will be involved & then to flatten them out—including Asquith, who will have taken his seat by that time if he gets in! D. is inclined to think he will, but the Labour people think they have won.

D. gave me yesterday the first note received by us from the German ambassador since his return here. I am keeping it with the telegram received on the outbreak of war.

February 20th 1920
Rather a bad day for the Coalition. The Wrekin result is appalling.[1] However, D. does not seem depressed. His spirits rise when he is 'up against it', & has his back to the wall. He is very fit, but Mrs. Ll.G. is watching him like a hawk. She is an extraordinary person. She goes away for weeks & does not bother about him, but when she comes back she is on the watch all the time. Most inconsistent.

February 21st 1920
Dined with Mrs. Beckett last night & we went & danced at Mrs. Burns'. Quite good fun. We started talking about the P.M. at dinner, & Lord Pembroke said he wanted to put a question to me. 'Years ago we hated the P.M. & he hated us; now we admire & respect him—but does he like us?' I replied at once that the P.M. both admired them for the splendid way they had behaved in the war, & appreciated & was grateful for their loyalty to him, & he would never forget it. But the fundamental point was that socially you have nothing in common. Lady Pembroke talked to me again about it after

---

1. Coalition Liberal seat lost to an Independent.

dinner, & I explained to her how the P.M. loathed big dinner parties & week-end parties. 'We hate it too', was her reply, 'and I can't think why we do it.'

Mrs. Beckett is rather a dear, & very nice to me. Her daughters are sweet.

D. goes down to Cobham today. Is taking several people with him to take the edge off his 'domestic bliss'.

February 23rd 1920
The Peace Conference had a very hot discussion. I could hear Millerand shouting and evidently protesting very strongly. As the discussion was about Russia, this was not surprising. The French are very much against any dealings with the Soviet Government. When Millerand had concluded his outburst, D. informed him: 'We have had English Statesmen, seated at this table more than a hundred years ago, who used your very words as an argument against having any dealings with the French revolutionary Government. And here are you, the inheritor of that Government, using the very same arguments, against the Russian Government.'

D. brought me beautiful camellias from Cobham. He has been so sweet to me today. He says he wants me to have a bigger flat. Mine is not nice enough now, he says, and he also wants me to have my share of his (Carnegie) luck.[1] I am rather glad he wants me to have a bigger flat, though I love the one I have got, but it is getting too full of treasures (mostly his gifts) & they will look much better in a bigger space.

February 24th 1920
Last night went to see a film of D.'s life which Captain Guest had put on the screen in No. 12—a perfectly appalling thing. The idea was all right, but the man who was supposed to be D. was simply a caricature. I begged D. not to let it be shown. Mrs. Ll.G. very angry with D. because she said I had put D. against it because I objected to the domestic scenes in it!

February 25th 1920
Well, so Asquith is in! I wonder how the Liberals will like his having got in with *Unionist* votes—and with the help of the Northcliffe press, too! The two very things they can never forgive the P.M. for. D. was not very depressed at the result—he had accustomed himself to the idea, I think. And what is more, when adversity comes it never finds him downcast. He may be a little quiet—a quietness that is rather pathetic sometimes—but he is always cheerful and good tempered & full of courage. So today, when the news came, he was quite resigned & cheerful. It is only when he is uncertain what to do, or when there is a chance of a catastrophe that might be averted, that he is morose and irritable.

---

1. Andrew Carnegie, American steel magnate, had bequeathed to Lloyd George an annuity of £2,000.

Personally, I think when the *fact* of Asquith's having got in is over, it will be all the better for D. As D. himself says, he will be able to get at him in the House, & they will come to grips & I will back D. any time.

D. went to the Leathersellers' Luncheon today & was given the honorary freedom of the Company. He was given a very good reception, & made, so I am told, a very good little speech.

February 26th 1920
Dined last night at Philip Sassoon's. D. & the Prince of Wales were there, & a few others. Had a cinema, The Last Days of Pompeii, which pleased D. extremely—so much so, that he did not take it very much to heart when he heard that the Gov. had been defeated in the House—not a very important defeat, however, but it shows how weak our Whips are. This is not a very good week for D. I saw the new moon through glass last Sunday, which is a bad sign. I hope D. will do well in the House this afternoon. They tried to get Asquith to come there today, but he would not. The Turkish debate could not be held next Monday as the P.M. will not be there owing to the St. David's Day dinner, & Tuesday is a half-day, so, as the House wanted the Debate soon, there was nothing for it but to have it today. Asquith's journey to the House is being widely advertised, so he ought to get some sort of a crowd—at any rate outside the House.

February 27th 1920
D. made a first-rate speech yesterday, & once more carried the day. The question of Constantinople will not be raised again. Bob Cecil made a poor show, & came out very badly. D. was very angry with Carson, however, for forcing him, as he did, to speak early in the debate. D. wanted to wait till Cecil and the others had spoken, & then to wind up. But for some reason or other—whether malicious or otherwise it is difficult to tell—Carson so put the point that it was impossible for D. to refuse to speak & that upset all his plans. However, it did not really make much difference, excepting that D. was very angry with Carson. Carson was at Sassoon's dinner on Wednesday [25 February], & I must say I did not care much for his face.

February 28th 1920
D. has at last gone off to Cobham (7 o'clock). His family are down there, so that explains his reluctance. Also, he has arranged a meeting tomorrow evening at 6.0 to give him an excuse to come up again. I feel really sorry for him, as he needs a weekend rest so badly, & would take it if it were not that he cannot stand being there with that crowd. He has had Peace Conference meetings all day today. He told me in confidence that he *guides* the Conference much more than Clemenceau used to. Clem. used to let them all go their own way, but D. shepherds them like a sheep dog—Millerand bolts off in one direction—& Nitti in another—but D. brings them back to the fold. I can well imagine that. It is what D. excels in.

March 1st 1920

D. was very troubled in his mind this morning as to whether he should go to the House. In the ordinary way he would *not* have gone, & the question was, should he go simply because Asquith was going to take his seat? Of course it would be humiliating to him, as he thought Asquith would get a great reception. However, I said I thought it would be better if he faced the music, as then no-one would accuse him of being afraid or bitter, & everyone would think it more chivalrous of him. So he made up his mind to go, fully expecting it to be a disagreeable incident. To his surprise, however, Asquith had a most feeble reception, but instead, when D. got up to go out, the House made a great demonstration. D. came back very pleased. Of course the Northcliffe papers are playing a disgusting game, & none of the other papers —except perhaps The Standard—seem to have the courage to stand up to them.

March 2nd 1920

D. went to the St. David's Day dinner last night. The Prince of Wales & Mr. Bonar Law & J. H. Thomas & other distinguished people—including self! were also there. It was a huge success. D. made a first-class speech & the Prince of Wales also—he talks very simply—just like a school boy—saying little things that come into his head as he goes along, & then coming back again to the prepared speech. He charms everyone. Bonar Law made a most witty speech—posing as one who is entirely in the P.M.'s hands—telling the story of 'pity the man who's chained to our Davy'.

March 15th 1920

Today was to have been the first sparring contest between D. & Asquith. The debate was on 'high prices'. D. had read carefully through all the Memoranda prepared for him on the subject & went to the House intending to speak after Asquith had spoken. Everyone expected an attack from A. against the Government; indeed it was rather a good opportunity for him. But it was a 'damp squib'. So far from attacking he practically apologised for making the speech & made it quite clear that he was in no sense criticising the Government. So harmless a speech was it that D. could find nothing to answer in it & consequently did not speak at all, much as he wanted to.

March 16th 1920

D. not very happy in his mind this week. He has his speech to Liberals this Thursday [18 March], & from what he has said I think he wishes it were later on. There is great talk of 'fusion' in the Coalition. D. went to see Bonar this morning & came back very bad-tempered. He says Bonar is funking it now. However, Bonar always jibs a good deal before taking a long jump, & in any case I am perfectly certain that he is loyal to D.

D. went to see the Prince of Wales off this morning. The King & Queen are very sniffy with D. because the latter has been listening to the Prince's objection to going to India after his Australian tour, & to the suggestion that Prince Albert should go instead.

Anyhow, the Prince when he came last Friday [12 March] to see D., again touched on the question of India, & begged D. to get him out of it, & to send his brother. It certainly is hard lines on the boy to be away from England practically till next July twelve-months. D. said he would think about it. Apparently the Prince went to the King & Queen & told them about it, & they were furious that D. had discussed the subject with the Prince before discussing it with them. On the station this morning they were extremely frigid with D., indeed D. says that the Queen would scarcely shake hands with him, and seemed openly to resent D. making a fuss of the boy. However, it only amuses D., who is really very fond of the Prince, who appears to be just as fond of him.

March 18th 1920

D. & I went down to Cobham first thing yesterday morning, & worked nearly all day at his speech. D. was very excited about it. I have rarely seen him more highly-strung. He told me that in his opinion the time was not yet ripe for fusion, and that there was still some work to be done before that was tackled. 'I am not going to ask for fusion in my speech tomorrow', he said— 'but for "closer co-operation". That is the first step. My tactics are those of the Saracen warriors', he went on. 'Do you know how they used to fight? They would prepare their forces for the charge, sweep down towards the enemy, then suddenly pull up in front of them, and if it did not appear to be the right moment to charge, they would sweep round again & ride away. Then they would make another onset from another angle, & again, if it did not appear to be the right time & place, return again without attacking. They might do this several times. But at last they would see that the right moment had come, & would drive the charge home. That is what I am doing. I have come right up to the attack, but I can see that the time is not quite propitious, & shall wheel round & return to the charge another time.'

Nevertheless, his speech today has been a great success. We came up this morning before eleven, & D. went straight off to the Committee Room. The Liberals are delighted with it, & he has made a wonderful case. Asquith must find himself in a hole—& there is nothing he can do. He is finished—You could see on Monday [15 March] that he has no fight left in him.

D. is also very angry about his speech to Liberal Ministers having been given away to the Press. It was a most confidential meeting, & one would have thought that Ministers would have been above giving away such confidences. But some one did. D. suspects Macpherson.

March 19th 1920

D. said we really must go down to Cobham last night, after he had got his speech off his mind. So we did, & were very happy, & came up again first thing this morning. The country was simply beautiful—just the beginning of spring. D. & I seem to be fonder of each other than ever. He is so sweet to me.

March 20th 1920
D. just gone off to Walton Heath to play golf. We were to have gone to St. George's Hill, but heard last night that the Club House has been burnt to the ground, so that we could not go there. So D. went to Walton Heath instead, & it is better for me not to go there with him. It seems a long time till Monday to see him. But Mrs. Ll.G. is probably going down to Wales next week, so we shall be able to spend next weekend together.

Diary 1921

Here there is another long gap. When the diary resumes, the country was in the grip of a coal strike. The Troubles were still raging in Ireland. Allied conferences were still trying to settle German reparations. Law had resigned, and Austen Chamberlain took his place as leader of the Unionist party. Churchill was now colonial secretary, and Sir Robert Horne chancellor of the exchequer. Lloyd George's plans for fusion had come to nothing. An Imperial Conference was held in London during the summer. In June Birkenhead, Beaverbrook and Churchill plotted to overthrow Lloyd George —or so Lloyd George thought.

April 11th 1921
Went down to Trent over Sunday [10 April], after hectic week of unfruitful negotiations over coal strike.[1] P. of Wales came on Sunday. He spoke of Strachey's Life of Queen Victoria which had just been published, and the Prince said: 'That must be the book the King was talking about this morning. He was very angry, & got quite vehement over it.' P. of W. had not seen the book, so we showed it to him, & presently was discovered in roars of laughter over the description of the Queen & John Brown.

Had a perfect Sunday—ideal weather—& returned Monday morning.

April 16th 1921
Peace—comparative after a very anxious week. On Thursday night [14 April] thought Gov. had been betrayed by action of some foolish M.P., who asked the coal owners to state their case. The latter made a terrible mess of the whole thing & D. was furious. He said it was like the battle of Dunbar, where, after the battle was almost won, the clergy persuaded the Scottish Army to go down into the plains and fight. They did, & were beaten.

---

1. On 1 April 1921 the mineowners began a lockout to enforce a reduction in wages and a return to district rates. The miners demanded a national pool to equalise wages. On 14 April Frank Hodges, the miners' secretary, told a meeting of M.P.s that he would accept a standstill on wages without insisting on the national pool. On the following day the miners' executive overruled him by a majority of one. At this the railway and transport unions called off the sympathetic strike which they had projected.

However, the Gov. were saved by the action of Hodges, who played his game badly, though I think that in any case the Railway & Transport men did not want to come out.

April 20th 1921

Returned this morning from Lympne—motored up with D. & Hankey. *A most interesting weekend.* Went down with D. on Friday [15 April] for dinner, intending to return the next day; but when it came to the point D. wanted me to stay, & as Lady Rocksavage[1] was there, this was possible. Briand just as woolly and vague as ever, talking a lot & with great effect, but unwilling or unable to be tied down to anything definite and practical. Berthelot, the real brains, striving hard to get the utmost for France, anxious and industrious. On fundamentals the P.M. agreed with them, & much may be hoped from the Conference which has been arranged to take place in London on Saturday [23 April]. Berthelot very attentive and sweet, but above all remarkably interesting. His is a very powerful brain, capable of intense concentration & industry. He tells me he dislikes politics, which he dissociates from his Quai d'Orsay work, but I think what he really means is that he takes little interest in home politics, whereas world politics are his whole life and interest. He is very witty, but has very little sense of humour, a subtle but possible distinction. Briand on the other hand is both witty and humorous. D. asked Berthelot at breakfast yesterday morning what country he would prefer to live in if he had to leave his own. He replied at once: 'Italy—but without the Italians.'

At dinner D. asked members of the party what they would do for a living if they landed, unknown, in America, without a penny in their pockets. Berthelot said: 'I would invent a new religion, and preach it to the Americans.' Briand remarked: 'That is the first practical proposal I have heard emanate from the Quai d'Orsay.'

Briand is essentially a cynic—I am not sure that Mrs. Asquith's remark on meeting him for the first time was not very near the truth—'Vous êtes un rigolo'.

Berthelot has a very brutal tongue when he likes. I said to him (he hates Jews) 'Do you not think Lady Rocksavage is beautiful?' He replied— 'Negroes are beautiful.' He loves talking about himself, introspective things, and philosophy. Fortunately he kept off the line he had taken in his letters, & was strictly sensible. He is a curious character.

Lunched on Friday [15 April] with Pertinax and Millet.[2] The former has become much more friendly as the result of being fussed over a little, & we invited the two of them up to Lympne to tea yesterday. They were delighted.

---

1. Sassoon's sister, who had married Lord Cholmondeley's son, and who was often hostess to her brother.
2. Two leading French journalists.

April 26th 1921

Went for a walk with D. in Richmond Park. He went over his speech on resolution to the Speaker[1] on leaving the House. D. had taken a lot of trouble over it and was afraid he wd. not be able to remember it. He always thinks Asquith can do things of this kind much better than he can—with great ponderous phrases and plenty of sentiment. However D.'s speech in the House turned out to be a first-rate one. One of the Reporters told me that it was the best-phrased speech he had delivered for years. Asquith, this man said, was going off, whereas D. was getting steadily better at things of this kind. I must say Asquith's speech this afternoon did not strike me as being particularly brilliant. I was very glad to be there to witness the ceremony— a most moving one. The Speaker when he rose to move the resolution had difficulty in controlling his voice, but he subsequently recovered himself and made a very good speech. Afterwards, however, when he read the second resolution, he barely succeeded in reaching the end, & when he turned & left the Chair he quite broke down. It was a most touching scene, and a very trying ordeal for the Speaker himself.

Carpentier was in the Gallery, & I subsequently talked to him as he came to our room. His face is becoming more brutal. I imagine he must be fast becoming very spoilt as the result of his success. Women of course go mad over him.

Winston still very vexed with the P.M. as a result of, as he thinks, having been neglected in the recent promotions. D. says Winston fully expected to be made Chancellor of the Exchequer. It was the joke of the moment his being away when all the changes were made, & he has not been to see D. since his return. D. has only seen him in Cabinets & meetings of the kind, & Winston writes him 'Dear Prime Minister', whereas it used to be 'Dear Ll.G.' or 'My dear David' even.

D. very pleased his speech in the House is over, & pleased also with his success. I love these walks and drives with him alone. He is such a wonderful companion, & very sweet to me.

April 30th 1921

Came up this morning from Chequers, where D. & I spent yesterday. We went down late on Thursday [28 April] after D. had made his speech in the House on the Irish Debate. Yesterday a perfect spring day, & Chequers was heavenly. D. & I walked about all day all over the place, very lazy, & thinking of nothing in particular. I think it did D. a lot of good, especially as he had no rest last weekend. I am beginning to appreciate what the Lees must have suffered in giving up Chequers.[2] The peacefulness of the place is indescribable. There is healing in the atmosphere. We were sorry to leave this

---

1. James William Lowther: speaker 1905–21; cr. Viscount Ullswater, 1921.
2. Lord and Lady Lee of Fareham had lately given Chequers to the nation.

morning but had to come up very early this morning as the other Allies arrived last night & the conferences begin today.

May 1st 1921

Saw Berthelot at tea yesterday, when the members of the Conference had tea in my room. He presented me with a very sweet letter, a copy of La Vie des Martyrs, which he and Briand say is a most wonderful book, and a quaint old Indian necklace, which Berthelot says is 'sans valeur', but which I have reason to think is not. I like him much better than I did, since he has ceased to be sentimental, and is just friendly and interesting. I dined with Pertinax & M. & Mdme. Millet at the Carlton last night. The former very upset because his paper is on strike today (being May 1st) & so he cannot write an article! Apparently he & Millet had managed to get some good stuff after the Conference. How they get it I do not know. I know they did not get it from the French Ministers for they had not seen them. Berthelot has a supreme contempt for journalists. He says the French ones would sell the Government and the country for the sake of publishing a piece of news. Mdme. Millet tells me Pertinax is much tamer now (The Times says so too!) because—so she says—he is afraid of offending me! However that may be, I think our attention to them last time they were here has certainly borne good fruit.

Tonight D. was to have dined with Eric Geddes, to meet a lady of the stage with whom Eric is enamoured. D. did not care to do so, so arranged a little Welsh political dinner which we are having at the Carlton. The Great Eric will be furious, but I love doing him in, as he is such a hypocrite over affairs of the heart—thinks nothing of having violent affairs with people like Delysia, but forced Rhys-Williams to leave the Transport Ministry because he was in love with his secretary (whom he has since married).

May 3rd 1921

Had a little dinner party last night. Philip Kerr and Muriel Beckett & Berthelot. Asked D. to come but he would not. I suspect he did not like my giving the party much, though I told him of my intention before I asked them. But he got his own back by prolonging the Conference till after nine o'clock, so that it was nearly 9.30 when Philip & Berthelot turned up. The latter said: 'Il me semblait que M. Ll. George voulait prolonger la Conférence!' Berthelot was in excellent form, and told us the most thrilling stories of the war. He told us of a Dutch journalist (naturalised French) who was terrified at the prospect of being called up, and tried to get into a safe job. He succeeded for some time, but Clemenceau got his knife into him & succeeded in getting him called up. He was however put in a safe billet. Some time after he asked to be sent to a more dangerous post. 'I have found my self-respect', was his reason, when asked why. Some time afterwards he asked to be put into the trenches. 'My self-respect demands it', he explained. He became Captain, Major, & Colonel and was eventually killed leading his men. His mistress, with whom he had lived for many years, was left unprovided for, and some rich friends took her in for a while; but eventually her pride refused to let her stay there any longer and she came to Berthelot asked him for a loan, saying she was going to seek work & would repay him. This she did, & he has since lost sight of her, but it is a touching story of two people whose self-respect became the governing feature of their lives.

Berthelot spoke of Clemenceau and the cruel side of him. He told how Joffre at the beginning of the war used to go and spend every Friday afternoon on a boat—a sort of barge—with his wife. This was a real pleasure and relaxation to him. Clemenceau however found out how Joffre was in the habit of spending his Friday afternoons, and promptly had the barge chartered for war service, and filled up with coal!

Berthelot has evidently an admiration & even affection for Clemenceau, owing no doubt to his victorious war policy, but he has a horror of his cruelty and viciousness. 'Ce sont une famille de loups!' was his comment. It appears that Mdme. Clemenceau was given away to her husband by her daughter. Mdme. C. used to meet her lover in the afternoon. She would take the daughter out, apparently for a walk, and leave her at a neighbouring dressmaking establishment for an hour or two or more. The daughter conjectured what was going on, & gave her mother away to her father. The story goes that Clemenceau, gaining knowledge of what was going on, surprised the lovers together. 'I am at your disposal, sir', said the lover to M. Clemenceau. 'Not at all—she is at your disposal', was Clemenceau's reply.

But Berthelot's most interesting story was of Foch—'une nuit du Général Foch', he calls it. It appears that Foch was sent for one night by Joffre early in 1915, when things were going badly. 'Ça ne va pas, mon ami', was Joffre's remark to Foch, & then he commissioned the latter to help him set things straight. 'Castlenau's army is broken; Maud'huy is on the point of retreating; the Germans are pressing the British hard, and the Belgians have completely broken up. You must put it right.' Thus Joffre to Foch, & the latter, nothing daunted, set about his task, beginning at 4 o'clock in the afternoon. First of all he visited Castlenau (for whom apparently he—and Berthelot too—had supreme contempt). He ordered him to stand and face the foe at all costs, 'But we shall all be annihilated', was Castlenau's protest. 'Very well', was Foch's reply, 'your men must stand & be annihilated & if necessary you must die at your post too.' 'That is all very well', said Castlenau, 'but who is to take the responsibility for it? I will not.' 'I take the responsibility', said Foch. 'Give me a piece of paper.' And he wrote: 'I, General Foch, order General Castlenau to stand at his post and to give up his life.' And he went away. Castlenau stood—and still lives.

Next Foch visited Maud'huy (in company all this time of course with Weygand) and learnt the state of things at Arras. Maud'huy insisted that it was not possible to withstand the enemy & said he would have to retreat and give up Arras. 'I will go away & dine', said Foch, '& will come back in an hour. Think it over, and I will then ask you to give me a different answer.'

He came back in an hour, and Maud'huy said he would make a stand and would defend Arras. 'That's the right answer', said Foch, & congratulated him. 'Arras will not be taken now.' And it was not.

He then went to Lord French, at Ypres, and found him in bed. He got up and received Foch and they talked over the prospects. French was cheerful but not over sanguine, but he promised to try & reorganise his line and stand his ground: which he actually did. (I cannot help thinking that if French had not been the British general, Berthelot's description of Foch's visit to him would have been more vivid!)

Foch then visited the King of the Belgians for whom, strangely enough (according to Berthelot) he seems to have had the utmost contempt. The King was in despair and in a state of blue funk. He could not stand and face the enemy. 'Sire', said Foch, 'if you stay where you are, you are still King of Belgium. If you retreat, Belgium exists no longer, & you cease to be her King.' Foch remained a long time in conversation with the King, and eventually succeeded in convincing him that he must face the enemy, which he did.

Thus in a single night—from 4 o'clock in the afternoon until the following morning—did Foch reconstruct the whole of the Allied line, and through sheer force of personal will and influence persuade the various chiefs to rally and face the enemy.

May 4th 1921
Dined last night at Philip Sassoon's—D. as well, and Berthelot among others. D. in great form, hilarious and very talkative, but keeping everyone amused. Berthelot quite silent and extremely dull, so different from the previous evening. He looked ghastly. D. rather jealous, especially when I suggested we should drive B. home. However, the latter refused saying he would prefer to walk.

Millet called to see me this morning. Says the French noticed that the P.M. deferred much more to his colleagues in the Allied Meetings than he had been in the habit of doing & they could not help wondering if the reason was that his power over them was not so great as it used to be. I could not very well tell M. that D. did it deliberately, calling upon the opinions of Churchill, Worthington Evans,[1] etc., to let the French see that D. was much more pro-French than the majority of his colleagues, & to let the French see also what his difficulties were. However he has got his way. Berthelot told me last Monday that Briand *must* stick to his original plan—i.e. to march on the Ruhr at once. But D. has persuaded him to do otherwise, though the old Breton has looked very bothered & harassed the last day or two. Millet also told me that Briand had received a wire this morning from Millerand, apparently demanding a decision of some sort. So that it looks as though French opinion was becoming impatient.

---

1. Sir Laming Worthington-Evans (1868–1931): secretary for war, 1921–2, 1924–9; postmaster general, 1923–4.

May 5th 1921

Conferences went on all yesterday & apparently very late last night. I left at 11, as there was no sign of a finish. The Reparation Commission, summoned from Paris & very much on their dignity, came in for a lot of sarcasm on the part of Briand, who kept everyone in fits of laughter. (The Commissioners had kept the Conference waiting for an hour the previous night while they decided whether they should or should not come.) Bradbury[1] I believe is sending in his resignation which the P.M. says he will certainly accept.

On arriving this morning found on my desk a note from Berthelot lamenting the fact that they had departed suddenly—also a note from M. Briand saying: 'Les Conférences Interalliées ne sont pas les champs de batailles les moins dangereux.' I think there is a double entendre and D. thinks so too. I think he is rather glad B. has gone. He was getting very jealous, though it takes a lot usually to rouse his jealousy. D. made his statement in the House this afternoon, a most able speech—very concise and clear, with a wonderful reference to France. He is now worrying over his Maidstone speech on Saturday, for which he has very little time to prepare. Also, he has a bad tooth, which he keeps on getting patched up but will not give the necessary time to get it properly attended. I got the dentist down to the House this afternoon to look at it as it was hurting him.

May 7th 1921

Philip Kerr said 'Goodbye' last night. He has gone on a tour round Midlands preparatory to taking up his new work on The Chronicle. I could not bear to say 'goodbye' & he was upset too. I have grown to love him like a brother, and he knows all about D. & me and understands. He is the most Christ-like man I have ever known, and he seems to shed his personality around and radiate happiness. However I suppose we shall see a good deal of him still, but the fact of his leaving Downing St. makes me very sad.

A hectic morning. D. preparing his speech & in a tearing hurry. Lord Fitzalan just come in very cheerful about the news from Ireland—Craig[2] & De Valera[3] met. D. very annoyed that he has to go to the Cazalets' afterwards. I know he will hate it, but it is his own doing, & he will see for himself what they are like. I feel quite certain he will not stay out the weekend!

May 9th 1921

Went down to Maidstone on Saturday & heard D. A most successful speech, & a very enthusiastic audience. He looked & spoke wonderfully well. He went on to Cazalets' afterwards, but I thought he would not stay there very long. Early yesterday morning he rang up to say he must see Horne & would come up to town if necessary. This of course meant that he wanted to come up, otherwise he would have asked H. to go down there. Apparently he sent

1. Sir John Bradbury: the head of the Treasury.
2. Prime Minister of Northern Ireland.
3. President of the Irish Republic.

for Hankey to go to lunch with him, & then returned to Hankey's house for tea, & came on up to town. He told me he was not very happy at the Cazalets'. The great thing was that they should be entertaining the Prime Minister, not that he should enjoy himself and have rest. He was very tired after his speech, but was not allowed to rest, but was trotted round the house and garden. 'I don't mind telling you a secret', he said to me. '*I'm not going there again!*'

We had dinner together, alone. D. was very sweet, & very pleased with his speech. He talked to me about his old uncle. Olwen's new baby (a photograph of whom has just arrived) is amazingly like him. She has called the baby Eluned, (Mair's other name) and D. was very moved when he heard, and wept. He can never forget Mair's death. I think he will be very fond of little Eluned.

May 10th 1921

Dined with D. in his room in the House last night. D. in very good form, though news had come of an impending railway strike. Geddes & D. compared notes on the M. of M. days. G. says Robertson is writing his book. D. says if he makes false statements in it, he (D.) will be forced to write *his* account of the war. (I rather hope R. will make false statements.) I want D. to write his book. He talks of doing it in the autumn recess.

Lord French came to lunch today & I sat by him. Megan on his other side pricked up her ears when he referred to our meeting at Lympne at Easter, & our drive over to Canterbury. She knew her father was there. She is a little too clever, but not clever enough to do her father in, which she is constantly attempting. One of these days they will come to grips over something & then there will be a row. Lord French talked of Foch, whom he loves. 'He would say to me', he said of Foch: 'Eh bien—nous avançons, bras dessus bras dessous.' Albert Thomas was also at lunch—a nice pleasant old thing but rather heavy. 'Foch was nearly shelved in the middle of the war', said French to me. 'I should like to hear Thomas' opinion of it, & who was responsible.' We asked him. 'Briand', was his reply—'Et moi! We did it together. He was tired, & we thought he wanted a rest.' This was a most unexpected reply, and French was frightfully amused, especially at the *explanation*!

This morning the German Ambassador came to see D. He thinks his Government will accept the terms. They are particularly gratified that Clause 238 (I think it is) has been left in the Treaty. This clause D. had a great fight with the French over (especially Loucheur). 'We tried to be strictly fair', said D. to Sthamer. 'Fair to the Germans as well as to ourselves.' D. is very hopeful as a result of the conversation.

May 12th 1921

We had dinner in D.'s room in the House again on Tuesday night [10 May]. This is becoming an institution. He just asks one or two people with whom he can let himself go, & it is a great relief for him. Since Bonar left he has lost an ideal companion with whom he could laugh & joke and enjoy himself.

He cannot do that with Chamberlain, who is pompous to the last degree, &
has become increasingly so since he took Bonar's place. He is a vain man. He
is very fond of relating an interview which he once had with Bismarck, &
what the great man said & what he said. Someone told me the other day—
I think it must have been Berthelot—that Bismarck also spoke of the incident,
but his comment was that nothing very great could ever come out of so poor
a head!

Yesterday the Germans accepted the Allied terms and the G. Ambassador
brought along the official document. D. very pleased indeed. It is a great
triumph for him, & I think he is very justly proud. It marks the end of a very
worrying period, & is a real step forward in the direction of general peace.
He made his statement in the House after questions. He said they were all
very pleased—excepting Lord R. Cecil, who sat, D. said with a look of
despair on his face. He saw the downfall of the Govt. further removed than
ever! D. said he had the same look on his face when Bonar's resignation was
announced—he realised what a mistake he had made in crossing the House,
as he would have been Chamberlain's rival for the leadership.

May 15th 1921
D. made an amazing speech in the House on Friday [13 May]. I knew it was
going to be something out of the ordinary, as he sent to get me up to the
House & waited to begin his speech till I was there. He had fortified himself
with a strong dose of port wine, & just let go about Poland—and the French!
It was a remarkably able speech—he was never in better form—full of the
most sparkling passages and trenchant phrases. But I am afraid it will cause
trouble! In fact the French press are already busy and beginning to howl. All
the same, I think D. was right, though we nearly had a row after his speech
about the things he said of the French. But they are certainly not playing the
game in this instance. And the Germans will—and are—making the most of
D.'s speech.

My articles appearing in The Sunday Times.[1] D. very pleased & of course
is telling no end of people that I have written them! Then he will be surprised
when it gets known.

Went to see 'Othello' with D. & Philip Sassoon & M. Beckett on Thursday
[12 May]. A wonderfully good show, & very well acted. What a marvellous
man Mr. Shakespeare was! A play like Othello has the same effect as the
Greek tragedies must have had on their audiences—moving one to pity and
fear!

D. entertaining the Crown Prince of Japan at Chequers today. Mrs. Ll.G.
was down at Criccieth & did not want to come up, so D. did not over-
persuade her & thought she was not coming. Megan however, who is playing
her mother off against D. & me, telephoned her mother all day Friday and

---

1. A series which the Editor had asked me to do, and which later appeared in book form.
[F.Ll.G.]

yesterday morning told her that D. insisted on her coming up! So she got into the next train & came, much to her disgust & very angry with D. at making her come. I am left high & dry, everyone else having gone away for Whitsun. However it is the fortunes of war, & cannot be helped. D. frightfully angry with Megan, but of course he hasn't much of a case!

The French terribly angry with D. as I knew they would be. All the English press however back D. I suppose when the storm has blown over the air will be clearer!

May 16th 1921

D. staying down at Chequers but scheming to come up tomorrow—also to get Mrs. Ll.G. back to Wales again.

May 20th 1921

D. has again attacked the French attitude towards Silesia in his statement to the Press. I begged him to make it less violent, & succeeded in persuading him to omit a few violent words which would have made all hope of a reconciliation impossible. I hope this quarrel will not go on for long, as it is terribly bad for the Entente. But I agree that the French want a little plain speaking, & D. is the best person to do it! But they are furious with him & I hear Englishmen are not very popular in Paris just at present.

Went down to Chequers on Wednesday midday [18 May] with D. & Megan. Came up again yesterday evening as D. had to be present at the Pilgrims' Dinner in the evening. We walked about all day at Chequers preparing his speech, which was a very good one (Megan had gone back to town early in the morning) and then came up to town after tea. A most peaceful and sweet day.

May 24th 1921

Went down to Philip Sassoon's at Trent on Friday [20 May] to lunch—found quite a large party there—Lord & Lady Rocksavage, Mr. Dudley Ward, & others. D. & I very unsociable & went for a long walk after lunch by ourselves. When we returned to tea found that the 'Dolly Sisters' had arrived, much to the annoyance of D., who does not shine in such company. After tea D. said he would go to Chequers, though Philip wanted us to stay the night. But there is always a spirit of restlessness about Philip's houses—always a crowd of people trying to be bright—& D. loves peace & quietness—so we sailed away. D. said it was the same road—from Elstree—that he took the Sunday years ago when he came to Allenswood to see me—the first Sunday in July 1912—when we both of us realised for the first time that something serious was happening—when I asked him to come to the garden party the following Saturday & he said he would. From then we never lost touch with each other & events marched more or less rapidly! However this is back history. We got to Chequers in time for dinner—a glorious evening, & then walked in the garden till bed-time.

Saturday [21 May] passed uneventfully—glorious weather—& various
people arrived in the evening—Seebohm Rowntree, Sir Dennis Bayley,
William Sutherland & Ned Grigg. Sunday—many talks on coal strike &
unemployment & Sir Robert Horne came over from Ascot. In the evening
we all went for a walk & D. & Rowntree went in front together. We lost
sight of them & later saw some people skirting a wood which we thought
were D. & R., but discovered them to be 4 strangers. However as there was
a right of way there we thought no more about it & took the direct route
home. We found that D. & R. had not returned. About $\frac{1}{4}$ hour later they
came in & informed us that they had run up against 4 strangers hanging about,
& whom they thought to be Sinn Feiners, as on going into the little summer-
house on the hill, D. found written up: Up the Rebels: Up Sinn Fein; I.R.A.
The men had been seen coming from that direction. D. sent one of the
detectives in the direction they had gone. I spoke to another, who rather
pooh-poohed the whole idea, saying that they were only visitors making
their way across the estate. However Sir Dennis Bayley, seeing that the P.M.
took a more serious view of the matter, went off with a third detective &
brought the 4 men back! Whereupon they were promptly locked in a shed
and questioned. They turned out to be actually Irishmen, one of whom confessed to having only been in this country a fortnight. They were taken off
to Aylesbury Gaol for the night, as their answers were not satisfactory,
though one of them turned out to be the Editor of The Statist! Today they
were brought up to London & examined & 3 of them let off. We found later
that they had only been very scantily questioned & that Sir Basil Thomson
admitted that he had forgotten to make any mention to them of the writing
in the summer-house! Also he'd not sent to Ireland for information. The man
who is detained turns out to be an Irish medical student.

D. very annoyed about the way the whole thing has been managed & had
Thomson, Shortt & Gen. Horwood up this afternoon for a talk. It turned out
that the Superintendent to whom the report was first made was an Irish
Catholic, & he had censured Randall, the P.M.'s detective, for allowing the
men to be arrested. 'If they had been Englishmen you would not have arrested
them', was his comment! Also it transpires that a very detailed plan of
Chequers which Randall had had made when the P.M. first went there, &
which he had handed in at Scotland Yard, is missing!

Megan takes a contemptuous view of the whole affair; says it is only a
practical joke, and thinks her father is making a great fuss about nothing!
Lady Greenwood is furious with her, especially since M. informed her that
she 'considered father was becoming quite impossible: it was time someone
taught him a lesson'. Margot's remark was: 'I shouldn't like to be the person
who set out to teach him that lesson!'

May 25th 1921
It now appears that the man who was released, the Editor of The Statist, was

in the Irish Rebellion of 1916 & was imprisoned in Stafford Gaol after it. Scotland Yard released him before making any inquiries!

D. very annoyed at Winston, who is being difficult, as he has returned from his voyage very disgruntled. He was furious at all the changes which were made in his absence, and is making mischief behind D.'s back. He declared his intention this morning of opposing the Government's Irish policy, & D. told him he would have a chance of doing it immediately, as the question was coming up at once. This put Winston rather in a fix, as he must either go back on his statement to D., or else show his hand at once in the Cabinet, & be no doubt in a small minority, since he has not yet had time to work up his Cabal.

May 31st 1921
D. very worried & cross all day yesterday. Things are not going very well & he does not quite see his way. Coal Strike going badly, & D. does not see the end of it. A beastly article in The Evening Standard yesterday rather upset him, especially as he is being very kind to Hulton.[1] Winston is going to prove troublesome, & F.E. [Lord Birkenhead] is half inclined to back him. Horne told me on Saturday [28 May] that Beaverbrook is getting hold of Churchill, & Horne thinks we ought to keep Churchill in with the P.M. But D. is so sick with C. I don't think he cares if he does go. Horne says Churchill is criticising the Government on Finance and Ireland in the Clubs & lobbies. H. wanted to go to Churchill & have it out with him but I advised him not to. I said the P.M. will give him 'one on the nose' sooner or later, & he is the best person to do it!

June 1st 1921
D. dined with some of his colleagues at P. Sassoon's last night. Very pleased with the talk, which he says was most useful. Geddes stated that there was only one person that the people cared about & would listen to and that was D. D. said that when Geddes said this Winston could not conceal his anger & irritation & others noticed it too. D. says he is going to detach F.E. from Winston. He (D.) wants a general election in the autumn, as he thinks it would be useful then. But all the same he is a little worried at the way things are going, & would not mind, at times, getting away from it altogether. Poor old thing, my heart aches for him sometimes.

June 2nd 1921
D. & I went for a lovely walk in Richmond Park, & then he went on to the House afterwards & had a very heavy afternoon. We *think* we can manage to be together at Chequers on Sunday [5 June] but it doesn't do to count on it.

Lost all my Derby bets yesterday. 'From him that hath not shall be taken away even that which he hath!'

D. picked the bluebells for me in Richmond Park.

---

1. Sir Edward Hulton, owner of The Evening Standard.

June 5th 1921

D. & I went down to Chequers on Friday afternoon. D. *very* cross & irritable all the way down, but made it up very sweetly before we arrived, explaining that he felt very tired & overstrung. He looked it, & I was so sorry for him, and though I can't help being upset when he is cross to me, it is almost invariably when he is over-tired. When we got to Chequers, D. went straight out into the garden & picked me some red roses as a peace-offering, & was very sweet to me the rest of the evening. Yesterday morning, however, he did not feel or look at all well, did not want anything for breakfast & I was really alarmed about him. I rang up Bertrand Dawson who happened to be at Penn & he came over during the morning. D. very sorry for himself at the prospect of the doctor's visit! Lord Dawson cheered him up, however, & assured him that with rest and carefulness, he would soon be all right again. Dawson told me that D. was very over-strained & must cancel all his engagements till the Imperial Conference (16th). This is not a bad thing as the next 10 days were going to be very heavy ones for D., & I was getting very worried about it. He was to have dinners (with speeches) tomorrow & Tuesday [7 June]. Oxford Thursday & Friday (3 speeches) and Carnarvon & Portmadoc Tuesday & Wednesday the following week. However all that is off now though I think he will try & get down to Criccieth for Gwilym's wedding.

I cannot go down to Chequers today as the family are there, but D. is in bed at present & will have a restful day.

Went to see the polo at Ranelagh yesterday afternoon with Stern. The Americans are beating us into fits.

June 11th 1921

Just got back from Chequers. Went there on Tuesday [7 June] as the family came up to town. D. was waiting on the station for me—I did not see him until I was on top of him, & was so taken back as he very rarely goes to a station nowadays. We went off in the car and he had brought me some red roses & a basket of strawberries, in case I was hungry! It was a glorious sunny afternoon and we drove to Hughenden to look at Disraeli's house. A beautiful old park, but the house very pretentious and ugly. We saw his grave in the peaceful little churchyard. D. looking much better but still a little pale, though I did not tell him so. We have had a heavenly week together. I thought I should have to go away again on Wednesday [8 June], but the family did not return, & last night they decided to go by train from London, & to pick up D. at Bletchley, & go on to Wales with him. This was a most delightful piece of luck, as I drove to Bletchley with him early this morning & then returned by train to London. It seems desolate so far from him. He has been so sweet and gentle, and we have had a wonderful time together. Dawson says he ought to stay down in Wales till Friday & then stay at Chequers till the following Monday.

On Thursday [9 June] he had a meeting of Ministers at Chequers to talk foreign policy (Silesia, Greece & Turkey) Winston, Curzon, Montagu, & W. Evans. D. said that every one of them was more or less hostile to him—Winston was obviously disappointed at finding the P.M. looking so well; Montagu always hostile and cynical; Curzon hopes to be the next Prime Minister, & has just entertained the King & Queen lavishly. The latter by the way have dined this week with the Crewes, & lunched with the Asquiths! D. says it looks as though they were expecting a change of government, but I told him that he does not pay the King very much attention—he always gets out of going to the Palace if he can, & has constantly refused invitations to Windsor. He cannot be surprised if the King is a little hurt.

D. is a little worried about the whole political situation. He says we have been on the crest of the wave—politically—and are now going down again into the trough & will have a bad time. It looks likely. D. is bent on cutting down expenditure but I think it will be a terrible mistake to cut down pensions, as he talks of doing, until everything else has been tried. There is no doubt he has a lot of enemies in the Government, who will leave him if they think they can better themselves. Austen he thinks will stick to him. He certainly gets on with him much better than he expected to. Austen plays the game, & he sees that he can trust the P.M. who conceals nothing from him. D. has just had a letter from Bonar, who evidently does not dream of coming back to politics, & commiserates with D. on the bad time he is having—a thoroughly typical letter, not tending to cheerfulness!

June 18th 1921
D. returned last night from Wales looking fit, but a little tired by the journey. This not surprising as the heat had been terrible all day. He says he has not had much of a rest in Wales. Everywhere he went he had to make speeches, & this in addition to the wedding & the big meeting at Portmadoc. Also Mrs. Ll.G. insists on his seeing & shaking hands with everyone who happens to call. D. intended to go to Chequers (hoping Mrs. Ll.G. would stay at Criccieth) but as she returned, too, he came to London. We went to P. Sassoon's last night to dinner & as Philip took his guests to the theatre afterwards D. & I had a nice talk. He still has a cold in the head, & I do not think he is as well as he ought to be after a fortnight's rest. D. saw Smuts before dinner. The latter is inclined to be tiresome over Ireland, & suggests we should give them Dominion Home Rule. D.'s reply was: The Br. Isles are a federation: you do not contemplate giving Dom. Home Rule to Natal, or the Orange States. Why then do you suggest it for us? But Smuts is always a little slim, & is probably running with Asquith & Co. in case this Gov. falls.

D. said last night that he thinks we shall very soon have to do what Smuts has done—take our courage in our hands—commit suicide as a Coalition & like the phoenix rise from Coalition ashes as a new party. Should not be at all surprised if there was a general election in the autumn. D. has gone down to Windsor this morning to talk to the King about the Imperial Conference which begins on Monday. I hear that the Crewes are staying at Windsor for the weekend: evidently the King & Queen had forgotten that they had asked them, for at Ascot this week the Queen asked Lord Crewe where he was going for the weekend, & the King asked Lady Crewe the same question!

Went to Ascot Tuesday & Wednesday [14 & 15 June], a beautiful scene & glorious weather. Bertie Stern invited me, and was very nice & attentive, arranging so that we drove together there & back. He is a curious person—told me for the first time about his past gay life (which I already knew from others), Winifred Barnes, etc. Can't think why he suddenly unburdened himself in this manner, as he is usually so reserved. Went to Cuckoo Bellville's[1] party on Thursday night—lots of celebrities, including the King of Spain and the Prince of Wales, who had come up from Windsor after his father's dinner party & intended returning there before morning. He must have had one of his gloomy fits, for he came up to me & remarked: 'There's more trouble about India—Have you heard?' For the moment I thought he meant a rebellion, but then it occurred to me that he must mean his visit there, & I said: 'But I thought it was all settled. Don't you want to go?' 'Of course I don't want to go', he replied petulantly—'I know', I replied, 'but I thought you had become more or less reconciled to the idea.' 'Oh, I suppose I can become reconciled to anything', he replied. 'Does the P.M. think I ought to go?' I could not understand why he brought the subject up again, as I knew it had been all settled ages ago, but I suppose he must have been feeling particularly depressed about it. Apparently he had been having an argument with his father about it, for I heard that the Prince said he would ask the P.M. whether he really wanted him to go. Whereupon the King said: 'I don't care whether the P.M. wants you to go or not. *I* wish you to go & you are going.'

Spent last weekend at Cuckoo Bellville's cottage at Hurstmonceux. A lovely spot. She had had the McKennas there a week or two back, & McK. had spent the whole time running D. down. Cuckoo eventually lost her temper, and asked whom he would put in D.'s place. 'Any one of the other 700 members of Parl.', was his reply. Later he asked: 'What is the matter with Winston as Prime Minister?' Which looks as though he were working with Winston against D. Cuckoo asked McKenna why he did not dine at the Embassy Club sometimes? 'A man in my position could not be seen there', was McK.'s answer. 'Why, everyone goes there—Horne, Montagu, Churchill', Cuckoo said. 'Oh, but as the head of a great bank I consider myself to be in a far more important position than a Cabinet Minister', was McK.'s answer.

June 20th 1921
My last article (serial) on Clemenceau appeared in The Sunday Times yester-

---

1. A Mayfair socialite who was running a very successful dress shop.

day, & the articles are shortly appearing in book form.[1] Very proud of myself.

D. having trouble with Addison.[2] The former says he cannot possibly persist in retaining him, especially as Addison has not been too loyal & is intriguing with Winston on Ireland. McCurdy[3] had 3 hours with Addison this morning, & an arrangement was come to whereby Addison is to go at the end of the Session, & D. will defend this in the House on Thursday [23 June]. McCurdy says Addison has no conception of the real position—says that the whole conspiracy is against him as a Liberal & progressive, & to separate D. from his Liberal colleagues. Addison has no idea how unpopular he himself is.

Meanwhile intrigues are seething everywhere. Winston is very hostile, but D. is watching him & F.E. Beaverbrook is clearly engineering for a coup. Bonar Law came home for the weekend—not for any ostensible reason, but I think it looks a little suspicious—he is so entirely in Beaverbrook's hands. Am dining tonight at the House with D.—and Mrs. Ll.G. is away . . .

June 22nd 1921

D. did a very skilful thing yesterday. He had heard that F.E. was going to make a statement in the House of Lords yesterday afternoon—he had also heard quite by accident that F.E. was going to make a sensational statement off his own bat on fiscal autonomy. D. realised that the whole of the intrigue against him was centering round Ireland. F.E. & Winston had already in the Cabinet tried to engineer a crisis on policy, but D. had so turned the debate that if the break came, it would have been on *tariffs*—and the intriguers realised that this would not do. F.E.'s coup was a new idea. But D. sent for him half an hour before his speech in the Lords, & in the course of conversation asked him what he was going to say in his speech. After that, F.E. could not very well in decency have gone away & said something entirely different. Today however he has been asking *why* the P.M. sent for him, which shows that he realises that D. must have guessed something, & F.E. would doubtless like to know *how much* he had guessed!

June 24th 1921

An amazing article in The Manchester Guardian yesterday, exposing the whole plot, with details. We don't know who wrote it, or how he got the information, but it is all correct. Last night D. had an emphatic letter from F.E. denying the whole thing—but 'protesting too much'. But no word from Winston, who is openly accused of treachery in the article. D. says that Winston does not tell actual lies, & that is why he will not deny it. But F.E.

---

1. Makers of the New World.
2. Christopher Addison, the minister of health, was attacked by the Conservatives for his housing plans.
3. Charles Albert McCurdy (1870–1931): food controller, 1920–1; Coalition Liberal chief whip, 1921–2.

does not care what lies he tells. However, the whole plot is exposed, and the intrigue, I suppose, finished for the time being. D.'s speech on Addison in the House yesterday put the finishing touch to it. He took the ground from under the critics' feet & there was not even a division! All the week Winston has been trying to work Addison up in order to make him stubborn & so make things more difficult for D. Beaverbrook & Winston between them have been working the papers up against Addison, to try & make him take a stand & so have a fight in the House, where the Gov. might possibly have been beaten. But they failed hopelessly, & D. was very pleased with himself last night.

Today Rees[1] of The Sunday Times rang up, & told me that Bonar *had* come over last weekend with a specific purpose. When I queried it, he said: 'But we know for a fact, & we know of course who was behind it (meaning Beaverbrook) but he found things unsympathetic.' It is difficult to believe these things of Bonar, but Beaverbrook seems to be able to make him do anything. The trouble is that when Bonar's brother got into difficulty during the war—trading with Germany I believe—Beaverbrook helped him out of it, & this has of course put Bonar under an obligation to Beaverbrook ever since.[2] It is practically blackmail. I haven't told D. yet, but I know he will hardly believe The Sunday Times story. D. said to Bonar last Sunday [19 June], (knowing he would repeat it to Beaverbrook): 'I may go out of office, but if I do go it will be because I want to go, and not because I am turned out.'

We are trying to get a house in Scotland for September, as Dawson will not allow D. to go abroad—D. was going to take me for a motor tour through the Tyrol & the Italian Lakes, ending up at Venice. But Dawson says it would be too tiring. So Scotland is the alternative.

Meanwhile the Wee Frees[3] are making frantic advances to D.—lunches—dinners, etc. A meeting was held on Wednesday [22 June] when they discussed their position, & *all but four* voted for taking D. as their leader (with certain conditions of course). The four opponents were Asquith, Maclean, Wedgwood Benn & Thorne. Hogge has given an interview to The Evening Standard saying they are willing to join D.—with certain conditions. It appears that Hogge's great grievance at the moment is that he has never met D. socially! What a change of front from 6 weeks ago, when they were hauling down D.'s portrait from the walls of the Nat. Liberal Club. But they find Asquith is no leader, & they have no hope or trust in him.

---

1. The Editor.
2. This story is not true. Bonar Law's brother John was a partner in William Jacks and Company, but was not one of the two partners prosecuted for trading with the enemy. The offence was little more than technical, and the two, found guilty, received brief terms of imprisonment. Beaverbrook played no part in the affair.
3. The Independent Liberals were loosely known as the Wee Frees—originally a small sect in the Scottish Church.

July 4th 1921

Had a divine weekend at Chequers, though Megan rather troublesome, & turning up just before lunch on Sunday [3 July] resented things being in my hands & was very cross and rude. Everyone noticed how bad-tempered she was. Her frivolous life is taking from her charm and looks. No one seems to have any control over her or to be responsible for her comings & goings. She just goes wherever she pleases & does what she likes—avoids her father when she has something else to do and resents finding me there when she condescends to turn up.

Last week a terribly busy week for D. The bubble of political intrigue burst with a further article in The Manchester Guardian. But still no explanation or denial from Winston. However, his mother's death has had a sobering effect on him, & he is now very civil to D., who wrote him a nice letter. The Coal Strike is settled & events in Ireland are marching rapidly. It looks as though De Valera might come over, but he still hesitates.

D. very pleased with himself over the Japanese Alliance which came up for discussion at the Imperial Conference last week. The question was as to whether the Alliance should be *renewed*, & it would have proved a difficult question. It suddenly occurred to D. that under international law the League of Nations ruling probably did not hold good, & on looking it up found that instead of *renewing* the agreement this year, it had never been legally terminated, & it required a year's notice to terminate it & no notice had yet been given. It would therefore leave a whole year in which to make up our minds. D. led the debate round in such a way as to leave it to the Lord Chancellor to make the point. The L.C. saw what D. was driving at & took up the cue— with great success, much to the disgust of Meighen who had just made a 2 hours speech against the renewal. F.E. was much amused & passed D. this note[1]—So the difficulty has been tided over for the present.

There is a talk of a Conference to be held between representatives of the British Empire and America. Several places have been suggested & D. is very keen on Honolulu, but I am afraid it would be too far. Another suggestion is *Cuba*. It is to be in October and ought to be rather fun.[2]

Geddes came to Chequers for the weekend. He has a most enervating effect upon me—he is so insistent on what *he* likes & what *he* thinks and what *he* wants. He is, I think, the most aggressive and pushful personality I know, & he doesn't appeal to me in the least. He is in love with Margot Greenwood who is keeping him at a distance at present, though rather liking him and flattered by his attentions. D. has persuaded him to stay on after his Railway Bill is through, & take over an 'economy campaign' in Gov. Depts. Geddes has agreed, but he will I know demand an addition to his long row of decorations in return!

---

1. Not preserved.
2. A conference over the Far East and naval disarmament was held in Washington in the autumn. Balfour was the British representative.

July 5th 1921

Lord Midleton returned from Ireland this morning, having seen De Valera. The latter will probably come over, but will not meet Craig. Smuts has gone over to see De Valera. They say he waited to see whether D.V. was likely to come, & now will take the credit for having persuaded him to come.

D. very tired this evening. We are going to have dinner quietly with Philip Kerr and then I shall play to him afterwards. He has had a terribly heavy day. Philip Kerr is about to take over the management of The Daily Chronicle, though Freddy Guest as usual has muddled the arrangements, and Philip will not have complete control till next January.

F.E. is *most* amiable to D. now. He keeps on denying that he had anything to do with the conspiracy against D. Said it was all Beaverbrook, and that he (F.E.) had seen him during the weekend and told him that it was no good trying to upset D. That if he did it, there would be no one to put in his place; & that in any case he would not succeed. 'No', was Beaverbrook's reply 'but I can *try*.'

July 6th 1921

Another *very* heavy day. D. worried by all sorts of things. He really has too much to do. Horne has been telling him that people are talking about us, and that we are too reckless. He said someone asked him the other day how long it would be before there was a bust-up in Downing St.? Meaning I suppose D. & Mrs. Ll.G. Horne says that Megan also has been talking to people about me, & criticising her father, thinking I suppose that she would put a stop to it in that way, & not realising that all she would succeed in doing is to discredit her father. But I don't think she would stop at anything to obtain her ends. D. told Horne that he would rather go out of public life than do without me, & that if it came to the point he would do that. I think Horne is right that we are too reckless, & go about too much together, & we shall have to be more careful about that.

Smuts has returned from Ireland, but not having accomplished much. De Valera would not discuss anything with him, but simply said that their demands were for a Republic. De Valera keeps repeating that if he comes to London D. will have him in a trap. D.'s retort is: 'If he *doesn't* come he will certainly be in a trap.'

July 11th 1921

Went down to Chequers with D. on Friday evening [8 July], as he was very tired & wanted to get away but would not go without me. However, to be prudent, I went by train & he came on afterwards by car. He arrived in great excitement and while he was changing, in my room, the telephone rang, and D. on answering was told that it was a message from Dublin Castle for me. D. then spoke to Macready himself, & learnt that events had been happening very quickly in Dublin. De Valera had agreed to come over this week, was going to issue orders for a truce, & had sent for Macready. The whole atmosphere was changed & Macready had been given a wonderful reception by the Dublin crowd. Naturally D. very pleased, as it looks as though there is every prospect of a settlement.

D. & I had a very happy morning on Saturday [9 July], but I left in the afternoon, as the arrival of the family would have made things unpleasant. The Dominion Premiers & their wives spent the weekend at Chequers, but Mrs. Ll.G. did not even trouble to be there in time to receive them. But D. very pleased with the weekend, & evidently it was a great success. Everyone seems to have enjoyed themselves, & D. took a great deal of trouble so it is not surprising.

July 12th 1921

D. & I had dinner together last night. He had a Cabinet afterwards at 9.30 to consider the question of the Egyptian delegation which had just arrived. I played to him after dinner. He is going down to Chequers tomorrow to have a conference with Austen & Balfour & some others as to the meeting with De Valera which is to take place on Thursday [14 July].

July 13th 1921

Just returned from looking at a lovely little house at Penshurst, but it has no view, so D. won't consider it. He has just rung up from Chequers to say that De Valera has asked to see him alone, & naturally D. is delighted, as it is a great score after what the Irish & others have been saying about his 'not to be trusted'. But D. told me on the telephone that his colleagues down at Chequers are rather sticky about it & do not quite like the idea. Although they don't object to D. taking the responsibility they hate to be left out of things—Austen particularly. However, D. is going to see him alone.

D. & I had dinner together with Philip Sassoon at Park Lane last night. D. in very good form. He was saying what an extraordinary volte-face has happened during the last few weeks. It was not so very long ago that he was politically in deep waters, and in the trough of the wave. But now, as he said last night, we are riding up to the crest of the waves, and a very steep and sudden rise, too.

July 14th 1921

De Valera just gone, after having been with D. nearly 3 hours. I have never seen D. so excited as he was before De Valera arrived, at 4.30. He kept walking in & out of my room & I could see he was working out the best way of dealing with DeV. As I told him afterwards, he was bringing up all his guns! He had a big map of the British Empire hung up on the wall in the Cabinet room, with its great blotches of red all over it. This was to impress DeV. In fact, D. says that the aim of these talks is to impress upon DeV. the greatness of the B.E., and to get him to recognise it, & the King. In the course of conversation today D. said to DeV.: 'The B.E. is a sisterhood of nations—the greatest in the world. Look at this table: There sits Africa—English & Boer;

there sits Canada—French, Scotch & English; there sits Australia, representing many races—even Maoris; there sits India; here sit the representatives of
England, Scotland & Wales; all we ask you to do is to take your place in this
sisterhood of free nations. It is an invitation, Mr. De Valera: we invite you
here.'

D. said he was very difficult to keep to the point—he kept on going off at
a tangent, & talking in formulas and refusing to face facts. And every time D.
seemed to be getting him & De Valera appeared to be warming, he suddenly
drew back as if frightened and timid. D. says he is the man with the most
limited vocabulary that he has ever met! When D. had put forward all the
points of the invitation to Ireland, he (D.) turned to another tack, & said:
'I shall be sorry if this conference fails: terrible as events have been in Ireland,
it is nothing to what they will be if we fail to come to an agreement. The
British Empire is getting rid of its difficulties; its industrial difficulties are
being settled: Mesopotamia is settling down—we shall be able to withdraw
our troops from Mesopotamia & Germany & other parts of the world. I
hesitate to think of the horror if war breaks out again in Ireland.' 'But', said
De Valera, getting very excited: 'This is a threat of force—of coercion.' 'No,
Mr. De Valera', said D., 'I am simply forecasting what will inevitably happen
if these conversations fail, & if you refuse our invitation to join us.'

However, they seemed to get on well on the whole. All our information
goes to prove that they are genuinely in earnest, & the fact that the outrages
have ceased shows that DeV. has authority.

Poisonous articles in The Times yesterday & today. Riddell rang up yesterday & said that Northcliffe had rung him up & apologised for the one in
yesterday's paper, saying that he knew nothing about it, & it was written by
someone who had been severely censured for doing so. However, I am not
quite sure as to how much was Riddell's invention, in order to make peace
for the Northcliffe journalists, who have been having rather a thin time in the
Gov. departments they had visited.

July 18th 1921
D. saw DeV. again on Friday [15 July], but D. says he had evidently been
afraid he had gone too far the previous day, & was bent on impressing on D.
the idea that he had proposed nothing & consented to nothing. He (DeV.)
insisted that what the people of Ireland wanted was a republic, & asked D.
if the *name* of republic could not be conceded at any rate. D. replied that that
was just what they could *not* have—that the people of this country would not
tolerate it after all that had happened. 'There must be some other word,' said
D. 'After all, it is not an Irish word. What is the word for republic in Irish?'
'Poblacht', was DeV.'s reply. 'That merely means "people",' said D. 'Isn't
there another word?' 'Saorstaat,' said DeV. 'Very well,' said D. 'Why do you
insist upon Republic? Saorstaat is good enough!' D. said that for the first
time DeV. simply roared with laughter.

The trouble, however, is simply going to be Ulster. D. has drafted a summary of terms which he will send DeV. on Wednesday night [20 July], & which DeV. will reply to on Thursday. D. had the draft yesterday, but did not give it to DeV., as he thought the time was not ripe. He saw DeV. yesterday, & arranged to let him have the draft. Smuts saw DeV. yesterday morning & impressed upon him the great difficulty with Ulster, but S. says DeV. doesn't really appreciate that the Gov. have any real difficulty, & thinks that they are just using Ulster to frighten him. On the other hand, D. saw Craig yesterday and the latter is quite obstinate and so are his Cabinet, & they think on their part that D. is trying to use Sinn Fein to persuade *them* to concede something. So the position is tightening a little, & it looks very much as though Ulster would again prove a stumbling block in the settlement. D. is a little worried about it, but I can't help thinking that in his heart of hearts he is bent on settling it, but does not like to appear too confident in case anything may happen. There are lots of people who don't want a settlement & who would be very glad to see him fail.

There is considerable trouble in The Times circles. I understand the foreign editor Long, resigned, as he told Northcliffe & Wickham Steed frankly that he put his country before anything, and they were doing it real harm by the line they were taking. Northcliffe, who is starting round the world on a tour of investigation, pacified his irate staff by putting in a substitute for Wickham Steed & taking the latter along with him. Whether this is a preliminary or not to the dismissal of W.S. remains to be seen. Meanwhile D. had to answer a question in the House today about the boycott of Times journalists by Gov. departments. D. was not really responsible for the order, though the F.O. approached him about it & having got what they thought was D.'s approval, rushed the thing through, & D. was confronted with a 'fait accompli'. However, he stood by it, & trounced The Times in the House to the delight of the majority.

D.'s speech last Thursday [14 July] at the McCurdy dinner was a masterpiece. He did not intend to come, he was so tired after the meeting with De Valera—utterly exhausted & very highly strung. But they sent urgent messages to him from the Hotel Cecil, & he turned up after 9 with no speech prepared at all. He made an amazing speech, & at the end was almost inspired. He told me afterwards he had quite forgotten the audience & his surroundings. It completely changed the meeting, which before he came had been absolutely lifeless & depressed. But on his arrival they gave him a wonderful reception, and the air became electrified. But he was terribly tired, & I was almost afraid he would break down.

Relations with America are rather strained. Having been allowed to take all the credit for the proposal of the Conference, they now wish to force us to hold both conferences—disarmament *and* Pacific in America. The Japs refuse to hold the latter in America, & we are against it too. Meanwhile, the American journalists are getting busy & bid fair to make mischief, & the

American Ambassador, Harvey has been making mischief too, while the attitude of the Northcliffe papers has also done us harm in America. Meighen and the Canadian crowd however are anxious to make up to America and they give all the Imperial Conference stuff away to the Northcliffe Press. Hughes on the other hand is anti-Meighen, & attacks him on every conceivable occasion. D. says he does not want to go to America—loathes the idea—but I think eventually he must go. Everyone expects it. Personally—and naturally—I think he is the only person who can carry off disarmament. But so many feuds and prejudices have been roused by this proposal & by the attitude of America that it is difficult to say what will be the outcome of it.

July 20th 1921
D. very interested in the Greek advance against the Turks. He has had a great fight in the Cabinet to back the Greeks (not in the field but morally) & he & Balfour are the only pro-Greeks there. All the others have done their best to obstruct & the W.O. have behaved abominably. However D. has got his way, but he is much afraid lest the Greek attack should be a failure, & he should be proved to have been wrong. He says his political reputation depends a great deal on what happens in Asia Minor, though I don't think people care a hang what happens there. But D. says that if the Greeks succeed the Treaty of Versailles is vindicated, and the Turkish rule is at an end. A new Greek Empire will be founded, friendly to Britain, & it will help all our interests in the East. He is perfectly convinced he is right over this, & is willing to stake everything on it.

D. told me today that if he settles Ireland, he is prepared to go out of office—after the American conference. He is quite serious about it. He will support Austen he says, & if Austen is overthrown then D. can easily go into opposition, which is what he would like. I think he really means it this time. If he did so he would destroy the remnant of the Wee Frees, & gather the Liberals round him. If he settles Ireland, he can go no higher, & the rest would do him good.

Things look more hopeful with regard to Ireland today. Last night they looked black. De Valera had taken exception to a statement Craig had made & wrote D. saying that if D. took that view it was not worth while continuing the conversations. D. replied in a very curt note saying that he was no more responsible for Craig's views than he was for the statement De Valera had made to which Craig's statement was a reply. De Valera did not answer, but did not publish the letters, & Smuts saw him this morning & reports that he is in a better state of mind & not nearly so obstinate. D. sends them the terms this evening & meets De Valera tomorrow: it will be the critical day, & D. is getting very excited about it.

July 22nd 1921
D. had a not too satisfactory interview with DeV. yesterday. For the first moment when I saw D. afterwards I thought it had been a failure. D. was

very depressed. DeV. had not even taken the terms away with him—but we now find this was a mistake, as he has since sent for them—How Irish! After DeV. had read the terms he told D. he could not advise his people to accept them. 'Very well, Mr. DeV.', was D.'s answer, 'then there is only one thing more left for us to discuss.' 'What is that?', asked DeV. 'The time for the truce to come to an end', said D. D. says DeV. went perfectly white, and had difficulty in controlling his agitation. He then said that at any rate he would put them before his people, and let D. know what their answer was. Although D. thought the meeting pretty hopeless at the time, I am perfectly convinced DeV. was only bluffing & what we have heard since confirms this view. We hear that they are very pleased with the terms, that they are more than they ever hoped to get, but that of course it is only policy to refuse at first in the hope that they may get even more. They have returned to Ireland today & meantime the Irish papers are behaving very well, & it is evident that the bulk of Irish opinion wants peace. D. says if they refuse there is only one thing to be done—to reconquer Ireland. He says Balfour squirmed at the Cabinet when the terms were discussed preliminary to sending them to DeV. They were so contrary to all the views the old man had ever held on Ireland. But he gave in gracefully, & in the end D. had a unanimous Cabinet, which was a great achievement. He took the terms along to the King himself late Wednesday evening [20 July]. We dined together previously, after D. returned from the Cabinet. After D. had seen the King, Grigg took the terms along to the Grosvenor Hotel.

Went to the Royal Garden Party yesterday & was introduced to Mrs. Asquith, above all people. She was very nice, & I was agreeably surprised in her. She does not repel: on the contrary she rather attracts. She is a sort of kind Nancy Astor, whereas Nancy A. is a good looking Mrs. A. She mentioned Megan and I said the P.M. always said how kind Mrs. A. was to her. 'Not so kind as my husband was to him', was her retort. She does not approve of Megan, says she is disappointed in her—says she dresses badly, & altogether has not improved. That is what most people say, though judging by the papers one would think she is the most charming & beautiful & wonderful girl that ever existed. The comments one hears, are far from complimentary, & D. is getting a little worried as to the way she behaves.

July 25th 1921

Went down to Chequers with D. on Saturday morning [23 July], but returned in the evening, as the family went down. D. very tired, & we only walked to the top of the hill, & then sat down and lazed for a long time. He has had a terrible fortnight, & unfortunately there is still such a lot to do to the end of the session.

July 26th 1921

Went to a topping dance at Cuckoo Bellville's last night, but very weary today. Crankie has returned from America & is just as sweet as ever, & everyone made a great fuss of him—Sir R. Horne very annoyed because I preferred to talk to Crankie to dancing with *him*. Really very sniffy, & would not look at me or dance with me the rest of the evening. D. dined 'en famille' as Mrs. Ll.G. goes away today, & D. wanted her to go away in a good humour. He intends to take her up to Scotland, going first to Sutherland's wedding & then driving up to Gairloch[1] in short stays, stopping at Glasgow & other places & making a great show of the fact that they are going up there together. He does not expect her to stay long there, however, as she will want to return to Wales. But things are so uncertain now that we cannot tell whether he will be able to go up north then. The W.O. have made an awful mess of the American Conference. The weekend we were at Lympne, I telephoned to Grigg instructions to get the F.O. to see the Japs & tell them that we did not want the Conference at Washington & to tell them that we would back them up if they suggested something else. D. knew they would prefer another meeting place. We now find that nothing was done in this direction, & that the Japs being under the impression that we had definitely accepted, thought there was nothing left for it but for them to accept too, which they have done. Curzon simply muddles everything. D. says he doesn't know what he does do, as he never seems to do any work. He went over to Paris a few weeks ago, presumably to settle the Silesian question, but now it appears to be in a greater muddle than ever. Lady Curzon says he is very depressed—and no wonder.

July 27th 1921
Smuts received letter from De Valera today. Apparently not very hopeful, but personally I think it is bluff. However, F. E. Smith has been making foolish statements about Ireland & a general election in the Lords, much to D.'s annoyance. F.E. is taking a good deal upon himself, but apparently he is aiming at getting the leadership of the Tory party. He is in Beaverbrook's hands, & the rumour goes round that he is doping, but we think there is not much truth in it.

July 29th 1921
Great fuss over an interview Northcliffe is supposed to have given in the States, alleging a conversation with the King about Ireland. Apparently it was sent over here to Campbell Stuart, who refused to publish it, but it has appeared in certain newspapers who have copied it from America. D. has obtained a statement from the King denying it, which he is reading in the House this afternoon. D. however wanted to prosecute for libel, & got Poole from Lewis & Lewis here this morning. He then sent for Lord Stamfordham, & found out in the course of discussion that Lord S. had seen Wickham Steed and had obviously been talking to him in such a way as to give him the impression that the King & D. had been at variance, & that is the explanation

---

1. He had rented a house at Gairloch for a summer holiday.

of the interview. D. was simply furious, & said to Stamfordham: 'This means that the King's secretary is seeing the Editor of the chief Opposition newspaper, & gives him the impression that there is a difference of opinion between the King & his Prime Minister. I cannot allow this to happen again.' D. said S. was very frightened, as he is evidently the culprit. It will prevent the prosecution taking place, but D. has secured a denial from H.M., & this will do Northcliffe a lot of harm both here & in America.

Great trouble also with the French, who have sent a very insolent note yesterday, which is attributed to Berthelot. They are seeing red, but the weather is much cooler today & D. says it will do them good. He says the French always make war in July. They talk now of a rupture with us, & goodness knows how it will end. Have not answered Berthelot's last letter as I simply did not know what to say, & I certainly shouldn't know what to say now.

D. had dinner last night with Rothermere. He says the latter is in a state of exaltation over his Anti-Waste Party—says he can sweep the country—has 180 candidates & no-one can stand against him. He and Esmond Harmsworth are going to run the party together. D. told him he would resign at once if he thought Rothermere's people would get in, as he wd. rather like to see how they got on in practising the policy they were preaching. 'Oh, I shouldn't dream of taking office', was Rothermere's reply, & I don't think I should recommend my party taking office, either!' Which seems to be a very cowardly way of looking at things. D. made a faux pas. He had heard that Rothermere was going off on the Continent for a year or two with a lady he is fond of. D. had heard of a lady *last* year whom Rothermere was keen on, & naturally thought it was the same one, so started singing her praises. Rothermere broke him off: 'Oh, it isn't *that* one', he said. 'It's another one.'

During the interval, there was a prolonged exchange of letters between Lloyd George and De Valera. Finally the Irish agreed to a conference in London. It met on 11 October 1921 and reached agreement on 6 December. Arthur Griffith and Michael Collins were the principal Irish representatives.

October 28th 1921
Went to see Ruddigore last night with D., the Attorney General, the Greenwoods, & others. A very good show. D. had had rather a full day, but thoroughly enjoyed the play. He had thrown a bombshell after questions when the question of Ireland came up & the 'Diehards' were making trouble. They have put down a resolution for Monday condemning the Gov. for their action on Ireland, & D. said he would accept the challenge and treat the resolution as a vote of censure. This scared the enemy & though they dare not withdraw they do not seem eager to go on. D. is of the opinion that anything

might happen next week. He even talks of going out of office & is making preparations in order to be ready for all eventualities. He has seen Bonar, & the latter says he will come in if D. goes out on Ulster. D. would prefer this. He says he is anxious to go out & that this would be a good moment & a good excuse. It depends of course primarily on the Irish, but a good deal hangs on how the Tories behave. D. had Winston and F.E. to lunch today & impressed upon them the fact that B. Law would come in if he went out. This, he thinks, will make them loyal to him (D.) for they will not desert him in order to put B. Law in. Strangely enough no-one seems to contemplate the possibility of D. going out on this Irish crisis. They simply think it means the failure of the Irish negotiations. Carson came to dinner with D. on Thursday & D. says he is quite obdurate—says he cannot possibly give in on Ulster. Muriel Beckett met him in the Park this morning and tried to pump him. He simply answered: 'Isn't it a good thing I am out of it all!'

November 6th 1921

Colleagues

Irish negotiations the whole week. D. has hardly taken his mind off them for one minute. Divided into three groups. He has successfully wangled Churchill & Birkenhead so that they are now all out for it. Strangely enough, and contrary to all expectations, Bonar Law showed signs of proving difficult, and D. heard that he was inclined to come out and lead the Diehards if there was a break. D. saw Bonar on Friday morning [4 November] at breakfast & for his benefit drew a lurid picture of what would happen if Bonar tried to form a Ministry—how the Liberal & Labour & D. & his colleagues would all be opposed to him, while Bonar would only be able to get people like Page Croft & Rupert Gwynne to form his Ministry. D. added that of course they would always be friends, but it was inevitable that if this came to pass they would both say things for which they would be sorry afterwards. Bonar is influenced by Carson, & also by the hope that this may be his chance of becoming Prime Minister. The extraordinary thing is that Beaverbrook is all out for D., supporting him most vigorously in his papers. D. says he will only be for him for a short run, but over a thing like this it is worthwhile taking all the support you can get. Beaverbrook is trying to influence Bonar Law, but unfortunately Chamberlain is seeing the latter this morning, & D. says that he is so hopelessly tactless that he may do harm.

Sinn Feiners

The other group that D. has been in touch with the whole week, & has been exerting his utmost influence to bear upon them, are the Sinn Feiners. And he has actually succeeded in extracting from them the condition he was bargaining for, the chief of which is allegiance to the Crown. Having done this, he says he cannot possibly coerce the South. It now remains, if he is to settle the Irish puestion, to persuade Ulster to make concessions.

Yesterday D. saw Craig for the first time on the question of concessions.

He had heard that C. was quite obdurate & would concede nothing, & D. was rather hopeless about it. However, he talked to Craig on and off all day and by the evening he had extorted from him considerable concessions, the most important being an all-Irish Parliament, which we believe will satisfy the Sinn Feiners. If D. succeeds in getting these confirmed, things will be extraordinarily hopeful. It is going now much better than he expected. He is still worried about Bonar, whom he wants to get on his side. Then Carson will be the only important person standing out. D. has repeatedly pointed out to Bonar that he (Bonar) will come in expressly to coerce the South. For D. will go out on the principle that he cannot coerce the South after the concessions they have made. Bonar jibs at this. He longs to have the great job, but the risk is a great one, & D. thinks he will funk it. Next week will bring forth great things.

November 8th 1921

Ulster resistance appears to be hardening a little. Bonar Law still appears to be trying to collect forces to back him in his Diehard attitude. D. is going to try to get hold of Lord Derby as he thinks it important to have him on his side. Meantime D. has seen Craig again but has not got much further. C. is apparently taking heart from the fact that Bonar is with him. D. thinks Ulster might agree to an All Ireland Council provided the 'two countries' remain as they are. D. has sent a message to the Sinn Feiners telling them that he will stand by them, & could never be a party to fighting them now that they have made the concessions they have, but pointing out to them that it is worth their while to bargain a little more in order to bring peace, i.e. in order to persuade Ulster to come in. Arthur Griffith sent back a message to say that they were willing to leave it in D.'s hands. D. says that they do not want to go back to fighting at any cost. Michael Collins does not want to be killed, any more by Craig's men than by D.'s.

Northcliffe, who apparently has not had accurate information as to what is happening here, & who evidently thinks that F.E. will not be backing D., but will be among the Ulster Diehards, has wired to Marlowe, The Daily Mail editor. Northcliffe instructs Marlow to give F.E. a message to the effect that he (N.) will give F.E. all the backing he wants. N. has further instructed The Daily Mail to take all further instructions direct from F.E. F.E. has taken N. at his word with the result that the articles in The Daily Mail for the last two days have been thoroughly friendly to D.'s policy! After all, D.'s policy is the one which The Times have been advocating all along as the only possible one for a settlement; but Northcliffe is quite unscrupulous if he thinks he has a chance of doing in D.

November 9th 1921

The note is being sent to the Ulster people who are coming to London today. D. feels that their resistance is hardening, but this makes him all the more pugnacious & determined to get a settlement *in spite of* Ulster if he can. He says he is inclined to try & get the S.Fs. to accept Ulster's attitude of remaining separate, & then point out to them (Ulster) that as they are not participating in the proposals which affect the South, they are not entitled to the lower taxation which Southern Ireland will obtain under these proposals. If the S.Fs. will agree to this, D. will put it up to Ulster & he thinks they will climb down.

D. is frightfully hurt about Bonar Law & the attitude he is taking. This is all the more extraordinary as Beaverbrook is fighting for D. & a settlement for all he is worth. D. says he knows he can only get him for a short run, but it is worthwhile. D. is seeing F.E. & Winston & Beaverbrook almost every night, so as to keep them on his side. F.E. is fighting splendidly but D. says that Winston is contributing nothing—he is just not going over to the other side.

November 10th 1921
Went last night to the Lord Mayor's dinner. D. spoke very well, but had nothing very exciting to say, so that the speech was not exciting. But D. got an extraordinarily good reception. Things are not developing *very* rapidly, though Ulster resistance seems to be hardening & B.L. is still obdurate.

November 11th 1921
Armistice day—with all its sad, tragic memories and regrets of young lives lost and all 'that might have been'. Flanders poppies everywhere this year. D. said he watched at the Cenotaph wreaths being laid on, for Britain, for Canada, for Australia, for India, & so on. Worthington Evans turned to him and said: 'Next year perhaps a wreath of shamrocks.' D. told this to Arthur Griffith later in the day. A.G. was very moved, & said: 'If this scheme of yours goes through, you'll get it.'

D. has now evolved a better scheme for getting a settlement even if Ulster refuses our terms. The S.Fs. are very doubtful of his previous one, in which they might lose the All Ireland Parl. for which they are fighting. D. therefore suggests that an All Ireland Parl. be set up for a year. If, after the first 6 months or before the end of 12 months, Ulster wishes to withdraw, she can do so, but only by coming back as part of the U.K. & paying the same taxes as the U.K. D. says that he knows the Presbyterians. They have their hand on their hearts all the time, but if it comes to touching their pockets they quickly slap their hands in them. 'I know', he said to me. 'My wife is a Presbyterian!' D. says the Ulstermen, once having paid lower taxes, will not volunteer again for the high ones.

Great indignation among many circles as to B. Law's attitude. Rees, the Sunday Times Editor, came to see me this afternoon & told me of a conversation he had with Horder, B. Law's doctor, a little while ago. Horder is a friend of Rees. 'You know', he said to the latter, 'Bonar's plea of illness and his sudden departure to the south of France were due to one thing only— cold feet about Ireland. Some excuse had to be made, so I was deputed to give the excuse about illness. But there was really nothing the matter with him.' If that is true, then B.L. is a double-faced hypocrite. There was no need for all the protestations he made at the time about his undying affection for D. And in any case there was no need for him to come out and embarrass D. now at this critical time. D. saw Bonar yesterday but could not get much further with him. D. said Bonar would have to become P.M. B.L. asked what D. would do when Parl. met in Feb. 'Well, Bonar', said D., 'by that time I shall have been recuperating in the S. of France and shall come back prepared to embarrass my friends in their difficulties.' B.L. flushed scarlet.

November 14th 1921
D. & I went down to Trent for the weekend. But D. first of all went to Philip Sassoon's house in Park Lane for lunch, & got Arthur Griffith along to have a serious talk with him so that he might know exactly where he was. The Ulster people had definitely refused the terms in the morning—refusing even to come into a discussion so long as it involved a question of an All I.P. D. therefore wanted to decide on his next move, for he is determined to pull this thing through. I do not think I have ever seen D. so excited about anything before. He talked to A.G. for a long time, & D. came up from below very jubilant—but very excited & said that A.G. would agree to his new scheme, & that the Ulster people would be 'done in'. Then F.E. & Chamberlain came along & they talked over the form in which this was to be drafted, and eventually we went off to Trent, arriving in time for dinner. Horne came on Sunday morning [13 November] & D. asked Bonar Law & Beaverbrook to come down to dinner, as he wanted to have a final talk with Bonar in order to know where he stood. Unfortunately I had to go to bed as my cold was bad, so I did not hear any of what passed. D. told me, however, that he had a talk to B.L. before dinner privately & D. told him quite plainly that he was not playing the game. Bonar flared up & said if that was the case he would refuse to discuss the matter any further & for a short time there was real unpleasantness. However, D. eventually talked him round, & they sat up discussing till nearly one o'clock. D. *thinks* that Bonar has agreed not to oppose his new proposals for the All Ireland settlement. But of course he has not told Bonar of the underlying scheme, i.e. the taxation part. D. says that if the Ulster men accept they will do so in the hope that the S.Fs. would refuse it. They (the Ulstermen) are quite ignorant of the fact that the S.Fs. have already agreed. It is a very subtle plan & I hope it will not have any hitch. D. is quite determined that it shall go through. Bonar has put his back up.

D. says the S.Fs. have behaved splendidly all through this fight. They have backed D. whole-heartedly & loyally, they have given nothing away to the press, & have shown great courage in the face of difficulty and even danger, for they have plenty of extremists on their own side.

D. says Carson is animated by a desire to get back into the limelight, as well as by his passion for Ulster. Carson has not found Lord of Appeal a very exciting job, & F.E. is the principal figure in the House of Lords. Carson referred the other day to the H. of L. as a place 'into which the rays of the sun never penetrate'. Lady Carson, too, would like her husband to become once again the popular politician.

Beaverbrook has offered D. a price of £1 a word ('including the "the's"') when D. goes out of office, if he will write for The Express. This Beaverbrook says, is at the rate of a thousand pounds a column, & he will commission him to write two columns to every article. D. is very pleased with the offer.

November 23rd 1921

Irish negotiations not going too well. The S.Fs. have got scared. They say Ulster will concede nothing as yet, & they are being asked to concede their points one by one. They are asked to sign a document which has now been drawn up to agree to a status quo as far as Ulster is concerned, but giving them (U.) the right to *come in* to an All Ireland Council (with reduced taxes!) at the end of 6 months or within a year. (D. says he thinks Ulster will come in.) The S.Fs. say however that if they sign this & it is shown to Craig, it will immediately become public, as everything that is shown to the Ulstermen does, & they (the S.Fs.) will not dare to go back & face their people having given so much away without being sure of anything in return. They therefore yesterday sent an impossible reply, retracting practically everything they had conceded. D. sent back a message to them to say that unless they took it back all negotiations would be broken off. They are seeing D. today, & from what I hear negotiations will not be broken off yet. But things seem very shaky. D. is worried & irritable. There seems to be so many snags and he is almost worn out with these protracted negotiations.

A most amusing Cabinet yesterday afternoon to decide whether the Goetze pictures should be hung in the F.O. Curzon has been violently opposed to it for some time, but the artist has been very persistent, & the agitation has grown until D. said the only way to decide it was for the pictures to be put up and for the whole Cabinet to view them & give a decision. This was done yesterday & the whole Cabinet—with the exception of Curzon—decided that the paintings should remain. Curzon said he did not know how he could possibly subject the morals of his ambassadors to these paintings, but D. said (sotto voce I presume) that probably they would do the morals of his ambassadors good!

We went with P. Sassoon & P. Kerr to see Patience afterwards. A very good show, & D. enjoyed it immensely. He is looking rather tired these days however, & I am a little worried about him.

November 24th 1921

D. has not yet seen Craig, but sees him tomorrow. Meanwhile the S.F. are being very difficult and D. says tonight that it looks as though a break may occur at any moment. F.E. saw them this morning & apparently the interview was not very satisfactory.

D. & I motored down to Hindhead this morning, starting at 9.0 & getting back at 1.30. D. wants to start building the house as soon as possible. He is very keen on it & it makes a diversion for him.

Last night D. dined with F.E. to meet Stinnes,[1] & had a very interesting conversation with the latter. Stinnes wants a big financial combination, between England, Germany, America & possibly Russia. He says however that if France goes to the Ruhr Germany will go to pieces. The South will break away. Stinnes said that if Grey had made it quite clear in 1914 that if Germany attacked France England would have come in, there would have been no war. But he said von Bethmann Hollweg was convinced we would not come in. 'England will never come in to a war which turns on the murder of a crown prince', he said. D. told Stinnes that he always thought v.B.H. a third-rate man. 'Oh you thought him third-rate?', queried Stinnes, insinuating that he would not even put him as high as that. He continued to say that they did not think France would come in to the war to support Russia—a republic supporting an autocracy. D. said he could not understand why, when the crash came in August 1918, the Germans did not make an orderly retirement say to the Rhine & then make a stand. S. said that the people were in a terrible condition and could not put up a fight. 'But people fight often more desperately when they are at their last gasp', said D. 'Yes, but we had no-one to lead', was S.'s answer. And eventually the Kaiser ran away, & the Crown Prince ran away. 'The Kaiser lost the war for us', was his comment.

The diary does not record the final stages of the Irish negotiations, though Frances Stevenson was involved in them throughout. Articles of Agreement for a Treaty between Great Britain and Ireland were signed in the early hours of 6 December 1921. Lloyd George came out of the conference room and handed Frances Stevenson the document with the words: 'Lock it up carefully.' She did so, and it remained with his papers until claimed by the cabinet office after his death.

---

1. German coal and steel magnate.

Diary 1922

The Irish treaty, though accepted by parliament, did not improve Lloyd George's standing with his Unionist supporters. Lloyd George's hopes were set on a great settlement of reconciliation at the Genoa conference. These hopes were not fulfilled. Lloyd George continued to talk of resigning. In the autumn (after the diary entries end) events made up his mind for him. The government brought Great Britain to the brink of war with Turkey. The Unionist party vowed to withdraw from the Coalition. Lloyd George resigned on 10 October 1922 and never held office again.

February 3rd 1922
D. has been in a very worried & restless condition all the week. He is always like this when he cannot make up his mind. He is undecided at present as to what is the best step to take in the political situation. There is no doubt that everything is in a seething state and anything may happen. D. is anxious to have a 'go' at the Wee Frees & especially Grey. On the other hand the Unionists are very disgruntled and there are rumours that some are making an effort to get rid of the Coalition. The Genoa Conference is rocky, & the fall of the Italian Government yesterday does not help matters at all. D. himself has not been feeling very well, & Mrs. Ll.G. has been very troublesome & is likely to make more trouble. The net result has not been to improve D.'s temper, especially as I said before as he cannot make up his mind. At one time, when he came back from Cannes, he thought of going to the country with a Liberal programme & if he could not get a majority, at any rate come back with a very effective minority. Then he saw Austen still wanted to keep the Coalition & was willing to play the game, and as long as that is so D. cannot oppose him. Now D.'s plan is—or was till yesterday—to say to Austen that he wanted to go out—that he would give Austen & his followers every support, & would advise his own followers to do so, on the ground that national unity must be maintained. D. would preside over the Genoa Conference, & be the Gov. representative, but after that he would sit on the opposition bench, but give the Gov. his support. D. was inclining more and more to that view. No one could then say that he was conspiring to keep his

office, & as there would be no election they could not say that he was doing it to catch votes. The delay which the Italian crisis must cause to the Genoa Conference must however make a little difference, though exactly how much it is difficult to estimate. D. is becoming more & more anxious to get out of Office, partly because it is becoming irksome to get so much criticism for all his efforts, partly because he thinks it is better to retire gracefully than to wait till people begin to sling mud, & partly because he wants to get a little rest and then to write his book. His family, too, are becoming very troublesome and he will be more independent when he is out of office.

Yesterday he saw the King. The latter does not like the idea of the Genoa Conference. 'I suppose you will be meeting Lenin & Trotsky?' he asked. 'Unfortunately, Sir', D. replied, 'I am not able to choose between the people I am forced to meet in your service. A little while ago I had to shake hands with Sami Bey, a ruffian who was missing for the whole of one day, & finally traced to a sodomy house in the East End. He was the representative of Mustapha Kemal, a man who I understand has grown tired of affairs with women & has lately taken up unnatural sexual intercourse. I must confess I do not think there is very much to choose between these persons whom I am forced to meet from time to time in Your Majesty's service.' D. said the King's only reply was to roar with laughter.

Winston & F.E. will be furious when they learn of D.'s plan to go out & leave the field to the Conservatives. That will not suit their book at all. D. dined with them both on Wednesday [1 February], & F.E. became quite drunk towards the end of the dinner. D. said he was very amusing. He has lately taken to spirits again & says he 'means to make up for lost time'.[1]

Winston is still nursing his ambition. He is determined to oust Horne from the Exchequer, if he can, & is trying to defeat the Geddes recommendations & then to blame Horne for not economising. He & F.E. tried to persuade D. at Cannes to give Horne another post. F.E. told D. he thought Horne wanted to go to the House of Lords. 'If Horne really wants to', said D., 'that is another matter; but I shall not ask him.' F.E. then went & told Horne that D. has commissioned him to ask Horne whether he would like to go to the Lords. Horne thought D. wanted to get rid of him. Fortunately in an expansive moment, & feeling very miserable, Horne told me about F.E. but made me promise not to tell D. I knew I ought to tell him, & finally did, & he reassured Horne & everything was all right. But had I not got to know of it, Horne would have gone on being disgruntled & thinking D. had not played fairly with him.

More trouble over Ireland. Craig & Collins cannot agree about boundaries & a very serious position has arisen.

---

1. Birkenhead had made a bet with Beaverbrook that he would remain teetotal throughout 1921. He decided that it was worth losing his bet to celebrate the signing of the Irish treaty.

June 22nd 1922

Just heard the sad news about Henry Wilson[1]—Will the Irish trouble never end? D. very upset, as we all are. Whatever he has done lately, he was a most loveable person, & we were very near him during the war. Can scarcely believe the news. It will put the whole Irish question back into the melting pot again. D. had been warned by Shortt that there were dangerous Irishmen in London, & S. advised him not to go to Chequers, but we had been rather inclined to discount the warning at this juncture. However Shortt was right.

And Northcliffe under restraint! Rothermere told D. that he had been queer for some time, but now he is really off his head. The day before yesterday he started telephoning first thing in the morning & continued for seven hours without ceasing. So yesterday they cut the telephone off. Northcliffe is cursing Rothermere & others, saying there is a conspiracy against him. He has made up the quarrel with Wickham Steed, & D. says the danger is that N. will sign over the control of The Times to W.S. D. would like to get The Times & if it is to be sold will try & get it bought by a friendly syndicate. He is very much afraid that Beaverbrook may try & get control, as B. is trying very hard to get at Northcliffe & pretends not to believe that the latter is mad. The whole thing is very complicated & it will be interesting to see what happens. D. says he would not mind resigning if he could become Editor of The Times at a decent salary & with a decent contract.[2]

Last Friday [16 June], Marshall, representative of The New York Times, came to see me with a view to getting D.'s book. I think they will make a substantial offer. I lunched with Butterworth the previous Tuesday. He said the most he would be able to offer would be £40,000. Marshall told me that Butterworth had subsequently approached him & offered him the *American* rights for £50,000!

Poincaré's visit passed off very satisfactorily. D. got everything he wanted out of him & Poincaré went back giving the impression that he had been quite firm with D. However D. will never like Poincaré. He thinks he is poor stuff. Someone said that it was quite possible that he had many sterling qualities. 'Well', said Balfour, 'he has no business to look like that, then.' I talked to the Editor of the Petit Parisien, & could see that the French are really intensely jealous of D. for the power that he has in Europe. They want to see him fall.

June 26th 1922

Have just been watching the funeral procession of Henry Wilson pass. How different from the procession we witnessed last week when the Prince of Wales came home! That one, so gay and quick, so full of life; this one so

---

1. Assassinated by two members of the I.R.A.
2. Apparently Lloyd George made a determined attempt to become editor of The Times. There is no evidence that Beaverbrook contemplated buying it, and he himself denied the story. After Northcliffe's death, The Times was sold to John Walter, the former proprietor, and J. J. Astor.

solemn and slow, almost heartrending. He was a great and loveable man. It is a pity that his death has roused such bitterness, & I am afraid the debate in the House this afternoon will be a very angry one. D. will have to put up a defence for the Home Office. He sat with me yesterday evening & we went through the evidence, & I think he will be able to make quite a good case. Beaverbrook is as usual playing a dirty game, and stirring up the public against Shortt. D. says that if Shortt went, it would mean that the whole Gov. would have to resign. Nevertheless I think Shortt is a great handicap to the Gov.— very slack and inefficient.

Rathenau also murdered. It makes one frightened. One good effect of these murders will be to make Scotland Yard more careful and to increase the protection of Ministers & prominent people. Also not to relax their efforts against Sinn Fein in this country.

Sat next to General Ronald Storrs at lunch at Lady Cunard's on Friday [23 June]. He had met H.W. two days before, & asked him to make holiday plans with him for his (Storrs') leave from Palestine next year. H.W. assented. 'But', he added, 'I have a presentiment that something will happen to me before then.'

They reprinted my article on H.W. in The Sunday Times yesterday.

Nancy Astor distinguished herself again on Saturday at the American Ambassador's dinner. She went up to Lady Curzon & asked her why she turned her step-daughter out of doors! Lady Curzon complained to Mrs. Ll.G. who is also beginning to find N.A. out. I am not on speaking terms with her (Lady Astor) now, owing to the insulting things she said to me one day when D. was at Criccieth in March. I allowed her to say everything she wished, & then asked her not to come here again and walked out of the room. This exasperated her so much that before she left for America she seemed to have gone quite mad.

D. says if there is a big row on the Irish debate, today, he would not be at all sorry to clear out. He wants to write his book, for which he has had very big offers.

Diary 1926

By 1926 Lloyd George was back in the Liberal party and dreaming of a Liberal-Labour coalition. Asquith, losing his seat in the general election of 1924, went to the house of lords as Lord Oxford and Asquith, while remaining leader of the Liberal party. After the general strike an attempt was made to drive Lloyd George from the Liberal party because of his conciliatory attitude during the strike. Instead Lord Oxford was driven to resign the leadership. Lloyd George became leader of a disunited Liberal party and tried to devise a new Radical programme.

April 1st 1926

D. made a great success in the House yesterday, on the Economy Bill, in relation to raiding of Insurance Fund. He was in tremendous form—spoke three times, each time with great effect. The papers today are full of it. They say it was his old form of back-bencher days. He himself says he felt that he was in the same vein as when he was fighting the Education Act. Today, for the first time, the Labour benches cheered *when he got up*—very significant. Labour & Liberal benches have been entirely united in this Debate. Also very significant.

The most amazing thing about D. since he went out of Office is his gradual conquest of Labour. At first they had a regular system of howling him down, and boasted that they would break his authority in the House. Once he sat down without finishing his speech (though nobody guessed it) the opposition was so overwhelming & the interruptions so intolerable. But gradually the interruptions became less frequent, & their attitude more friendly, as they saw that he was really the same D. and prepared to fight for the underdog. Lately there have been many friendly passages between the two sets of Benches. When D. took the corner seat next to the Labour benches I said at the time that it was a very dangerous seat from the point of view of Labour—that he was in far too close contact with them for them to be able to avoid infection! Now he speaks almost as the Leader of the Opposition, with the Labour & Liberal benches around him, the former hanging on his words and loud in their praises. The other day after a similar performance, Kirkwood and Jack

Jones said in the Lobby that he was the real leader of the Labour Party. Yesterday Ramsay [MacDonald] took no part in the Debate at all. There are rumours that he is ill, but D. says that ever since he can remember Ramsay has always been ill, always talking about his complaints. He is one of those people, says D. who is supposed to be on the verge of the grave, but who manages to outlive everybody else. Herbert Lewis is another. Thirty-seven years ago he was supposed to be dying of consumption. Last year he broke his back, & (at 67) wrote a final farewell letter to D. This week he has been writing to the papers, and receiving medals of recognition of his work for Wales. He is still alive.

April 2nd 1926
Lord Reading is about to leave India & the Vice Royalty. It seems much more than five years ago since he came down to Lympne one afternoon with Hewart, & D. told them both of the intended changes—Reading for India and Hewart for the L.C.J. They stayed the night. After dinner we had a singsong—I played the piano—all sorts of tunes, & Reading sang some sea shanties & Hewart a comical song of the circuit—very effectively. Everyone in great high spirits & very pleased with themselves. Everyone now acknowledges that Reading's appointment has been an unqualified success, though many were against him at the time, on account of his being a Jew.

May 15th 1926
D. has had an anxious fortnight during the General Strike. 'The Nine Days' Blunder'. He took a line peculiarly his own, and for this he has been howled at by the Tories, and cold-shouldered by all the Liberals with the exception of Kenworthy, Hutchison and Garro Jones. But he stuck to his guns, unpopular though it made him. He criticised the Government for having dallied and dawdled when resolute action might have avoided the strike—and for this was called unpatriotic, because he did not support the Government wholeheartedly in the emergency—an emergency which ought never to have happened.

The Labour people are pleased with him. He has proved more of a friend to them than Ramsay Macdonald, who got cold feet, or even J. H. Thomas, who showed up very badly, and who D. thinks is broken as a result of the strike. When D. spoke in the House the first week of the strike, the Labour people cheered him. Hartshorn overheard Ramsay Macdonald say to those next to him, 'There they go, the b..... fools, cheering him again.' The Labour Party have been getting more and more friendly to D. all the session. In the fight over the Economy Bill [sic] he led the Opposition, and they practically acknowledged it, and the last time D. got up to speak during the Debate the whole Labour Party cheered him.

D. is pursuing a definite policy, and the strike has helped him in forwarding it, though it has had the effect of making him temporarily unpopular in the country, whereas there is no doubt that Baldwin has temporarily made strides.

D.'s idea is to go definitely towards the *Left*, and gradually to co-ordinate and consolidate all the progressive forces in the country, against the Conservative and reactionary forces. Thus he will eventually get all sane Labour as well as Liberalism behind him. His Land Campaign will help, and will go forward simultaneously. D. will not leave the Liberal Party. I begged him not to offer himself to Labour, saying that he must be *solicited* by them. Whereupon he began to reminisce. He said the word *solicitous* reminded him of an article he read in one of his father's old schoolmaster journals; the article being called 'the unsolicitous, much solicited Solicitor-General'. These are the only words D. remembers of the article, but they have stuck in his mind ever since. These old journals were stacked away upstairs in the cottage at Llanystumdwy, and on rainy days D. used to go and pore over them and over some books which he also found there. He remembers finding an old Greek history—a school manual of some kind—and in this way he first became acquainted with the history of Greece—Rollins' Ancient History he also found there, and read from cover to cover, and then later Macaulay's Essays.

D. told me how it was just a chance that he did not become either a teacher, like his father, or a preacher. He would certainly have become the latter, to which he was very drawn, but for the fact that in his uncle's sect there were no paid preachers, & D. could not afford of course to take up unpaid work. As to the teaching profession, the only schools in his neighbourhood were Church of England schools, and he would have had to join the established Church, which of course he would never have done. The authorities tried to persuade him to take up teaching, and said that it would be quite sufficient if he went to Church *once* on Sundays, but they did not realise the fierceness of the Non-Conformist sects!

May 21st 1926

A new development. Last night D. dined with me. I left the office about 6.30. & he was to come on at 7.30. He was a little late, & came in very excitedly, so that I could see something had happened. He said to me: 'I have been expelled from the Party.' And handed me Oxford's[1] letter to read. I read it & remarked that it was clearly a letter intended for D.'s resignation. It was a shock to both of us, & I don't think we discussed it very connectedly, or at least definitively, but rather speculated as to the influences which had led up to it. In brief it was obvious that the Old Gang thought D.'s luck and popularity were down as a result of the strike, and that this was a time to get rid of him. Dirty work. The Asquith women are of course at the bottom of it. My chief concern last night was to get D. into a calm frame of mind. It was a blow for him—rather a cruel one. It faced him with a crisis the like of which he had not quite experienced before. He has now before him a fight for his political life. He left at 9.30 to meet Masterman & McCurdy, with whom he

---

1. Lord Oxford and Asquith. Asquith's letter is summarised by Roy Jenkins in his biography of Asquith, p. 515.

was to discuss the thing. In the meantime Sylvester called. He had been to see Reading with a copy of the letter & Reading had said that it was meant for D.'s resignation. He wanted D. to breakfast with him this morning—which D. did. Have not had an opportunity of knowing what passed there. D. has now left for Manchester, to see C. P. Scott, en route for Wales for Whitsun. Before going he sent a preliminary acknowledgement to Oxford, & asked for time to consider further reply. He had also drafted a long reply which he discussed with Masterman, McCurdy, Tweed and others, and which he took with him to Wales. He went off very cheerful. I go to Churt till he returns.

Reading has seen Oxford twice since the strike, with the idea of trying to patch things up between D. & O. R. had not realised they were so bad, & he felt certain that if D. & O. could meet, everything would be all right. But to his dismay O. demurred at seeing D. & R. eventually returned & told D. that he realised that there was only one thing that could heal the breach, i.e. if D. handed over his funds to them, & that as long as D. refused to do this there could be no reconciliation—in other words: 'Your money or your (political) life!'

May 30th 1926
An exciting week. On Sunday [23 May] D. telephoned from Criccieth saying he had posted a draft reply to Oxford, & he wanted me to get it in the morning & take it round to Masterman. I went up to town early Monday morning, got the letter and took it round to M. who made several suggestions and alterations, which I subsequently telephoned to Criccieth. D. sent the final letter that night from Criccieth, but it was delayed in the post and did not reach the office till 6.15.[1] At 5.30 we heard that Oxford's letter had been sent to the Press, & so were relieved to get D.'s reply, which could now be published simultaneously with the other.

On Wednesday [26 May] everything in a ferment of excitement. From then onwards all the Liberal Press (except Westminster) violently pro-D.— even Nation. Hosts of telegrams and letters from all over the country supporting D. His speech on Wednesday at Llandudno greatly praised for its restraint. He himself returned on Thursday, outwardly very cheerful & determined, but inwardly trembling with excitement, keyed up to the highest pitch— higher than I can remember—and deep down hurt, almost like a child unjustly punished, at the treatment he had received. He will not resign. His tactics are perfect. He is giving them a long rope with which to hang themselves. He has already succeeded in driving them right into the arms of the Conservatives. Lincolnshire referred in his speech on Friday [28 May] at Grey's luncheon to 'our leaders, Oxford, Grey & Baldwin!'.

The rumour is that Oxford will not reply to D.'s letter, but that they intend to ignore him—more easily said than done. Meanwhile there is talk of a party

1. Lloyd George amended his letter on the advice of C. P. Scott. J. L. Hammond, C. P. Scott, 294.

meeting being summoned next week in the House to pass a vote of censure on D. If they fail, it will be amusing to see what they will do. It is quite likely that D. will eventually succeed in driving *them* out of the Party.

D. saw Snowden yesterday. S. says this makes things easier for an understanding with the Labour Party.

July 27th 1926

D.'s prestige with the Labour Party in the House is increasing enormously. Last week, after a speech in support of the Miners, a Welsh Liberal member came to him and said: 'The people are with you.' 'And I am with them', replied D. in Welsh. 'I was born amongst the people, and I will die amongst the people.'

Yesterday after his speech on the Coal Mines (a very weighty and powerful one—but very moderate) another Member (Labour) came to him and said: 'The Miners will be grateful to you for your speech today.' And during the Debate, when the Tories got angry because the Labour benches were interrupting Baldwin, the Labour people shouted back: 'Well, you interrupted Lloyd George.' Very significant when you remember that two years ago D. found it difficult to get a hearing owing to Labour howling him down. Even last July they jeered at him when he was speaking on the Coal Subsidy, and he turned on them and said the [1] had taken the matter into his own hands without consulting them, and he was not surprised.

Today we were looking up the passage in Leviticus about the Jubilee, for D.'s speech at the Summer School on Friday [30 July], and I said I had just been reading the Epistle of John, and how beautiful it was, and D. said that James was his man, and read me out the chapter denouncing the rich, which I think is very appropriate to him!

---

1. Missing in the original.

Diary 1927

February 3rd 1927

D. & I walked in Richmond Park in the morning yesterday, & then picnicked on sandwiches & fruit which we had bought in Putney on the way down. A bright cold morning. D. benefited much from the air, he had left the office feeling rather rattled owing to numerous petty worries. He had dined with members of the Industrial Council the night before—Samuel turned up—is obviously trying to make himself the rallying point for all 'pure' Liberals. Does not approve of D. but thinks it better to be civil to him—now at any rate.

D. is most anxious to resign the Chairmanship of the Party. He finds the duties attached to it becoming more & more irksome. He hates having to get up in the House with a cantankerous group of Liberals behind him, most of them looking unpleasant & disgruntled & hardly ever giving him a cheer. If he were released from the Chairmanship he would be free to attend the House whenever he pleased, or to stay down at Churt. He could pursue his Land Campaign & make speeches when he liked. His friends are divided in their advice. Masterman and Keynes are against it. They are against giving Simon or Runciman a look in—or even Samuel if he got in. They think it would be foolish of D. to give it up just when he has beaten them. But D. thinks that is the time when he can do it best. Before when he wished to do it there was first of all the Wedgwood Benn challenge to his authority in '24, then last year at Naples, when he had practically made up his mind to do it, there was Mond's secession. Ramsay Muir is for it, but most of D.'s friends are against him. I don't know what to advise—I always think it best on these occasions for him to follow his own instinct—it is rarely wrong. I know he is not entirely happy in his present position, & I hate to see him bothered & wasting his energy & mind over trifling little matters, when it is the *big* things he is made for.

Simon came in to see D. the other day on the subject of China & the Liberal line in relation to it. Simon asked him what the expression 'Shanghaied' meant. 'It's what you & the Liberal party tried to do to me last May', said D. Simon flushed. 'You defeated us successfully', he replied. 'Yes', retorted D., 'with a division.' I could not make out why Simon looked so red and uncomfortable when he came out through my room, but I understood when D. told me.

D. thinks the China situation looks serious. The Gov. are in a hopeless mess, & there is no one strong enough to deal with it. It appears that while the major members of the Cabinet were abroad during the recess, Bridgeman took command of the situation & insisted upon forces being sent there.

The party seems to receive one blow after another—Kenworthy—the Liberal Council—Wedgwood Benn. And yet the members of the Liberal Club at Oxford have doubled since the beginning of last term. If we could win Market Bosworth it would be a tremendous fillip. Max [Beaverbrook] told D. when the latter saw him at Cannes last month that we *must* win it. Max says that he spent £15,000 on winning the Newport election in 1922.[1]

D. spent the afternoon here yesterday making his speech for Middlesboro' on Saturday [5 February]. He told me an amusing story. When the Prince of Wales was preparing for his investiture in 1911 D. went to the Palace to teach him a few words of Welsh. D. was standing with his back to the window, & was surprised to see the Prince looking uncomfortable & red. The latter suddenly dashed to the window & shouted 'Get away George, you little rascal!' Prince George had been standing at the window pulling faces to try & make his brother laugh!

August 18th 1927
Muriel & I were discussing Disraeli yesterday, (we have been reading Maurois' Disraeli). He was apparently very popular with young men—very kind & understanding to them—remembering probably his own difficulties & experiences. D. on the other hand, does *not*, I think, *understand* young men. He is always of course kind to them, & encouraging to young politicians in the House, & they in turn admire him & are attracted by his personality. But he had so little youth of his own, his responsibilities came up on him so early, & his life at that time was so different from that of the average young man of today, that I think it prevents him from entering on a plane of actual sympathy with them. I may be wrong, but that is what I feel. Disraeli on the other hand had lived the life of a fashionable young man of his day, & had done all the things expected of him as such. D. as a young man belonged to no clubs—went to no theatres, did not dance or dine or have any social life at all. His sole interest was politics. Even now he shuns any regular social life. Theatres bore him, & dances & parties of any kind except political.

He is in a mood now to retire from politics & write his book. I do not think he will do this. He has had these moods before, & now he is less able to leave

1. This was the by-election just before the fall of the Coalition when a Coalition candidate was defeated by an Independent Conservative. There is no other evidence that Beaverbrook provided any financial assistance to the victor. Even if he did, the sum of £15,000 is certainly an exaggeration. Beaverbrook never gave more than £1,500 to any individual candidate.

the Party to itself. Rothermere came over to Criccieth to see him last week. He is going to back D. & his land policy, & says he will be P.M. again soon, he has been defending D. over the Morning Post articles on honours. Max on the other hand seems to be in league with The Morning Post & intended to write an article defending Bonar Law at D.'s expense.[1] D. told him, however, that if he did so, he would contradict it flatly, & give the facts, which would not be flattering either to the Conservatives or to Bonar. I gather he and Max had words on the telephone. D. is furious with him.

D. says he wants to leave the Party to get on without him for the present & see how H.S.[2] can manage. I don't think he will be allowed to do it, however. Besides, things are going so much better now, it would be a pity.

1. Lloyd George's suspicion seems to have been unfounded. There is no evidence that Beaverbrook supplied The Morning Post with information about the sale of honours which was in any case well-known, nor did he write any article at this time about Bonar Law.
2. Herbert Samuel.

Diary 1934

The entries for the last three years are in the nature of an epilogue. Lloyd George had a prostate operation in August 1931 and so missed the financial crisis. The Liberals supported the National government. Lloyd George opposed it. In 1934 he was isolated and largely withdrawn from politics. The National government under Ramsay MacDonald were in difficulties over unemployment, foreign affairs and India. Lloyd George sometimes dreamt that he might be called on once more as saviour of the nation. Alternatively he planned yet another one-man campaign. Meanwhile he worked with Frances Stevenson on his War Memoirs. Her diary entries are therefore often retrospective and sometimes unchronological.

February 12th 1934
A sententious American Professor with an inferiority complex expatiated on the British Character—held up the Middle West as the type of all that is best in America—and quoted the inevitable Abraham Lincoln 'God loved the common people—that is why he made so many of them.' D.'s comment— 'He made many more fleas.'

D. on his grandmother—her business-like capacity—her method of collecting accounts—she took D. with her as a boy of 4. Paid a casual visit—having carefully put account in her pocket. Leading up to it by way of conversation. Brushing offer of payment aside—any time will do—The account lost? Well, well. Perhaps she has a copy in her pocket. Produces it, by accident. Difficult under these circumstances *not* to pay the bill on the spot.

D.'s uncle, on the other hand, neither sent in bills nor collected accounts. Would have run the little business on the rocks if it had been left to him— very nearly did so. Delighted in turning out a finished and beautiful article.

D.'s women-folk always spoilt him. His grandmother doted on him and would never allow him to be scolded or punished. Loved to take him with her on her walks—often lengthy ones—amounting to 3 or 4 miles when he was only a little chap. (D. always walked a great deal when he was a boy & young man. Would walk to and fro from Llanystumdwy to Portmadoc when an articled clerk—miles.)

His mother also spoiled him—waited on him—he could never find his socks—& apparently was never made to do so. (What effect would this have on him in after-life—*marked* effect.) After married, position reversed—He always spoilt his own women-folk—wife & daughters—It was they who expected to be waited on.

His uncle loved him—stern but never punished him. Looking at him as he returned from school one day: 'I wonder what will become of this boy?'

February 13th 1934

D. on Winston. (We had been inserting contemporary comments in the Memoirs.) Winston's great idea of himself. D. said he was justified in giving Winston office. Had he not, W. would, with his ability, have been bound to break through somewhere, where the first opportunity offered. 'Just like a geyser bursting through a crack', said D. Described conversation before war at Criccieth, where what constituted a genius was discussed. Various people mentioned. Winston said, 'What about me?' Chalmers[1] replied laconically: 'Ability, yes: genius, no.' At another time D. describing Winston's ambition said to me of him: 'He would make a drum out of the skin of his own mother in order to sound his own praises.' But D. & Winston love each other, & have never quarrelled throughout. D. took enormous risks when he put Winston back into the Cabinet in 1917. Asquith sacrificed him to the Tories. Orpen described to me a scene in his studio while he was painting Winston just after he had lost office. W. came to Orpen for a sitting, but all he did was to sit in a chair before the fire with his head bowed in his hands, uttering no word. Orpen went out to lunch without disturbing him & found Winston in the same position when he returned. At four o'clock W. got up & asked Orpen to call him a taxi, & departed without further speech. D. said it must have been gall & wormwood to him to be useless & inactive in the war to which he had been looking forward all his life—But he did not repay D. in very good coin.

February 18th 1934

D. & I sitting & smoking (& discussing Garvin or Samuel) after Sunday breakfast [today], when the P.A. rang up to know whether we had heard of the death of the King of the Belgians. Greatly shocked & distressed. Gave D.'s appreciation of the King over the telephone to the P.A. D. very upset as he genuinely admired & liked the King. I only saw him once when he came to the Rue Nitot in Paris during the Peace Conference to have a talk with D. Very simple & unassuming but bearing his kingship with an obvious dignity. A man with a difference.

We talked of Kings, D. saying that now there was no King of outstanding strength in Europe, with the possible exception of the King of Serbia. I suggested our own, but D. said: 'Quite frankly, he is not a man of strength.

---

1. Then head of the Treasury.

He is admirable and reliable, but has never interfered in any emergency, and would not be capable of doing so should any emergency arise. If he had someone strong behind him to act, he would carry out orderly, faithfully & with courage. But nothing more. I look upon this event', said D., 'as an ominous one for Europe. It may have serious results in the present unsettled state of the Continent.' There were just two or three pillars one regarded as being bulwarks against trouble—Mussolini, & the King of the Belgians amongst them, (& incidentally he is not a Belgian, said D.). D. regards Hitler as a very great man.

In the evening Mottistone (General Seely)[1] came to supper, bringing with him two daughters of considerable character and amiability. He is a genial but vain man—though with plenty of courage. But D. always contends that if a man boasts of his prowess, it does not mean that what he says is untrue. He quotes the Alan Breck of Robert Louis Stevenson as an instance of this. Seely once referred to his chauffeur, who had been his batman during the war, as 'a very brave man—one deserving of the V.C., for he followed me without hesitation wherever I went'.

D. chaffed Seely on being the Father of the National Government, 'And I will tell you who is the Mother', he added—'Lady Londonderry.' Seely rather embarrassed at the accusation, did not deny it. It appears that in the early summer of 1931 he gave a series of dinners, with the best of possible intentions, i.e. of preparing the way for the formation of a Government consisting of the best brains of all parties. D. was naturally to be included in this, & was invited, and went, to the first dinner. By the time the second was held, D. was ill and out of politics pro. tem. for any useful purpose. As everyone knows, his enemies rushed the position & formed the Nat. Gov. without him, which was not by any means what Seely had initially intended. But the thing was out of his hands by then. D. admitted last night that he never suspected what Seely's object was in holding these dinners, though he ought to have seen the way things were shaping even at that time.

Seely still contends that Ramsay[2] is the key position of this Gov. unless D. were to come in & take his place. But I suspect that the latter remark was made partly if not chiefly out of courtesy to D., his host. Seely is a very affable and rather obvious flatterer. I doubt (1) if the present Gov. desires or would welcome the inclusion of D. in any reconstruction (a certain section of the Tory party would oppose it bitterly, though Baldwin[3] himself might not be averse, and a man like Elliot[4] might be glad) (2) if D. himself would

---

1. John Edward Bernard Seely (1868–1947), secretary of state for war at the time of the Curragh incident; cr. Baron Mottistone, 1933.
2. Ramsay MacDonald, the prime minister.
3. Baldwin, leader of the Conservative party, was the real power in the government. He first achieved fame by leading the revolt against Lloyd George's Coalition in 1922.
4. Walter Elliot (1888–1958), minister of agriculture, 1933–6; secretary for Scotland, 1936–8; minister of health, 1938–40; a progressive Conservative, often regarded as a future prime minister.

be glad of an offer (3) if he were asked to come in, whether he would sustain physically a job of work which demands concentration & continual attention. He has got so accustomed to ease and leisure, not to say self-indulgence, since his illness, that he would find daily application to a job very onerous. I think he realises that. In any case, he has allowed it to become very widely known that he would not join any Government of which Ramsay was a member. And as, according to Seely, Ramsay is the 'key position', the occasion is not likely to arise for D. to be called upon. One hears conflicting reports as to Ramsay's health. I was told on first-hand authority that he is suffering from hardening of the arteries of the brain; but on the other hand, Seely says that he is 'physically fit, but spiritually sick'. However, time will show.

Seely had seen Hitler in Germany recently & was greatly impressed by him, S. says he prophesied 10 years ago what course events would take in Germany. He has lately been to see D'Abernon (who is in weak health, having had a stroke) & D'A. clearly remembered Seely's prophecy, made to him when he was Ambassador in Berlin. D'A. in his return reminded Seely that at that time he (D'A.) had counselled us to make friends with Germany. 'The French are fundamentally our enemies', was his line, 'but the Germans like us.' Seely told us how D'A. became a rich man. 'He escaped over the roofs of Constantinople with a document in his pocket which subsequently brought him half a million pounds.' Very romantic and exciting, but slightly libellous, even if true.

We talked of H. A. L. Fisher (à propos of the alternative merits of writing in one's own handwriting as against dictating). D. said he thought Fisher was an admirable writer and historian, 'better than Trevelyan'. We discussed his brilliant book on Mrs. Eddy, which has been entirely suppressed by the Christian Scientists, and done him a certain amount of material harm. Christian Scientists no longer go to New College,[1] for instance, and when H.A.L. F. went to America on a lecture tour he was largely boycotted. 'Never quarrel with a religious sect', was D.'s remark. 'This applies, too, to the Jews.' 'But Hitler had to', commented Seely.

S. told us of Hitler's amusement at a letter he had received from Dr. Temple, the Archbishop of York, in which the latter said that before recommending one of his congregation to go to Oberammergau, he would like Hitler's assurance that the performance did not contain any anti-Semitic propaganda! Seely swears this is true & that Hitler himself told him, with a twinkle in his eye!

February 21st 1934
A nephew of Green, the historian, wrote to D. asking him if the story were true that a small boy (D.) had been discovered sitting on the doorstep of a cottage in N. Wales, devouring a book. When asked what the book was, he

---

1. H. A. L. Fisher, the historian and a Liberal minister in Lloyd George's government, was now warden of New College.

said, 'Green's History of England'. D. says the story as to his having been found reading a history book was true, but the book was Macaulay's history. The man who spoke to him was T. J. Williams, of Criccieth, a life-long friend & loyal supporter. He lost both his sons in the war, and is now himself dead. He said to D., 'You ought to be out on a lovely day like this. Why aren't you fishing down by the river?' 'I haven't any flies', was D.'s reply. 'I'll give you some', said Williams. D. soon laid the book down & went off. The book was one of his father's. Amongst the little store of books that his father left was this & Grote's History of Greece, & a translation of Thucydides, all of which D. read at an early age and now knows almost by heart.

D. went to the House of Commons yesterday, to the Resolution of Condolence on the death of King Albert. He was uncertain whether to speak, but in his heart of hearts I think he had intended to, having a speech prepared. But Samuel spoke more shortly than he anticipated, & D. having to decide in a hurry whether he should get up or not, missed his chance, & the Speaker was up before D. He was very sick about it, as evidently people had expected him to speak, & were enquiring why he had not. He said Megan was pale with fury. When he went out he told her how annoyed he was with himself, & he added, 'especially so, as people may say that I lost my nerve.' 'Yes, that is what they *will* say', was Megan's comforting reply.

D. talked with Baldwin, who wants to have the MS. of his book to read over Easter. He also talked to Kingsley Wood,[1] who is evidently not satisfied with the progress the Gov. is making. 'The time is coming', he said to D., 'when you will have to take your place as P.M.' D. says he would be very loth to do so. He would hate the worrying responsibility of P.M. & would rather have a job of work such as Minister of Reconstruction or even Chancellor of Exchequer if he had a free hand to deal with slums, the land, etc. I wonder if his opportunity will come? He was rather pathetic last night, obviously needing sympathy but I did not realise why until this morning.

Have discovered an interesting letter from Tom Bridges, written to D. in July 1917, in which he says, 'Yesterday I had a long talk with King Albert, who is one of your great admirers. He is quite ready to face another winter if necessary, but regards the whole condition of Europe (including Thrones!) as shaky. This he puts down of course to discontent due to depression, dear food, overwork & the revolutionary wind that is blowing from the East. I pointed out to him that with so strong a backing *his* throne at any rate should be safe, but, as he expresses it, if there is a storm at sea, one is better in a good sized ship than in the dinghy. . . .'

We talked at lunch today of India—D. thinks Baldwin is going to press the White Paper[2] through, & may come to grief over it. He was just off to a

---

1. Sir Howard Kingsley Wood (1881–1943), postmaster general, 1931–5; minister of health, 1935–8; secretary for air, 1938–40; lord privy seal, 1940; chancellor of the exchequer, 1940–3.
2. Preliminary to the Government of India Act.

party meeting when D. met him yesterday, & not relishing it. D. is anti-white paper. He persuaded Winston & Reading not to serve on the Commission of Inquiry so as to have a free hand after the Report was made. He thinks we should keep a strong hand in India. 'So long as the natives stick to rice', he said, 'we shan't have much trouble. But when they take to eating wheat, that is when we shall have to look out.'

February 21st 1934
Ivor Nicholson sent me a book by Henry Lunn to look at. He is publishing it, & it contains some questionable passages about D. Just what one would have expected from him. Sanctimonious phrases on the one page, and mean, spiteful, scandalous matter on the next. D. says it has always been the attitude of the 'unco-guid' towards him. Even when he was a very young man, before, as he himself says, he had acquired any vices, they looked askance at him. They fought against him when he was first put up as the prospective candidate for Carnarvon. One man was heard to say, 'How can you vote for a man like that, who takes his dog down on a Sunday morning to meet the postman?' (Incidentally, I think D.'s memory must be at fault here, either about the day or the postman, as there was certainly no Sunday post in Criccieth in those days.) On his election platform there was but one Methodist, and he was his wife's cousin, and appeared more as a relation than as a Methodist. D. says their attitude was, & always has been, due to an instinctive dislike of his unorthodoxy, 'Such men are dangerous' was the feeling. And so they are.

   D. says he once helped Lunn to get out of a financial mess—persuaded Pethick Lawrence & a Mr. Wilson of Sheffield to put up some money which would settle his debts. But it is possibly an illustration of the theory that to put a person under an obligation to oneself is the most certain way of making an enemy of him.

February 23rd 1934
The Jenkins's of Little Brown & Co., D.'s American publishers, came to lunch yesterday. We talked of Wilson & the Peace Conference. D. said Wilson ought never to have come over. The behaviour of the French to him as the Peace Conference went on & he stood in the way of their ambitious demands, was execrable. Shameful caricatures and poisonous Press articles. The Princesse Murat, who had lent him her house, demanded it back. D. was always against holding the Peace Conference in Paris, foreseeing such drawbacks. But the allure of Paris was too strong for everybody!

February 26th 1934
R. T. Evans, formerly one of D.'s henchmen, & now, because he joined the National Government, in his black books, has written to Sylvester to ask if it is true that D. has told Dan Hopkin (R.T.'s Labour opponent in Carmarthen), that he will support him at the next election, & possibly go down to speak for him. It is true—R.T., after having got everything he could out of D.,

joined the National Gov. & D. has no further use for him. He is a man of
certain parts, included in which is a certain oratorical gift consisting of one
speech with variations, according to his audience. This speech went down
very well in Wales, but the House of Commons had very little use for it.
R.T.'s maiden speech was received I believe rather coldly. D. says the House
in these days is on the whole more tolerant than of old. There was small
consideration shown in the old days for boring speakers, but now the members are rather more polite. D. recalled how he delivered his maiden speech
to a House which included Gladstone, Chamberlain & Balfour. He spoke on
compensation for publicans (against it) for nearly 20 minutes, & did not
realise he was nervous until he sat down, when his mouth was so dry that he
could scarcely move his tongue.

March 6th 1934
Very hard at work on the book. D. just written a character sketch of Winston, but wonders whether he is too hard on him. He is very fond of Winston
& does not want to hurt his feelings. The sketch is biting but so true, & D.
cannot well say less. But Winston won't like it. D. says that Winston's failure
is due to self-centredness—Whenever he has an opportunity he throws it
away through a desire to focus all the lime-light on himself—D. quoted the
instance of Dardanelles—a marvellous opportunity completely bungled
because Winston would not wait until he could get military help for the
enterprise—he did not want to share the glory.
            'When self the wavering balance shakes
                  Tis rarely right adjusted.'
D.'s particular brand of egotism is at any rate not such as to risk a failure of
his schemes through a miscalculation of that kind.
    D. & I went though a list of Winston's gaffes—
            Home Office—Sydney Street fiasco.
            Admiralty—Dardanelles.
            Ministry of Munitions—12½% rise in wages.
            War Office—War with Russia.
            Colonial Office—Drafting of telegram
to the Dominions which I consider was the immediate fall of the Coalition
Gov. in 1922. D. & Winston came into my room from the Cabinet room &
W. read me the telegram. My heart sank. 'If they sent *that* . . .!' But, I thought,
they won't. D. would never allow it. I tried to get hold of D. to tell him of
my misgivings—thought of sending him in a note to the Cabinet. But then
I thought, 'He will never allow it—It is all right.' But the telegram went.[1]
    D. says that if anything should happen to him now, he thinks Malcolm
Thomson & I could finish the book up to the end of 1918. 'But', he said to
me, 'if anything should happen to me to prevent me from completing the

---

1. This was the appeal for aid during the Chanak crisis which was sent to the Dominions
by Churchill on 15 September 1922.

story of Unity of Command, *don't forget*: Unity of Command was arranged at *Beauvais*, not at Doullens—Foch simply got the job of co-ordinating the armies at Doullens: he was made Allied *Commander in Chief* at *Beauvais*.' This is very important, D. says.[1]

March 9th 1934

Complete landslide in the L.C.C. elections—M.R.—majority and wipe-out of Liberals. D. says this is the most significant thing that has happened to the Liberals. Megan went down to Camberwell to speak for a Liberal candidate and had a rowdy meeting. She managed to pull through—I heard from a friend subsequently that she managed to secure a hearing by constantly bringing in her father's name, when the audience ceased their noise & listened to her. I told D. this, & he expressed surprise, saying that Megan had given him to understand that the demonstration was one of personal hostility against him. He is bitter about his children, saying that they all now take the line that he is more of a hindrance than an asset to them, after having benefited by all he has given them. Megan is the worst of them all in this respect, being rude and indifferent to him in private, & in public taking any reflected glory there may be, and playing the 'little daughter' most prettily. They all spend the minimum of time with him, for which he is not sorry. Perhaps they know this and it influences their behaviour. There is always something to be said on both sides!

Debate last night in the House on Air—strong demonstrations in favour of increased no. of fighting planes. D. says it could have been avoided but for Simon's mismanagement.[2] At Geneva other countries would have agreed not to use aeroplanes for bombing purposes, but we insisted on reserving the right, as D. puts it, to bomb niggers! Whereupon the whole thing fell through, & we add 5 millions to our air armaments expenditure. But D. is not yet ready for his attack on them. He would rather wait until the autumn. Meanwhile The D. Mail has done a volte-face and is giving the Gov. support.

March 10th 1934

We listened in last night to Oliver Lodge on the other world—profoundly moving and somewhat painful in its simple touching message of comfort to those who had lost their loved ones. D. deeply moved by his reference to dead children. He has an ever-open wound which bleeds again and hurts terribly when he is reminded of little Mair, who died when she was seventeen & was the apple of his eye. She was the most charming of all the children, & had not been spoilt as D. had only just taken office when she died. She was at school with me, and stayed on after I had left. I remember hearing the

---

1. The meeting at Doullens, which Milner attended on behalf of the war cabinet, was on 26 March 1918. The meeting at Beauvais on 3 April, attended by Lloyd George, gave Foch the strategic direction of military operations. The British war cabinet named Foch commander-in-chief of the Allied armies on 14 April. The only surviving copy of the Beauvais agreement is in the Lloyd George papers and is reproduced facing p. 227.
2. Sir John Simon was now foreign secretary.

news just after I had gone up to College & the tragic impression it made upon me. She was a very sweet and gentle girl, and clever too—much loved by all at school. But there was always a certain sadness in her face, & a thoughtfulness beyond her years. Megan took her place, which D. had to fill with someone in order to console himself. I believe at the time he was unconsolable. He would have felt his loss fiercely and unrestrainedly. He says his wife seemed to feel little emotion and to recover from the blow very easily.

Sir Walter & Lady Layton came in the evening & stayed to dinner—a long talk on the political situation. Agreement that Liberalism (or rather the Liberal party) had missed the boat and was a complete washout. D. said: 'We ran away at the last election, surrendering everything, and leaving all the bag and baggage behind.' He thinks there is no hope at the next election. Layton & indeed all the management of The News Chronicle are inclined to go Labour. D. had already told me of a talk he had had with Vallance,[1] in which the latter gave a hint of a combination & understanding with the Herald on a progressive policy. And a young friend of ours who has got a job as leader writer on the Chronicle was told that his line was to be 'half-way between Maxton and Samuel'. This evening after dinner Layton went still further and outlined a scheme for extending the News Chronicle-Star group into a much larger group of papers. (This included the purchasing of the Starmer group or the controlling interest in them, and the founding of a Sunday paper on the lines of The Observer.) These would operate on an advanced progressive policy, & Layton suggested that Elias (proprietor of the Herald) should have a large share in the management. Indeed he had evidently broached the subject to Elias. Then Layton put the question, which was obviously the reason of his visit: Would D. put money into the scheme? D. said he would. Funny enough, a short time ago, we were discussing how he should invest the proceeds of the Inveresk shares if he sold them, & I said: Why not buy a newspaper? But that was before The News Chronicle was reorganised under Vallance, & I had in mind the purchase of the N.C. if it should go first. We are to be informed of the progress of Layton's plans.

March 17th 1934
The Nathans came down to dinner tonight. His wife, candidate for Bethnal Green in the L.C.C. elections, was like every other Liberal, defeated; and as the election was run, as Nathan himself puts it, on general election lines, i.e. funds, organisation, speakers, etc., on a grand scale, he has come to the conclusion that he will lose his seat—as a Liberal—at the general election. *Therefore*—he is going Labour! He had an idea, I think, that he might even stand as Labour in Bethnal Green, but we speedily disillusioned him of that! He asked D.'s advice on various constituencies. Putting a nice time limit on his principles, in order not to appear to make a volte face too soon after the

---

1. Aylmer Vallance, editor of The News Chronicle.

L.C.C. defeat, but in time on the other hand to avoid the Borough Elections which occur in November, he will change his coat in *September* and wait for the General Election. I expect he will pull it off.[1]

D. had dined with Lord Dawson on Thursday [15 March], and D.'s Memoirs came up. Trenchard was there, and defended Haig. 'Ask the soldiers what they think of him', he said to D. 'If by "soldiers" you mean the men at G.H.Q.', was D.'s retort, 'who never soiled their boots with the mud of Passchendaele, then I will not contradict you. But by soldiers I mean the men who fought right through the mud—I have asked some of these men, and they are unanimous in their condemnation of the men who planned this campaign.' And Dawson's son-in-law, an ex-soldier, burst out 'It was a *crime*,' he said. The dialogue seems to have been a little heated, & I am wondering whether Dawson was completely satisfied as to the success of his dinner party. I was present at just such a one when H. G. Wells and D. came to blows about the war—and the peace, of which H.G. did not completely approve. It was nearly, if not quite, unpleasant. D. took the line (a) that the peace was good in all respects (b) that it is very easy to talk now, but he defied anyone to do better at the time. Some of his friends think that he would do better sometimes to admit that he has occasionally made mistakes, and been in the wrong, but he seems to be incapable of doing this—possibly because he is able always to make out such a completely good case for everything—the instinct of the clever lawyer at all times.

March 19th 1934
We talked on the subject of self-confidence at dinner tonight. D. says he lacks self-confidence, but possesses the quality of love of approbation, which to a certain extent supplies the stimulus which lack of self-confidence needs. He said that Uncle Lloyd realised this failing in him, and for that reason sought to encourage him whenever he did well. The old man would always write him after his speeches, & if he did moderately well, the letter would begin with 'Bravo'—scrawled across the page—But if he did outstandingly well, there would be many 'Bravos'—sometimes 'Bravissimo' occupying nearly the whole of the page. I have many of these letters. He would write also *before* D. was going to make an important speech. Sometimes these letters would include tiny pieces of liquorice in case D.'s throat became tired or sore. D. says that in the early days, when perhaps he had failed to make a contribution to a Parliamentary Debate, or when perhaps, he had allowed too long a time to elapse before speaking, the old man would write & say casually in his letter that he 'had not observed D.'s name in the account of the Debate'. I have never been able quite to estimate how much D. loved him. I think he respected him and had a certain affection for him, but I think he loved him not at all. Indeed, I do not think D. is capable of feeling love for any *man*, even for his own sons. And unless he loves, no other feeling counts with him

1. He did.

—friendship, affection, respect, gratitude. That is probably why he has few men friends.

March 21st 1934

Went up last night to accompany D. on his 'Whither Britain' broadcast. A success—The substance was what he has said many times before, but it is a policy he means to stick to until some part of it at any rate is adopted. His belief in the land as the solution of all our troubles is an ancient one—he has always been an advocate of land settlement since his cabinet days. He says he has the land in his bones. I expect he will force it on the Government before he finishes.

We dined before the broadcast with John Reith[1]—He is a curious character —a cross between a canny Scot and a mediaeval saint—but more of the fanatic in him than the academic. He firmly believes in the mission of the B.B.C. to purify the life of the nation. He had the day before been subject to a cross-examination by Tory M.P.s from which he had emerged triumphantly, using no arts but the simplicity of singlemindedness. Beaverbrook has been running a campaign against the B.B.C. & Reith says it is a purely personal one against him, and that B. is out to bust the B.B.C. Reith asked me if I remembered when he had given D. a certain quaint little picture of St. George & the Dragon, & I said, Yes, during the 1922 election. It was—Reith was working with the loyal Tories who refused to back Baldwin, helping them to organise their side of the election. 'But', I said, 'what has been puzzling me ever since, is what you were doing in that galère.' 'It's a queer story', said Reith. 'I had been working in Beardmore's for two years in Scotland, & I loathed it, and decided to come south & perhaps take up politics. Sir William Bull, whom I knew, asked me to help him during the election. I had some amazing experiences. The machinations that went on behind the scenes, the money that passed—the working of the political machine—these things were a revelation to me.' He did not add, but I guessed, though neither of us voiced it in front of D., that his experiences then decided him *not* to go in for a political career. He is a singularly honest man. He joined the B.B.C. immediately afterwards.

D. saw Sir Wilfrid Greene again. The latter was at G.H.Q. when D. came there on a visit in September 1917. D. had asked to see specimens of German prisoners, and Greene said instructions had been given for the 'down-and-outs' to be produced for D. in order to show how the type of German soldier had deteriorated. D. would have liked to use this in his book in order to help in his case against the military (not that he needs it!) but I fear Greene will refuse.

Still very busy on the book. The more one reads of Passchendaele & Cambrai, the more one is shocked at the hell it was, and angry at the men who were responsible for it.

---

1. Director General of B.B.C.

March 23rd 1934

D. had been up to London the previous day. These late nights don't suit him. He is always upset after them now. But he wanted to be in the House for the Unemployment Debate. His broadcast speech was referred to repeatedly in the course of the Debate, & he was much congratulated on it in private. He dined with some young Conservatives, who told him that Horder has forbidden Ramsay to be in Downing Street more than two hours a day. Rather a narrow limit for a Prime Minister in these strenuous times! Ramsay insists however in public that he is *not* retreating to Hampstead to live—but this statement under the circumstances seems to me rather equivocal.

March 25th 1934

Milner Gray came down yesterday to ask D. on behalf of the National Liberal Executive to ask D. to go down to Bournemouth to speak at the Annual Federation meeting. D. refused. He said quite frankly that he has no desire to take an active part in leading the Party—that the N.L.F.[1] have always made him feel that he is the prodigal son and that he has in the past been sojourning with swine; that he has his time full with his book & his farm & is therefore, perfectly happy; and that anyhow at the next election the Liberal party will not return more than six members from England. The utmost he would promise Milner Gray was that he would not say all this openly, but would give the book as his excuse.

D., worrying about some trifle today, said that Broadhurst once said to him: 'Young man, the things that worry you in life are not the big things, but the ones that are so small that you would be ashamed to confess them to your own wife.' Lord Morley corroborated this one day when D. remarked to him at a Cabinet Meeting: 'You seem to be worried today, Lord Morley.' 'You will find that the things that upset you most are the trifles', was Morley's reply. 'At the present moment I am worrying as to whether I shall accept a dinner invitation.'

Lord and Lady Snowden to dinner; she looking worn and saddened, he with all the pain and suffering of the world in his face. I have never seen a countenance so crucified with anguish of body & mind, for he is a very bitter man. I do not think he is long for this world. Much talk of Ramsay, who is his mortal enemy—a feeling that he will resign soon. Lady S. thought it a portent that he had smiled at her when he met her yesterday, not having previously spoken to her for 2 years. But D. explained this by saying that Ramsay was obviously afraid that Snowden was going to pillory him in his forthcoming book. D. said that in the last century there had been some Prime Ministers who were failures, and some who were hated, but he could not recollect one that had been a figure of fun—until Ramsay.

A consensus of opinion taken at dinner on Elliot did not reveal a very high opinion of his ability. He is said to have his eye on the 'crown' and to be run

1. National Liberal Federation.

by one Street, a very able civil servant, who is responsible for all these market-
ing schemes. Twelve years ago, when D. was still Prime Minister, I was
invited to a luncheon parly to meet some young men of whom big things
were expected. As far as I remember, they consisted of Evan Morgan (now
Lois Sturt's husband), Brendan Bracken, a satellite of Winston Churchill, & a
financial mystery Ralph Glynn, now one of Ramsay's Secretaries (Parliamentary, I think)—and—Walter Elliot.

March 28th 1934

For some months now, D. has been trying, at the initial request of the Free
Church leaders, to get going a movement amongst all the churches of all the
denominations, to preach a crusade for peace. The movement was to start
here and become an international one. It seemed a practical idea. The first
discordant note was sounded by one of the Free Church leaders who said he
refused to take part in anything with which D. was associated; as the fact that
he was connected with it would taint any movement from the outset. Next
came a blow from the Roman Catholics.

March 29th 1934

Great struggle to get draft of Memoirs completed to send to Baldwin in order
that publication of documents may be sanctioned. The usual last-minute
alterations, corrections, recriminations, leaving everyone utterly exhausted
and extremely bad tempered. D. is incapable of *achieving* anything, without
reducing all round him to nervous wrecks. In this way he *distributes* his own
nerves in a crisis, and, I believe, saves himself in the process. I always used to
think it was an unnecessary bother and a crisis over nothing, but now I
perceive the more subtle psychology of it, and realise that it is necessary for
him to produce this state of enervation in everyone else, in order that he himself may derive some sort of nervous energy which fortifies him. Anyhow the
MS. is now gone. I have a feeling that this time they are not going to be so
easy over passing the documents. The prosecution of Lansbury's son for the
publication of a perfectly innocent memorandum is going to set an awkward
precedent—I am not sure that it was not done deliberately. But D. says that
if they refuse to allow him to publish he will take all the stuff abroad and
publish it there. He is quite serious about the idea. He is wrapped up in the
work, and considers he is doing more important work by writing his
Memoirs than by anything he could be doing at the moment in politics.
There is some consternation amongst the Liberal rank and file at present at
his refusal to go to Bournemouth. I think they see him definitely leaving the
Party.

I must say these volumes are shaping into a fine and impressive piece of
work—He is doubtful as to whether he ought to include his devastating
examination of Winston's character. I think that is all right, but don't much
like his account of 'What Kitchener said about Runciman'. I was impressed
by what Mrs. Sidney Webb said when she was here and was discussing auto-

biography—that she did not think it permissible to include what so-and-so said about someone else—in other words, gossip—but only one's own impressions and experience. D. says quite flatly that he does not agree with her —that is just what he would have expected from a statistician and mathematician.

April 2nd 1934

Rothermere to tea today. Much talk of a war, which, according to him, will occur next year, for which we are utterly unprepared—no aeroplanes, no submarines. R. said he had just come from Gibraltar, where the Fleet were carrying out the same antiquated manoeuvres as they did before the war— & as far as I can gather as they did 100 years ago, with a few aeroplanes & practically no submarines.

As regards politics, Rothermere says that the Socialists will have a majority at the next election. He admits Ramsay is gaga and Horder says he cannot & ought not to carry on, but (which is news) Baldwin himself wants to get out of office, and looks to Elliot to succeed him. This D. thinks is because he would like at all costs to avoid seeing Winston step into his shoes. Winston, by the way, seems to be making headway in his party.

Rothermere thinks the trade revival is only temporary. He thinks there will be another crash. He has the greatest contempt for the Government, & seems—which is queer—to be reconciled to the prospect of a Socialist Government. There must be something more behind it, I feel.

April 6th 1934

D. developed a temperature yesterday & returned to bed with a touch of flu. He is much better today, & became quite cheerful & talkative as he took his broth at lunch. His family are *very* much 'off' him at the moment, but as usual are quarrelling amongst themselves. Little William George, D.'s nephew, is now the object of anger on the part of the Lloyd George family. He has dared to criticise the Welsh members, saying that as *Welsh* members they are no good at all; D. is inclined to agree with him. He says that when he was a young Welsh member he & his co-Welsh members would not have tolerated the sort of things that are now allowed to pass. He gave me an example of this—the L. & N.W. Ry. Co. had dismissed some Welsh platelayers because they could not understand English, & the Company said there was a danger of their misunderstanding orders. As a result, D. and other Welsh Members held up the Company's Bill for obtaining greater facilities in N. Wales and defeated it. There is no sort of spirit of that kind amongst the Welsh members now. But then Megan and Gwilym would not be members at all but for the fact that they bear D.'s name. Arising out of this conversation, D. told me of an amusing tale of Spencer Leigh Hughes, whom D. approached in support of the candidature of one John Thomas. 'Oh, he'll get in if he stands', was S. L. Hughes' reply—then he added: 'He'll get in all right, because there's a split in the opposite party.' D. says it is one of the wittiest impromptu retorts he has ever heard. D. met him one night during the Boer War after a British victory. S.L.H. was quite drunk. 'I'm drunk', said he to D. 'I dare not go home to my wife—She would forgive me if I told her that we had won a victory, but by that time I shall be too drunk to explain!'

Horne rang up this morning to ask D. if he would meet Winston on Tuesday [10 April]. Apparently the Manchester Chamber of Commerce gave evidence to the India Select Committee which they were asked, & persuaded to withdraw by a member of the Gov. Winston has evidence of this, and intends to raise it in the House on a question of privilege. They want to consult D. about it. Winston is working extremely hard to undermine the Gov. and appears to be gaining ground.[1]

April 7th 1934

D. still rather seedy, but quite cheerful. Childs, the American Ex-Ambassador came down to lunch with his wife. He was at Genoa with D. in 1922 & they reminisced about the Conference. D. said he had everyone against him, which was true—Childs had supported him in his endeavour to get America to come in—'If she had', D. said, 'I say now, as I said at the time, that we stood a good chance of clearing up all our difficulties—War Debts, Reparations, Armaments.' D. tried hard to get Hughes, the American Foreign Minister, to come to Genoa, but he would not. That was the first blow. Then Barthou obstructed everything, taking his instructions from the 900 telegrams sent by Poincaré, who from the first was out to wreck the Conference. He was determined to go to the Ruhr to collect his reparations, 'expecting to find', as D. put it, 'the roads there littered with gold as in some celestial city.' (What Poincaré wanted, I fancy, was the Ruhr itself.) D. had a heartbreaking task, but the Conference was doomed to failure from the start. D.'s reign was nearing its end. At home the wolves were howling, headed, strangely enough by Garvin, who loves D. but hates the Versailles Treaty. When D. came home he knew it was the beginning of the end. He was sick and preoccupied, though he never lost heart nor courage. I could not go to Genoa, and was infinitely sorry to have missed it. Philippe Millet said that if I had been there things would have turned out otherwise, for there would have been a contact between D. & the French, which they failed to obtain through Ned Grigg, who was there with D. But I know it would have made no difference. The forces against D. were too great, too powerful, too determined to wreck him and the Conference—D. said that Childs was his one friend there.

Childs said that when D. went to see Coolidge at the White House on his American trip, he (Childs) was behind the scenes. Coolidge sent for him and said: 'Lloyd George is coming to see me today. What will he talk about?' 'Oh, War Debts, I expect', said Childs. 'What will I talk about?' asked

---

1. Churchill accused Lord Derby and Sir Samuel Hoare, secretary for India, of tampering with the evidence prepared by the Manchester Chamber of Commerce. The charge was investigated by a committee of the house of commons and found to be groundless.

Coolidge. 'I should talk about German West Africa', said Childs. 'Get me the papers on German West Africa', said Coolidge. As a matter of fact, D. said, they did not touch on either subject. They discovered that they had both been brought up in the same kind of surroundings, a small mountain town, that they had both been lawyers & had for their clients the same kind of country folk, & they fell to comparing their early youth and their experiences, and spoke of practically nothing else.

April 10th 1934
Last night listened in to Riddell talking on the Peace Conference & the sign-ing of the Treaty. A banal and jejune account of a vast and dramatic topic. Riddell is heavy-footed in his narrative & he is one of those people who always ruin an amusing story in the telling of it. His own humour is of the elephantine type—clumsy and lumbering. What a wonderful panorama he could have unfolded of those thrilling months. And Riddell was right at the heart of things in D.'s confidence—there was nothing he did not know of the drama enacted behind the scenes as well as before the footlights. He was in & out of the flat in the Rue Nitot as much as any of us, as his book on the Treaty shows. What wonderful times those were! Every meal was a feast of interest —Hankey to breakfast to discuss the agenda of the day's conference, & the latest items of interest. Philip Kerr there also to advise and to receive instruc-tions. Riddell told the story of D. being without a seal to sign the Treaty. I rushed to the Rue de la Paix at the eleventh hour to secure him one & to have it engraved, & he afterwards gave it to me to put amongst my treasures, though I rather think it should be national property. It was an insignificant little object for so great an occasion but it was the only thing I could get at such short notice.[1]

We celebrated today D.'s 44th anniversary of his election to Parliament A host of messages arriving for him all day. D. very cheerful and completely recovered from his attack of 'flu. In very good humour, excepting when an uninvited journalist tried to interview him against his will. I think it is time we put up a determined stand against these vulgarians who think they have a right to cross-examine us on any subject they think fit at any time. It is becoming a real inquisition—D. really resented it today, & I was glad to see him turn on the impertinent young man. 'I will not be *bored* into making statements I have no wish to make', he said angrily. The man winced at the word bored, but in his account in the evening paper (of course he made an interview out of the encounter) I see he substitutes the word 'manoeuvred' for bored!

We had a little celebration dinner & D. gave us an account of his taking his seat 44 years ago. He was accompanied (introduced) by Lord Rendel and G. Trevelyan (the father of the historian). All the great men were there, as it was Budget Day, Goschen being Chancellor of the Exchequer—Gladstone

---

1. It is now in the Lloyd-George Memorial Museum at Llanystumdwy.

was there, Chamberlain & Balfour. He says he does not remember his feelings on that day. He has been asked to write an article on the most memorable day of his career, the journal which asked him probably thinking that the day he took his seat would perhaps be the most memorable. But he says no, not that day, nor the day that he became Prime Minister. The outstanding day seems to him now to be the one on which he heard that he had passed his preliminary law examination. On that day he was treading on air, the future was heaven, everything seemed possible. Never at any time since does he remember having experienced the same sense of exhilaration and general happiness. I can understand him, as I remember feeling just the same sense of exhilaration on learning that I had a first in my Matriculation examination. The whole world seemed beautiful and fine. I had a marvellous sense of achievement and satisfaction, and life in all its full potentiality lay before me.

D. said that the only sensation he remembers when he made his maiden speech was that when he sat down his mouth was very dry. Otherwise he does not remember being nervous—though he probably was.

The outstanding feature of the Goschen Budget was a scheme for compensation for publicans. D. opposed it vehemently in the country, and spoke at a meeting at the Free Trade Hall in Manchester, where Morley was the chief speaker. D. says he made the best speech he has ever made, the whole audience standing up and cheering when he sat down. Irving happened to be amongst the audience, having strayed in by chance, happening to be in Manchester on tour & having a spare hour. He afterwards said that he was greatly charmed by D.'s speech. D. quoted a passage from the Merchant of Venice, quite unaware of the presence of the great actor.

April 20th 1934

D. went up yesterday to dine with Rothermere—to discuss the war which is to take place next year. A large dinner and a great deal of hot air. D. disagreed with R. & Winston & others, that there would be war. His question is: Where will it come from? And no-one seems to be able to supply a definite answer.

He lunched with Winston and Horne, to discuss the Motion for Privilege which W. is to bring against Derby and Hoare. D. thinks he has a very strong case. Horne had just returned from Trent where he had seen Baldwin, who talked a lot about D. and said, according to Horne, that there would have to be a reconstruction of the Gov., and that he could not visualise a reconstruction which did not include D. D. not keen. He says he would rather envisage a change next year with a *chance* of his getting office, than a change now with a *certainty* of office.

April 14th 1934

Went up to London on Monday [9 April] to hear Winston make his accusations against the Gov. A successful speech but the forces against him are very powerful and D. does not think he will succeed in establishing his case—at any rate, Derby & Hoare will get off—Winston was very excited and excitable. Yesterday the Budget, which D. attended, but loathed it. He loathes Neville Chamberlain too. We were glad to get back to Churt, which is beginning to look lovely in its spring finery.

April 24th 1934

D. feeling very much under the weather the last 3 days. I got Nicoll[1] to come & examine him & N. says that he has been doing too much. He has been working very hard at the MS.—too hard, trying to cram into one year what would normally take 2 years. However, the MS. is now complete, & D. can take it easy. Today we decided to try some new orchard lamps to save the fruit blossoms from frost. It seems to me rather a fantastic and expensive idea, but D. has made up his mind to 'make his farm pay, whatever it costs', and tomorrow we have a large consignment of lamps coming down with several tons of crude oil, & the farm men are fighting amongst themselves as to who is to stay up all night to look after the fires! I expect D. will be up very early the first morning to see the operations in progress!

Today we had back from the King the chapter D. had submitted to him containing the references to H.M. The latter very gratified with what D. says about him, but requesting that certain derogatory references to Ramsay MacDonald should be deleted. D. furious & says he certainly will not do this, & that H.M. has no right to make the request.

The only effect of the King's interference is to make D. rewrite the passage on Ramsay MacDonald in the chapter on Labour Unrest, and strengthen the case against Ramsay in doing so—make it more hostile & more vehement. He says that he has not refrained in his book from attacking certain people, e.g. Asquith & Kitchener, who were doing their very best according to their own lights to *help* during the war. He is therefore not going to spare one who, like Ramsay, did his best to thwart and hinder every effort to prosecute the war vigorously.

It is evident that Ramsay has been complaining to one or two of his friends including H.M. who are now busying themselves to try to get D. to hold his pen. But every fresh appeal that comes only strengthens D.'s determination to publish his denunciations.

I read to D. while he was resting—Essays of R.L.S.—the one on Victor Hugo—D. says that Victor Hugo and Carlyle had a greater influence on him than any other writers. He admires tremendously Victor Hugo's understanding of human nature and his descriptions of human impulses. He says Les Misérables is one of the greatest stories ever written. He described the play in the mind of Valjean when a poor wretch is arrested for a crime he himself committed—the struggle between conscience and reason. We could not help comparing this description of the power of a man's conscience with Julian Huxley's description of the meaning of conscience during his wireless talk on

---

1. The Churt doctor.

Rationalism—'a natural phenomenon, due to the forcible repressions of certain impulses in early childhood'.

I accused D. of not liking the French. This is true, but it does not prevent him from admiring the dramatic power and insight of Hugo, and indeed he says there is a tremendous similarity between the Welsh & the French peasant, their thrift, their religious side which nevertheless does not debar them from ribaldry and even obscenity. 'The garden and the midden are very close together with the Welshman & the Frenchman', he said—I think the reason why D. likes both Hugo & Carlyle is because they go right down to the bedrock of things, probing and exposing relentlessly & remorsefully, as D. himself does when he likes & wants to get at the root of anything.

April 26th 1934

Went up to London yesterday for one or two interviews. D. still feeling a little cross and not himself. He ran across Baldwin in the House, who said he was feeling worried and depressed. D. thinks there are signs of trouble in the Conservative Party and that this is the cause of Baldwin's worry. D. says that one day he will say, publicly, that he wonders how Mr. B. is enjoying the insistence of his party to return to one-party Government & to break up a Coalition—Mr. B. says that a national Gov. is best for the country. Since when did he discover that a post-war Coalition was necessary to solve the nation's difficulties? Mr. B. claims that they must stick to Ramsay MacDonald because he saved his country in an hour of national emergency. But surely the leader whom Mr. B. turned against in 1922 had a claim to something of the sort. If Mr. B.'s party followers are making trouble in order to get a Conservative Gov. instead of a National Gov., it was Mr. B. himself who taught them to do this kind of thing.

I have a feeling that Baldwin got off too lightly for his wrecking of the Coalition Gov. in 1922 and that he will still have to give compensation for his baseness on that occasion. As Mr. Balfour remarked at the time, after the meeting at the Carlton Club, with his habitual laconic incisiveness: 'It is the sort of thing gentlemen don't do.'

May 7th 1934

The gardens at Bron-y-de were open yesterday to the public in aid of the Surrey Nurses. The Speaker of the House of Commons—ignorant of this, called on D., and was amused at being made to pay 1/- to be allowed to enter. He discussed the political situation with D. & said he thought Winston's Committee on Privilege might work up into a serious crisis. Apparently Winston has some remarkable evidence, including indiscreet remarks in a letter by Derby in reference to the dinner that was held at Derby house, to the effect that he would do all the best that good champagne could do to persuade the Manchester people to alter their evidence.

The Speaker has no opinion at all of Walter Elliot. He thinks he is a 'confounded windbag'.

D. said to the Speaker: 'You have a very useful gift of deafness on certain occasions.' The Speaker said: 'Well, if I see that a man is interesting the House, & there is no harm in continuing, I let him go on.' D. says that is the art of a good Speaker. Gully & Whitley were strict in the letter, & would stop an interesting speech which was interesting the House if it were not strictly in order. D. says that on one occasion Gully kept on pulling him up, & eventually he made up his mind that he would not be stopped, & went on speaking for three quarters of an hour, keeping strictly to order, but saying absolutely nothing of any importance or interest. But he was determined that he should not be stopped!

May 11th 1934

D. went up to town, but much against his will, as it was one of the most glorious spring days I have ever in my life experienced. The brightness of the atmosphere was almost unearthly, & all day I have experienced a sense of exaltation that I can only account for by the sunshine and the beauty which extended over the whole landscape—a brilliance which only an English May can produce—so they say—but I confess I have experienced an equally thrilling spring in the French countryside.

D. came back having seen Winston, who gave him his deposition (on the Select India Committee Investigation) to read, and wanted his opinion on it. Winston says the two people who have given him the most valued advice have been D. and Balfour—D. says this document is a very powerful one. Ramsay has sent for Winston & harangued him on the duty of everybody to pull together, at a time when the position here & in Europe, & in the East, is getting worse & worse (according to Ramsay). He added that the position in the Dominions was also getting worse, & suggested that the Government were thinking of asking someone of good standing, & a knowledge of the Dominions, to go and talk to them. Winston, scenting a trap, said: 'If you are going to suggest that I should suppress the result of my inquiry, I tell you frankly that nothing will persuade me to do so.' Of course Ramsay protested that he meant nothing of the sort—what they wanted most of all was to have the actual facts, & to have them published, without bias one way or the other. Winston thinking that Ramsay meant what he said (he so rarely says anything that is even comprehensible) wrote to the Secretary of the Committee saying that Ramsay had told him that what the Gov. wanted was a statement of facts. The Secretary referred this to Ramsay, who said he had said nothing of the kind, & wrote Winston himself accusing him of disclosing a private conversation. Whereupon Winston in turn wrote a snorter to Ramsay. And there the matter stands at present. But D. says, as he told the Speaker, that he thinks that is what the Committee will probably do—put in a statement of the facts, and get the Speaker to give judgment. Derby has certainly given the whole case away.

May 10th 1934

A heavenly day today. We walked in the orchards & saw the trees dazzling in their splendour of blossom. It was a marvellous sight, & at some points almost took our breath away. D. leaned on a gate and said he wanted to say like Nebuchadnezzar, when he looked at the hanging gardens of Babylon: 'Is not this Bron-y-de the great, which I have built?'

We found a large brown owl & 3 owlets—the sweetest little things. Porter, our fruit foreman, took 2 of them—a pity I think—& we are going to try to rear them.

Harold Nicolson's book on Curzon came out this morning. He shows how poor C. winced under D.'s lash of contempt and cynicism. I must say the old boy did have a bad time—I remember one day when D. turned on him because he brought the Archbishop of Canterbury (whom D. disliked) to a Cabinet meeting, when the question of the taking over of the British Museum for the Air Ministry was to be discussed, the Archbishop being a Trustee of the Museum. D. took Curzon on one side & asked him what the Archb. was doing there, & why he had come without an invitation. Curzon explained, whereupon D. said that he had not invited the Manager of the Hotel Cecil (which was an alternative to the B.M.) to attend the meeting. Curzon was deeply hurt, for the incident took place in the presence of his colleagues.

May 12th 1934

We were surprised & rather excited this morning to read Baldwin's eulogy of D. in his address to the Conservative women. He seems to have gone out of his way to drag in D.'s name & to proceed to praise him in a most enthusiastic and unqualified manner. More significant still—he drew attention to the dangers of Dictatorships & the need for our avoiding what has happened on the Continent, & ended up by saying that the Party would not mind whom they worked with in order to avoid these pitfalls & save the country from threatening dangers.

D. says that he has no doubt that Horne reported to Baldwin all that he (D.) said when he lunched with him recently. On that occasion D. stressed the necessity for a change of façade, & the dangers which awaited the Gov. over the White Paper. Horne is no doubt very much in touch with Baldwin, & he told D. at the time that they all realised that no reconstruction would be possible without D. D. said, as he has said many times, to many people: (a) That he did not want in any case to be Prime Minister. (b) That nothing would induce him to join a Government which included Ramsay Mac-Donald.

May 14th 1934

And now today Ned Grigg rang up and asked if he could come to lunch and his visit has lent a new significance to the situation, and appears to have been dictated by a new urgency. The Conservatives it appears are genuinely frightened at the prospect of what will happen at the next election unless the tide of unpopularity is stemmed. They realise that either Fascism or Socialism will be the alternative and they do not want either. Moreover, the crisis may come much earlier, over the White Paper, on September 1st, when Baldwin is due to meet.

There may be a serious rupture in the Party with incalculable consequences. Grigg has a special angle from which he views the situation & its possibilities, i.e. the Imperial one. He says that the Dominons & Colonies are already disgruntled at the way their cases have been handled on various occasions, especially by the Labour Gov. If there is trouble in the Gov. over the White Paper, & it wobbles and weakens, India will be lost to us, says Grigg. Firmness alone will deal with the situation, & firmness he does not see in the Gov. as at present constituted. He is alarmed at an imminent crisis—perhaps even a fall of the Gov. and then what! He frankly asked D.'s advice. Drop the White Paper, says D. Baldwin is too committed to it to be able to agree to modifications, & the only alternative is to drop it, and govern India. 'The real Ll.G. showing himself', laughed Grigg—'The Imperialist—the Diehard!' But all along D. has said that unless you can come to definite terms with Congress (& this he does not seem to think so out of the question as is supposed) the only thing to do is to govern India with a strong hand. Grigg realises this, & also that with a reconstruction of the Government it would be quite possible to put the White Paper out of the way. But that would have to be done *soon*, and Baldwin, although he *wants* a reconstruction, and *wants* D. in and *wants* to get out of his White Paper difficulties, nevertheless will not make a move. He *cannot* take action, says Grigg. Someone else must take it for him. The question is, who? The break-up said D. must come on something quite unconnected with the White Paper. If you had a George Younger for a Whip, he would find a way. But you have not. Who, then? The King, suggested Grigg. He is anxious for Ramsay to go, knowing he is a weakness to the Gov., & on the other hand H.M. is definitely against a Tory Gov. But D. does not think that is a good suggestion. He does not think H.M. has any action left in him—he is obviously a sick man. I suggested Fitz Alan, who is versed in all these arts, & friendly to D., but Grigg says he is one of those who think you can get a purely Conservative Gov.

We talked round the subject for a long time, & eventually D. gave Grigg a plan. He says the way is for a number of the young Conservatives to attack the Gov. in the House of Commons, to say that it has lost the confidence of the country, & their confidence, & urge a reconstruction with a strong, small Cabinet. (According to Grigg, Neville Chamberlain is to be given the Foreign Office—there has thus evidently been a good deal of important discussion & planning already.) Baldwin will then find it easy to suggest a reconstruction, & once things definitely being to move in this direction, they gather impetus.

Grigg made it quite clear that they took it for granted that D. would be included in the new Government. In fact, he said, that it was a well-known fact that Tories had always done their best work under a Liberal Prime

Minister. I took this as an indication that they would want D. to be P.M., but he does not appear to have seized on that point. He says he would not accept, but personally I think his acceptance of that position would be the only alternative to getting rid of Ramsay MacDonald, and forming another National Gov., which is apparently what is wanted by everyone.

It was evident that Grigg came as an emissary—whether from Baldwin or not, we cannot be quite sure. That he and his confederates mean business is also evident. Grigg is a keen imperialist and a sincere patriot, and an honest politician—as politicians go. He sees the Empire going to pot under the present régime, and Britain losing her prestige. We shall await results with interest.

May 23rd 1934
D. returned from Wales in a very bad humour—3 days of sea fog, & raining most of the rest of the time. He is in a dreadful state of nerves, and says he cannot go back to Criccieth again. 'I can't stand it', he said over & over again. They don't leave him alone, and insist upon his attending all sorts of silly little functions which he dislikes and yet cannot very well refuse. He met the Prince of Wales at Carnarvon & received him as Constable of the Castle. The Prince made a bad impression, evidently disliking the ceremonies he attended, & being unpunctual and ungracious in his appearances. As far as I can see, N. Wales had the same effect on him as it has on D. But D. was alarmed at the impression the Prince was making, & took him in hand and livened him up & forced him to respond to the welcome that had been prepared for him.

May 29th 1934
D. went up to London to lay a wreath on the Memorial to W. S. Gilbert. He adores Gilbert & Sullivan, & was much taken back yesterday when B. J. Lynd, Robert Lynd's daughter informed him that in her opinion it was 'all right for children to act—then it was funny and suitable'. D. says that the music of Sullivan and Edward German will last long after that of Elgar and Vaughan Williams. Of Elgar, little will survive beyond his Pomp & Circumstance, & of V.W. nothing except Linden Lea and For All The Saints. I am inclined to agree with him—I have no taste for the modern discords. To me, La Bohème is exquisite, and listening to its sheer beauty on the Radio tonight, D.'s statement (read from the evening paper) that 'Germany had now re-armed to the point which she had reached in 1913' left me quite cold and unmoved.

D. met Herbert Morrison and asked him what exactly Stafford Cripps was up to. (Cripps has lately delivered a violent speech outlining an extreme programme for the coming Socialist Government.) D. says it is exactly the way to prevent a Socialist Majority. If Cripps were a little cleverer, he would accuse him of deliberately playing to lose votes, in order to avoid having to form a non-majority Government after the next election, which is the likeliest thing to happen. But on the other hand, D. does not think he is clever or

subtle enough for that. 'He reminds me', says D., 'of Balfour's comment on
our Generals during the war. "If they had been traitors they could not have
played their part more cleverly."'

May 31st 1934

D. greatly amused at the trouncing Barthou[1] has given Simon at Geneva,
but his elation is a little tempered by the fact that he also loathed Barthou,
who, with Poincaré's help spiked the Genoa Conference in 1922. He and
Barthou had many bitter passages then. Barthou made some offensive references to Protestantism, & D. intended to ask him (he had it down in his notes)
why the French had not warned the British in 1914 of their dislike for
Protestants. Had they done so, there would have been a million more
Protestants alive in Britain now. These peace conferences!

D. says it would be amusing if he turned up at the House of Commons
Debate on the Disarmament Conference as a strong supporter of Simon's!

June 13th 1934

D. felt ill yesterday as we walked, and I did not like the look of him, so
telephoned to Dawson, who came down in the evening. He reports heart
tired and blood pressure up & says local symptoms are due to this. D. to stay
in bed & rest. I feared there was something wrong & have suspected it for
some little time past. D. has looked so fagged from time to time, but has
appeared to be unconscious of it himself, probably his enormous energy has
disguised his tiredness from himself.

Winston has been unlucky again. The Report of the Committee on Privilege went unanimously against him, & the Debate today, while not being
exactly a triumph for the Gov. was not exactly a triumph for Winston. He is
unpopular in the House. Nevertheless the Gov. must feel the backwash,
Baldwin having been forced to say that the India Committee is not a judicial
one.

Ned Grigg reports that he finds everywhere a feeling that 'something must
be done'; on the other hand, no one seems to know quite what!

June 14th 1934

Further slight complications in D.'s indisposition—glycosuria. He is terribly
depressed, thinking he surely must have diabetes. He hasn't & I think I convinced him of this. He told me stories of men he had known who had *really*
had diabetes but who had survived it many years. He told me how, in 1888,
he was dining in the House of Commons with Tom Ellis. The latter pointed
to a man who came in, and said, 'That is Charles Broadhurst. He is dying of
diabetes.' Twelve years afterwards, D. was attending the funeral of Tom
Ellis, and Charles Broadhurst was also there. He lived for several years even
after this. The telling of the story cheered D. Altogether he is much brighter
today. I dashed up to London to procure sugarless & starchless foods for him.

---

1. French foreign minister.

June 27th 1934

D. a little bit annoyed, having written to Weygand[1] proposing a meeting
while the latter is in London, and receiving a perfectly courteous but quite
definite refusal. D. now says that if he had considered more carefully he
would not have asked Weygand, as he ought to have known that it would be
difficult for Weygand to meet him at the moment, seeing how unpopular D.
is there, and that Weygand's supporters are those who dislike D. most. It is
very true that the French hate D., so much so that the Echo de Paris will not
publish this series of articles from his Memoirs & say quite frankly that they
do not wish to have them because he is so unpopular. Nor will any other
French paper take them. However, he has other friends and other compensa-
tions but there is no doubt that it hurts his pride to receive such a snub.

July 19th 1934

D. entertained the London Cardiganshire Society here, at the request of his
old schoolfriend, Bob Jones (tho' quite how Bob comes to be associated with
the Cardis we don't know, he being a Llanystumdwy man). Bob was in the
seventh heaven, being a hero on the one hand to the visitors he brought with
him, & being fêted by D. as his old pal! Bob is only a working tailor, but an
attractive, dear old man with a humorous face & mind, & a romantic touch
about him. I can understand he & D. being school friends together—he is in
fact the only real school friend D. ever had. The other boys, D. said left
school to go to work at the age of 10 or 11, & few of them stayed after that.

Speaking of his Sundays, D. said the thing that redeemed his chapel going
from utter dreariness was the fact of the one & a half mile walk there and
back. When his mother was too unwell to go—and she became an invalid
early in life—he & his brother went alone to chapel (Uncle Lloyd having
gone in advance) 'and', said D. to me, 'you can get lots of fun in the course
of a mile and a half!'

D. tells stories by the hour of the people of the village—many of them
simple and great hearted, honourable & full of faith and as a pendant no doubt
to their own hard lives—they were most of them very poor—vastly occupied
with the life to come. There is the story for instance of the old man who lay
dying, & was reminded by those around him of the glories of the life to come;
'What frightens me', he remarked, 'is the greatness of the change.'

September 17th 1934

Admiral Grayson[2] came down yesterday to lunch with D. It is fifteen years
since I last saw him in Paris at the Peace Conference but he is just as charming
and suave as ever—a genial and rather fascinating Virginian, who reminds me
a little of Lord Dawson, having the same easy manner & understanding of

---

1. French chief of the general staff and Foch's principal assistant during the first world
war.
2. President Wilson's medical adviser.

human nature which appertains to the doctor who is a man of the world & has had dealings with the great.

Grayson was strongly attached to President Wilson, & was with him to the end. He told us that the refusal of the Senate to pass the League of Nations killed him. When he heard the news, he said to Grayson: 'They will not accept the League of Nations until the heart of the world is broken—and perhaps its pocket-book too.' 'He was something of a prophet', said Grayson.

He discussed with D. Grey's mission to America in 1919,[1] when D. & Clemenceau sent Grey over (Wilson had already returned) to tell Wilson that they would have no objection to modifying the Constitution of the League if it would make it easier for Wilson to get the U.S.A. Government to pass it. (They had heard that Wilson was having trouble and felt he was in honour bound to Clemenceau & D. not to modify it in any way.) Grey went to Washington but never went near Wilson, for there was trouble in the British Embassy over an official who had made insulting remarks about Mrs. Wilson, and Grey refused to accede to Wilson's request that the official should be removed. 'It would injure the young fellow's career', was his reply. That it wrecked the career of the League was a minor matter, apparently. 'But', said D., 'it need not have wrecked the man's career either. Grey could have seen that he was promoted. That is what I always did in such emergencies.'

We asked Grayson if it was true that Pres. Wilson had had a stroke while in Paris. D. never thought he had, but Harold Nicolson has taken the other view, & wrote me only the other day on the matter, asking if D. still took the same view in spite of evidence to the contrary. Grayson says he definitely did *not* have a stroke, only a touch of influenzal disorder which he caught from Clemenceau. The slight twitching of his face was the remains of a nervous condition which he had suffered from years before, and which he always gave evidence of under great strain.

D. & Grayson compared notes about Hoover,[2] whom D. and Wilson both disliked. Wilson received him during the war & afterwards asked Grayson's opinion of him. 'Well', was G.'s reply, 'if he was a horse in Virginia, & I was buying one, I wouldn't buy him. Your boots are pretty good, but as far as I can see, there was no reason why he should look at them all the time, instead of looking you in the eyes.' Some years after, when Wilson was lying ill, the news came that Hoover had taken a house a few doors away from Wilson. Grayson, going to see W., said: 'I see you've got a new neighbour'—and added 'Don't you agree with me now, that he is a skunk?' 'Not a skunk', W. replied. 'A skunk has a *white* streak down his back.'

Grayson made me play to him the tunes I used to play in Paris in 1919— Missouri Waltz and the old S. American songs: Dixie, Swanee River, etc.

---

1. Viscount Grey went on a special mission to the United States in the autumn of 1919. He failed to see President Wilson, though probably not for the reason given in the text.
2. Herbert Hoover, head of the American Food Mission during the first world war, and president of the United States, 1929–33.

He reminded me of the evening at the Rue Nitôt, when I played Chopin for Balfour, & Grayson made me end up by playing *his* tunes, at which Balfour was slightly puzzled & quizzical. 'I didn't understand the music he liked', said G., 'and he didn't appear to appreciate mine.' Nor did he. But, as always, Balfour, even when he didn't understand the opposite point of view, always took an amused interest in it.

Grayson was most anxious for D. to go over to America to see Roosevelt, & give him encouragement in his tremendous and rather lonesome task. D. begged G. to send him a message to tell him *not* to give way to the money bags, and not, on any account, to be persuaded to fire on the strikers. G. says R. is without any friends that count, but that his courage is tremendous when he knows he is doing the right thing. We planned a tour for D. to Los Angeles, Virginia, etc., but I don't suppose for one moment that it will come off. But Grayson says, & I believe it is true, that if D. and Roosevelt could get together at this moment, the history of the world might be altered.

September 21st 1934
We went to lunch yesterday with the Lees at White Lodge, & then on to the New Gallery to see the film of Palestine which Lee has made. It is quite impressive, though its evident object is to tell the audience about (1) Lee (2) Jesus Christ & Palestine. Lee is an able and fastidious man, of tremendous obstinacy & self-interest, & try as I can I never wholly succeed in liking him. His selfishness destroys to my mind his merit & achievement. Nevertheless he is a loyal friend of D., & indeed a loyal friend to all his friends, who, once established, he never deserts.

Today is published Vol. III of the War Memoirs. D. is very satisfied, as is also Ivor Nicholson—6,000 advance copies (more than double previous vols.) & an amazing press. D. very pleased because for the first time there is a general reference to his literary ability. He has certainly taken infinite trouble over the preparation of this vol. & vol. IV—and I am nearly dead from my labours! We drank a bottle of champagne tonight (forbidden, because of D.'s excess of sugar) but much enjoyed. D. said: 'There is a great advantage in virtue—it enables you to enjoy sin so much more.'

There is a certain amount of criticism & some of the critics fasten on the Smuts Memo.[1] I wish he had asked Smuts' permission. I pressed him to write many times or to let me write, in view of what Hankey said, but he would not. He said: No, it was a memo. written at D.'s request, & therefore it was not Smuts' private property.

We listened tonight to the Eroica Symphony (very badly played) on the B.B.C. from Queen's Hall. D. says that the first time he heard it was at Gladstone's funeral.

---

1. This is the memorandum by Smuts of 20 April 1917 on the General Strategic and Military Situation and particularly that on the Western Front. War Memoirs, pp. 1531–43.

D. has been immersed in the Esher Diary, just published. He says that the account of Rosebery's retirement reconciles him to his own, which is so much happier & so full of interest. He quite definitely shrinks from the possibility of having to go into active politics again. Harold Macmillan writes saying things are going from bad to worse, & that he is worried about the political situation and wants to see D. He is coming down on Tuesday, but D. is not very interested.

September 25th 1934

Macmillan[1] came down yesterday, seeking D.'s advice. The young Conservatives are worried (1) about the present political situation which they do not like for reasons connected with Policy (White Paper, Unemployment, etc.) and (2) because they think that the most progressive of them are bound to lose their seats at the next election. D. advised him not to try to force a crisis, as he personally does not think anything can be precipitated before the next election, the Gov. being too secure & Ramsay having no intention of going. Moreover he is not anxious to be drawn back into politics at this moment, & he told Macmillan that nothing on earth would induce him to take office with the present Gov. He knows (but this he did *not* tell Macmillan) that the Conservatives would simply make use of him to consolidate the position for them up to and during the next election; after the election they would throw him over, and his plans, and he would be left high and dry with no sort of political future whatever—much less than he has now. It is certainly not worth his while to be drawn back into politics now for such a purpose.

The conversation turned on Baldwin, who, Macmillan said, although having a high regard for D. seemed particularly reluctant to consult him about things or to concede anything to those who suggested that D. should be asked to take a hand in setting things right. 'I don't know why he should be afraid of me', said D.: 'I have never done anything to harm him.' 'It is not what you have done to him', was Macmillan's reply, 'but what he did to you.'

What D. has at the back of his mind is the consolidation of a small block of progressive opinion behind him after the election, in the hope that the Gov. majority will be so small that a block of votes of even 20 or 30 would influence things one way or another. Then D., with his little party, would be all powerful, and could dictate policy, which is just what he would like.

I cannot help feeling, however, that the next election—or at any rate some sort of political reconstruction—will come sooner than D. cares to admit. But there is no doubt that he does not want to be drawn back into politics at the moment, & at any rate, it is a good thing to be *able* to tell any inquirers that nothing would induce him to do so!

---

1. Harold Macmillan, then an outstanding progressive among the young Conservative M.P.s.

September 28th 1934

D. dined last night with Ned Grigg & Vansittart,[1] at their request. They form part of the body of young Conservatives who are worried at the trend of things politically, but they are especially worried about foreign policy, & the position we are drifting into on the Continent. D. however is not worried about the prospects of an immediate war, & told them so. For the rest, he talked to them very much as he had talked to Macmillan. He is not going to pull Tory chestnuts (even young ones) out of the fire for them. Once bit, twice shy!

October 4th 1934

Sir James Lavery has been down here this week making a painting of D. He has also made one of D. & me working together at the book, & D. is buying it from him and giving it to me for a birthday present, partly, & partly for helping him in the great work. Lavery is a most charming and delightful old Irishman, simple & courteous and gentle. He has had less trouble with D., than I have ever known any artist to have. Usually D. is quite impossible & the sittings have ended as often as not in unpleasantness. But Lavery simply disregards any attempt at unpleasantness. For a man of 78, he has a fine sensitiveness and exquisite tact.

Lavery told us some amusing tales of Whistler, whom he evidently knew well. Whistler was very jealous of Burne-Jones, who at one time secured a great success at the Paris Salon where he exhibited his picture The Mermaid. The Paris papers gave him large headlines, & Whistler meeting Lavery one day said to him 'What is all this fuss about "Mr. Jones"?' Lavery explained that it was over B.J.'s picture, The Mermaid (representing a mermaid dragging down a sailor to the bottom of the sea). 'Oh', was Whistler's contemptuous comment, 'you mean that picture of two unfortunate people in a tank!' On another occasion Whistler met Swinburne, who referred to Rossetti as an artist. 'I thought he was a poet', was Whistler's reply.

Lavery told us of how he painted both Redmond & Carson, a great achievement—but as he explained, he was a bit of an anomaly himself, being a Papist born in Belfast! Redmond, when the portraits were finished & he learned that they were to be exhibited, said: 'Well, Carson, I always said that one day you & I would be hanging together!' Carson, who did not like his portrait (though Lavery says it is an excellent piece of work!), said that it was easy to tell which side Lavery was on. (He probably thought as a man who was painted by Whistler, & who said: 'Well, the portrait may be like *me*, but thank God I'm not like *it*!')

Lavery speaking of Papists told the story of Fitzalan, who on becoming Viceroy was taken up by one of the Castle officials to see the view from the top. 'You can see for 30 miles, your Excellency', said the man, 'and there's

---

1. Sir Robert Vansittart, permanent under-secretary at the foreign office and leading advocate of a strong line against Germany.

not a bloody Papist in sight.' Fitzalan himself (much amused in spite of his hereditary Papism) had told the story to D. at the time.

October 5th 1934

The surprising vote taken at the Cons. Conference at Bristol yesterday on the White Paper has altered D.'s view of the political situation.[1] He now thinks a general election may be precipitated as it looks as though Baldwin may find it impossible to continue the leadership of the party under the circumstances. D. cannot help but be sardonically amused at the trend of events—which are somehow repeating themselves, with Baldwin instead of himself as the central figure. In 1922 it was D. who had trouble with the Diehard Conservatives (which included Baldwin). Now B. himself is the one who seems likely to be ousted. 'But there is this difference', said D. to me. 'I had on my side the most powerful of the Tories. Balfour, F.E., Chamberlain, Horne, Worthington-Evans—they all stood by me. Baldwin will have no one with him who counts.'

Have been reading up the events connected with the Maurice Debate in order to help D. with this Chapter in Vol. V, and am uneasy in my mind about an incident which occurred at the time & which is known only to J. T. Davies & myself. D. obtained from the W.O. the figures which he used in his statement on April 9th in the House of Commons on the subject of manpower. These figures were afterwards stated by Gen. Maurice to be inaccurate.[2] I was in J. T. Davies' room a few days after the statement, & J.T. was sorting out red dispatch boxes to be returned to the Departments. As was his wont, he looked in them before locking them up & sending them out to the Messengers. Pulling out a W.O. box, he found in it, to his great astonishment, a paper from the D.M.O. containing modifications & corrections of the first figures they had sent, & by some mischance this box had remained unopened. J.T. & I examined it in dismay, & then J.T. put it in the fire, remarking, 'Only you & I, Frances, know of the existence of this paper.'

---

1. The annual Conservative conference endorsed the government's India policy only by 540 votes to 523.
2. There has been much controversy over this affair. The account given in the text is not altogether accurate. On 9 April 1918 Lloyd George stated in the house of commons that British manpower on the Western front was greater on 1 January 1918 than on 1 January 1917. This statement was correct. A Unionist M.P. asked for the figures of combatant manpower. The Department of Military Operations, then headed by General Maurice, supplied a statement showing that combatant manpower, too was greater, and this statement was given as a parliamentary answer on 18 April. The statement was, however, incorrect (it had mistakenly included the British troops on the Italian front), and a correction was sent shortly after. Maurice was absent when the incorrect statement was supplied and ceased to be director of military operations on 20 April. Apparently he never noticed the parliamentary answer of 18 April and was of course unaware that it had been corrected. On 7 May in a letter to The Times, Maurice impugned Lloyd George's figures of 9 April. Lloyd George was able to answer that these figures had been confirmed by Maurice's own department. It is impossible to ascertain whether Lloyd George knew that the confirmation had itself been corrected.

There is no doubt that this is what Maurice had in mind when he accused D. of misstatement. But the amazing thing was that the document was never fixed upon. How was it that the matter was never clinched, & Maurice or someone never actually said: 'The figures supplied by us were so & so'? They argued round & over the point, but never did one of them put any finger on it. I was waiting for the matter to be raised, & for the question to be asked: 'Why did D. not receive these supplementary figures? Or did he?' But the questions never came & I could not voluntarily break faith with J.T., perhaps put D. in a fix, & who knows, have brought down his Government! The only explanation is that Maurice & Co. were relying on getting their judicial Committee where every point would have been thrashed out in detail. When the judicial committee was turned down, it was by that time too late to bring up details again, & by that time also Maurice was beaten.

I suppose it is too late now for the matter to be cleared up, & I had better keep silent. But I will talk it over with J.T. In any event, no good could come of any revelation made now, but the amazing thing to me still is that in all these years no one has fastened on this particular point. There is a slight allusion in Colonel Repington's book (Diary) about a discrepancy in figures, but this also seems to have escaped attention. And as the Official Statistics since compiled seem to justify D.'s statement at the time, it were better perhaps to let sleeping dogs lie.

October 8th 1934
Ned Grigg came down to dinner last night, hot from the Conservative Conference at Bristol. He is afraid the Conservative Party won't hold together for very much longer, & would like a Reconstruction—D. is against it, & advised Grigg that any reconstruction would be a tragedy for the new blood that joined it, as the Gov. would inevitably come down in their Majority at the General Election, even if they were returned, & it would be put down to the reconstructed Nat. Gov. and not to the old one. Grigg was forced to agree to this, but he says the trouble is that the people who will lose their seats at the Election will be the young progressive Conservatives. Nevertheless D. is in favour of keeping the present Gov. in & working in the meantime on a vigorous policy of reconstruction on which to fight the election. His idea is to back wholeheartedly any candidate of any party, who will accept his programme. The whole scheme is a bit loose & vague at present, but I expect it will materialise before the Election.

October 11th 1934
Sir John Lavery still painting. He asked in the first place to come down for an hour, saying that was all he would require. Each day he says tomorrow will be the last sitting. Today he apologised to D. saying: 'I gave you my word of honour that this would be my last sitting, but I'm afraid I shall have to break it.'

'Never mind', said D. soothingly, 'you are an artist.'—'And I put art before honour', finished Sir John for him. But D. thoroughly likes sitting for him and is enjoying it. Sir J. is a very lovable old man. He is full of interesting reminiscences. He told us of how he painted Cardinal Logue, who looked down all the time with his eyes hidden by shaggy eyebrows. At last, Sir J. asked him if he would mind looking up, & the Cardinal did so. 'This is the first time I have seen the colour of your eyes. I see they are black', said Sir J. 'No! Grey!' barked Logue. When Sir J. & Lady Lavery said goodbye to the Cardinal when the picture was finished, the Cardinal endeavoured to be nice to them & said he hoped they would visit him again. 'Ah, Your Eminence', said Lady Lavery chaffingly, 'I expect you will forget us as soon as we are gone.' 'Well, I shan't forget the colour of *your* eyes', was Logue's gallant reply.

October 10th 1934
Horrible news of the assassination of the King of Yugoslavia & Barthou— D. much affected by the latter's death. He was a genuine admirer of Barthou, in spite of his opposition to D. at the Genoa Conference. Poincaré had determined that it should be a failure & sent constant wires to Barthou, bidding him oppose D. on this & that. 'I've received my 900th telegram today', said Barthou to D. one morning. It is a sad story of incompetence & mishandling.

October 16th 1934
And now Poincaré. D. is a little mournful as they drop out, one by one—all the outstanding figures of his great days. But he really hated Poincaré, whom he conceived to be the stumbling block in the restoration of Europe. Poincaré baulked D.'s plans time after time. Wilson hated him too. When D. went to America in 1923, the two of them discussed Poincaré. The occupation of the Ruhr had just taken place. 'He is a cheat and a liar', said Wilson, with as much vehemence as his palsy would allow. And he repeated—'a cheat and a liar'.

D. was asked to go up to broadcast a short appreciation of Poincaré, but he refused. He could not, he said, say anything nice about him without being a hypocrite. But he was probably glad of an excuse not to have to leave Churt!

Weekend conference of Welshmen to help in the drafting of the new Welsh policy—I wonder if it will come to anything? I think some of the members themselves are a little sceptical, & being technical people they are I think very scared of being mixed up in politics. However, when D. sets his mind & his hand to anything, someone has got to shed blood. And even if the net result is negligible, there is bound to be a vast amount of publicity!

October 19th 1934
We discussed (D. & I) Megan and her fondness for her constituency & for running about there so busily. We decided that it satisfied her innate appetite, which she has had ever since she was a small child, for appearing all the time as it were upon a stage, & being the centre of attraction. D. says that he has never had any such desire, & I do believe him, to the extent that he is still shy,

as he says he always has been, of the actual public appearance & not of the speaking & all that that involves, but rather of the glances and notice of strangers—he says his Uncle was just the same, to the extent that he could not bear to see a stranger enter his congregation. Nor did he ever wish to go much abroad & meet new people. He could go occasionally to the neighbouring little towns, but for the most part, people would come to see him, & sitting in his workshop he would not mind who came there to talk—indeed would welcome anyone who would give him news of the outside world. Indeed that was the way, says D. that Uncle Lloyd, listening but often questioning too, would inform himself of current affairs. D. himself, in very much the same way, now sits at Churt & welcomes all and sundry, & in this way gets a very fair account of all that is happening in the outside world whilst remaining far from it.

October 24th 1934

Lord Derby sent D. a haunch of venison, which unfortunately, when it was unpacked, was found to be alive with maggots. I told D. this. 'Well, write and thank him for his moving present', was his reply.

October 27th 1934

Received a pessimistic letter from old George Barnes.[1] He was on the whole I think the sanest of all D.'s colleagues at the time of the peace conference. His calm, rather slow but completely unprejudiced mind could take stock of a situation in the shrewdest way, while he had the courage to express his judgments even when they were unpopular and unpalatable. If D. could have listened to him in 1919 it would have been well, but as D. rightly said, Barnes was not in a position to make allowances for D.'s difficulties. The letters that passed between them are illuminating as a record of what D. knew he ought to do, but what circumstances prevented him from doing. He was in the whirlpool of international complexities & Barnes was more or less a spectator of his struggles. Barnes has a great affection for D. He has tremendous deep loyalties, which make for a charm which he would otherwise lack.

October 29th 1934

D. very delighted at the reviews of Vol. IV. It is obvious though that some are a little shocked at the ferocity of his attacks. Bernard Shaw asked D. when he met him a short time ago: 'Aren't you frightened of attacking people in the way you do?' Whatever the reason, D. never hesitates to hit out, but I know that often he does not realise how hard he is hitting. He says, for instance, that when he made his Limehouse speech, he had no idea that he was saying anything which would arouse such a storm of indignation and anger as it proved to do. It was a carefully prepared speech.

D. pleased to find that Wells takes the same view as he does about Grey.

---

1. George Nicoll Barnes (1859–1940), member of the war cabinet, 1917–19; member of the British peace delegation, 1919.

D. was surprised that there was not more anger at his attack on Grey. It was allowed to pass almost without reproach. 'He was a mean man', said D. to me today. 'I am glad I trampled upon his carcase. He would have pursued me even from his grave.'

Ben Tillett asked him some years afterwards: 'Did you realise, in making that speech, that you were undermining the whole foundations of Society as it is at present?' D. telling me of this last night, broke out vehemently, saying: 'Of course I did! I *loathe* them! I cannot tolerate the system which decrees, in Cromwell's words, that "one man shall wear a saddle on his back, and another shall sit in it".' The violence of D.'s demeanour and tone as he said this, took even my breath away for a moment. And I got an insight into the whole of his political purpose when Hobson,[1] lecturing on economies last night on the B.B.C., referred to the revolution which had occurred in our Society by the imposition of taxes upon wealth, & the heavy death duties which prevented it from being passed on. And D., looking at me significantly, pointed his finger to his own breast, meaning: I did it.

He told me how after his speech at Limehouse, he went to dine at the Carlton, with Sydney Buxton & Harold Spender & Edwin Cornwall. The two former were terrified at his speech, & at what they thought would be its effect. Sir E. Cornwall was not apprehensive (probably says D. because he had not enough intelligence to anticipate the results). But Spender & Buxton were in the depths of despair & the extreme of terror. D. was amazed when he realised this. Not that he had not planned his speech deliberately. It was indeed part of a deep-laid and long-term plot to destroy the power of the Lords, which he did. They reacted perfectly to all his manoeuvres, and threw out the Budget a second time as he meant them to do, thereby making it possible to curtail their powers. D. tells how King Edward sent him a message during his election campaign, just before his speech at Newcastle, and tried to coax him not to make a violent speech, saying that that was not the way to get his Budget through the Lords—it was the way to make the Lords throw it out. And since D. *wanted* them to reject it, he made a still more violent speech, to Edward's sorrow and anger.

D. said that the night of the Limehouse speech, the Duke of Norfolk sat at the next table at the Carlton when they dined. Some time afterwards, D. was introduced to him, and the Duke reminded him of Limehouse. 'During the election campaign', said D. to the Duke, 'I thanked God that the other Dukes were not like you.' Norfolk had behaved with sanity and intelligence, never allowing himself to be provoked into mad outbursts against D., as the others did, thereby benefiting D. & not themselves. Marlborough, for instance, behaved like an ass, says D. D. never forgave him because after he had visited Blenheim with Winston rather unwillingly at Marlborough's invitation, Marlborough subsequently made remarks to the effect that D. in spite

---

1. J. A. Hobson, an heretical economist.

of his dislike of Dukes, was not averse to visiting them & drinking their champagne.

October 31st 1934

Have been reading H. G. Wells' fascinating autobiography. He says that his God fell to pieces when he was 13. D. & I, comparing notes, recalled that our faith in God dissolved at the age of 11. D.'s doubts reached a crisis when he was thinking things over in bed one night. The whole fabric of his faith dissolved, & the horror of the discovery was so great that he leaped out of bed with a shout of dismay.

H.G. and D. never seem really to hit it off when they meet. There is a clash of intellects, which is disappointing. Dinner at Max's [Beaverbrook] one night, when the question of Oliver Cromwell was being discussed. I remarked to H.G. that D. claimed Cromwell as a Welshman & H.G. was contemptuous. 'I suppose we shall be told that we must in future refer to "Williams the Conqueror",' he said.

The Martyrdom of Man is according to H.G., one of the most remarkable books ever written. I rather suspect that it was from this book that he got his idea for his Outline of History.

November 1st 1934

D. and I read Poincaré's Diary, the parts relating to the details of March 1918, as D. is now making notes of this event for his Memoirs. We wished to find what Poincaré said about the Unity of Command, & find him critical of Clemenceau, who, he says, pays too much attention to unimportant things, & is influenced by personalities. D. says that was quite true of Clemenceau. He was, for instance, always suspicious of his colleagues. Loucheur told D. that Clemenceau had them all watched by his police, and first thing each morning would be presented with a dossier recording where each member of the Government had been the night before. Poincaré represents Clemenceau as belittling Foch (it was of course well known that C. was hostile to Foch, & did not wish him to be made Generalissimo). Winston, whom D. saw yesterday in the House, said that Haig, whom W. saw just before the March offensive, was also contemptuous of Foch, & remarked that he was in his dotage. It was on this occasion that Winston, keenly interested in & apprehensive of coming events, asked Haig why he had not accepted D.'s suggestion of a Reserve behind Amiens. Winston pointed out that Haig would have the advantage of having the Reserve behind his own lines. But Haig evaded the question, simply saying that he had arranged with Pétain what they would do in an emergency. As events proved, he had no such arrangement with Pétain, for when the line broke on March 22nd, they neither of them knew what the other was doing, & it was some time before they could get contact & draw up a scheme of hasty and belated co-operation.

D. reading on later into 1918, the German accounts, says he is at a loss to understand why the Germans signed the Peace Treaty. They need only have withdrawn to the Rhine, & stood there. We were suffering frightful losses, the Americans had failed in the Argonne, we had failed to capture Maubeuge, & the Germans could have stood out for terms. We would not have gone on fighting to help the French get Alsace Lorraine. At the moment he cannot find any adequate explanation of why the Germans gave in so completely. He said the Crown Prince, if he had taken a stand & gone into action with his men, could have rallied them sufficiently.

November 2nd 1934
Lunched—D. & I—with the Guedallas and Cummings.[1] Discussed Labour gains at the Municipal elections and probabilities at the General Election. D. gives Labour 300 seats at the General. Cummings astonished. He only prophesies 230.

November 6th 1934
Lothian came down last night, having just returned from a visit to the States. He is full of the Pacific (metaphorically), & urges on D. the necessity for rousing the British public to an awareness of the trend of events there. The Japs will, he declares, before we know it, dominate the position, making it untenable for us and U.S.A. We should, he says, make a clear statement of our policy & D. is the one to do it. D. rather impressed, & inclined to make a speech in the House on the subject. He outlined the speech to me tonight, after Lothian had gone, & I think he could make a very powerful indictment against the Gov. on the subject of defences, especially of air, together with constructive suggestions. I think in particular his idea of a Territorial Air Force a magnificent one, & one which would catch the public imagination. I hope he will go on with the plan. Lothian says that the time has come when people will listen to D.

D. says that the trouble is that power all over Europe is now in the hands of the anti-Democratic forces, & one has got to accept that situation in formulating any policy. All the same, he thinks Hitler is a great man. 'They condemn him for persecuting the Jews, but he has not shown half the ferocity which Cromwell showed towards the Irish Catholics—as for instance, in the siege of the fortress of Drogheda and the burning alive of its inmates.'

L. is very patient, & D. treats him very roughly, cutting him short & trouncing him when L. expresses an opinion which does not quite fit in with D.'s. But they understand each other after all these years, & Philip still loves D. in spite of the fact that he left him because he felt he was becoming a slave, deprived of freedom both of thought and action. He had a hard struggle to get away, for D. fascinated him & dominated him. However, Nancy Astor helped.

Today D. & Philip went for a walk together, and came back each com-

---

1. A. J. Cummings, leading Liberal journalist; political columnist in The News Chronicle.

plaining that they had not been allowed by the other to get a word in edgeways!

They have decided to call together a group to frame a foreign policy which will form part of the programme to be urged upon candidates at the next election at the price of Liberal support. The economic programme will be drawn up separately—D. getting keener on politics as the election draws nearer.

November 7th 1934

D. very angry because a Welsh Broadcasting Committee had been treated de haut en bas by a B.B.C. official (not Sir John Reith, but a subordinate). He always rises in wrath when anything like this happens, having an inferiority complex about his race. He says he can understand the hatred of English officials abroad, with their air of self-satisfaction & their contempt of 'lesser breeds'. It took him back to his early days when he, as a young solicitor just beginning practice, confronted English magistrates in Wales. The rich English residents always managed to get themselves elected as magistrates and would treat the native Welshman with contempt. This used to rouse D. to fury & he would go out of his way to insult the magistrates to their immense surprise and indignation. In this manner he would often turn a Welsh jury against the magistrate, and get his man off. He attacked an English lawyer once in this way—Samuel Pope—and when Pope attempted to lecture & reprove him, D. retorted: 'We are not accustomed in Wales to being ruled by Popes.'

November 8th 1934

D. very critical of his brother's book on Uncle Lloyd, which has just been published. He says he has used Uncle Lloyd as a vehicle for expressing his own narrow views on religion. Uncle Lloyd was anything but narrow-minded & intolerant. His greatest friend was a curate of the Church of England, & he would, says D., take in all the journals of all the various sects and study them. He brought up D. to admire the great Welsh preacher, John Jones Talysarn, above all others, & this man was a Methodist.

William George gives an account of Uncle Lloyd's last sermon, which he left what was practically his death bed to deliver. He had to be helped into the Chapel, but when the time came for him to mount the pulpit he did so with an alert step, & preached vigorously on the text—'Yea, though I pass through the valley, etc.' All who were there say that he spoke as a man inspired, with the light of heaven in his face and in his mind. D. says that at the end, when he knew death was at hand, Uncle Lloyd had no other thought but of God. D. himself, on the other hand, when he knew he had an even chance of living or dying under his operation in 1931, had no more thought of religion (he himself admits it) than a pagan. I wonder what Uncle Lloyd would have thought of that! As far as I can see, he never really talked religion to D., and certainly never wrote it to him in his almost daily letters. I have so many of them, and must get them translated, as they reveal the tender solicitude of the old man for his foster-son. It was a marvellous thing that he should have lived to see D. at the top of his fame, though he himself was apprehensive of D.'s giving up the Exchequer & becoming Minister of Munitions in 1915. He thought he was taking a tremendous risk—and so he was.

I often wonder what the old boy really thought, towards the end, of the man who had travelled so far away from him. Did pride predominate over sadness at the separation? Was D. still to him the little boy who belonged to him, or was Uncle Lloyd, with his uncanny understanding, aware of the inroads which the world, the flesh and the devil had made upon his teachings? D. certainly never denies that the thought of Uncle Lloyd in the little Welsh village influenced him many times. He would not hurt the old man's feelings by getting into scrapes, by doing things which would bring him into disrepute. This influence kept him during his early parliamentary career from associating with the more dare-devil Welshmen in London—Sam Evans, for instance, who drank & kept bad company, but who was jolly good company for all that! It would have been easy for D. with his rather reckless temperament & his love of women, to go very wrong during those days. But the fear of hurting the man who was so devoted to him & had given up so much for his sake, acted as a safeguard.

D. has not up to date received an invitation to the Royal Wedding. Though he hates admitting it, he is a little perturbed, not that he wants to go—he hates such functions—but because he is apprehensive of a snub, which he would find it difficult to tolerate. It is possible that H.M. is annoyed because D. refused to delete the passages in Volume IV (Labour Unrest) reflecting on Ramsay MacDonald, as H.M. asked him to do. D.'s only reaction to this was to make the passages stronger and more scathing! (Invitation subsequently received.)

November 14th 1934

D. went up on Tuesday [13 November] to dine with a group & discuss a possible policy—chiefly on foreign affairs. For his domestic policy he has the other group which are meeting here at weekends to evolve a programme. On Tuesday however, Lothian had arranged for Smuts, Lee, Admiral Richmond, Gen. Fuller, Lionel Curtis, & one or two others, to dine with D. & talk frankly on foreign affairs. D. was pleased with the talk, but even more pleased with a talk he had beforehand with Smuts. The latter says that the country is ready to listen to D. He says that he has noticed a great change in this country since his visit a year ago. Then he thought the Government was becoming less popular, but he says that now it is tumbling down. 'I have seen a great many people', he said to D., 'and they talk to me very freely because they know that I belong to no political party. And I say to you in all sincerity that you will soon have to come back & take your part in governing this country.' Smuts went on to say that he had told Baldwin that wherever he went there was a feeling that D. should be brought in. 'Could you & would you work with D.?' he asked Baldwin. And B. answered that he could and would. Today he received the following letter from Smuts, confirming the talk:

'My dear L.G.

I much appreciated our talk last night and the most interesting company at the Dinner. I have written to Baldwin expressing the hope that you and he will meet and discuss procedure on the India Bill, and the preceding consultation in some form with Indian leaders. In view of what I told you about future possible developments I am very keen that all appearance of party attacks over India should be avoided, and the course you adopt should appeal to the nation as high and patriotic statesmanship on a question of the highest Imperial importance. The tackling of the grave question of Foreign Policy in the same high detached spirit will also have far-reaching effect. And I expect only good from such a line of approach by you.

With kindest regards and all good wishes,

Yours very sincerely,

J. C. Smuts.'

D. is beginning to fear that he may be called in sooner than he thought. He is not committing himself however to this government or to the Conservatives. Yesterday Dr. Addison[1] came to lunch and they discussed the possibility of D. & Labour coming to a bargain over seats at the next election. D. thinks he can promise them a good dozen seats in Wales, & more in England, if Labour will give him a quid pro quo. Addison thinks it is possible, and has arranged for him to see Lansbury on Thursday next [22 November], and have a very confidential talk with him as to a bargain about seats.[2] If this could be brought about, it would entirely change the situation, and might ensure a minority for the Government. But I doubt if it is quite as simple as D. seems to think. In any case, events may move faster than he believes. Winston seems to think the Gov. may break up in the next few weeks. They are doing some extraordinarily stupid things. D. says their policy for the distressed areas is fatuous and futile, and that was the general opinion of the House including the Conservatives, on Wednesday [14 November]. Then there is India looming ahead. Lothian says that Baldwin will throw over the White Paper rather than risk a break-up of the party, but there are many who do not take that view. D. thinks there is a possibility that he will be defeated in his Party meeting in December, & if so he will have to resign & Ramsay too, who is equally committed. Who then? Neville? Possibly. D. still sticks to his opinion that he does not want to be brought into any Government

---

1. Dr. Christopher Addison, now an influential member of the Labour party, had been one of Lloyd George's closest associates during and after the first world war.
2. George Lansbury, at this time leader of the Labour Party.

before the Election. But what if the general election came upon us now? It is not impossible.

November 16th 1934

D. in a reminiscing mood. He talked of Gladstone, and how he (D.) had attacked him in his very early days in the House of Commons on the Clergy Discipline Bill. D. had been very insolent (as only he knows how, and evidently did in those young days) and said (inter alia) that drunken parsons were as a rule nicer than sober ones, and that in Wales they knew how to deal with unruly parsons and did not need to come to the House of Commons to get powers to discipline them. At least, that is what D. *says* he said. I must look up the speech. When he sat down, Gladstone rose in a fury, and spoke for 40 minutes, in reply. D. says that Birrell says that D. turned to him on the bench while Gladstone was speaking, and remarked: 'I don't think much of this old boy.'

When D. went down to Wales afterwards, & the more proper folk reproached him for his attack on Gladstone, he said: 'I give you the same reply that Cromwell gave, "If I meet the King in battle, I will fire my pistol at him".'

D. says that he thinks Gladstone as a Churchman had a fundamental dislike for Dissenters, and the Dissenters felt this lack of sympathy, and disliked him in return. This did not prevent their admiring him as a Liberal, however! 'I admire him, but I never liked him', is D.'s qualifying comment always.

D. told us how he discovered the secret of Rosebery's limitations, one night when there was an important debate in the House of Lords. He overheard Rosebery's valet say to him, 'Your grouse is done to a turn, my lord', and Rosebery disappeared, leaving the Debate to take care of itself. 'He was self-indulgent and everything could take second place to his own personal enjoyment', was D.'s comment. The fact that his grouse was waiting was the determining factor in that debate.

Lulu Harcourt was another, D. says, who always liked his food. He always ordered special food at the Ministerial table—a thing which no-one else ever did. Harcourt, said D. was one of his bitterest opponents when it came to the question of an increase in Death Duties. Always the best of good Radicals outside the Cabinet, inside the Cabinet Harcourt fought D. strenuously. 'When it comes to a question of tackling the big estates, these rich Radicals show their real attitude.' Asquith, on the other hand, according to D., was no respecter of property. He gave D. firm support with his Budget.

November 19th 1934

Beaverbrook came over to see D. yesterday to tell him that he intended to work hard to secure Baldwin's defeat at the Party meeting on the White Paper. D. asked him if he realised what Baldwin's defeat would mean, & proceeded (probably without waiting for an answer!) to say that the King would have to send for Winston, as the leader of those who defeated Baldwin, since Ramsay would also have to go, being committed equally with Baldwin to the White Paper policy. Max said that in his opinion Salisbury would be sent for—which is probably correct.

We discussed why it is that Max 'has a down' on Baldwin, & concluded that it is the complex of the 'tall poppy'. Max does not like tall poppies & on seeing them with their heads in the air immediately wants to strike them down. If D. ever becomes one again, Max will change his attitude & strike at the newly-appeared tall poppy. The only exception to this rule was of course Bonar, whom Max worshipped. He still worships his memory.

November 22nd 1934

D. returned from London, having been there 3 days, fogbound, much to his disgust. He had however, his important interview with Lansbury, which turned out, as it happened, to be rather non-productive. Lansbury seemed to be doubtful as to whether he could persuade his party to come to any sort of national agreement or agreement on a national policy. It is, he says, a hopeless party—all at sixes and sevens. 'Parnell had the same sort of difficulties with his party', said Lansbury to D. 'But he managed to dominate it.' Rather implying, said D., that Lansbury failed to dominate his. D. was I think, disappointed with his talk, & feels that in any case he would rather come to terms with the Conservatives. Personally, I think he was optimistic ever to think that he could come to terms *before* the election, with both parties at once. It must be either one or other. *After* the election, if it were a question of forming another National Government, that would be a different matter. But to attempt to fight an election, as an opposition, on those lines, is I think an idea impossible of realisation. I think D. is beginning to see that.

D. spoke on Tuesday [20 November] at the Printers' Pension Dinner, but the only part of it he enjoyed was meeting Winston. They always enjoy a talk, even if they don't agree about anything. Winston is of course full of the White Paper & the fight that is about to take place upon it. Full of contempt as usual for the Governmental Tories. 'That half-wit Charlie Londonderry', he said contemptuously to D.

Randolph Churchill says that the proof that there is no emergency in this country is the fact that neither D. nor Winston are in the Government. D. genuinely hopes that there will be no emergency to call him into any Government, but with his lifelong training in politics he cannot divorce his mind from what is going on in the political world, or refrain from taking part in it to a certain extent. What is quite clear is that he has finished with the Liberal Party except in Wales. The general opinion is that there will be no Liberal Party in the House after the next election, with the exception of the Welsh Members.

D. discussed the foolishness of the Labour Party in not working with him before the 1929 election, when they could have had an agreed programme, & even afterwards, from 1929–1931, when he would have willingly helped them to carry an extensive programme of reform, they only accepted his help very grudgingly. And then came the deluge.

Talked of what would happen after death, & D. said the people he would like to meet & talk with would be such men as Caesar, Hannibal, Napoleon, Mahomet, Jesus Christ, Cicero, & Alexander. Of the great poets, only Shakespeare. 'The others', he says, 'would not be very interesting from a point of view of personality, only because of their writings.' This I thought rather a sweeping statement.

November 27th 1934

Had a marvellous morning hunting for holly with D. in the woods behind Old Barn. It was a divinely beautiful day, the little mauve clouds in a sunny blue sky reminding one of early spring rather than late November. But the woods were autumnal, the larches dropping gold from their boughs, the birches looking more ethereal than ever in their slender bareness, the hollies almost vulgar in their wealth of red berries. D. knew exactly where to seek for the holly treasure: he seemed to have marked down at some time or other every holly tree on the estate, & made for them unerringly. It is the same instinct which made him when a boy mark down wild cherry trees in the woods at Llanystumdwy, or a fern in the river bank, & then come back to it again & again & watch & note its progress. I think these rambles through the woods for a definite treasure take him back to his childhood: in fact, he is the boy D. again, with all the eagerness and enjoyment of boyhood.

This afternoon he went through the speech with me that he intends to make in the House of Commons tomorrow, on defence. He is *very* nervous. He says it is a speech which will please neither one side nor the other, but I think it is a very good one. It all depends on his mood & how he will deliver it. He has not been feeling very well the last day or two.

November 30th 1934

Went up on Wednesday [28 November] with D. for the Defence Debate in the House.[1] D. looking a little cheap & under the weather, but decided nevertheless to make his speech, for which I was glad, for it was an excellent one. He spoke I thought very slowly, even for him, and his voice rather lower than usual. But the speech has been much praised since especially by Tories. Simon too sent him a congratulatory note (D. says he was so pleased that he had not been attacked in D.'s speech, for D. has on occasions handed him some stingers). Today Gwilym telephones that the Tories are talking of nothing else, and that some say that an entirely new political situation has been brought about. They speak of a possible combination of S.B., Winston,

---

1. This was the debate in which Baldwin, when challenged by Churchill, asserted that the German air force remained inferior to the R.A.F. Subsequently Hitler claimed that Germany had reached parity in the air, and Baldwin confessed to the house of commons that he had been wrong. In fact Hitler's claim was a tactical boast, and Baldwin had been right.

& D. Winston, by the way, had almost an ovation when he sat down after his speech, at which I was somewhat suprised, for I did not consider that he spoke as well as usual. But I suppose it was the *matter* of the speech that was more important than the delivery, & there is no doubt that Winston's line greatly pleased the Tory party, as did D.'s speech, than which he has never delivered a wiser, or, I think, more statesmanlike. There was imagination in it, too, coupled with a patriotism that was almost imperialistic. I was unable to stay to hear the end of a speech as we were all turned out of the Ladies' Gallery at 7.30 in accordance with an absurd rule to that effect. The Sergeant at Arms found difficulty in getting us out, & he said to me as I went: 'I wish you would get your man to sit down before 7.30. I always have the greatest difficulty in getting the ladies out of the Gallery if he is speaking!'

However, D. did not feel very well afterwards, having developed a cold. But he managed to survive the wedding & came down here directly afterwards, when I put him to bed & discovered that he had a slight temperature. This morning he was all right again, but rested in bed most of the day, & was very happy at the reports that came through as to the success of his speech. He is not very thrilled at the prospect of a reconstructed Government in which he might be included, saying that he would far rather this Government went to the country & was beaten. But I think he realises that *his* speech may have a special effect upon the Tories in view of the discontent already existing in their ranks & the Party Meeting which takes place next Tuesday [4 December].

December 3rd 1934
The critical day in the Tory party arrives tomorrow. D. however does not think the vote will go against Baldwin.

December 5th 1934
As anticipated, Baldwin got his majority easily, though D. says the vote against him is a formidable one.[1] D. took it very quietly, but is no doubt disappointed. 'They're safe now till '36', he said. 'And that suits me.' Actually, that is true, for it gives him time to formulate a constructive programme, which will be more permanently useful than a sudden access to power gained by a crisis; and he knows this. But I feel that he knows also that he is working against time, which is rather pathetic. Still, he has never lacked courage, and hopefulness.

December 6th 1934
A mournful day, with news of Riddell's death. I feel it keenly; he was such a very good friend to me—kind, understanding, shrewd & always helpful. It was a pity he & D. parted company, but after the Paris Peace Conference, when D. became so bitterly anti-French, there was a rift between him &

---

1. The Conservative Central Council, meeting at the Queen's Hall on 4 December, endorsed the government's India policy by 1,102 to 190.

Riddell, who was pro-French & pro-Turk. There was an angry scene at Lucerne in 1920, when D. at the lunch-table openly called Riddell unpatriotic because he took a pro-French view. Riddell left for London the next day. After D. went out of office they rarely saw each other & D. says definitely that Riddell had no use for him as soon as he was no longer Prime Minister. This I do not consider fair to Riddell. His enemies worked on this theme & persuaded D. it was so. Some people believed it. Max Beaverbrook in a gathering one day where D. was being discussed, swung round suddenly & said to Riddell: 'We have no use for him now he is not in office, have we Riddell?' It is said that Riddell flushed & made no reply.

December 7th 1934

D. went up to London yesterday to the House. Met Baldwin, & they discussed the Queen's Hall meeting. D. congratulated B. on his success. B. said there were no really good speeches on the other side. Speaking of Winston, D. said: 'He is not a good verdict-getter.'

December 13th 1934

D. gone up to London to see Lansbury & Addison, at their request. He thinks they will turn down his offer of co-operation. Curiously enough, just before the telephone message came through that they wished to see him, D. had dispatched a letter to Addison making his position clear. The young Tories, (Macmillan, Astor, Grigg, Lindsay, & some others) are anxious to secure co-operation with D. for the next election, & D.'s programme which he has lately incorporated in the form of a Memo, has lately been submitted to them. The thing he is keenest on of course is land settlement, & there seems to be no divergence of opinion between him & the Progressive Tories on this. He is receiving a lot of attention from one source or another now that the election is drawing near. D. says they are saying to themselves, 'I wonder what the old b.... will do next?' This is what Michael Hicks-Beach is reported to have said in loud tones when passing Speaker Gully's Chair after Gully had refused to allow the Closure to a Debate.

The Brett Youngs[1] came over the weekend. D. submitted his Memo to Francis, who approved of it, but suggested that if D. was showing it to Baldwin's young Tories, he ought to show it to Baldwin himself! Francis's implication was that it was not cricket to do otherwise, but D. is strongly of the opinion that it is not politics to do it!

---

1. Francis Brett Young, the novelist.

Diary 1935

In the autumn of 1934 Lloyd George set up a new economic enquiry and announced the results at Bangor on 17 January 1935 as a British New Deal. His aim, though ostensibly non-party was to secure a Liberal-Labour coalition under his leadership or at any rate under his inspiration. Some younger Conservatives were also interested. Baldwin, who was now preparing to take over the premiership from MacDonald, agreed to consider including Lloyd George in his government. Neville Chamberlain insisted that if Lloyd George came in, he would go out, and Chamberlain was the second man in the Conservative party. No doubt Baldwin was merely playing with Lloyd George in order to conciliate the discontented Conservatives. Lloyd George sensed this and yet could not give up the hope that power might come to him again after all.

In June 1935 Baldwin duly became prime minister and reshuffled the existing team without calling in either Lloyd George or Churchill. Lloyd George answered by launching the Council of Action for Peace and Reconstruction, which was intended to appeal to the Nonconformist conscience. Though he spent £400,000 on this from his political fund, the movement was still-born. Baldwin found an alternative resource in professing a devotion to collective security and on this ticket won a general election in November. Henceforth Lloyd George was an isolated, though still a formidable, critic.

January 10th 1935
D. went up to London today to lunch with Max & Rothermere. He lunched with them last Friday [4 January] & came to the conclusion that Rothermere was with him over his new plan, & Max hostile, but he could not make out why. (We had dined with Max at Cherkley the previous Sunday & D. had then outlined his plan to Max, & D. had thought that Max was only half-hearted in his approval. Personally I thought that Max looked ill & distrait & seemed worried about his health—talking about diet, and a change, and so on.) However, D. says that today Max was in an uproarious good humour, & intent on destroying the Government. D. went with him to Stornoway House after the lunch, & in the course of conversation said to him: 'You want

this Government out, Max. Why?' Max stood up, and gesticulating with a diabolical look on his face said: 'Ll.G. I learnt one thing from father, and that was, to hate! to hate!' (Max's father was a Presbyterian Minister.) 'You don't hate MacDonald?' D. asked. 'No!' was Max's reply, 'not MacDonald! *Baldwin!*'

So, D., Max & Rothermere are all set on destroying the Gov. with different motives. But D. & Max want to destroy the Gov. wholly, & that at the election, and, in spite of everything said to the contrary, D. would not mind destroying Baldwin *qua* Baldwin. D. himself has often said that a Welshman never forgives, & will take his revenge long afterwards when everyone thinks he has forgotten all about it. And D. will never forgive Baldwin for what he did in 1922. Max is rather worried at the prospect of putting a Socialist Gov. in for this one, but D. assured him that such a Gov. would be the tamest and safest of all Governments—it would not be to their interest to play up to instability, strikes, etc. Max and Rothermere are to go & see Kingsley Wood on Monday [14 January]. It is supposed that the latter is going to attempt to persuade Rothermere to toe the line, as has happened before. So Max is going with Rothermere to see that he gives nothing away.

While D. was with Max, a message came that Jim Thomas wanted to speak to Max. 'This is what always happens before an election', said Max to D.[1]

It is not at all certain that the crisis will not come sooner than D. anticipates or wants, even if the crisis is only a reconstruction of the Gov. which is what Rothermere wants. D.'s plans have been somewhat precipitated by the results of his speech in the House of Commons, when he said that the present system had failed. He was interviewed by the Herald & others, & rather rashly disclosed that he had already drawn up his schemes to put things right. This resulted in an enormous rush of support from all quarters, & now that he has said that he will make his platform a non-party one, he is being hailed by all & sundry, as the Man. His speech on the 17th, is likely to be a momentous one. He has already drafted it, & Malcolm Thomson and I today went through it with a view to criticising it, which we have done rather drastically. I said to Malcolm: 'He will probably slay us for this', & Malcolm later typed out and passed me the following note:

Attitude of meek but stubborn sincerity in which the criticisms of Miss Stevenson and Malcolm Thomson are advanced:
'THOUGH HE SLAYS ME, YET WILL I TRUST IN HIM: BUT I WILL MAINTAIN MINE OWN WAYS BEFORE HIM.'
Job, xiii, 15.

As a matter of fact, I had already told D. that I should be slain for any criticism I should make. He said, 'Yes, I will probably slay you. And afterwards I shall adopt all your suggestions.'

---

1. J. H. Thomas was Dominions secretary. The government were ostensibly considering Beaverbrook's Empire programme as well as Lloyd George's New Deal.

Rothermere told D. that the Press Association had already ordered *four* columns of his Bangor speech. Ramsay is speaking on the same day, & the P.A. have only ordered *one* column of his speech.

The Young Tories meantime have been busy, for they mean to save their Party at the Election if they can, & they want D. to help them. Grigg has been working hard to effect a meeting between Baldwin & D. and Baldwin now says he would like to see D. when he (Baldwin) returns to London at the end of this week. But how far this is a genuine desire on Baldwin's part to meet D. and discuss things on the level, or how far it is just courtesy in acceding to Grigg's importunity, it is difficult to say. We shall soon know. One thing is certain: D. will not go into a Government with Ramsay Mac-Donald, nor will he take office with Neville Chamberlain as Chancellor or Simon as Foreign Minister. It is equally clear that Baldwin cannot get rid of Ramsay MacDonald or Chamberlain.

Nothing however will prevent D. going on with his plans for an election & forming, he hopes, a powerful Committee on Non-Party lines. Snowden came to dinner on Christmas Day, & is dining here again on Saturday [12 January], & he will come in with D. as much as his health permits. Melchett is willing to become the Chairman of the Committee. Lothian & Astor are eager & interested. Walter Layton is one day enthusiastic & the next day doubtful, as is his wont. The correspondence from every section & from all parts of the country is overwhelming. There are many comings & goings. Grigg, Melchett, Layton, Snowden have all been here since Christmas. It is becoming exciting. D. is in great spirits, & I hope he can see it through. He will have to guard his energies, as he easily gets overtired & overstrained. But it is the moment he has been waiting for all these years. I feel he is staking everything on the results of the next few months. If he fails, he will devote himself to the farm and his writing for the rest of his life. Meanwhile, the book is completely forgotten.

January 12th 1935
D. in bed with a temperature. Most ominous for his meeting next Thursday [17 January]. But he is already better tonight, so perhaps it can be done. I cannot help feeling that the upset is partly due to a letter which he received last night from Grigg, enclosing one from Baldwin, in which he says that he cannot meet D. yet. I think that secretly D. had been hoping that such a meeting might take place and have possibilities. But he says that he is glad now it is not to take place, as it gives him a free hand & he wants to see the Gov. beaten at the election. I expect the last is the wisest point of view in the long run. Grigg in his own letter is optimistic (unwarrantedly so, to my mind) of a reconstruction of the Gov. by Easter. This, although it would be immediately exciting and fruitful for D. would only probably give him a short innings & be ultimately unsatisfactory. I admire his courage in choosing the long view & the waiting game at his age.

January 20th 1935

Bangor is over, & a success, & I gather D. is very pleased with his triumph. I travelled up to Bangor with Ethel Snowden, who was going just to sit on the platform & represent Philip, who is all in with D. She has become most friendly disposed towards me, a change from her attitude of a few years ago. But she herself is changed, owing I believe partly to her conversion to the Oxford movement, partly I imagine to a 'change of life!' Whatever the cause, she is much quieter & gentler, but I think sadder. It must be a pretty terrible life for her, cut off from many of her political friends, & with Philip more a cripple than ever. It is painful to see him drag himself about, every step an anguish, every journey a martyrdom. His courage is almost terrifying.

E.S.'s great friend is apparently Queen Mary, whom she sees & writes to privately as one woman to another. Recently, however, E.S. had been out of touch with her. She wrote an indignant letter after she lost her job on the B.B.C., denouncing Ramsay & giving her own opinion of him. As H.M. is rather partial to Ramsay, the letter fell flat, & E.S. ceased to write until she received a note from Queen Mary, not so long ago, asking for news of her. E.S. says she is going to write them a full account of the Bangor meeting, & D.'s popularity & vitality. She says, however, that they are *not* unfriendly disposed towards D., as he imagines they are, but that they do attach a great deal of importance to the little courtesies and attentions, which D. refuses to bother about. He always says that he refuses to be a flunkey! I think he is oversensitive about it.

There is no doubt that E.S. has a secret passion for D. though she has learnt to be somewhat more subdued in her expression of it. She told me that she had had a dream, which apparently was more than a dream, in which she had been told that D. needed her assistance! The first time it appeared was when he was Prime Minister. She *did* actually seek him out a great deal in those days. I very nearly asked her if her interpretation of helping him was to slander me, & tell him that there was gossip of our relations on the Continent. She has probably forgotten that aspect of it, but at the time she succeeded in worrying D. a good deal about it.

January 29th 1935

Much fluttering of the political dovecotes as to D.'s position, now & in the future. The Press full of it, the Lobbies also. There is, they say, no other topic of conversation in the House. There is however no word from Baldwin, but Grigg & Macmillan have both visited Churt. Apparently Baldwin (so it is said) is anxious to have India out of the way, & asks D. to wait for a bit. Personally I think he is as crafty as the craftiest politician, & hopes that the situation 'solvebitur cunctando'. He is not going out of his way to bring in one who would in all likelihood challenge his sovereignty, usurp his position, & in any case make things damned uncomfortable for him. Meanwhile, as I say, the political haunts are buzzing with excitement and speculation. There is no doubt that D.'s proposals, mild as they are, have caught on in the country. We are overwhelmed with approval from every quarter, & of every political complexion.

Everyone all over D. in the House. Simon congratulating him & wanting to have a chat. But Hore-Belisha[1] told D. at Birmingham on Saturday [26 January] that Simon in his sneaking way is going round to Ministers individually & suggesting that if D. is given a job it will mean that someone will have to give one up.

D. apparently had an ovation at Birmingham on Saturday. 90% of the audience being Conservatives who are enthusiastic for his New Deal. Austen Chamberlain very affable & courteous. D. says that every time he goes to Birmingham he has memories of that time he went there in the Boer War. He feels certain that they intended to kill him, & that Joe [Chamberlain] was at the back of it. Joe's remark the next morning when he was told of D.'s escape, was that 'someone had blundered badly over his job' seems to bear that out. D. says that Joe was quite ruthless, & would stick at nothing, but all the same he has a tremendous admiration for him. He says his mistake was to resign too early. He ought to have stayed in, as D. did in 1915, when the Liberals were trying to make things impossible for him: then, when the psychological moment came, Joe should have struck, & become master of the situation—as D. did in 1916. 'I knew when the time had come', said D. to me in explaining this. 'I was not such a fool as to resign before the right time. But I went through hell before that, with McKenna & Runciman trying to force me out.' He scarcely ever attended Cabinet Meetings in those Munition days. 'What has happened to the Minister of Munitions?' asked Balfour once at a Cabinet meeting. 'We never seem to see him now.'

January 31st 1935
D. received a stiff letter from Rothermere—an ultimatum in fact. D. thought that when he last saw Rothermere the latter was inclined to be cool & even insolent towards him, & is at a loss even now to understand why he has suddenly veered round & gone back on his promise to back him (R. gratuitously informed D. at Riddell's funeral that he would give him full support).

February 7th 1935
We were discussing Germany & the fight for freedom she had put up throughout the ages—thence we went to the French Revolution—thence to the Russian. D. said the Czar had only got his deserts—he had ignored the just pleas of the peasants & had shot them down ruthlessly when they came unarmed to him in 1905. He then told me how when he was at Windsor in 1913, expounding his plans for his land campaign, the King said, 'Why, the agricultural labourer round here gets *14/- a week*', and he repeated '*fourteen*

---

1. Leslie Hore-Belisha (1893–1957): National Liberal M.P.; minister of transport 1934–7; secretary of state for war, 1937–40.

shillings a week.' And the Earl of Leicester, who was standing by, roared with laughter, saying, 'What! 21/- a week for an agricultural labourer! Ha! Ha! Ha!'

D. delighted, though, like everyone else, surprised at the Wavertree result.[1] The Gov. are alarmed, & angry. Everyone wonders what will happen next. Will there be a reconstruction? Will D. be asked to come in? Will opinion harden amongst the Conservatives *against* his being asked? D. thinks for a time they will hold back from asking him—there will be a reaction *against* him.

He is not well. I doubt if he could stand any continuous exertion or excitement. That is why I would rather see him go into the Gov. & do a real job of work than engage in a campaign against them which at the moment is practically a single handed one. But there is no doubt that his political instinct is unerring. He struck at the psychological moment, & has transformed the political situation.

February 15th 1935
Everything quiet down here, & no messages from the political front. D. thinks that the Gov. have decided to bluff the situation, & have made up their minds not to have him in. This means that Neville Chamberlain has won the day. His speech in the House last night was an indication of the Gov. attitude. He proved that trade & unemployment had improved under this Gov., in spite of the fact that this month's unemployment returns are up by 300,000, and that the traffic returns are steadily going down. They mean, it is clear, to go on as they are until the General Election. Their majority enables them to do this. D. says it is the same policy that Balfour followed in the years preceding 1905, when Chamberlain was urging him to go to the country on Tariffs, but Balfour, having his majority in the House did not see the red light in the country. D. says he will go on with his campaign in the country, & keep away from the House of Commons. It means, I fear that Labour will come in next time, but D. says he does not mind that. He will help all he can to help them destroy the Tories. Meanwhile he thinks his persistent campaign will gradually detach a number of the Left Wing Tories.

A letter from the Home Office (Gilmour) announced that the Prince of Wales will *not* go to Carnarvon in May for the Jubilee celebrations, but to Cardiff. This after D. had personally seen Gilmour & begged him to get the P. of W. to favour Carnarvon, the place of his Investiture. The excuse given is that Cardiff is easier of access. But D. will look upon it as a personal affront, & it will be another black mark against H.M. and the P. of W. It is a pity. The P. of W. however was *not* pleased at his last visit to North Wales, which was I believe badly muddled. He used to be very fond of D. We had friendly and amusing times at P. Sassoon's house parties.

---

1. A Conservative seat lost to Labour.

March 3rd 1935

A letter from Ramsay came on Friday [1 March], asking D. to submit his plans for the relief of unemployment. I think *they* think they are calling D.'s bluff, in the hope that the plans he has referred to are mere repetition of the Green & Yellow Books. But if they don't want D. to take charge eventually, they are fools to give him any sort of opening. From now onwards they will perforce be on the run. They have given D. such a chance that with his political flair he will have the situation at his feet. He is immensely pleased, as the letter was entirely unexpected, & came so to speak out of the blue.

Lady Maureen Stanley came down to lunch yesterday with Brendan Bracken. *She* says that her husband & other of the young Tories are desperately anxious that D. should be called in. Stanley of course has got into a dreadful muddle over the Unemployment Regulations. D. hinted to Lady M. that the person who *could* help to further the situation is her father-in-law (Derby) who, so D. reminded her, was his coadjutor when D. became P.M. in 1916. Derby is always friendly disposed towards D. but the trouble is that his will is of the consistency of jelly, and the last person he sees dominates him. D. had tremendous trouble with him in 1917–18 when there was a question of dismissing Robertson & possibly Haig, & Derby was Minister for War. He would agree whole heartedly with D. & go away fortified for action, & then would come back, having seen the others, all his will power gone, & no action having been taken. Still he is a dear, and a great and lovable personality, with no guile of any kind in his make-up, & a winning kindliness and good nature which endears him to everyone—a real gentleman. He is at the moment abroad, but I received a message the other day from Hutch that Derby was anxious to see D. on his return. That was before the recent development, & I do not know whether this will influence the situation at all. There is no doubt that if Derby chose to step in and take a hand, he could bring matters to a head. If he thinks it is his patriotic duty to do so, he will.

March 11th 1935

The Stanleys (Lady Maureen & Oliver) came down to lunch yesterday. She is seized with the ambition, I think, to get D. as her pet lion, & possibly to push her husband's chances as a future Prime Minister. Her mother has Ramsay of course as her tame lion, & the old Lady Londonderry had a regular Zoo. I remember her in the Speaker's Gallery during the debate on D.'s Land Proposals in 1914. She could scarcely contain herself, so great was her indignation while D. was speaking. Her objections were made in a loud tone, which greatly irritated the other occupants of the Gallery, including Violet Bonham Carter, who ordered her angrily to be quiet. Finally the Sergeant-at-Arms mustered up sufficient courage to ask her to refrain from voicing her objections quite so loudly. It was on that occasion that F.E. failed so dismally in his attempt to pick D.'s land policy to pieces. It was a poor speech, with no heart in it, & bitterly disappointed his party, who thought he was going to pulverise D. D. himself was treading on very thin ice in this particular speech as he had been badly briefed on a previous occasion and had used facts which he could not now substantiate. But he cleverly manoeuvred his time so as to leave the challenge on which he was unsound until the last, only to find that no time was left, under the rules of the house, in which to complete his case, which he assured the House, was a devastating one! The House almost howled with rage when they saw how they had been tricked. The speech was a tour de force from this point of view, & F.E.'s poor show added to D.'s triumph. I often think that even at the time F.E.'s affection & esteem for D. possibly cramped his style in attack.

Work is going on furiously in connection with D.'s Memo. which is to be submitted to the Gov. this week. It will be I think a magnum opus, as D. has put all his energy & thought into it, realising that it is an epoch-making document. His industry on such occasions as these is unflagging, and that to my mind is one reason why he is able to get the better of his opponents. It is of course one expression of his almost superhuman energy. The document is being touched up & strengthened & added to, & is going in in a few days. The experts whom he is consulting are very pleased with themselves & at the turn things have taken. D. himself is looking better than he has done for a long time, & younger. I wonder what will come of it all?

The pressure upon the Cabinet by the younger Tories is increasing. They want D.'s help for they sense danger, & according to all accounts the West Norwood bye election is going none too well for them. 'But I don't see why you should pull the chestnuts out of the fire for them', I said to D. 'They are my chestnuts', was his quick reply, '& they are going to put them into the fire for me. Then, if they provide me with the necessary implements, I will help them to pull the chestnuts out.'

D. listened in to a Welsh sermon yesterday by which he was profoundly moved. It was by Philip Jones, one of the old type of preachers whom D. admires so much, & who are able to move their audiences to a pitch of extreme emotion so that they are beside themselves and almost frenzied. It was the same Philip Jones who when D. was Prime Minister kept him talking at breakfast one morning, discussing the old Welsh sermons, so long that J. T. Davies eventually came up to the dining room to say that the Cabinet had assembled and had been waiting ten minutes.

March 17th 1935

A thunderbolt from Germany.[1] It is too soon for anyone to envisage what it all means. D. seems to think that properly and firmly handled, it might lead to a settlement of all the problems of disarmament. Everything depends on what action the French may take. Young Jouvenel, who came down to lunch the other day with the Stanleys, says that the word that is upon all French

---

1. On 16 March 1935 Hitler repudiated the restrictions on armaments imposed on Germany by the treaty of Versailles and announced the introduction of conscription.

lips today is 'Sadowa'. Ominous memory. 1870 & all that led up to it governed French mentality until the war and continues to do so, and the thought that if then they had acted sooner, instead of waiting to let the Germans invade them in 1870, that humiliation would have been spared them, influences them now. 'But what man', asked D., 'if he were given the choice of dying now or ten years hence, would not choose the latter?' D. thinks on the other hand that Hitler is right, & that this position was inevitable since all the European countries around Germany have broken the Treaty of Versailles by adding to their armaments. But logic never governs international situations, & the present one may be perilous.

March 19th 1935
The following letter from Cummings, who spent Sunday [17 March] here, & then went on to Max's for dinner:

'. . . It was an outstanding transition! It was just as if I had been suddenly transported from an atmosphere of wise & sagacious statesmanship into a den of jingoes. The moment I arrived I was assaulted by Garvin who talked furiously without ceasing for half an hour like an inspired war maniac. I hope I replied in kind . . .
P.S. I gave Beaverbrook your messages. He wants to meet you and loves you. *But he is cold about the New Deal.*'

Just as we thought. Though just why he is opposed to the New Deal, we cannot fathom. D. thinks it may be just that Max does not like tall poppies, and must perforce, like Tarquin smite them down. Then again Max has no sympathy with the underdog, & for this reason would not be stirred to enthusiasm for D.'s plans to help the unemployed. Continuing the comparison, D. commented that he had always felt more sympathy for the man who was a failure than for the man who succeeded. 'Caesar, Scipio, for instance, I never felt very drawn by; but Hannibal always secured my sympathy.' (Which after all comes to very much the same thing as Max's reaction. In any case, it isn't strictly true, as D. has an enormous admiration for the great ones of history—Napoleon, for instance—but perhaps because he ended in St. Helena—And J.C. for much the same reason?)

March 24th 1935
Max came over yesterday, very friendly, and in the greatest good spirits. He is right in with the Government who he says intend to have a reconstruction after the Jubilee (probably in July) and an election in the autumn (probably in October). They are going to give Max office (probably the Colonies) and they are going to include D. in their scheme of reconstruction.[1] D. says, 'Not unless they give me my Scheme.' But I think in any case he will be in.

---

1. These were characteristic fantasies. No such offers were ever made. Beaverbrook would have accepted nothing less than Empire Free Trade. He was also attacking the government's foreign policy in the name of Isolation.

Max thinks he is playing the same role as he played with D. in 1916, only this time instead of delivering Bonar Law to D., he will deliver D. to the Government.

D. says that some of the Labour Members are very sick at the rumours that are going round that he is to join the National Gov. Grenfell, a very decent Labour man, tackled D. on the subject in the House of Commons. 'You ought to be with us', said Grenfell. 'I would rather have been with you', replied D. 'But your leaders thought otherwise.' And D. told him about his meetings with Lansbury, etc., & how nothing had come of it & he had been given to understand that Labour did not want him. 'We were never consulted about it', was Grenfell's comment.

April 9th 1935

D. went up to London to lunch with Lothian today. He asked Lothian whether, supposing the Cabinet made an offer to him in connection with his New Deal, he (Lothian) would come in and work with him. Lothian gave D. to understand that he could count on him. D. then told Lothian that he wanted to make it quite clear that under no circumstances would he have anything to do with Samuel, in any development that might take place. Lothian thought this was a pity, but D. stands firm on this point. Lothian then asked what people D. *would* agree to work with. D. said Reading, Crewe or Layton were the sort of people he would like. Lothian thinks the Gov. mean to come to terms with D. Tom Jones also thinks so.

D. also saw Addison, who told him that the Committee of the Labour Party had never turned down D.'s offer of co-operation. It had never been put before them to decide. D. was under the impression that they had discussed it officially & that it had been definitely handed back to him. Lansbury certainly gave him to understand this. Anyhow, it is much too late now for the thing to be reconsidered.

D. joined a deputation of the Welsh Churches to the P.M. to petition for help for the distressed areas of Wales. The Rev. John Roberts made a most telling appeal on behalf of the Welsh miners. He is the son of the man who walked into D.'s office at Portmadoc to offer D. a word of cheer & encouragement when he, at the age of 21, was apprehensive and worried about the future.

Ramsay's attitude seems to have filled everyone with dismay & indignation. One thing he said was that it was not for those who waited on the deputation to paint pictures, but to suggest remedies! Another, that their business was to look after the morals of their people! It was an ill-tempered, almost insane harangue. D. said that it was the speech of a man who was nine-tenth's gaga, & it made him angry that such a man had the affairs of the country in his hands, & was about to represent it at a foreign conference. The House afterwards was teeming with criticism of his speech. It seems to have been an incredible performance.

April 17th 1935

D. returned from Scotland, very pleased with his meetings & not in the least tired. His vitality & resilience are amazing. He regretted his gaffe at the luncheon in honour of a retiring journalist of the Scotsman staff—one Tom Fergusson—whom D. referred to as 'my old friend Tom Robinson.' But D. says that as no one of the 300 present appeared to notice the slip, they were evidently there to do honour to D. & not to Fergusson.

He is very high-spirited at the thought of meeting the Cabinet tomorrow, & not in the least nervous. He talked to Beaverbrook after breakfast on the telephone, & B. thinks the outcome of the meetings will be a break, as they do not mean to offer good enough terms. Moreover Neville is pleased with his Budget & somewhat tête montée & I suppose intransigent as a result. D. also thinks that will be the inevitable outcome, & says he rather hopes he will. He longs for a fight, he says. He says Gladstone was the same. Ostensibly a man of peace, & working for peace, nevertheless when the fight came the Old Man warmed to it. D. said he had a terrible eye even to the last. He & Sam Evans once baited the Old Man in the House of Commons, & he glared across at them in reply. Sam Evans nudged D. & whispered: 'I wish he would take that terrible eye off us.'

D. held forth about the mean mindedness of Liberals as a race. They are frightened of reforms that will mean increased taxes—always have been. He remembers when as a very young boy the news came of the Education Act. A leading local Liberal opposed it, saying it would mean heavier rates. The local Tory agent supported it, saying that the boys of the neighbourhood should be properly educated. D. has never forgotten the difference in attitude of the two men. I cannot understand how D. ever became a Liberal, but for the fact that he would in his then circumstances have had no chance as a Tory. But he is instinctively drawn towards Tories for his friendships, and hates the sanctimonious humbug which seems to characterise the majority of successful Liberals. His great friends have been people like Winston, F.E., Horne, Geddes & Riddell. He always says there are no Liberals who would make a jolly dinner party such as we used to have in the days of the old Coalition.

April 18th 1935

An interesting and, I think, profitable day. We went up early this morning in order that D. should be at the House by 11.0 for his meeting with the Cabinet. He was in excellent form and spirits, not in the least nervous. It appears that they were all friendly in manner towards him, with the exception of Runciman, who barely acknowledged D.'s greeting. J. H. Thomas very friendly, & anxious to allow D. to have his way in the matter of seeing the Ministers of the Departments concerned individually, Ramsay deprecating Thomas's friendliness to the suggestion in an impatient aside. Neville, to D.'s great surprise, very friendly & propitiating. S.B. not taking much part in the discussion, but by his manner friendly.

This afternoon D. held a miniature Cabinet in his *own* room, the various Ministers coming in turn & receiving instructions from him as to what he required of them. It was really amusing. 'Hullo Godfrey', said Hore Belisha to Godfrey Collins as the latter came out, 'Have you passed your exam? How many marks have you got?'

D. says that on the whole the impression he got from today's meeting is that they want to make terms with him, but that of course they want to get as cheap terms as possible. D. is to meet them again the week after next.

April 21st 1935

We listened in to the St. John Passion music; grand, & so comforting & satisfying. D. reminded me of the Good Friday in March 1918 when the reports from the front were so bad, & the Germans had driven the Portuguese back in the North. It looked as though the enemy might really reach the seaports. D. & Hankey went off to St. Anne's Soho to hear the passion music, & on entering during the service the first words D. heard were: 'O Lord, make haste to save us.' He thought they were singularly appropriate & fervently endorsed them. When they got back to Downing St. they found the news much better. Plumer had succeeded in holding the Germans.

April 23rd 1935

Very busy this week, D. furbishing up his apparatus for the Cabinet meetings on Monday & Tuesday next [29 & 30 April]. He is very happy—très content —& in better form than I have seen him for a very long time. The H. A. L. Fishers to dinner last night—he looking handsome & distinguished, & also more happy than he has for a long time, owing to the success of his History. He & D. talked of the state of Europe, the prospect of war, & the conversation turned on the Peace Conference, when the Allies took, to their misfortune, the word of Beneš (the little French Jackal, as D. always calls him) as against that of Apponyi.[1] H. A. L. Fisher then called to D.'s mind the Conference of the B.E. Delegates at the Rue Nitôt summoned to consider the position after Brockdorff Rantzau had sent in his protest. 'It was the fairest and most impartial conference that ever deliberated, and the most creditable', said D. All the Dominion representatives were there, including Botha. H. A. L. Fisher recalled that when Botha was asked for his contribution, all he remarked was, with a beautiful smile, 'It is the 17th Anniversary of the Treaty of Vereeniging, as my friend here well knows', & he patted Milner, who was sitting beside him, on the knee.[2]

April 27th 1935

D. went up to town last night to Lord Birkenhead's dinner to his friends on the eve of his marriage. Rothermere was there. R. has had a series of articles in the D. Mail this week against a general election, saying that no recon-

---

1. Representatives respectively of Czechoslovakia and Hungary at the peace conference.
2. The treaty of Vereeniging ended the Boer war. Milner was the British representative.

structed Gov. wd. be any better than this one, as there was no personality of
outstanding capacity who could be included. This D. takes as a direct insult
to himself. It may indeed be intended as such, being Rothermere's riposte to
D.'s ignoring of his letter & his terms. R. & one other were there when D.
arrived, & D. shook Rothermere by the hand with a casual, 'How do you do?'
apparently not even glancing at him, & passed on to the other man. He did
not look at or speak to Rothermere for the rest of the evening. He (D.), must
have discussed the position with Winston, for the latter said to him: 'I should
make it up, if I were you. He is a good enough fellow.' To which D. replied
that it was not a question of making up, but simply that he had never been
bullied by anyone & that he was not going to eat corn for Rothermere. There
is no disguising the fact that Rothermere has been extremely insolent to D. &
that D. resented it, & I imagine that last night's incident carried things a stage
further.

The Gov., so D. says, are very cock-a-hoop on account of the success of
Neville's Budget, & moreover Ramsay has come back from Stresa very tête
montée.[1] D. thinks he will find that their attitude towards him will have
hardened when he meets them on Monday [29 April] again. He still says it
would suit him better in the long run if they rejected his proposals, but I still
think this is chiefly self-delusion in an effort to prepare himself against a
possible blow—'holding out his arm to shield his head'.

May 4th 1935
No definite news yet. The Gov. still appear to be attaching importance to
D.'s proposals, but now he begins to suspect that they are keeping him on the
end of a string, & that their game is to keep his hands tied while they prepare
for an election. They do not know their Ll.G. though. He is already thinking
out a plan of opposition campaign, & an organisation, the result of which
would be the bringing down of the Gov. majority so that they would be
impotent after the election. Rothermere in the meantime blows hot and cold,
and with true Harmsworth megalomania gives away offices, first to one, then
to another. One day Beaverbrook is Colonial Minister, the next day he is
nothing, but D. is made Minister of Munitions!

We talked tonight with Cara Copland[2] about Margot & her indiscretions.
D. told us how she wrote him a most offensive letter in 1910, saying that his
policy was losing Liberal seats, & ruining the Party. D. sent her a stinger in
return, saying that if she could hear what people said about her she would
realise that it was she who was doing her best to ruin her husband & the
Liberal Party. He said it was as brutal a letter as ever woman could have had
written her. But she put his back up by her insolence. As a matter of fact, he
said, it was he who saved the Party at that time. They were losing bye-

---

1. The international conference which set up the Stresa Front of France, Great Britain
and Italy to preserve the existing treaty settlement.
2. A relative of Mr. Asquith's and a friend of Beaverbrook's.

election after bye-election, & Bonar Law said to him: 'You won't get 50 seats at the next election.' D. by his Budget changed the whole venue of the political situation.

May 10th 1935

We came back to Churt today after the Jubilee festivities. D. however has to return to London tonight, as the Prince of Wales insisted that he should go down to Cardiff tomorrow, & brought the King in at the State Banquet last night to bring pressure to bear on D. The King said the P. of W. was representing him & he hoped D. would go, & the P. of W. said he would take D. down on his private train, so there was no getting out of it. The King was most charming to D. in his audience last night. He thanked D. for the article he had written in The Sunday Pictorial. D. said it represented his true feelings about the King—his admiration for the courage he had displayed in very difficult times. 'For after all, Sir, you have been through most anxious and arduous times'. 'Yes', replied His Majesty, 'I never expected to have all these responsibilities. After all, I was only the second, & never expected to become King.' 'If you will pardon my saying so, Sir', said D., 'it was a merciful intervention of Providence that stepped in & made you King.' The King was very moved. They then spoke of the international situation and the possibility of war. D. said he hoped His Majesty would not listen to the warmongers like Mussolini. H.M. fired up and broke out vehemently, 'And I *will* not have another war. I *will* not. The last war was none of my doing, & if there is another one & we are threatened with being brought in to it, I will go to Trafalgar Square and wave a red flag myself sooner than allow this country to be brought in.' D. says it was a most extraordinary outburst. H.M. asked D. to go to his private apartment & hear his pipers & wrote down the names of the tunes they played. D. says everyone there was most charming to him— even Lady Londonderry!

D. had seen (Lord) Lloyd earlier in the day, who said that there will certainly be a reconstruction in July and that D. will certainly be included. From the fuss everyone has made of D. at the functions this week it looks as though there may be some truth in it!

Cromer informed D. that he had worn the wrong uniform at St. Paul's on Monday (this after a most unholy fuss about it, & all because Dame M. sat on the invitations, which indicated which uniforms should be worn, in case they should be taken away from her & she not allowed to go!). D. therefore took care to broach the subject first to H.M., who laughed it off, but admitted that he had spotted it, 'I saw it in the photograph in The Daily Mirror', he said.

May 18th 1935

D. had a long chat with Tom Jones,[1] & said a number of things which he

---

1. Tom Jones, formerly deputy secretary to the cabinet and an inveterate political busybody. His account is in Thomas Jones, A Diary with Letters, pp. 145–8.

wished passed on to Baldwin, to bring matters to a head. They are explained in the letter which T.J. subsequently wrote. D. thinks that at the next meeting they will show their hand & probably break off negotiations. But to my mind they can do nothing with him even if they want to until they have made up their minds what they are going to do with each other—and at present they are in a hopeless confusion as to who is going to resign, who is to go to the Foreign Office, etc. Meanwhile D. gets extremely impatient and somewhat irritable. He plans a meeting with heads of Nonconformists to arrange a campaign.

May 23rd 1935

D. just gone off to the Cabinet. He dined last night with Tom Jones, who says Baldwin intends to try to buy off D. by offering a post to Gwilym. Of course Gwilym will not be allowed to take it even if he wanted to. D. says that is what Balfour did to Chamberlain—gave Austen Cabinet Office to buy off his father, who never recovered from it. D. has gone to Downing Street in a very truculent mood. If this state of things goes on much longer he will burst—or someone else will.

Later

D. returned well pleased with his interview. He thinks T.J.'s letter must have had an effect on Baldwin, who was most pleasant and even ingratiating. D. has now got Macmillan (Harold) to support him in his industrial schemes.

Later

D. had an unpleasant conversation on the telephone with Macmillan, who said he had not understood that D. was putting him forward as one of his experts, that he certainly was not that in any sense, that all his proposals were independent proposals & that he imagined that they were being put forward as such—in fact, he conveyed in great heat that he thought D. had let him down. D. retorted that if that was the way he regarded things he had better act by himself. I wish D. would not lose his temper so easily when confronted with any sort of difference of opinion. I fear that his quarrelsomeness is doing him great harm—he has already told Jim Thomas off at one of the meetings.

July 1st 1935

The Council of Action has been initiated, & D. has burnt his boats (I think) so far as this National Gov. is concerned. The last meeting of D. & the Cab. Committee was rather a grim one, most polite and studiously pleasant, 'But', said D. to me, 'they knew in their hearts they were about to knife me. What they did not know was that I too had a dagger in my sheath for them.' He was referring to his plans for the Council of Action, but I am fearful lest he is relying too much on those Free Churchmen. Francis Brett Young, who came to see us, is melancholy at what D. is doing. He says if only he had waited, Baldwin & he would certainly have been able to come to terms and work together, but that now a breach has been created which cannot be spanned.

D. himself is I think a little unhappy about the whole situation, and says alternately (1) that he is glad of the break, that he never wanted to work with the Government and that he will smash them ultimately; and (2) that he and Baldwin will probably be able to come to terms after the election. And in the meantime this somewhat comic convention has been summoned and forces itself upon a somewhat inhospitable world tomorrow. D. goes so far as to say that if he sees that the Free Churches won't fight, he will throw up the whole thing. But I know him too well to believe that he will give up any idea once he has started on it, & that the more opposition he receives the more determined he will be to force the thing through.

July 13th 1935

Went up to hear D. speak on the Foreign Affairs debate on Thursday [11 July]. He made an excellent speech, of the attacking order, & was in great form, but rather spoilt the effect by a stupid passage of arms with Austen [Chamberlain], in which, to my mind Austen behaved with dignity & D. with a certain lack of dignity. I found it painful and was sorry, but we can at least say that the incident was redeemed by D. offering Austen a complete apology which was welcomed very graciously.

D. & Austen have never been close friends, although A. was always one of the most loyal of D.'s colleagues & identified himself with all that D. stood for when P.M. I remember most vividly the day of the Carlton Club meeting in Oct. 1922, when we waited for the news of the proceedings. I sat in the Cabinet room with D., who was very quiet, and talked to him of anything but the thing we were both thinking of. Then a telephone message came to say that the vote had gone against D., & almost immediately Austen burst into the Cabinet room, more agitated than I have ever seen him & exclaimed, 'Well, we must resign. We are beaten.' I slipped out of the room & left them to make their plans for speedy action. The dreary time that followed I try to forget—the long stream of scarcely courteous notes of resignation from the disloyal Tory Ministers—the quick evacuation from Downing Street—the losing fight of the election. D. sitting distrait in an uncomfortable armchair in Ned Grigg's uncomfortable house which he lent to D. (at 16 guineas a week) until D. could find a permanent home. Then the journey south to the sun at Algeciras at Xmas, & D.'s spirits revived by the extreme courtesy and interest of everyone abroad (to whom he has always been Lloyd George, whether P.M. or not). But never once did I imagine that he would be in the wilderness for 13 years at least. When D. said 'Ten' in 1922 I laughed & did not believe him or think that he meant it.

The Council of Action, though successfully begotten with a certain amount of travail, is scarcely yet a robust infant, and has I fear a stormy future.

July 16th 1935

A happy day. D. pleased with the tremendous publicity accorded to his 'new deal' proposals. Even the opposition papers give him long leading articles, though they turn it down with thick-skinned & paradoxical inconsistency on the grounds (a) that his proposals are far too costly & would ruin the poor taxpayer and (in the same para.) (b) that the Gov. are already doing what D. proposes. The one thing they are unable to do is to ignore D. apparently!

July 17th 1935

D. discussed today the prospects at the General Election. He calculates that if we come to no arrangement with Labour, Labour may win 275 seats, on the analogy of the 1929 election. If then the Liberals have only 20, that would give the Government a majority of only 25 to carry on with, which would make things impossible for them after a very short time. If on the other hand Labour win 290, and we win 40, then the Gov. would be defeated. But in that case, even by combining forces with Labour, we should not have a sufficient majority to carry on a vigorous policy. 'Under those circumstances', said D., 'I would form a Government with Lansbury as nominal Prime Minister, but retaining the active leadership for myself. I would then proceed to formulate a devastating progressive programme, & go to the country again immediately upon it with a terrific campaign, & return with a majority of 150.' I believe he could do it, too. But in the meantime I feel he ought not to play about with the Harold Macmillans, who would not be in on a programme of that kind. 'They won't even be returned to Parliament next time', said D. No, but D. must lay his plans *before* the election, & with a Council of Action tied to his tail!

July 22nd 1935

The papers (morning & evening) full of D.—the Gov.'s reply to the New Deal, & D.'s reply to them. Tonight we went to see the Paramount Film of him & the farm at Churt—first rate. But he had to undergo a heavy fire in the House this afternoon, from Eyres Monsell,[1] on account of his statement regarding submarines & the naval agreement. Either Gerothwohl misled D., or Eyres Monsell lied. But D. stood up to E.M., who sat down very much rattled, his urbanity disappeared. But of course he had 400 cheering Tories behind him, which is not pleasant for D. He voted in the Opposition Lobby, & Rhys Davies, on seeing him there, said 'Well, have you thrown away the scabbard?' Seymour Cocks, another Socialist member who was standing near, said: 'There never was one.'

July 24th 1935

Distressed Areas Debate in the House. D. went up with speech fully & carefully prepared, & intending to speak, & left without having done so. He went up to the Speaker after Mannering[2] (the Rhondda Member, who made a most moving & eloquent speech) sat down, & asked him whether it would not be better to leave the Debate to the Members who actually represented Distressed Areas. The Speaker demurred: 'I would like to change the bowling a

1. First Lord of the Admiralty.
2. Correctly, W. H. Mainwaring.

little', he said. However, D. finally put his notes in his pockets & went out, much to everyone's disappointment. Much comment in the papers today about it, & D. himself a little uneasy. My own opinion is that he decided not to try to compete with Mannering's masterly appeal.

July 29th 1935
Had a pleasant weekend, with Tom Jones & Burbidge among others as guests at Bron-y-de. T.J. very worried about D.'s new campaign. He says it has destroyed the chance of co-operation with Baldwin which was still possible in spite of his turning down of the 'New Deal'. S.B.'s idea was, according to T.J., to wait until he had been P.M. for some little while, in the hope that, once he had the supreme power, he would be able to influence his colleagues to take in D. He thought that D. would be prepared to wait in patience, but he little knew his Ll.G.! Now, says T.J., D. has destroyed everything by his new move, & S.B. is angry thinking D. is out to wreck. 'That is precisely what I am out for', said D. when T.J. told him this. T.J. unhappy about D.'s own prospects, for he does not consider his new campaign has much chance of any great success. Personally I am inclined to agree with him.

We had great fun, however, talking over the old days especially the events of the Peace Conference—at which T.J. was present. We teased him about his interview with Mussolini at Cannes. M. came as editor of the Popolo d'Italia asking for an interview with D., but T.J. turned him down on the grounds that D. would not give an interview to the Editor of a Socialist Journal while the Italian P.M. was sitting in Conference with him. T.J. took M. out to dinner, but was not greatly impressed. D. says he knew nothing about M.'s request for an interview, but he probably did.

July 30th 1935
Message from John Simon, who is busy about the Speaker's seat. D. did not agree with his suggestion & sent a message to this effect. Late in the day Simon sent word that he & the P.M. agree that D. was right, & had withdrawn the question which had been put down for tomorrow on the subject.

D. says he feels that Fitzroy has always been fair, & fair to the weaker parties in the House, & for this reason D. will do all he can to assist in making his seat safe, but that Simon's proposal would simply have had the effect of precipitating a dog-fight. D. loathed Whitley, whom he considered to be partial to the detriment of his own party. When the Liberals were under the weather during Whitley's Speakership, W. made things harder for them by his partiality to the Tories, & D. never forgave him for the snubs he inflicted upon the party & upon D. personally. Whitley came down here after he had resigned the post, D. thinks to try to make amends, but although D. treated him with scrupulous courtesy, ('as I did Jowitt when he came here to tell me he had betrayed me') yet he regarded him as a traitor. He did not even attend Whitley's funeral.

A string of 'regrets' in tonight's bag from people who had promised to support D.'s Council of Action but who are now crying off & do not want to attend a wedding feast which looks like being a frost. D. however is not daunted & continues preparing his plans. He is confident that he is going to smash the power of the National Gov. at the election.

August 4th 1935

The H. A. L. Fishers to dinner last night, Mary[1] having just secured a first in Greats, & the whole family very jubilant. The talk naturally turned on Abyssinia,[2] & Fisher asked D. what *he* would do if he were in power now. D. replied that first of all, he did not think that he would have allowed things to drift into their present impossible position, i.e. he would have insisted on the League taking a stronger line with Japan, in the first place. The moment they abandoned their authority in that question it was practically impossible for them to deal with any other dispute. However, things being as they are, he would see that an enormous amount of equipment & ammunition were supplied to the Abyssinians, which would enable them to put up a good fight. He says he feels sure that that is what Palmerston would have done.

An American business man who had also come to dinner rather surprised us by backing up Mussolini. 'After all', he argued, 'if this had happened a few (sic) years ago, no one would have taken any notice. All of you other European countries have done the same as Mussolini from time to time. The only difference is that M. says quite frankly that he is attacking Abyssinia because he *wants* it, whereas Gt. Britain for instance pretended that she was doing it for the good of the people whose land she proposed to annex.'

Discussion as to how far the French Press is being subsidised by the Italian Gov. in order to support their policy and decry us for opposing it. D. said that Clemenceau told him at the Peace Conference that practically the whole of the French Press was bought by one country or another who wished to obtain support upon any particular issue. One of the reasons why Britain was attacked so fiercely and so continuously during the whole of that time (and since) was because we scorned to stoop to those methods. I suggested that as between subsiding French papers with money to secure a particular object, & subsidising the Abyssinians with arms for a similar end, I did not think there was much to choose. Which remark was not very popular.

August 12th 1935

A long session with H. Macmillan, Lord Allen, Layton, etc., on the possibility of getting a joint policy out of the two documents 'Five Years', & 'Organising Prosperity' (Macmillan very sticky at first—and very nearly not wanting to play, as the Press had somehow got wind of the Conference beforehand). Allen very difficult & pernicketty, until D. lost his temper & taunted them with being cowards. In reply to Allen's suggesting that all the candidates

---

1. Daughter of Mr. and Mrs. Fisher.
2. Italy was preparing to attack Abyssinia and did so in October.

should be purely Lloyd George candidates, D. said, 'I've had enough of this. At the first dinner I had with you all you suggested that I should go first into the jungle, & when the tigers had finished mauling me you would come cautiously after.'

Later, when one of them tentatively suggested that what they were afraid of was that the movement should become a Lloyd George one, D. suggested that there was an easy way out of that difficulty. 'I will withdraw altogether from it, and you can run the thing yourselves. I ask for nothing better. I will have nothing to do with the campaign, and will retire to my own constituency & occupy myself with that.' But this did not seem to suit them either.

However, he is meeting them again on Wednesday [14 August].

If anyone doubts D.'s industry, let them see the notes he made for his Eisteddfod speech—three separate careful drafts.

August 16th 1935

A trilogy of tragedies—poor Gareth Jones, Basil Blackett, and now Will Rogers. The last had become a great friend of D. under the auspices of Nancy Astor, and visited D. when in England. On one occasion he was present at a Debate in the House when D. delivered his 'Kyabram' speech, poking fun at Beaverbrook. Marjoribanks, who was championing the Beaverbrook cause of Empire Free Trade, made fun of the Liberal Party and the divisions in it. 'In the Liberal Party there are many mansions', he jibed, & D. in his reply, retorted, 'And in the Conservative Party there are many flats.' Will Rogers was hugely pleased with this 'mot'. 'I wish I had said that', he said to D. afterwards.

Just returned to Churt after 3 days of very hard work on the part of D. in London, including a speech to the leaders of the T.Us., which was very subtle and a great success. The Gov. will soon begin to realise that D. is gingering up all sections which may do them harm at the next election, & probably when they have at last woken up to the fact, they will decide to hurry on the election.

Lothian came in this morning, & enquired what were D.'s movements in the immediate future. I told him he was going down to Wales next weekend for a preaching meeting. 'He's going to be holy', said L. 'And I suppose have an outburst afterwards, like all the revivalists.'

We dined on Wednesday evening [14 August] with Mottistone at Prunier's. D. & Mottistone recalled the old days, when they were Members of a group of Liberals that included Winston, Masterman, Elibank, Reading. M. reminded D. of how they dined night after night at the Café Royal while the C.-B. Government was being formed, & how one after another of their number disappeared as he was summoned to be a Minister, Mottistone's story is that D. was the first to be called.

August 21st 1935

D. went up today to the Foreign Office to talk with Hoare & Eden on the situation.[1] (Great sensation in the evening papers—'Ll.G. called to the F.O.', etc.) He told Hoare that he did not think that we were in a strong enough position morally to lecture Italy, seeing that even since the war we had added one million square miles of the earth's surface to the 12,000,000 we already ruled over. In any case we could not act alone. Hoare thought there was a chance of France joining with us in taking sanctions against Italy, but D. is doubtful of this. Eden said that Laval did not seem ever to have read the Covenant of the League of Nations!

We lunched at Pruniers, & went into see Emlyn Williams in his play, Night Must Fall. A marvellous piece of acting, & study of Welsh psychology.

August 28th 1935

D.'s Nonconformist friends are running away again from the Council of Action—D. saw some of them (Scott Lidgett & S. Hughes) in Wales on Monday, and last evening, no sooner had he arrived back at Churt, than Hughes rang up & said he *must* see D. that night. D. was furious, knowing that it meant that Hughes had gone back *again* on his agreement of the previous day. When Hughes came, bringing Wilson Black with him, D. turned on them and rent them [sic]. 'Gideon knew how to distinguish between the funks and the brave men', he said. 'I wish someone would give me that power.' 'He only had 300 left at the finish', said Hughes. '*But he won*', retorted D. The interview was extremely unpleasant, & D. was considerably upset by it. I *wish* he had not embarked upon this enterprise. I almost wrote this folly. It seems to me to be the most complete muddle, & scarcely anyone believing in it. The only thing that reassures me is that Lothian is taking a keen interest in it. He has just written an excellent memo. on the Peace—? or War—situation. His clear statement of the position however makes me realise how hopeless it seems to be. D. had another letter from Hoare today—quite hopeless & helpless. Snowden whom I went to see on Sunday, was livid at the feebleness of the Gov. in such a crisis. He is all for strong action with the French if possible—if not, without. It is amazing how he has recovered from his operation. All the lines of pain have disappeared from his face. She however looks sad and restless, & seems to be neglecting him for social activities which seem to me to be quite unnecessary. I am coming back to my original estimate of her—a hard, ambitious, clever—and now disappointed—woman. After having been up in London all the summer—rushing down to Churt for a bare weekend—she is now off to Switzerland for 3 weeks, leaving the old boy alone except for an elderly companion-nurse, and incompetent domestics.

September 3rd 1935

Lunched with Lothian & D. at Prunier's. L. in an agitated state of mind as to the international possibilities. Not one of our Cabinet at their post—all on

---

1. Sir Samuel Hoare was now foreign secretary, and Anthony Eden was minister without portfolio for League of Nations affairs.

holiday, except the Foreign Secretary, who is ill in bed. (D. thinks as a result of his failure to carry his policy of raising the embargo through the Cabinet). Lothian went on to say that we were utterly unprepared should there be any outbreak, either military or naval. He had seen the Secretary to the Admiralty (on holiday in Scotland) yesterday, & he had admitted that if there were an outbreak in the Mediterranean our naval base would have to be Devonport, as we were unprepared for anything else. 'What I want to see', said L., 'is the whole place bristling with arms.' 'What I would like to see', retorted D., 'is Abyssinia bristling with British arms.'

There is certainly a war scare on in London. D. & I walked from the dentist in Grosvenor Street to St. James's (D. twice nearly run over as he stepped unconcernedly into the road) & in that short distance, 3 separate people, entire strangers, had come up to D. & asked him if he thought there was going to be a war.

September 9th 1935
Left for Freudenstadt. *Very* tired and right at the end of my tether. D. very busy preparing for his several meetings in connection with the C. of A. In very good form & extremely optimistic. He is always happy in action. It is doing nothing & marking time that bothers him.

September 22nd 1935
Returned yesterday—a most interesting if somewhat uneventful holiday. Germany today is rather terrifying in her quiet and earnest preoccupation. Feel my holiday was not long enough, as I spent the first 2 days in travelling & the next 2 in bed with a temperature.

September 26th 1935
Went to Bristol yesterday with D. who made a first rate speech, almost entirely on the international situation. His reconstruction campaign has unfortunately been almost killed by Abyssinia. D. yesterday spoke his mind, & came down in favour of action by Britain, in co-operation with other European powers, but without France if she did not wish to come in. I anticipated his having to seek police protection against possible Italian assailants after this speech, but today comes an invitation, slightly reminiscent of Borgia methods, from the Italian Ambassador, asking him to lunch at the Italian Embassy tomorrow, in company with Lothian.

D. looking I think rather tired, & his temper is not of the best. He is feeling the reaction no doubt after his month of meetings, & Bristol being the last, he unconsciously feels a flop. I cannot make up my mind how far the Council of Action campaign is making an impression, apart from D. Everything will ultimately depend I expect on how the Gov. handle the foreign situation. D. receives hosts of suggestions from people who imagine they could settle it if given the opportunity. One gentleman suggests persuading Abyssinia to become part of the British Empire, & then Italy would have to leave her alone.

D. at dinner however very happy, & entertained us with stories of his childhood, how it really belonged to another civilisation, when most of one's travelling was done by coach, and ballads were sold in the markets and fairs which took the place of newspapers.

September 27th 1935
D. returned from London very pleased with his interview with Grandi.[1] They talked first of all on art, about which D. confessed he knew nothing save whether he liked a thing or not. Grandi said after all this was the ultimate test (I don't quite agree). Then they talked about the war, and finally about the present crisis. Grandi said that Mussolini was a great admirer of D., and had had every utterance of D.'s sent him during the last 3 years. 'And now that you have turned against him', said Grandi, 'he still wants to be kept informed as to what you are saying. He says you are the only person who understands him.'

It was agreed that it would be extremely difficult for Mussolini now to turn back. D. said that if he had had authority he would have suggested giving Italy some of the German Colonies and bringing the Germans themselves into the deal. 'You could have your whack and they could have theirs', said D. Grandi said that if the Italians thought they could have got that, they would not have proceeded in their war preparations. And he thought that such a possibility might influence them even now. 'But in any case', advised D., 'don't go on once you have reached Addis Ababa. And don't bomb villages, & women & children.'

Grandi said that as early as January last Mussolini had made his intentions known to Laval, who must have, & did in fact pass them on to Simon. Moreover, Mussolini had 'made his arrangements' with the French. Grandi hinted that this meant some agreement by which the French had been able to remove garrisons from the Italian frontier. 'We have made our bargain', said Grandi.

D. assured Grandi constantly that the British were sympathetic to Italy's claim for expansion.

October 11th 1935
A general election now almost certain to take place next month. D. dispirited & discouraged. It has come far too early for him. 'I feel like the Abyssinians must be feeling', he said to me, 'knowing that all the guns and ammunitions are with the other side—and the poison gas, too.'

He puts the Labour figures still at 275. Nathan who came in this morning says the Labour Party itself only hopes for something between 150 & 225.

October 23rd 1935
House met yesterday. D. attended reluctantly. He is out of heart at the Gov.

---

1. The Italian ambassador.

election changes, & realises that the Gov. have torpedoed his plans, probably deliberately. He will speak today, however, & put questions to Hoare, asking for information on various points on which the public have been kept in the dark, notably the negotiations which are now obviously going on as regards mutual help by the 'sanctioning' countries. He does not expect to get much sympathy or support.

He ran into Ramsay in the House, & scarcely knew him, he was looking so changed & ill. Ramsay told him that he was feeling bad, & that he began sentences & forgot what he had been going to say. 'You have never had that, have you?' he asked D. twice, almost appealingly. And D. said he realised too late that Ramsay hoped to be reassured by D. saying that he too had suffered from the same disability. D. says it is pitiful to see the present condition of the man who four years ago was so full of insolence & power. Now he is obviously treated by his colleagues with indifference and contempt.

There have been many attempts to bring D. & Samuel together for the election, but up till last night they had failed. But last night Reith telephoned to say that Samuel had offered to give D. one of the Liberal broadcasting dates, & would D. see Samuel & arrange it. So D. took the bull by the horns & sought out Samuel in the House & they dined together.

D. wants Samuel to make a statement before polling day, advising Liberals, in constituencies where there is no Liberal candidate, to vote for the candidate who supports the Council of Action questionnaire. Samuel sticky, but will see what he can do and let D. know.

November 17th 1935

Election over & results out & D. returned to Bron-y-de, not one atom the worse for his strenuous campaign, in which he virtually won three seats—his own & those of Megan & Gwilym. The Gov. large majority is no more than I had expected, or at least not very different.[1] D. nevertheless in good spirits & thinking already of organisation for the future. His resilience is amazing. He is pleased with the Welsh results—sorry that one or two did not get in who might have done had they not clung to the fetish of Free Trade. One of them he advised to leave free trade alone. 'I must stick to my principles', was the reply. 'Do you want to get to heaven or to Westminster?' was D.'s slightly cynical retort.

Waiting for the results to come in, & hearing one after another of Gov. victories—or rather 'No Change'—I could not help thinking of that other election under such different circumstances—when the Gov. victories first of all elated, & then frightened us—the victory of D.'s government in 1918. We were gathered together in my room in Downing Street, & as defeat after defeat came in to us from the Whip Room, D. became very quiet. 'I did not want this.' He was wise enough to realise that such a huge majority would have a serious reaction later on. Moreover, it placed him very much in the

1. Conservatives and their associates 432, Labour 154, Liberals 21, I.L.P. 4.

hands of the Tories. When the news of Asquith's defeat came he was genuinely upset.

Last night at dinner, arising out of a discussion on food, & fish in particular, D. said: 'I attribute the downfall of the Liberal Party to an oyster.' He went on to explain that Percy Illingworth[1] died of typhoid caused by a bad oyster. Had he lived, he would never have allowed the rift between D. & Asquith to take place. He would have brought them together, patched the quarrel up, cursed them & saved the Liberal party. He would have held up to the light the intrigues of McKenna & Runciman, whom he knew well. After his death, there was no one who could take his place, & could put the party before persons & personalities. Gulland, the Chief Whip in 1916 did nothing. Long after, D. told Asquith that Gulland never came near him at that time to see if anything could be done. 'You may not believe me', was A.'s reply, 'but he never came near me either.'

November 18th 1935
A *very* quiet weekend. Not a single telephone call for D. from any political source, newspaper or otherwise. One would say that he had suffered a total eclipse. But he is already busy with plans for the future. Today had a conference of the Council of Action H.Q. Staff & tomorrow a meeting of Area Heads. He means to go on with it & is very cheerful. It gives him a semblance of activity & so long as he has this he will be happy. He is already making arrangements to cover the next two years, & it is more than a possibility that at the end of that time he will have become again a political force.

At dinner last night Muriel mentioned James Hilton, & said that his philosophy of life was marred by his extreme pacifism. 'You forget', said D., 'that the greatest philosopher of all (meaning J.C.) was also the greatest pacifist— that is, he would have been regarded as a philosopher if they had not made a religion of him.'

Strangely enough, the subject of might v. right came up again at dinner tonight. D. recalled Clemenceau's retort to President Wilson, when the latter pleaded the potency of right against might. '*Might* is right', he asserted. D. went on to talk of Clemenceau, how he revealed at times strange inconsistencies. He expressed a doubt, for instance, as to whether the Revolution had been good for France. 'It destroyed', he said, 'a great part of the cultured aristocracy, and it brutalised France.'

---

1. Percy Illingworth, who died in 1915, was Liberal chief whip from 1912 to 1915.

Diary 1936

April 9th 1936

Discussed with D. his successes in the House—2 excellent speeches, received with praise in many unexpected quarters. His articles also have attracted much notice & support. I told him I thought if he so wished, he could lead a successful attack on the Gov. & perhaps get them down. He says he does not wish to do so—would not take office if it were offered him now. I said, why not, provided it did not mean too strenuous work, & that this was understood. He said he could not undertake anything unless he flung himself wholeheartedly into it, he was constitutionally incapable of doing a job without using his whole strength to it. 'I could not do as Balfour did, for instance', he said, 'saunter down to the office at 11.30 & then play games in the afternoon, & only half understand what was going on.' He went on to tell me of what had been instilled into him when a boy, first by his uncle, then by one of the solicitors into whose office he went, that the work to hand must be thoroughly done, whatever it happened to be. The *habit of work* had been instilled into him in those early days, & it was impossible for him now to get away from it. When he was articled to Breese Jones & Casson at Portmadoc, it was Casson who told him to apply himself to the *work*. 'You may find it to be only licking stamps, at first, or taking letters to the post, or turning the duplicating press; but you will find yourself in this way learning the *habit of work*, and when the more important things come along, you will be ready for them'. D. said there was another clerk articled in the same office at the same time as he—the son of a Carnarvonshire squire. This man disdained the little jobs that the articled clerks were expected to do. He did not form the habit of work, but acquired other habits instead, including drink, & he never came to anything. It sounds like a moral story from a Sunday school book, but it happens to be quite true. Even now D. cannot half do a job, but if anything he does it too thoroughly, as those around him know to their cost!

He is thinking of writing an article on Baldwin, entitled 'Tomlinson'—after Kipling's Poem—the story of the man who was fit for neither heaven nor hell.

April 27th 1936

Basil Liddell Hart looked in today. He is vetting the military part of Vols. V & VI which are now ready in a rough state. He quoted Lawrence (of Arabia) as saying that D. was the only man he knew who could dominate Winston. He said that Winston with D. was a completely different person from Winston with anyone else. D.'s power over Winston was very obvious at Marrakech, when D. intervened more than once to allay a quarrel between Winston & Randolph, on the subject of the Ross candidature. Winston was—and is—very anxious to appear favourably in the eyes of this Gov. as long as there is a possibility of his securing a job, & he was very wrath with Randolph for queering his pitch by standing as an anti-Gov. candidate.

D. & I discussed Parnell today, à propos of a play now being acted in London. D. told me how he saw him come into the House after his disgrace, erect & defiant, amidst a dead silence, with everyone shunning him. And how Jacob Bright, the Quaker, stainless of character, & ultra-respectable, got up from his seat behind the Gov. benches, and went over & sat down by Parnell, shook hands with him & chatted with him. D. said that one day when William Parry was in the Gallery, he (D.) asked Parnell if he could introduce him to a Welshman who was an admirer of his. 'Ah!' said Parnell, 'I did not know I had any friends left in Wales.' The Welsh Liberals all took the side of Gladstone in the controversy. D. says that Parnell's great mistake was not to resign the leadership of the Irish Party before the divorce. D. is very anti-Kitty O'Shea. But he is always inclined to blame the woman when it is a question of a man choosing her & his career—he is always for the immolation of the woman.

He says that the suggestion in the play, that Gladstone was actuated by mean motives, is grossly unfair. He says that it was Morley, who was at that time himself living with a woman to whom he was not married, who persuaded Gladstone that he would not be able to carry the Nonconformist vote if Parnell remained as Leader of the Irish Party. In any case, G. was never a mean figure, but grand & terrifying, even at the age of 80.

D. admits that Gladstone did *not* care about the condition of the poor. Home Rule, nationality, & such large issues appealed to him, but he did not care how the poor lived or what were their injustices. Joe Chamberlain on the other hand did, & D. and he had much in common for this reason.

May 30th 1936

D. spoke today of his 1909 Budget & his difficulty in carrying his revolutionary taxes through the Cabinet. He said by far the most difficult fight he had was in the Cabinet, not in the country. Harcourt was the most inveterate in obstructing his proposals, while posing all the time as an ardent Radical. Crewe, while not liking them, said very little, Grey said nothing. But at heart they were all against him. Chalmers, then the Head of the Treasury, walked up to the Cabinet door one day when D. was going in to thrash out his proposals, & when D. went in, Chalmers turned to someone at his side & said: 'That little man goes in to the fight absolutely alone.' And when D. came out, Chalmers said to him apprehensively: 'Well? . . .' 'Oh, I carried them all right', was D.'s cheerful reply.

Asquith alone was helpful, when it came to a vote, although he never supported the proposals actively. But once, when nearly everyone around the table had raised objections to a certain proposal, Asquith summed up with the words: 'Well, I think there is substantial agreement on this point!' (At that time no minutes of Cabinet meetings were taken, & no votes recorded.) It was left to the Prime Minister to record the sense of the decisions taken. It is stated that at the end of Asquith's Ministry in 1916, after a debate on Air Defences, there were 3 different versions of the decisions taken, given by Ministers who each thought they had carried their point.

May 31st 1936

D. was discussing with me the dislike of the Liberal intelligentsia for him. 'As a matter of fact', he said, 'the aristocracy have always been far more partial to me than these people—and even than they were to Bonar Law & Baldwin. When the Coalition broke up in 1922, the majority of them stuck to me. Balfour, Crawford, Anglesey, Pembroke, the Devonshires, Salisburys, Milner, etc. Actually Ormsby-Gore was the only member of an aristocratic family that went with Baldwin, & when I asked someone the other day the reason for Ormsby-Gore's promotion, I was told that it was because he went with Baldwin at that time.'

June 7th 1936

Went to Cherkley to lunch with Max who has just returned from abroad, where he went to recuperate from a mysterious illness. I asked Lonsdale,[1] who was there, what had been the matter with him. 'Nerves', he replied: & then added in a confidential tone. 'He is frightened of God.'

June 11th 1936

Went yesterday to lunch with Muriel Beckett at her new house in Hyde Park Terrace. Bee Pembroke, Horne, etc. also present—brought back memories of the great days—D. Prime Minister, & Horne a Minister also. The Peace Conference, with the Pembrokes & Derby & Henry Wilson, & all the glory & excitement of the post-war days. Horne, à propos of an argument as to whether argument was any use in persuading really stubborn people, quoted D., on the occasion of a ticklish situation during the Railway strike in 1921, when Horne was Labour Minister. He came to D. just before a Cabinet Conference with the Labour Leaders, & told D. how he had found an irrefutable argument which would drive the Labour people out of their position. D. brushed him on one side, saying: 'No one ever convinced anyone by an

---

1. Freddie Lonsdale, the playwright.

argument.' They went into the Cabinet room, & D. unfolded his tactics. He spoke at some length on the situation & then said: 'I cannot help thinking, when I am faced by a crisis of this kind, what those who come after me, & sit here where I am sitting, will do when they are faced by a similar situation. You, Mr. Henderson, will probably be sitting here. What would *you* do, if you were in my place?' Henderson was completely bouleversé. D. had appealed to a latent, perhaps subconscious, vanity & ambition in the man, & achieved, by attacking & playing upon this, what he would never have gained by reasoned argument. In this method of D.'s lies *nearly* the whole of his success in dealing with men, (his energy the other factor).

Tonight D. has gone up to attend the Diamond Jubilee of Gypsy Smith. He has an excellent little speech. He told me how he was the first person to canvass the gypsies in the Carnarvon Boroughs, in 1890 during his first election. He went to the gypsy encampment & spoke to them, & said that he had a sympathy for poachers, as he had the poaching instinct himself. He held that he had as good a right to the salmon & trout in a river as any man. They were completely won over by this, and voted for him always after.

June 20th 1936
D. had smashing success in House on Thursday [18 June], a real resurrection of his old fighting days.[1] The House almost hysterical & so was I. The Front Bench literally cowed before his onslaught, & Baldwin's reply was pitiable. There was consternation on the faces of the Tory back benchers. After the speech a young Tory Member went up to Winston & said he had never heard anything like it in the House. 'Young man', replied W., 'you have been listening to one of the greatest Parliamentary performances of all time.'

July 2nd 1936
On Monday [29 June] we dashed up to London to the Duff Cooper debate—Dyer's day off, so we trained from Guildford and had a picnic supper in the train. D. was fully armed with a good speech, but he did not deliver it—only asked one or two pertinent questions. On the way back D. said to me: 'I have come to the conclusion that success unnerves one as much as failure. I seem to have completely lost my nerve since my success in the House a fortnight ago', which is true. Most people expected D. to speak & were disappointed that he did not, as Simon rather got away with a clever but tricky speech. However, perhaps Duff Cooper was not worth D.'s while!

D. lunched with the Russian Ambassador. It was a tête-à-tête lunch, & the Ambassador evidently talked to him freely. He was very upset to learn that D. was contemplating a visit to Germany. G. is the arch-enemy of Russia, but D. begged Maisky to use his influence with Moscow to prevent them from any act of aggression. Britain, said D., would stand by the Covenant, & if Russia committed any act of aggression she would be on the other side.

---

1. An attack on the government for the failure of their Abyssinian policy.

But again, if Germany aggressed, Britain would come to the aid of Russia, with economic sanctions—not with an armed force. Maisky says that Moscow is convinced that Germany intends to have a great Mittel-Europe state—she will attack Czechoslovakia & take the corridor, Lithuania & Latvia, & then with the help of Poland, invade Russia.

Diary 1937

March 17th 1937

D. shocked and upset last night by the news of Austen Chamberlain's death. He is the last survivor (bar George Lambert) of D.'s first parliament. D. was very sad last night, & this morning. 'I am becoming very solitary', he said to me. But apart from that, I am sure he was fond of Austen, as no one could fail to be who had worked with him, because of his complete integrity. He was very loyal to D. during Coalition days, & when D. wished to retire after the Genoa Conference in 1922, Austen begged him to remain, although he (Austen) could have had the Premiership. Austen said at the time that he did not wish to cause a split in the Tory Party, which would be the result, so he was convinced, of some of the Tories wishing to have Bonar Law as P.M. but Max was willing, so D. says, for Austen to have it, & would have backed him up.

D. delivered an excellent speech in the House, & Members were much moved. Neville thanked him, & many members said it was by far the best & the most moving tribute. Privately, D. disagrees with those who say that Austen was a great statesman. 'His was rather the excellence of character than of capacity', he said to me.

D. dined at Buckingham Palace last night, his first encounter with the King and Queen as such. He was rather nervous about his reception, after what has happened & his championship of Edward, but they were most gracious to him, the King engaging in a long conversation with him. D. says H.M. is obviously the instrument of the Gov. but he (H.M.) harped with much amusement on the fact that De Valera had described him as such! D. tackled him on the subject of the Duke of Windsor's salary, & told him quite bluntly that it would be wisdom to see that he got a generous allowance. The King cordially agreed with him, but when D. asked him if the Duke had much money saved, he said he did not know what the position was! (This may indicate greater shrewdness than D. gives him credit for!) H.M. is most anxious that the Duke should not return to this country, but D. told him that he did not take that view & thought H.M. would be wiser not to oppose it. '*She* would never dare to come back here', said H.M. 'There you are wrong', replied D. 'She would have no friends here', said H.M. D. did not agree. 'But not you or me?' said the King anxiously.

May 17th 1937
Yesterday went with D. to the radiologist to have an X-ray of his sinuses, since he has been suffering badly from neuralgia. Dawson there. D. examined thoroughly—very little sinus trouble, but Dawson says that his blood pressure is too high, though it is no use disclosing this to D. D. rather exhausted after the examination, but we took Dawson back to Thames House for a picnic lunch in the Office. He & D. discussed personalities amongst their mutual acquaintances, including Baldwin. Dawson said that in his judgment Baldwin was a 'browser'—he loved to 'browse' on literature & the classics & all scholarly things. He was a man who liked to 'browse' on scholarship without being a scholar himself. Dawson did not quite like to admit that Tom Jones had actually written parts of Baldwin's books—as we are given to understand he did, but thought that Tom Jones' value was rather in having been able to *help* & *advise* Baldwin in his writings. D. remarked that B. would never be heard of in history but for the abdication. I said that the remarkable thing was that Baldwin & Chamberlain, both of whom have achieved fame in recent years, were regarded as duds in D.'s Ministry.

The Polish Ambassador was present last night, & Max Beaverbrook, & of course Winston. D. evidently drew the Polish Ambassador out, knowing the case thoroughly, as well as his man—& finally elicited the fact that the Poles did not wish to have the Russians in an alliance. He said he would give the reasons if D. wished. 'You need not tell me', said D. 'I know the reason.' D. must have talked brilliantly & amazed the company, for this morning Max rang up & paid him many compliments, calling him the greatest conversationalist of the day, and said that he had never heard him more brilliant than last night. 'Every time I hear you talk', he said, 'I am more impressed with your powers as a conversationalist.' So impressed had he been with the substance of D.'s talk that he straightaway sat down on reaching home last night & wrote a letter to the Prime Minister,[1] begging him to send for D. and have a talk on the situation, as he could give him better advice than anyone, and saying that Neville was foolish not to seek his advice. But it will make no difference. Neville will not send for D., and if he did, he would not listen to anything D. said.

---

1. Neville Chamberlain had just succeeded Baldwin as prime minister.

Diary 1944

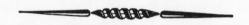

The two final entries are preserved on a detached sheet of paper. No year is given. The 24 May entry can be fixed to 1944 because of Churchill's speech. The 27 May entry, which appears first in the original, may belong to an earlier year.

May 27th

D. & I today discussed Lord Acton and his phrase 'I have no contemporaries'. I said the same thing might apply to D. He agreed, & said, 'I regard Winston as my only contemporary. We have always been friends. That is the reason that I have preferred to adopt an attitude of indifference to his policy and his Government—instead of openly quarrelling.'

May 24th

D. decided on Wednesday [today] to go to hear Winston's speech, and we are both glad, for the House gave him (D.) a touching welcome. I wonder if they realise how near it may be to his last appearances. Winston, whom we met in the corridor afterwards, was nice to us both. D. was rather inclined to be critical of the Government's policy, but I thought Winston very patient & I finally managed to turn the conversation to his pictures: we parted very happily. It was a perfect spring day, but as we drove through the smiling countryside there was a heavy sadness in my heart.

Index